Empire State Railway Museum's 37th Annual

# Guide to
# Tourist Railroads
# and Museums
# 2 0 0 2

KALMBACH
BOOKS

Front cover: Grand Canyon Railway steam locomotive no. 4960 at Williams, Arizona, on September 30, 2000. Scott Hartley photo.
Back cover: Durango & Silverton Narrow Gauge Railroad. Mike Danneman photo.

Cover Design: Kristi Ludwig                                ISSN: 0081-542X
Page Layout: Linda Wenzel

# To the Museums and Tourist Railroads

**Listings:** We would like to consider for inclusion every tourist railroad, trolley operation, railroad museum, live-steam railroad, and toy train exhibit in the United States and Canada that is open to the public and has regular hours and about which reliable information is available.

*2003 Directory:* To be published in February 2003. A packet that includes all pertinent information needed for inclusion in the 2003 Guide will be mailed to all organizations listed in this book. New listings are welcomed. For information, please write to:
    Editor—Guide to Tourist Railroads and Museums
    Books Division
    Kalmbach Publishing Co.
    P.O. Box 1612
    Waukesha, WI 53187–1612

On the web go to www.kalmbach.com/books/touristguide.html

**Advertising:** Advertising space for the 2003 Guide must be reserved by November 15, 2002. Please contact Mike Yuhas at 1-800-558-1544, extension 625, or Lori Schneider at 1-888-558-1544, extension 654.

**Publisher's Cataloging in Publication**

Empire State Railway Museum's 37th annual guide to
  tourist railroads and museums — 2002 ed.
    p. cm
    Includes index.
    ISBN: 0-89024-427-8

    1. Railroad museums—United States—
Directories. 2. Railroad museums—Canada—
Directories. I. Empire State Railway Museum.
II. Title: Guide to tourist railroads and museums

TF6.U5S75 2002                         385'.22'02573

# Contents

# Advertising Contents

iii

A-4

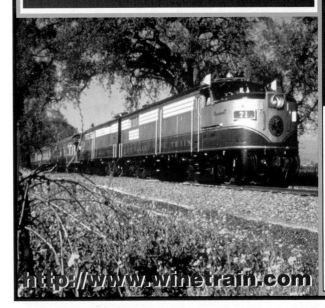

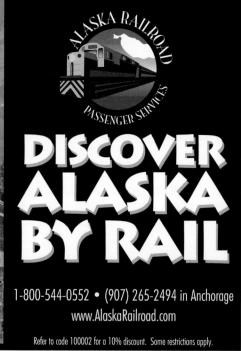

# McCLOUD RAILWAY OPEN-AIR TRAIN RIDES

*Bring the whole family for a delightful, inexpensive, excursion trip featuring either diesel locomotives or historic steam locomotive No.25. Try our new "double deck" car for incomparable views of unspoiled northern California.*

———

Hear the "clickety clack" as your trains winds its way around the base of Mt. Shasta. Open Air Excursion Trains depart McCloud, California, May through September 30th, with trips Thursday through Saturday in mid-summer. Call for schedule details.

# ALL ABOARD! SHASTA SUNSET DINNER TRAIN

*A nostalgic train ride through spectacular scenery in the shadow of Mt. Shasta featuring elegant four-course dining aboard restored vintage rail cars. A memorable evening riding the rails into yesterday!*

———

Experience true luxury in our 1916-vintage rail cars amid surroundings of mahogany and brass. Shasta Sunset Dinner Train departs McCloud, California, weekends year round, Thursday through Saturday June through September. Reservations are required.

———

To reach McCloud from I-5, take the McCloud/Reno exit and travel ten miles east turning left on Columbero Drive. Follow Columbero into town turning right after the railroad tracks.

———

For schedules & reservations call the
## Shasta Sunset Excursions
P.O.Box 1199 McCloud, CA 96057
**(800) 733-2141 (530) 964-2142**

A-8

A-9

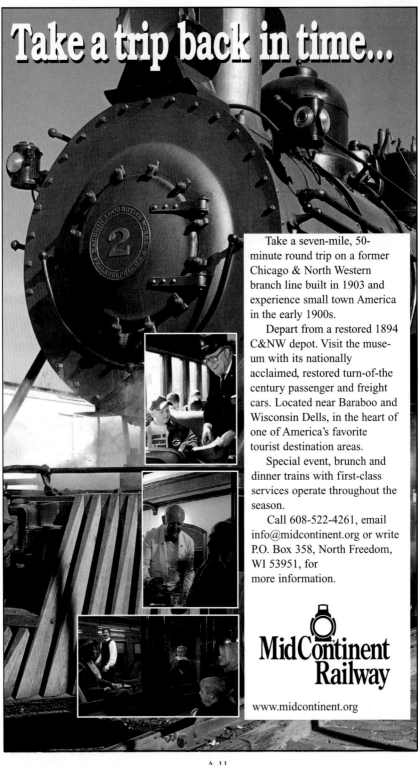

# Take a trip back in time...

Take a seven-mile, 50-minute round trip on a former Chicago & North Western branch line built in 1903 and experience small town America in the early 1900s.

Depart from a restored 1894 C&NW depot. Visit the museum with its nationally acclaimed, restored turn-of-the century passenger and freight cars. Located near Baraboo and Wisconsin Dells, in the heart of one of America's favorite tourist destination areas.

Special event, brunch and dinner trains with first-class services operate throughout the season.

Call 608-522-4261, email info@midcontinent.org or write P.O. Box 358, North Freedom, WI 53951, for more information.

## MidContinent Railway

www.midcontinent.org

# Leadership in Creative Railroading

**TRAIN, Inc.**, the Tourist Railway Association, Inc. was formed in 1972 to foster the development and operation of tourist railways and museums. Membership is open to all railway museums, tourist railroads, excursion operators, private car owners, railroad publishers, industry suppliers and other interested persons and organizations. **TRAIN, Inc.** is the only trade association created to represent the broad spectrum of what is called "creative railroading".

Our members included in the Guide to Tourist Railroads and Museums may be identified by the **TRAIN** logo on their listing page. Members receive our quarterly magazine, **TrainLine**, which contains articles on creative railroading and railroad preservation. Our annual convention provides educational seminars, speakers of national import, updates on federal regulations along with product and supplier displays.

**TRAIN, Inc.** is a leader on issues such as insurance, safety and legislation affecting the operation and display of vintage and historic railway equipment. **TRAIN, Inc.** serves as a voice for the total industry and keeps members informed on laws , regulations and actions that affect us all.

For More Information Contact:

## Tourist Railway Association, Inc.

P.O. Box 1245
Chama, NM 87520-1245
1-800-67TRAIN
(505) 756-1240
FAX (505) 756-1238
Email address: ranger@cvn.com
Visit our website at *http://www.train.org*

*Subscribe to TrainLine, the quarterly magazine of railroad preservation and tourist railroads. Send $20 and your address to the above address.*

A-13

# 18th Year 2002 RAILROAD TOURS

**CUBAN RAIL HISTORIAN ADVENTURE** - Feb 9-24 & March 2-17. Legal railroad tours for railfans to Cuba

**CHINA STEAM SPECTACULAR** - March 4-17 & Oct 12-27. The last of the great mainline steam in regular service. We now have a charter train pulled by steam & diesel for the March tour with photo run-bys. Call for our detailed China brochure.

**MEXICAN RAIL SPECTACULAR** - March 23-30. Charter train Chihuahua to Guadalajara through Copper Canyon and the Sierra Madre Mountains.

**MEXICAN RAILFAN ADVENTURE** - March 30-April 7. Charter train for railfans. Guadalajara to Chihuahua via Los Mochis with photo run-bys.

**SACRAMENTO RAIL & RIVER BOAT CRUISE** - April 27. Train and steamboat excursion for the entire family in the Sacramento area.

**GREAT CANADIAN RAIL ADVENTURES** - June 8-23. Tour British Columbia and Alberta. Includes Vancouver Island, Inside Passage, Prince Rupert, Jasper, Icefields Parkway, Lake Louise, Banff, Kamloops, Lillooet and Vancouver.

**ANDES RAIL ADVENTURE** - July 13-28. Charter steam-diesel-railcars in Ecuador and Peru, with photo run-bys and visits to Inca ruins.

**ROCKY MOUNTAIN TRAIN SPLENDORS** - July 27-Aug 7. Spectacular train rides and sightseeing in Oregon, Idaho, Montana, Utah and Colorado.

**GREAT BRAZILIAN RAILFAN ADVENTURE** - July 30-Aug 17. 18 charters using steam-railcars-street cars-interurbans. 21 different rail lines visited.

**CANADIAN MARITIME RAIL SPECTACULAR** - Sep 7-22. 8 wonderful train rides in Quebec, Maine, New Brunswick and Nova Scotia onboard Via Rail and the new luxurious Acadian Train running across Maine. Tour also includes Prince Edward Island and chartered Via Rail "Park Car" rear end dome. All this during the spectacular fall colors.

**INLAND PEACE RIVER COUNTRY TOUR** - Sep 7-15. Travel by charter RDC Budd railcars on the British Columbia Railroad.

**NEVADA NORTHERN RAILFAN SPECTACULAR** - Sep 28. A grand day for the railfans on the Nevada Northern Railroad with all steam including a double-header.

**RIO GRANDE PHOTO FREIGHT** - Sep 30-Oct 1. Charter photo freight with steam over Cumbres Pass in the New Mexico / Colorado Rockies.

**NEW ENGLAND FALL COLORS RAIL ADVENTURE** - Oct 6-12. Travel and sightsee by rail in New England during the fall colors.

**REDWOOD STEAM SPECTACULAR** - Oct 13. Charter steam on the California Western Fort Bragg to Willits through the Redwoods with photo run-bys. Possible double-header!

**FALL COLORS EXPRESS** - Oct 12-15. Private rail car charter LA-Oakland-Reno and return using the Silver Lariat, Plaza Santa Fe and Tamalpais.

**COPPER CANYON RAIL CRUISE** - Nov 3-9. Charter train through the Sierra Madre and Copper Canyon region of Mexico.

**RUSSIAN TRAIN TOURS.** Several departures in 2002 with steam & diesel.

*Please call for our 2002 all-color brochure*
*1-800-359-4870 USA     1-800-752-1836 Canada   (530) 836-1745     Fax (530) 836-1748*

**TRAINS UNLIMITED, TOURS**

P.O. Box 1997 • Portola, California 96122 USA
Visit our website
http://www.trainsunltdtours.com

A-16

# COUNTRY TRAINS
## GIFTS FOR RAILROADERS

- Engineer Pin Stripe Hats • Buckles •
- Herald & Engine Mugs • T-shirts •
- Rubber Stamps • Herald Hats •
- Copper Cuts • Prints • Neckties •
- Stickers • Signs • Belts • Pins •
- Postcards • Suspenders • Whistles •
- & The Unusual •

108 PAGE CATALOG AVAILABLE
$5.00
REFUNDED ON FIRST ORDER

**COUNTRY TRAINS
P.O. BOX 250
14009 S. GARDNER AVE.
ELLERSLIE, MD 21529-0250
TEL 301-759-3605
FAX 301-759-3609
www.countrytrains.com**

Dealer Inquiries Invited

A-20

Empire State Railway Museum's 37th Annual

# Guide to
# Tourist Railroads
# and Museums
# 2002

## Symbols

| | | | |
|---|---|---|---|
| ♿ | Handicapped accessible | 🏛 | National Register of Historic Places |
| 🅿 | Parking | ✉ | Brochure available; send SASE |
| 🚌 | Bus/RV parking | M | Memberships available |
| 🎁 | Gift, book, or museum shop | **arm** | Association of Railway Museums, member |
| ☕ | Refreshments | **TRAIN** | Tourist Railway Association, Inc., member |
| 🍴 | Restaurant | 🚆 | Amtrak service to nearby city |
| 🧍 | Dinner train/dining car | **VIA** | VIA service to nearby city |
| 📷 | Guided tours | MasterCard | Credit cards accepted |
| 🎋 | Picnic area | VISA | |
| 🚂 | Excursions | | |
| 🎨 | Arts and crafts | | |

# To the Reader

In 1966, railroad enthusiasts Marvin Cohen and Steve Bogen produced, and the Empire State Railway Museum published, the first *Steam Passenger Service Directory* (now titled *Empire State Railway Museum's Guide to Tourist Railroads and Museums*). At that time, tourist railroading was in its infancy, and the book featured 62 tourist railroads and steam excursion operations. Four years later, in 1970, the Museum and *Directory* sponsored a tourist railroad conference, and the Tourist Railroad Association, Inc. (TRAIN), was founded.

The tourist railroad industry has flourished over the past three decades, with local groups of rail enthusiasts and preservationists banding together to return to service locomotives and rolling stock that have sat dormant and neglected for too many years. The mission of these organizations includes educating and entertaining the general public. That's where the Empire State Railway Museum and this book fit in. Through the foresight and perseverance of the Museum, this book continues to be published so that rail enthusiasts, as well as those who are only casually interested in trains, can become aware of the hundreds of wonderful tourist railroads and railroad attractions available for them to enjoy and learn from. Kalmbach Publishing Co. is pleased and proud to be able to produce this book on behalf of the Empire State Railway Museum.

**Guest Coupons:** The reduced-rate coupons provided by many operations in this edition of the *Guide to Tourist Railroads and Museums* will be honored by the museums. Be sure to present them when purchasing tickets.

**Brochures:** Many operations offer brochures and/or timetables. Please see the symbol sections in the listings for those operations that provide brochures.

Every effort has been made to ensure the accuracy of the contents. However, we depend on the information supplied by each operation. Internet addresses, business office locations, and phone and Fax numbers are subject to change. We cannot assume responsibility for errors, omissions, or fare and schedule changes. Be sure to write or phone ahead to confirm hours and prices.

Finally, if you don't see a full listing in the book for a railroad or museum you know exists, check the abbreviated listings at the back of this book. These are organizations that did not respond to our mailings, but which we felt would be of interest to our customers. Again, in all cases, be sure to write or phone ahead.

If you know of an operation that is not included in the book, please send information to the publisher. See page ii.

1

# HEART OF DIXIE
# RAILROAD MUSEUM
*Train rides, museum*
*Standard and 24" gauge*

NEIL SMART, JR.

**Description:** Twelve-acre museum site displays two 100-plus-year-old depots, large shop, yard, and many pieces of equipment and memorabilia. Rides include 8-mile round trip on standard gauge 1910-54 vintage train and shorter trip on narrow gauge former Birmingham Zoo steam train.

**Schedule:** Museum: Monday through Saturday, 10 a.m. to 4 p.m., year round, and Sundays, 1 p.m. to 4 p.m. April 7 through December 15, except major holidays. Train rides: first and third Saturdays, April 6 to December 14, or on specially requested dates.

**Admission/Fare:** Museum: admission free. Donations appreciated. Train rides: adults, $8; children, $6. Less for narrow gauge.

**Locomotives/Rolling Stock:** Two 1951 EMD SW-8 locomotives; one 1953 Fairbanks-Morse H12-44 locomotive; one Whitcomb 25-tonner; and four steamers from 0-4-0 to 2-8-0; 15 passenger cars; more.

**Special Events:** Cottontail Express, March 30. Halloween Nightmare Special, October 25-26. Polar Express, November 29, 30, December 6, 7, 13, 14. Santa Claus Express, November 30, December 1, 7, 8, 14, 15.

**Nearby Attractions/Accommodations:** American Village, Oak Mountain State Park; Birmingham, 30 miles, has numerous museums, parks, etc.

**Location/Directions:** Take exit 228 off I-65, go ⅝ mile on State Route 25 south, turn left on Ninth St., drive to the museum.

Radio frequency: 151.515, 154.54

**Site Address:** 1919 Ninth St., Calera, AL
**Mailing Address:** PO Box 727, Calera, AL 35040
**Telephone:** (205) 668-3435 and (800) 943-4490
**Fax:** (205) 668-9900
**Internet:** www.heartofdixierrmuseum.org

2

## FOLEY RAILWAY MUSEUM
## CITY OF FOLEY MUSEUM
## ARCHIVES
*Museum*

**Description:** Museum houses L&N Railroad artifacts, as well as artifacts representing the history of Foley and Baldwin County.

**Schedule:** Monday through Friday, 10 a.m. to 4 p.m.

**Admission/Fare:** Free.

**Locomotives/Rolling Stock:** On display, two boxcars and one caboose.

**Nearby Attractions/Accommodations:** The Foley area has an array of interesting places to visit. The beaches at Gulf Shores, Riviera Outlet Center, all types of restaurants, and several museums.

**Location/Directions:** From I-10, take Gulf Shores Parkway (Highway 59) south to Foley. Depot Museum is one block east of the intersection of Highway 59 and Highway 98.

**Site Address:** 125 East Laurel Avenue, Foley, AL
**Mailing Address:** 125 East Laurel Avenue, Foley, AL 36535
**Telephone:** (251) 943-1818
**Fax:** (251) 971-1819
**E-mail:** foleymuseum@gulftel.com

**Description:** The depot is one of the nation's oldest remaining railroad structures. A tour includes a one-hour guided experience of the three-story building, including a glimpse into the depot's Civil War era.

**Schedule:** Monday through Saturday, 9 a.m. to 5 p.m. Closed Thanksgiving, Christmas, and New Year's Day. Call ahead for summer hours.

**Admission/Fare:** Depot–adults, $7; seniors, $6; children, 4-17, $6. Age 3 and under free.

**Nearby Attractions/Accommodations:** The depot is part of the EarlyWorks History Complex, which includes the Alabama Constitution Village and a large hands-on history museum.

**Location/Directions:** I-565 east, exit 19-C. The depot is directly on your right.

         arm TRAIN

**Site Address:** 320 Church St., Huntsville, AL
**Mailing Address:** 404 Madison St., Huntsville, AL 35801
**Telephone:** (256) 564-8100 and (800) 678-1819
**Fax:** (256) 564-8151
**Internet:** www.earlyworks.com

# NORTH ALABAMA RAILROAD MUSEUM, INC.

*Train ride, museum, display*
*Standard gauge*

HUGH DUDLEY

**Description:** The Chase Depot offers exhibits, a display passenger train, and a self-guided walking tour. A guided tour, "All Aboard Railroading," is available. Ride on a 10-mile round trip excursion on the museum's Mercury and Chase Railroad.

**Schedule:** Museum–April through October: Wednesdays and Saturdays; call for hours. Train–Usually third Saturday of the month; contact for information.

**Admission/Fare:** Museum, parking, and self-guided walking tour–free. Guided tour–adults, $4; children 6-11, $2. Train–adults, $10; children under 12, $5.

**Locomotives/Rolling Stock:** Excursion train–Alco S-2 no. 484; coach no. 6082; baggage no. 139; and dining car no. 1000. Display train–Boxcab no. 11; refrigerator car; RPO car; coach; 6-10 Pullman sleeper; more.

**Special Events:** North Alabama Railroad History Festival; Goblin Train; Santa Train; call for dates.

**Nearby Attractions/Accommodations:** Alabama Space and Rocket Center (home of Space Camp), Huntsville Depot Museum, Museum of Art, Botanical Garden, Dogwood Manor Bed & Breakfast.

**Location/Directions:** From east end of I-565 in Huntsville, continue east on U.S. 72 for 2 miles, take left on Moores Mill Rd. for 1 mile, cross second railroad track, left on Chase Rd. for ½ mile to museum on left.

      M

**Radio frequency: 452.325 & 457.325**

**Site Address:** 694 Chase Rd., Huntsville, AL
**Mailing Address:** PO Box 4163, Huntsville, AL 35815-4163
**Telephone:** (256) 851-6276 (voice Wed. and Sat., 8 to 2, otherwise recording)
**E-mail:** fredrrman@aol.com
**Internet:** www.suncompsvc.com/narm/

**WHITE PASS & YUKON ROUTE**
*Train ride*
*36" gauge*

DEDMAN'S PHOTO

**Description:** Built in 1898, the White Pass Railroad is a spectacular mountain railroad. The WP&YR offers round trip excursions from Skagway to the White Pass Summit, Lake Bennett, and through rail/bus connections to Whitehorse, Yukon.

**Schedule:** May through September: daily. Summit Excursion–depart Skagway 8:30 a.m. and 1 p.m., 3-hour round trip and Lake Bennett Adventure 8 a.m. (8-hour round trip). Through service northbound–depart Skagway 8 a.m. (train); arr. Fraser, B.C., 10 a.m. (change to bus); arr. Whitehorse, Yukon, 1 p.m. Through service southbound–depart Whitehorse, Yukon, 1:30 p.m. (bus); arr. Fraser, B.C., 2:30 p.m. (change to train); arr. Skagway, Alaska, 4:30 p.m. Steam Train–June through August: every other Saturday, departs at 8 a.m.

**Admission/Fare:** Summit Excursion–adults, $82; children, $41. Through service–adults, $95; children, $47.50. Bennett steam train–adults, $156; children, $78. Bennett diesel train–adults, $128; children, $64. Reservations recommended.

**Locomotives/Rolling Stock:** 1947 Baldwin no. 73 2-8-2; 1920 Baldwin no. 40 2-8-0; 8 101 Alco diesels; 11 GE diesels; 59 train cars; 1898 rotary snow plow no. 1.

**Nearby Attractions/Accommodations:** Klondike Gold Rush National Historical Park.

**Radio frequency: 160.325**

**Site Address:** Second and Spring Streets, Skagway, AK
**Mailing Address:** PO Box 435, Skagway, AK 99840
**Telephone:** (907) 983-2217 and (800) 343-7373
**Fax:** (907) 983-2734
**E-mail:** info@whitepass.net
**Internet:** www.whitepassrailroad.com

6

# MUSEUM OF ALASKA TRANSPORTATION & INDUSTRY
*Museum*
*Standard gauge*

PATRICK DURAND

**Description:** See Alaska Railroad locomotives and 26 items of rolling stock. These items were used to help build Alaska as we know it today. In addition, you will find aircraft, boats, automobiles, heavy equipment, and other varieties of transport important to Alaska's history.

**Schedule:** May 1 through September 30: open daily, 9 a.m. to 6 p.m.; October 1 through April 30: limited hours.

**Admission/Fare:** Admission charged.

**Locomotives/Rolling Stock:** Alaska Railroad RS-1 no. 1000; Chitina Autorailer; EMD F7A no. 1500; USAF Baldwins nos. 1841 and 1842; GM center-cab diesel; Pullman "McCord"; U.S. Bureau of Mines safety car.

**Special Events:** Annual Transportation Expo to be held fourth weekend in June.

**Nearby Attractions/Accommodations:** Alaska Live Steamers operates a miniature scale railroad for the education and enjoyment of all. They are located next door to the museum. Admission charged. They operate the first and third weekends of the month, May through October. You can find them at work on holidays and other weekends also.

**Location/Directions:** Traveling north out of Wasilla, turn left at mile 47 Parks Highway (onto Neuser Drive). Museum is ¾ mile west of highway, next to Wasilla Airport.

**Site Address:** 3800 W. Neuser Dr., Wasilla, AK
**Mailing Address:** PO Box 870646, Wasilla, AK 99687
**Telephone:** (907) 376-1211
**Fax:** (907) 376-3082
**E-mail:** mati@mtaonline.net
**Internet:** www.alaska.net/~rmorris/mati1.htm

**Schedule:** Labor Day to Memorial Day: Saturday and Sunday, 12 to 4 p.m. Tours can be arranged.

**Admission/Fare:** Donations.

**Locomotives/Rolling Stock:** S.P. 2562 Arm no. 1 30-ton Plymouth; S.P. 7130 and 7131 derrick and toolcar; "Imperial Manor" sleeper, S.F. 2870; coach "Janemarie" Rock Island private car; S.P. 5984 horse car; Southern Railway office car "Desert Valley"; 14 other cars of various models.

**Special Events:** Cotton Festival and Ostrich Festival.

**Nearby Attractions/Accommodations:** San Marcos Hotel, America West Arena, Bank One Ballpark, Scottsdale Railroad Park, Casa Grande ruins.

**Location/Directions:** U.S. 60 south on Arizona Ave., U.S. 10 east on Chandler Blvd. approximately 8 miles.

    M arm

**Site Address:** 399 N. Delaware Ave., Chandler, AZ
**Mailing Address:** PO Box 842, Chandler, AZ 85244
**Telephone:** (480) 821-1108

# MC CORMICK-STILLMAN RAILROAD PARK
*Train ride, museum, 15" gauge*

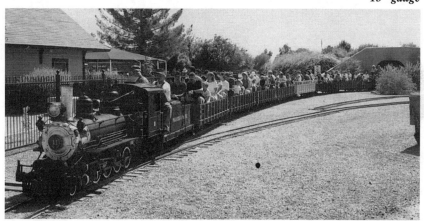

**Description:** A 30-acre theme park offering train rides, carousel rides, railroad museum, retail shops, picnic area, two playgrounds, snack stop, Hartley's General Store, and model railroad displays.

**Schedule:** Year round, seven days a week: daily 10 a.m. to sunset. Call for summer hours.

**Admission/Fare:** Train or carousel ride–$1 per person for anyone 3 or older. Museum–$1 for anyone 13 and older.

**Locomotives/Rolling Stock:** 5-inch scale locomotives. Steam–2-8-2, 4-6-0, 2-6-2. Diesel–GP7, SW1; 20 various cars.

**Special Events:** Railfair, October 14-15. Holiday Lights, December 15-30 (no December 24, 25, 31). Exclusively Little, March 4. Free summer concerts, May 14 through July 16.

**Nearby Attractions/Accommodations:** Shopping, resorts, restaurants, casino.

**Location/Directions:** Southeast corner of Scottsdale Rd. and Indian Bend Rd.

       M MasterCard VISA

**Site Address:** 7301 E. Indian Bend Rd., Scottsdale, AZ
**Mailing Address:** 7301 E. Indian Bend Rd., Scottsdale, AZ 85250
**Telephone:** (480) 312-2312
**Fax:** (480) 312-7001
**Internet:** www.ci.scottsdale.az.us/mccormickpark/

# GRAND CANYON RAILWAY
*Train ride*
*Standard gauge*

AL RICHMOND

**Description:** Relive the excitement of the Old West aboard a historic train to America's national treasure, the Grand Canyon. After a 2¼-hour journey, passengers have 3¼ hours to explore the canyon before the train returns to Williams. Many passengers spend the night inside Grand Canyon National Park.

**Schedule:** Year round: daily except Dec. 24-25. Williams departure–10 a.m., arrives Grand Canyon National Park 12:15 p.m., departs Grand Canyon 3:30 p.m., returning to Williams at 5:45 p.m.

**Admission/Fare:** Adults, $54.95; children age 16 and under, $24.95. Additional park entrance fee and tax. Upgrades available.

**Locomotives/Rolling Stock:** Steam: no. 18, 1910 Alco SC-4 2-8-0; no. 29, 1906 Alco SC-3 2-8-0; no. 4960, 1923 Baldwin O1A 2-8-2 Mikado type; diesel: no. 2134 GP7 Electro-Motive Division of GM Corporation, more. Many historic coach and other passenger cars.

**Special Events:** Memorial Day: Steam engine returns to service

**Nearby Attractions/Accommodations:** Fray Marcos Hotel and Max & Thelma's Restaurant. Historic downtown Williams and Route 66. Golf. Amtrak now stops in Williams for an all-rail trip to the Grand Canyon.

**Location/Directions:** I-40 exit 163 (Williams), Grand Canyon Blvd. ½ mile south to Williams depot.

**Site Address:** 235 N. Grand Canyon Blvd., Williams, AZ
**Mailing Address:** 1201 W. Route 66, Ste. 200, Flagstaff, AZ 86601
**Telephone:** (800) THE TRAIN (843-8724)
**Fax:** (520) 773-1610
**E-mail:** info@thetrain.com
**Internet:** www.thetrain.com

# YUMA VALLEY RAILWAY
*Train ride*
*Standard gauge*

**Description:** A 34-mile, 3- to 4-hour round trip alongside the Colorado River. Enjoy the native wildlife and agriculture as you journey through the desert in 1922, 1923, or 1950 Pullman coaches pulled by either a 1952 Davenport-Beshler or 1957 G.E. diesel-electric.

**Schedule:** October: Saturday, 10 a.m.; November through March: Saturday and Sunday, 1 p.m.; April and May: Sunday, 1 p.m.; June through September: by appointment only.

**Admission/Fare:** Adults, $13; seniors (55+), $12; children (4-16), $7.

**Locomotives/Rolling Stock:** 1952 Davenport-Beshler (former U.S. Army); 1957 G.E. center-cab (former USMC); 1922 Pullman chair car (former Apache Railway); 1923 Pullman club car (former U.S. Army ambulance car); 1950 Pullman Chair Car (former Rhode Island Railroad). Also, in retirement, a 1941 Whitcomb diesel chain-drive 30-ton mining engine (former Apache Railway).

**Special Events:** Yuma Crossing Day, last weekend of February.

**Nearby Attractions/Accommodations:** See web sites of Yuma Chamber of Commerce and local paper for up-to-date information.

**Location/Directions:** I-8 to Fourth Ave. exit. Next to Yuma Crossing Park.

*Coupon available, see coupon section.

            M

**Site Address:** 100 N. Second Ave., Yuma, AZ
**Mailing Address:** PO Box 10305, Yuma, AZ 85366-8305
**Telephone:** (520) 782-1583

# EUREKA SPRINGS & NORTH ARKANSAS RAILWAY
*Train ride*
*Standard gauge*

**Description:** Five-mile round trip excursion trains; also, diesel-pulled dining cars.

**Schedule:** Excursions, 10 a.m. to 4 p.m. Dining trains, 12 and 5 p.m. daily. Closed Sundays, except Memorial Day, July 4th, and Labor Day weekends.

**Admission/Fare:** Excursion: adults, $8; children ages 4-10, $4. Lunch: $14.95; dinner: $23.95. All plus tax.

**Locomotives/Rolling Stock:** No. 1, 1906 Baldwin 2-6-0, former W.T. Carter; no. 201, 1906 Alco 2-6-0, former Moscow, Camden & San Augustine; no. 226, 1927 Baldwin 2-8-2, former Dierks For. & Coal; six commuter cars, former Rock Island; no. 4742, 1942 EMD SW1.

**Nearby Attractions/Accommodations:** Tourist town with many opportunities.

**Location/Directions:** Eureka Springs is 45 miles northeast of Fayetteville, 9 miles south of the Missouri state line. Take Highway 23 north to the city limits.

**Site Address:** 299 N. Main, Eureka Springs, AR
**Mailing Address:** PO Box 310, Eureka Springs, AR 72632
**Telephone:** (501) 253-9623
**Fax:** (501) 253-6406
**E-mail:** depot@esnarailway.com
**Internet:** www.esnarailway.com

# FORT SMITH TROLLEY MUSEUM
*Trolley ride, museum*
*Standard gauge*

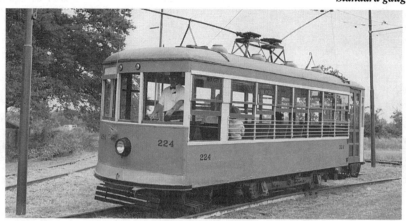

**Description:** Ride a restored Fort Smith Light & Traction Birney Safety Car over ½ mile of track in the downtown area.

**Schedule:** May through October: Mondays through Saturdays, 10 a.m. to 5 p.m.; Sundays, 1 to 5 p.m. November through April: Saturdays, 10 a.m. to 5 p.m.; Sundays, 1 to 5 p.m. Tours by appointment.

**Admission/Fare: Trolley ride:** Adults, $1; children, $ .50. Museum is free.

**Locomotives/Rolling Stock:** Fort Smith Light & Traction nos. 205, 224, 10; locomotives Frisco no. 4003 (steam); USAF no. 1246; August Railroad no. 6; ARR no. 7; diner MKT no. 100162; troop sleeper (power car) MKT no. 100186; three cabooses, more.

**Nearby Attractions/Accommodations:** Fort Smith Historic Site, Fort Smith Museum of History, Civic Center, Fort Smith National Cemetery.

**Location/Directions:** From west Highway 64 to Garrison Ave., Garrison to S. Fourth St., south four blocks. From east I-54 to Rogers exit, west on Rogers to S. Fourth St., south three blocks to museum.

**Site Address:** 100 S. Fourth St., Fort Smith, AR
**Mailing Address:** 100 S. Fourth St., Fort Smith, AR 72901
**Telephone:** (501) 783-0205 and (501) 783-1237
**Fax:** (501) 782-9289
**E-mail:** info@fstm.org
**Internet:** www.fstm.org

**FRISCO DEPOT MUSEUM**
*Museum*
*Standard gauge*

**Description:** Self-guided or interpretive tours upon request. Beautifully restored Victorian depot built in 1885/1886. Operated by the Frisco Railroad 1901 to 1968. Nine exhibits depicting 13 lifesize figures, dressed in historical costumes each with their own audio unit telling their story. Two videos are shown about history of the railroad in Mammoth Spring and life in Mammoth Spring in the 1900s.

**Schedule:** Year round: Tuesdays through Sundays, 8 a.m. to 5 p.m. Closed Mondays except Monday holidays.

**Admission/Fare:** Adults, $2.25; children, $1.25; age 5 and under are free; special rates for groups of 15 or more with 2 weeks notice; season passes.

**Locomotives/Rolling Stock:** Wooden Frisco caboose SL-SF no. 1176.

**Special Events:** Mammoth Spring Park offers events and programs March through October and by request. Call for information.

**Nearby Attractions/Accommodations:** Mammoth Spring State Park, Mammoth Spring Federal Fish Hatchery, camping, canoeing, trout fishing on Spring River, museums, antique stores.

**Location/Directions:** Located in Mammoth Spring State Park on Highway 63. Twenty-seven miles south of West Plains, Missouri, and 16 miles north of Hardy, Arkansas.

Radio frequency: 160.35000

**Site Address:** U.S. Highway 63, Mammoth Spring, AR
**Mailing Address:** PO Box 36, Mammoth Spring, AR 72554
**Telephone:** (870) 625-7364
**Fax:** (870) 625-3255
**E-mail:** mammothsprg@arkansas.com
**Internet:** www.arkansasstateparks.com

BARRY ROBINSON

**Description:** Located in the 1.5-acre former Cotton Belt erecting and machine shop. It contains the last two SSW steam locomotives and other railroad equipment and artifacts.

**Schedule:** Year round: Mondays through Saturdays, 9 a.m. to 3 p.m. Closed during periods of extremely cold weather. Call before your visit during hottest summer weather.

**Admission/Fare:** Free; donations appreciated.

**Locomotives/Rolling Stock:** SSW 4-8-4 no. 819; SSW 2-6-0 no. 336; GP 30; SSW relief crane and outfit train; cabooses; passenger cars; snowplow.

**Special Events:** Annual Model Train Show and Sale, April. Mainline steam excursions with SSW 819.

**Nearby Attractions/Accommodations:** Jefferson County Museum in Old Union Station; Band Museum; Arkansas Entertainment Hall of Fame.

**Location/Directions:** Highway 65, Port Rd. exit.

**Site Address:** 1700 Port Rd., Pine Bluff, AR
**Mailing Address:** PO Box 2044, Pine Bluff, AR 71613
**Telephone:** (870) 535-8819

15

CHARLES HOOT DESIGN

**Description:** Reader Railroad, the oldest all-steam standard gauge carrier to operate in the United States, offers a 7-mile, one-hour round trip. Open-platform wooden coaches are drawn by veteran logging engines, operations reminiscent of the railroad's earliest days.

**Schedule:** Write or call for information.

**Admission/Fare:** Adults, $6; children 4-11, $3.60; children under 4 ride free with parent. Group rates available. Fares may be slightly higher for special events.

**Locomotives/Rolling Stock:** Locomotive: no. 7, 1907 Baldwin 2-6-2, former Victoria, Fisher & Western. Rolling stock: open-platform wooden coaches; open-air car; caboose.

**Location/Directions:** Off State Route 24 between Camden and Prescott on Highway 368.

**Site Address:** Highway 368, off State Route 24 between Camden and Prescott
**Mailing Address:** PO Box 507, Hot Springs, AR 71902
**Telephone:** (501) 624-6881
**internet:** www.movietrains.com

# ARKANSAS & MISSOURI RAILROAD
*Train ride*
*Standard gauge*

**Description:** 134-mile scenic excursion over trestles and through Winslow tunnel with a 2½-hour layover in historic Van Buren for shopping and dining, or a 70-mile scenic excursion over high trestles and through the Winslow tunnel.

**Schedule:** Regular excursion days: April through September, Wednesdays and Saturdays. October through November: Wednesdays, Fridays, and Saturdays. There are other special excursion dates available.

**Admission/Fare:** Call or write for information

**Locomotives/Rolling Stock:** Six T-6s, nos. 12, 14, 15, 17, 18; two RS-1s, nos. 20, 22; one RF-32, no. 42; 12 C-420s; one C-630, no. 4500; all Alco.

**Special Events:** Mardi Gras of the Ozarks, Saturday before Fat Tuesday; Rodeo of the Ozarks, July 1-4; Frisco Festival, fourth weekend in August; Annual Christmas Train, December 15.

**Nearby Attractions/Accommodations:** Shiloh Museum, Walton Art Center, Terra Studios, Daisey Museum, Prairie Grove Battlefield, Roger's Historical Museum, University of Arkansas, Pea Ridge National Military Park, Devil's Den State Park, Beaver Lake, Best Western.

**Location/Directions:** On our website at arkansasmissouri-rr.com

**Site Address:** 306 E. Emma St., Springdale, AR
**Mailing Address:** 306 E. Emma St., Springdale, AR 72764
**Telephone:** (501) 751-8600 and 800-687-8600
**Fax:** (501) 751-2225
**E-mail:** Brendab@arkansasmissour-irr.com
**Internet:** www.arkansasmissouri-rr.com

17

# DESCANSO, ALPINE & PACIFIC RAILWAY
*Train ride*
*24" gauge*

GRANT KERN

**Description:** Passengers ride an industrial 2-foot-gauge railway to yesteryear among 100-year-old Engelman oaks in San Diego County's foothills. The train leaves Shade Depot and makes a ½-mile round trip, climbing the 6½-percent grade to High Pass/Lookout and crossing a spectacular 112-foot-long wooden trestle, giving passengers magnificent views of the surrounding area. At Shade Depot and Freight Shed is a display of railroad artifacts, including those of the DA&P. Mail service with mailer's postmark permit canceling is available.

**Schedule:** June through August: Sundays, 1 to 3 p.m., every half hour. September through May: intermittent Sunday operation. Rides and tours may be scheduled at other times with advance notice; please call to arrange.

**Admission/Fare:** Free.

**Locomotives/Rolling Stock:** No. 2, 1935 2½-ton Brookville, SN 2003, powered by original McCormick-Deering 22½-horsepower P-12 gasoline engine, former Carthage (Missouri) Crushed Limestone Company.

**Location/Directions:** Thirty miles east of San Diego. I-8 exit Tavern Rd., travel south on Tavern 1.9 miles, turn right on South Grade Rd. and travel .6 mile, turn left onto Alpine Heights Rd.; the DA&P is the fifth driveway on the right.

**Site Address:** 1266 Alpine Heights Rd., Alpine, CA
**Mailing Address:** 1266 Alpine Heights Rd., Alpine, CA 91901
**Telephone:** (619) 445-4781
**E-mail:** dapry@juno.com

# DISNEYLAND RAILROAD
*Train ride*
*36" gauge*

**Description:** Twenty-minute train ride that circles the perimeter of Disneyland and makes four stops. Also takes guest through major Grand Canyon Diorama and Primeval World, featuring lifelike dinosaurs. Steam trains pull open-air cars.

**Schedule:** Daily, according to Disneyland Park hours.

**Admission/Fare:** Included with admission to Disneyland.

**Locomotives/Rolling Stock:** Locomotives: C.K. Holliday, 4-4-0, 1955 Disney; E.P. Ripley, 4-4-0, 1955 Disney; Fred G. Gurley, 2-4-4, 1894 Baldwin; Ernest S. Marsh, 2-4-0, 1925 Baldwin. Various open-air cars used to transport guests.

**Nearby Attractions/Accommodations:** Located within Disneyland Park. Disneyland is located in Anaheim, which offers many restaurants, hotels, Anaheim Angels baseball, Mighty Ducks ice hockey, and shopping.

**Location/Directions:** Disneyland is located about 35 miles east of downtown Los Angeles. Take the 5 freeway south, exit at Harbor Blvd. in Anaheim, and turn right to the Disneyland entrance.

**Site Address:** 1313 Harbor Blvd., Anaheim, CA
**Mailing Address:** Guest Communications, Disneyland, 1313 Harbor Blvd., Anaheim, CA 92803
**Telephone:** (714) 781-4565
**Internet:** www.disneyland.com

# GOLDEN GATE LIVE STEAMERS, INC.

*Layout*
*2½", 3¼", 4¾", 7½" gauges*

JIM LOWE

**Description:** We are a club of some 200+ members. Our purpose is to build and operate live steam engines. We offer a 10-minute ride over ½ mile of 7½" gauge track.

**Schedule:** Sundays 12-3 p.m., weather permitting and depending on availability of club engine.

**Admission/Fare:** Donations appreciated.

**Locomotives/Rolling Stock:** Two club engines, a Pacific and an Atlantic, plus various club members' engines and cars.

**Special Events:** Open House, May 5. Spring Meet, June 1-2. Fall Meet, October 12-13.

**Nearby Attractions/Accommodations:** Redwood Valley Railway 15" gauge.

**Location/Directions:** In the Berkeley Hills of Route 24 use Fish Ranch Rd. exit, one mile to Grizzly Peak Blvd., right one mile to Lomas Contatas.

**Site Address:** 2501 Grizzly Peak Blvd., Berkeley, CA
**Mailing Address:** 130 Pereira Ave., Tracy, CA 95376
**Telephone:** (209) 835-0263

*Train ride*
*15" gauge*

**Description:** A 1¼-mile ride in the East Bay Hills through Redwood groves. Authentic scale narrow gauge steam equipment and trackwork.

**Schedule:** Year round: weekends and holidays, 11 a.m. to 6 p.m., weather permitting. Summer weekdays, mid-June through Labor Day, 12 to 5 p.m.

**Admission/Fare:** Single-ride ticket, $1.75, five-ride family ticket, $7, under age 2 ride free.

**Locomotives/Rolling Stock:** No. 4, 1875 2-4-2 "Laurel"; no. 5, 1890 4-4-0 "Fern"; no. 11, 4-6-0 "Sequoia"; no. 2, 0-4-0 gas/hydraulic switcher "Juniper." (Current project, no. 7, 1930 2-6-2 "Oak.") Passenger Gondolas with wood bodies, truss rods, archbar trucks; D&RGW-style caboose, 4-wheel work "Jimmies," and special purpose work cars.

**Nearby Attractions/Accommodations:** Tilden Regional Park with antique merry-go-round (with food service), 18-hole golf course, Botanical Gardens, pony rides, Little Farm, Environmental Education Center, hiking trails, picnic areas.

**Location/Directions:** Tilden Regional Park in Berkeley Hills. Grizzly Peak Blvd. at Lomas Cantadas. Off Highway 24 at Fish Ranch Rd.

**Site Address:** Grizzly Peak Blvd. at Lomas Cantadas, Berkeley, CA
**Mailing Address:** 2950 Magnolia St., Berkeley, CA 94705
**Telephone:** (510) 548-6100
**Fax:** (510) 841-3609
**Internet:** www.hometown.aol.com/rvrytrain

# LAWS RAILROAD MUSEUM
# AND HISTORICAL SITE
## *Museum*
### *Narrow gauge*

BOB HAYDEN

**Description:** Original 1883 depot and agent's house, including over 20 other historic buildings with exhibits, and 11 acres of mining, farming, and railroad equipment. Located on the original location of the Carson-Colorado and later the Southern Pacific site.

**Schedule:** Year round: daily, 10 a.m. to 4 p.m. except Thanksgiving, Christmas, New Year's Day and Easter.

**Admission/Fare:** Suggested $2 donation per person.

**Locomotives/Rolling Stock:** 1909 Baldwin 4-6-0, former Southern Pacific; Brill motor car, 1927; 12 boxcars; one A frame gondola; one stock car; one combination caboose; postal caboose.

**Nearby Attractions/Accommodations:** Fishing, skiing, hunting, camping.

**Location/Directions:** From Bishop follow Highway 6 north 5 miles, then turn right on Silver Canyon Rd.

**Site Address:** Silver Canyon Rd., Bishop, CA
**Mailing Address:** Box 363, Bishop, CA 93515
**Telephone:** (760) 873-5950
**Internet:** www.the sierraweb.com/bishop/laws

22

# KNOTT'S BERRY FARM
*Train ride*
*Narrow gauge*

**Description:** The Ghost Town & Calico Railway (GT&C) is America's only narrow-gauge passenger train operating on a daily, year-round basis. America's first theme park and the newest member of the Cedar Fair family of amusement parks and resorts nationwide, Knott's Berry Farm is 165 wild rides, live shows, and attractions designed for real family fun and adventure.

**Schedule:** Open daily except Christmas. Please call (714) 220-5200 or click on www.knotts.com for operating hours.

**Admission/Fare:** Adults, $40; seniors (60+) and kids 3-11, $30.

**Locomotives/Rolling Stock:** No. 41 "Red Cliff" Rio Grande Southern; no. 40 "Green River" Denver & Rio Grande and Denver & Rio Grande Western; railway coaches; special cars; Galloping Goose gasoline-driven railway car former Rio Grande Southern; more.

**Nearby Attractions/Accommodations:** Knott's is 10 minutes from Disneyland Park. The Radisson Resort Knott's Berry Farm is adjacent.

**Location/Directions:** Please call (714) 220-5200 or click on www.knotts.com for directions.

**Site Address:** 8039 Beach Blvd., Buena Park, CA
**Mailing Address:** 8039 Beach Blvd., Buena Park, CA 90620
**Telephone:** (714) 220-5200
**Fax:** (714) 220-5124
**E-mail:** pr@knotts.com
**Internet:** www.knotts.com

**Description:** Huge working model railroad passing by your table as you dine.

**Schedule:** Mondays through Thursdays, 11 a.m. to 4 p.m. Fridays and Saturdays, 11 a.m. to 8:30 p.m. Closed Sundays.

**Admission/Fare:** No charge for railroad, if dining. $8.50 per table, if not dining.

**Nearby Attractions/Accommodations:** Only 10 minutes from Roaring Camp Railroad. Just 5 minutes from the Santa Cruz Boardwalk. One mile off Highway 1.

**Location/Directions:** Exit California Highway 1 on 41st Ave., west one mile, turn left into parking lot at Capitola Station.

*Coupon available, see coupon section.

**Site Address:** 1820-F 41st Ave., Capitola, CA
**Mailing Address:** 1820-F 41st Ave., Capitola, CA 95010
**Telephone:** (831) 475-0150
**Fax:** (831) 475-0188
**Internet:** www.thetrainplace.com

## CLOVIS TOURIST INFORMATION & VISITOR CENTER AT TARPEY DEPOT

**Description:** A restored, century-old train depot, which currently serves as an information and visitor center. Self-guided tours.

**Schedule:** Tuesdays through Sundays, 10 a.m. to 2 p.m. Closed all major holidays.

**Admission/Fare:** Free.

**Special Events:** Clovis Rodeo: last weekend of April. Farmers Market: May through September, Fridays 5 to 9 p.m. National Pole Vault Championship: August.

**Nearby Attractions/Accommodations:** Yosemite National Park, 90 minutes. Kings Canyon National Park, 60 minutes. Sequoia National Park, 60 minutes.

**Location/Directions:** U.S. Highway 99 to Freeway 41 north, onto 180 east, then onto 168 east. Take the Bullard off ramp, go east ½ mile, then north on Clovis Ave., and one block to Fourth St., where the visitor center is located.

**Site Address:** 399 Clovis Ave., Clovis, CA
**Mailing Address:** 399 Clovis Ave., Clovis, CA 93612
**Telephone:** (559) 297-2696 and (888) 725-6947
**Fax:** (559) 297-5826
**E-mail:** tarpeydepot@ci.clovis.ca.us
**Internet:** www.ci.clovis.ca.us

# ORANGE COUNTY MODEL ENGINEERS, INC.
*Train ride*
*7.5" gauge*

**Description:** Free to the public, station store, guided tours of railroad roundhouse and facilities. 18,000 feet of track. Approximately 12-minute ride.

**Schedule:** Year round; third Saturday and Sunday, 10 a.m. to 3:30 p.m.

**Admission/Fare:** Free.

**Locomotives/Rolling Stock:** S.P.R.R. GS-1 4-8-4, Pennsy K-4 Pacific, 4-6-2 Streamlined Hiawatha Engine, 0-4-2T 3.75" scale "Joshua" and many more live steam and diesel locomotives.

**Special Events:** Annual fall meet, third weekend in September; up to 20 trains operating.

**Nearby Attractions/Accommodations:** Disneyland, Knott's Berry Farm. Easy access to all of So. California and its myriad of attractions.

**Location/Directions:** Highway 405 (San Diego) south from Los Angeles. Exit Brookhurst St. south (about 3 miles) to Adams Ave. Left on Adams (east) to Placentia Ave. (about ½ mile) right (south) on Placentia ½ mile to Fairview Park. Station is on the east side of Placentia.

         M

**Site Address:** 2501 Placentia Ave., Costa Mesa, CA (Fairview Park)
**Mailing Address:** PO Box 3216, Costa Mesa, CA 92628
**Telephone:** (949) 54-TRAIN (548-7246)
**Fax:** (714) 838-8646
**E-mail:** verno-hb@ix.netcom.com

# RAILROAD PARK RESORT
*Dinner train, display*
*Standard gauge*

C. MURPHY

**Description:** A 28-room caboose motel and restaurant, dinner house in refurbished train cars. RV park and campground on premises.

**Schedule:** Year round.

**Admission/Fare:** Room–$70 to $75 per night. Dinner average $15 per person.

**Locomotives/Rolling Stock:** Willamette Shay; snowplow, flanger; cabooses; speeders.

**Nearby Attractions/Accommodations:** Golfing, skiing, camping, hiking, lakes, fishing, boating, and state park.

**Location/Directions:** I-5, Railroad Park exit. Forty miles north of Redding, just south of city of Dunsmuir.

**Site Address:** 100 Railroad Park Rd., Dunsmuir, CA
**Mailing Address:** 100 Railroad Park Rd., Dunsmuir, CA 96025
**Telephone:** (530) 235-4440
**Fax:** (530) 235-4470
**E-mail:** rrp@rrpark.com
**Internet:** www.rrpark.com

California, Eureka

# NORTHERN COUNTIES LOGGING MUSEUM
*Train ride, museum*
*Standard gauge*

MICHAEL KELLOGG

**Description:** Fort Humbolt State Historic Park includes a logging museum. The exhibit emphasizes historic steam logging equipment used in redwood logging. Several artifacts have been restored to operating condition and are demonstrated on occasion by the Northern Counties Logging Interpretive Association. Two small steam locomotives provide short rides once a month during the summer. Cab rides for members.

**Schedule:** The museum is open daily, 9 a.m. to 5 p.m. Steam trains and equipment operate April 27-28 (Donkey Days), May 18, June 15, July 20, August 17, and September 21, 11 a.m. to 4 p.m.

**Admission/Fare:** Museum and displays–free. Train rides–adults, $1; children, $.50.

**Locomotives/Rolling Stock:** Bear Harbor Lumber Co., Marshutz & Cantrell, 1892, 12-ton 0-4-0, no. 1 "Gypsy"; Elk River Mill and Lumber Co., Marshutz & Cantrell, 1884, 9-ton 0-4-0, no. 1 "Falk"; more.

**Special Events:** Dolbeer Steam Donkey Days, April 27-28.

**Nearby Attractions/Accommodations:** Historic military fort adjacent; national and state redwood parks in the area.

**Location/Directions:** Off Highway 101 at the southern end of Eureka, opposite Bayshore Mall.

       M  TRAIN

**Site Address:** 3431 Fort Ave., Eureka, CA
**Mailing Address:** 3431 Fort Ave., Eureka, CA 95503
**Telephone:** (707) 445-6567
**Internet:** www.visithumboldt.com/loggingmuseum

28

California, Felton

# ROARING CAMP &
# BIG TREES RAILROAD
*Train ride*
*Narrow gauge*

**Description:** 75-minute round trip from Roaring Camp Depot to Bear Mt. Redwood Forest. Excursion about the Dixieanna Shay locomotive travels through magnificent redwood forest. Conductor gives brief history of locomotives, trees, and area.

**Schedule:** Open year round.

**Admission/Fare:** Adults, $15.50; children, $10.50. Parking, $5.

**Locomotives/Rolling Stock:** 1912 Lima 2-truck Shay, 2-truck Heisler, 3-truck Shay, former West Side Lumber.

**Special Events:** Civil War Re-enactment, Memorial weekend. Frog Jump and Race, July. Labor Day Roundup. October Harvest Faire. Thanksgiving Mountain Man Rendezvous.

**Nearby Attractions/Accommodations:** Santa Cruz Beach and Boardwalk, Longs Marine Library, Henry Cowell State Park, Monterey Bay Aquarium, Winchester Mystery.

**Location/Directions:** Off State Route 17/880 to Santa Cruz, Mt. Hermon exit, 3.5 miles to left on Graham Hill Rd., ¼ mile to Roaring Camp.

*Coupon available, see coupon section. †See ad on page A-17.

**Site Address:** Graham Hill Rd. and Roaring Camp Rd., Felton, CA
**Mailing Address:** PO Box G-1, Felton, CA 95018
**Telephone:** (831) 335-4484
**Fax:** (831) 335-3509
**E-mail:** RCamp448@aol.com
**Internet:** www.roaringcamp.com

# SANTA CRUZ, BIG TREES & PACIFIC RAILWAY
*Train ride*
*Standard gauge*

**Description:** One hour long journey from the Redwood Forest to the beach in Santa Cruz. Line runs along San Lorenzo River Canyon, through historic part of city. Coaches are turn of the century Lackawanna cars.

**Schedule:** June through Labor Day, southbound, 10:30 a.m. and 2:30 p.m. and northbound 12:30 p.m. and 4:30 p.m. September and October, weekends only.

**Admission/Fare:** Adults and seniors, $17.00; children (3-12), $12.00. Parking, $5.

**Locomotives/Rolling Stock:** Nos. 2600 & 2641, CF7 1500-horsepower diesels, former Santa Fe; no. 20, 50-ton center-cab Whitcomb; three 1900-era wooden passenger coaches; two 1920s-era steel coaches; seven open-air cars.

**Special Events:** Holiday Christmas Train, weekends.

**Nearby Attractions/Accommodations:** Henry Cowell State Park, Santa Cruz Beach and Boardwalk, Shadow Brook restaurant, Longs Marine Library.

**Location/Directions:** Six miles inland from Santa Cruz on Graham Hill Rd., off Highway 17.

*Coupon available, see coupon section.

**Site Address:** Graham Hill Rd. and Roaring Camp Rd., Felton, CA
**Mailing Address:** PO Box G-1, Felton, CA 95018
**Telephone:** (831) 335-4484
**Fax:** (831) 335-3509
**E-mail:** RCamp448@aol.com
**Internet:** www.roaringcamp.com

# FILLMORE & WESTERN RAILWAY
*Train ride, dinner train*
*Standard gauge*

**Description:** Day and evening diner car service, 2½- to 3½-hour rides; Murder Mystery dinners on Saturday evenings; barbecue; school field trips; Pumpkinliner; Christmas Tree excursion trains; dance car (with dinner) wine train.

**Schedule:** Year round; weekends. Group excursions by prior arrangement.

**Admission/Fare:** Day excursions: adults, $18; seniors (62+), $16; children, $8; infant-3 years, $5.

**Locomotives/Rolling Stock:** 1906 Baldwin steam locomotive no. 51; 1891 0-4-0 Porter no. 1 Sespe; 1949 F7 engines nos. 100 and 101; more.

**Special Events:** Railroad Days Festival, March (Fillmore town festival); Fourth of July (festival, arts and crafts, chili cook-off, etc.); Pumpkinliner, October; Christmas Tree Trains, December.

**Nearby Attractions/Accommodations:** Six Flags; Magic Mountain; Ventura County Beaches; Santa Barbara. All major hotels in Santa Clarita, Ventura, Oxnord, Camarillo and Santa Barbara.

**Location/Directions:** I-5 to Highway 126 (Ventura County, California) and Central Ave. in Fillmore. Two blocks north to Main St. Or, I-101 from Ventura, Hwy. 126 east to Central Ave. Two blocks north to Main St. Free parking.

**Site Address:** 351 Santa Clara Ave., Fillmore, CA
**Mailing Address:** PO Box 960, Fillmore, CA 93016
**Telephone:** (805) 524-2546 and (800) 773 TRAIN (773-8724)
**Fax:** (805) 524-1838
**E-mail:** fwry@earthlink.net
**Internet:** www.fwry.com

# YOSEMITE MOUNTAIN-SUGAR PINE RAILROAD
*Train ride*
*36" gauge*

JOSEPH BISPO

**Description:** The YMSP operates a one-hour narrated steam-powered excursion over a restored section of the Madera Sugar Pine Lumber Co. The 4-mile trip runs through the scenic Sierra Nevada at an elevation of 5000 feet, winds down a 4 percent grade into Lewis Creek Canyon, passes Horseshoe Curve, Cold Spring Crossing, and stops at Lewis Creek Loop. Ex-Westside Lumber Co. Shays provide the motive power for the train. Converted logging cars using sectioned logs are used for passenger cars.

**Schedule:** Railcars: April through October: daily. Steam train: May through September: daily. April and October: weekends.

**Admission/Fare:** Railcars: adults, $9; children 3-12, $4.50. Steam train: adults, $13; children 3-12, $6.50.

**Locomotives/Rolling Stock:** 1928 Lima 3-truck Shay, no. 10; 1913 Lima 3-truck Shay, no. 15; Vulcan 1935 10-ton switcher; four model A powered railcars; logging cars; covered and open converted flatcars, more.

**Special Events:** Moonlight Special with steak barbecue and music every Saturday and Wednesday night in summer; reservations advised. Gold panning, group tours, theme events, and private charters.

**Nearby Attractions/Accommodations:** Operating in the Sierra National Forest, 4 miles south of Yosemite National Park on Highway 41. Narrow Gauge Inn next door.

**Site Address:** 56001 Yosemite Highway 41, Fish Camp, CA
**Mailing Address:** 56001 Yosemite Highway 41, Fish Camp, CA 93623
**Telephone:** (559) 683-7273
**Internet:** www.ymsprr.com

California, Folsom
(Folsom City Zoo)

**FOLSOM VALLEY RAILWAY**
*Train ride*
*12" narrow gauge*

TERRY GOLD

**Description:** A ¾-mile ride through a 50-acre city park features vintage wooden freight cars drawn by a ⅓-scale oil fire locomotive representative of late 19th-century steam motive power.

**Schedule:** February through October: Tuesdays through Fridays, 11 a.m. to 2 p.m.; weekends and holidays, 11 a.m. to 4 p.m. November through January: weekends and school holidays., 11 a.m. to 4 p.m. All are weather permitting.

**Admission/Fare:** $1.50 per person.

**Locomotives/Rolling Stock:** 1950 Ottaway Locomotive old-time wooder; truss rod-style freight cars; cattle car; hopper car; five open gondola cars; bobber caboose.

**Special Events:** Train will operate all day until 10 p.m., week of July 4.

**Nearby Attractions/Accommodations:** Folsom City Zoo.

**Location/Directions:** Folsom is approximately 25 miles east of Sacramento off U.S. 50.

**Site Address:** 50 Natoma St., Folsom, CA
**Mailing Address:** 121 Dunstable Way, Folsom, CA 95630
**Telephone:** (916) 983-1873
**E-mail:** goldtown@jps.net and goldtown@juno.com

# CALIFORNIA WESTERN RAILROAD
## THE SKUNK TRAIN
*Train ride, dinner train*
*Standard gauge*

GARY RICHARDS

**Description:** In the heart of Redwood country. Come ride this historic train through the forest. 3½ hour half-day trips, 8½ hour full-day trips, and 5 hour sunset BBQ's.

**Schedule:** Daily service, March through November; regular service, December through February.

**Locomotives/Rolling Stock:** No. 45 1924 2-8-2 Baldwin, nos. 64, 65, 66 1955 EMD GP9, Coach nos. 655, 656, 657, 658, 659, 696, 697, 698, 699, 1925 M-100 and 1935 M-300.

**Nearby Attractions/Accommodations:** Fort Bragg is located on the rugged Mendocino Coast. Willits is located at the gateway to the Redwoods.

**Location/Directions:** 3½ hours west of Sacramento; 3 hours north of San Francisco.

**Site Address:** Fort Bragg and Willits, CA
**Mailing Address:** PO Box 907, Fort Bragg, CA 95437
**Telephone:** (707) 964-6371 and (800) 77-SKUNK
**Fax:** (707) 964-6754
**E-mail:** skunk@skunktrain.com
**Internet:** www.skunktrain.com

**Description:** Housed in the 1901 Southern Pacific Depot is a museum, along with an N scale and HO scale layout.

**Schedule:** Year round, first and third Sundays, 10 a.m. to 4 p.m.

**Admission/Fare:** Donation.

**Nearby Attractions/Accommodations:** The Niles District, home to many antique shops, is two blocks away.

**Location/Directions:** Between Nursery Ave. and the Sullivan underpass.

   M

**Site Address:** 36997 Mission Blvd., Fremont, CA
**Mailing Address:** PO Box 2716, Fremont, CA 94536
**Telephone:** (510) 797-4449
**Internet:** nilesdepot.railfan.net/NDHFhome.html

# SOUTH COAST RAILROAD MUSEUM
*Museum*
*Standard gauge*

**Description:** The centerpiece is the historic Goleta Depot, a Victorian-styled Southern Pacific country station. The museum features refurnished rooms and station grounds, and a variety of informative displays, including a 300-square-foot HO scale model railroad exhibit. Other attractions include miniature train and handcar rides, Gandy Dancer Theater, picnic grounds, and a museum store and gift shop.

**Schedule:** Museum–Wednesdays through Sundays, 1 to 4 p.m. Miniature train–1:15 to 3:45 p.m. Handcar–third Saturday of each month, 1:15 to 3:45 p.m.

**Admission/Fare:** Museum–donations appreciated. Handcar–free. Miniature train–$1.

**Locomotives/Rolling Stock:** 1960s Southern Pacific bay window caboose no. 4023.

**Special Events:** Depot Day, fourth Sunday in September, 11 a.m. to 4 p.m.

**Location/Directions:** Goleta is seven miles west of Santa Barbara, U.S. 101 north exit Los Carneros Rd.

       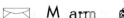     M arm

**Site Address:** 300 N. Los Carneros Rd., Goleta, CA
**Mailing Address:** 300 N. Los Carneros Rd., Goleta, CA 93117-1502
**Telephone:** (805) 964-3540
**Fax:** (805) 964-3549
**E-mail:** museum@goletadepot.org
**Internet:** www.goletadepot.org

# RAILTOWN 1897
## SIERRA RAILWAY COMPANY
*Train ride, museum*
*Standard gauge*

**Description:** Operated by the California State Railroad Museum; one of Hollywood's most popular filming locations. The Historic Sierra Railroad Shops and Roundhouse at Railtown 1897 have been in continuous operation as a steam locomotive maintenance facility for over a century. Six-mile, 40-minute round trip route passing through Gold Country.

**Schedule:** Open daily 9:30 a.m. to 4:30 p.m., except Thanksgiving, Christmas, and New Year's Day. Steam trains operate weekends April to October (selected dates only in November and December), departing hourly 11 a.m. to 3 p.m. Guided roundhouse tours available daily.

**Admission/Fare:** Roundhouse tours: adults, $2; children (6-12), $1. Train rides: adults, $6; children (6-12), $3; 5 and under are free.

**Locomotives/Rolling Stock:** Sierra Railroad 2-8-0 no. 28; 4-6-0 no. 3; combine no. 5; coach no. 6; former Feather River Shay no. 2; former Southern Pacific commuter coaches; more.

**Special Events:** April, May, July, August, September, December.

**Nearby Attractions/Accommodations:** Jamestown, "Gateway to the Mother Lode," Sonora, "Queen of the Southern Mines," preserved Gold Rush town of Columbia (State Historical Park), Yosemite National Park.

**Location/Directions:** Located 3 blocks east of downtown Jamestown on Highways 49/107 just west of the Highway 120 junction.

**Site Address:** Fifth Ave. and Reservoir Rd., Jamestown, CA
**Mailing Address:** PO Box 1250, Jamestown, CA 95327
**Telephone:** (209) 984-3953
**Fax:** (209) 984-4936
**E-mail:** railtown@mlode.com
**Internet:** www.railtown1897.org

# LOMITA RAILROAD MUSEUM
*Museum, display*
*Standard gauge*

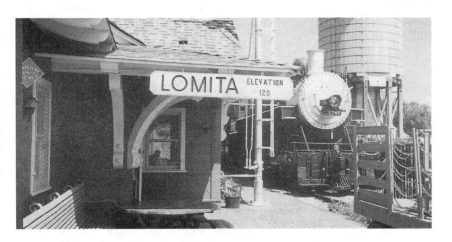

**Description:** A replica of the Boston & Maine station at Wakefield, Massachusetts. On display are lanterns of the steam era, chinaware, and silverware of the period, scale model live steam engines, spikes, tie date nails, insulators, prints, photographs, postcards, clocks, and a wooden water tower 35 feet high and 14 feet in diameter next to the engine.

**Schedule:** Year round. Wednesday through Sunday, 10 a.m. to 5 p.m. Closed Thanksgiving and Christmas.

**Admission/Fare:** Adults, $2; children under age 12, $1.

**Locomotives/Rolling Stock:** 1902 Baldwin 2-6-0 (Mogul) no. 1765 with a whale-back tender, former Southern Pacific. 1910 yellow caboose, UP OWR&N; 1913 UP boxcar; 1923 oil tank car, Union Oil Co.; Santa Fe red caboose no. 531.

**Special Events:** Golden Spike Day, call or write for details.

**Nearby Attractions/Accommodations:** South Coast Botanical Gardens, Torrance Cabrillo Museum, San Pedro, Banning House and Drum Barracks, Wilmington.

**Location/Directions:** 110 (Harbor Freeway) south to Pacific Coast Highway off ramp. Right (west) to Narbonne Ave. Right to second signal. Right (east) one block. Parking on 250th St.

*Coupon available, see coupon section.

     M

**Site Address:** 250th St. and Woodward Ave., Lomita, CA
**Mailing Address:** 2137 W. 250th St., Lomita, CA 90717
**Telephone:** (310) 326-6255

**ELDORADO EXPRESS RAILROAD**
*Train ride*
*18" gauge*

**Description:** A one-mile roundtrip in El Dorado Regional Park, with some narration.

**Schedule:** Thursdays through Sundays, 10:30 a.m. to 4 p.m.

**Admission/Fare:** Adults, $2; children (1-3) $1.

**Locomotives/Rolling Stock:** Built 1946 locomotive 4-6-2 Pacific, Tender, 3 open cars, each holds 18 persons.

**Nearby Attractions/Accommodations:** Knott's Berry Farm, Queen Mary ship.

**Location/Directions:** 605 Freeway and Spring St.

*Coupon available, see coupon section.

**Site Address:** 605 Freeway and Spring St., Long Beach, CA
**Mailing Address:** 4943 Lincoln Ave., Cypress, CA 90630

## TRAVEL TOWN MUSEUM
*Train ride, museum, display, layout*
*Standard and narrow gauge*

**Description:** An outdoor transportation museum celebrating the history of railroad in the western United States, concentrating on California and specifically on Los Angeles history.

**Schedule:** Year round: weekdays 10 a.m. to 4 p.m., weekends 10 a.m. to 5 p.m.

**Admission/Fare:** Free.

**Locomotives/Rolling Stock:** Locomotives, freight cars, cabooses, interurbans and motorcars.

**Nearby Attractions/Accommodations:** Griffith Park, Los Angeles Zoo, Autry Museum of Western Heritage, Griffith Observatory, Greek Theatre.

**Location/Directions:** Ventura Freeway exit 134 (Forest Lawn Dr.), located at Griffith Park and Zoo Drives.

       arm ᴛʀᴀɪɴ

**Site Address:** Griffith Park, 5200 Zoo Dr., Los Angeles, CA
**Mailing Address:** 3900 W. Chevy Chase Dr., Los Angeles, CA 90039
**Telephone:** (323) 662-5874
**E-mail:** TravelTown@rap.lacity.org
**Internet:** www.lacity.org/rap/grifmet/tt/index.htm

**NAPA VALLEY WINE TRAIN**
*Train ride, dinner train*
*Standard gauge*

**Description:** Year round gourmet dining excursions for brunch, lunch or dinner, 3-hour, 36-mile round trip. Three different restaurant options, special events regularly.

**Schedule:** Year round, daily, 8 a.m. to 10 p.m.

**Admission/Fare:** $30.00-$110 per person

**Locomotives/Rolling Stock:** Four Alco FPA-44 diesels, nos. 70, 71, 72, and 73; seven Pullman dining and lounge cars, circa 1915-1917; one 1952 Pullman Vista Dome car; one Pullman coach converted to professional viewing kitchen.

**Special Events:** Murder mystery dinner theatre, family fun, vintners luncheons, appellation dinners, dinner concert series.

**Nearby Attractions/Accommodations:** American center for wine, food and the arts.

**Location/Directions:** One hour north of San Francisco in downtown Napa off Soscol Ave. and First St.

†See ad on page A-5.

**Site Address:** 1275 McKinstry St., Napa, CA
**Mailing Address:** 1275 McKinstry St., Napa, CA 94559
**Telephone:** (707) 253-2111 and (800) 427-4124
**Fax:** (707) 253-9264
**E-mail:** www.winetrain.com
**Internet:** www.winetrain.com

# NATIONAL CITY DEPOT
*Museum, display*
*Standard gauge*

**Description:** One- and 3-mile rides on the Coronado Belt Line. The museum depicts the Santa Fe and San Diego Electric Railway Company.

**Schedule:** Saturday and Sunday, 12 to 4 p.m.

**Admission/Fare:** Adults, $5/10; Children, $3/7. Museum: Adults, $3; Children, $1.

**Locomotives/Rolling Stock:** Santa Maria Railbus; various LRV/Speeders.

**Nearby Attractions/Accommodations:** National City and Otay (NC&O) no. 1 Car Plaza across the street; Sea World; world-famous San Diego Zoo; Tijuana, Mexico.

**Location/Directions:** Five miles south of San Diego. Take I-5 south to Bay Marina Dr. exit in National City and turn right. Go west two blocks and the museum is on the right.

         M arm

**Site Address:** 922 W. 23rd St., National City, CA
**Mailing Address:** 1240 E. Plaza Blvd. #604-132, National City, CA 91950
**Telephone:** (619) 474-4400
**Fax:** (619) 474-4400
**E-mail:** ncd@trainweb.com
**Internet:** www.trainweb.com/sandiegorail/sdera

**NEVADA COUNTY
TRACTION COMPANY**
*Train ride*
*36" and 24" gauge*

**Description:** Take a 3-mile round-trip, 1½-hour train ride. View rolling stock dated from 1888 to early 1900s. Visit a 1850s Chinese cemetery.

**Schedule:** Summer hours, May through September: daily, 10 a.m. to 2 p.m. and 4 p.m. October: Halloween all month, with same time schedule (and Friday and Saturday night Haunted Forest of Terror at 7 p.m. and 8 p.m.

**Admission/Fare:** Daily rides: adults, $8; children, $5. In October, daily rides: adults, $9; children, $6. Haunted Forest, $10.

**Locomotives/Rolling Stock:** Argent no. 5 former Stone Machine Co.; Daisy Tenn. 2-6-2, 26-ton Lima Operational West Side Lumber Co.; railbus, 1939 0-4-0 Henschel 14-ton electric speeder; 1959 0-4-0 Plymouth 12-ton 1985 street trolley.

**Special Events:** October, Haunted Forest of Terror.

**Nearby Attractions/Accommodations:** Empire Mine State Park, Malahoff Digging State Park, Historical Nevada City (Independent Trail is wheelchair accessible), Sacramento Railroad Museum.

**Location/Directions:** On Highway 49 and 20, 55 miles northeast of Sacramento. Take Sacramento St. exit, right on Railroad Ave., ⅛ mile on right. Located at Northern Queen Inn upper parking lot.

**Site Address:** 402 Railroad Ave., Nevada City, CA
**Mailing Address:** 402 Railroad Ave., Nevada City, CA 95959
**Telephone:** (530) 265-0896
**Fax:** (530) 265-0869
**E-mail:** depotpeople@nccn.net
**Internet:** www.northernqueeninn.com

43

# HERITAGE JUNCTION
## HISTORIC PARK
*Museum, display*

**Description:** We offer a collection of historic structures, including 1886 Southern Pacific train station.

**Schedule:** Saturdays and Sundays, 1 to 4 p.m.

**Admission/Fare:** Free. Donations appreciated.

**Locomotives/Rolling Stock:** Locomotive 1639 Mogul.

**Special Events:** Christmas Open House, always second Sunday in December. Cowboy Poetry and Music Festival, March 30-April 1, 2001.

**Nearby Attractions/Accommodations:** Magic Mountain, Hart Park.

**Location/Directions:** Next to Hart Park.

**Site Address:** 24107 San Fernando Rd., Newhall, CA
**Mailing Address:** PO Box 221925, Newhall, CA 91322
**Telephone:** (661) 254-1275
**Internet:** www.scvhistoricalsociety.org

# SIERRA RAILROAD GOLDEN SUNSET DINNER TRAIN
*Dinner train*

**Description:** The "Golden Sunset" dinner train takes passengers on a 38-mile long trip through the countryside to the Sierra foothills. Along the way, the passengers enjoy fine dining and our lounge car.

**Schedule:** Trips every weekend, year round.

**Admission/Fare:** Brunch, $59; Dinner, $69; Murder Mystery, $69; Rail & Raft, $88; Party Train, $25; Wild West, $55; X-mas trip, $18. Children 7 and under are half off.

**Locomotives/Rolling Stock:** GP9 Sera 46, Baldwin S-12s, nos. 40, 42, 44; GP-7 no. 47; GP-20s, nos. 48 and 50; dining cars, lounge car, cabooses.

**Special Events:** Oakdale Chocolate Festival, May; Oakdale Rodeo, second weekend in April; Antique Festival, third weekend in June.

**Nearby Attractions/Accommodations:** Yosemite National Park; fishing; wine and cheese festival; Hershey's Chocolate plant; River Journeys; Oakdale Cheese Factory; Civil War living history reenactment.

**Location/Directions:** From San Francisco, take 580 and 120 east to Oakdale. From Sacramento, take Highway 99 south and 120 east 70 miles. From Los Angeles, take Highway 99 and J14 north 300 miles to Oakdale.

**Site Address:** 220 S. Sierra Ave., Oakdale, CA
**Mailing Address:** 220 S. Sierra Ave., Oakdale, CA 95361
**Telephone:** (209) 848-2100 or (800) 866-1690
**Fax:** (209) 848-8595
**E-mail:** sierrarail@aol.com
**Internet:** www.sierrarailroad.com

45

# IRVINE PARK RAILROAD
*Train ride*
*24" gauge*

JOHN FORD

**Description:** Irvine Park Railroad is located on 500 acres in Irvine Regional Park, the oldest county park in the state of California. The train departs from an old-fashioned depot, where railroad folk songs fill the air. The locomotive will make a scenic one-mile journey around the park during which riders can view two lakes complete with waterfalls and fountains, a grove of oak trees, and the Orange County Zoo. The ride is narrated by the engineer and lasts approximately 12 minutes.

**Schedule:** Winter–daily, 10 a.m. to 4 p.m. Summer–daily, 10 a.m. to 4:30 p.m. Closed Thanksgiving and Christmas.

**Admission/Fare:** $3; children under age 1 are free. School group rates are available.

**Locomotives/Rolling Stock:** A ⅓ scale replica of the 1863 C.P. Huntington; four coaches.

**Special Events:** Christmas train two weeks prior to Christmas. Call for times.

**Nearby Attractions/Accommodations:** Bicycle and paddleboat rentals, Orange County Zoo, food concessions, pony rides.

**Location/Directions:** From State Highway 55 take the Chapman Ave. exit and drive east to Jamboree Rd. Turn left into the park entrance.

**Site Address:** 1 Irvine Park Rd., Orange, CA
**Mailing Address:** 1 Irvine Park Rd., Orange, CA 92669
**Telephone:** (714) 997-3968
**Fax:** (714) 997-0459
**Internet:** www.irvineparkrr.com

# ORLAND, NEWVILLE & PACIFIC RAILROAD
*Train ride*
*15" gauge*

**Description:** The ON&P is an all-volunteer railroad operating in the Glenn County Fairgrounds. A 1-mile ride takes visitors past the original Orland Southern Pacific depot, the picnic site, and the demonstration orchard, then through a tunnel and along Heritage Trail. The train is normally pulled by a magnificent 5/12-scale live-steam model of the North Pacific Coast's 1875 Baldwin narrow-gauge locomotive "Sonoma." The picnic grounds at Deadowl Station are open whenever the train is running. Former Orland Southern Pacific depot, 1918 Southern Pacific 2-8-0 no. 2852, caboose, schoolhouse, blacksmith shop, print shop, 1920s gas station, miscellaneous steam machinery, old farm equipment. Livestock is also exhibited at fair time, during May and October.

**Schedule:** 12 noon to 5 p.m. Saturday and Sunday; Spring: March 23-24 through May 15-19; Fall: August 31, September 1-2 through October 19-20.

**Admission/Fare:** $1.

**Locomotives/Rolling Stock:** No. 12 replica of 1876 Baldwin 4-4-0; no. 2 4-4-0 amusement park type; Davenport switch engine; four open gondolas; covered car.

**Special Events:** Glenn County Fair, May 15-19. Harvest Festival, Oct. 19-20. Spook Train, Oct. 31, Father's Day, June 16. Independence Day, July 4.

**Location/Directions:** Glenn County Fairgrounds.

**Site Address:** 221 E. Yolo St., Orland, CA
**Mailing Address:** PO Box 667, Orland, CA 95963
**Telephone:** (530) 865-1168 and (530) 865-9747
**Fax:** (530) 865-1197

# ORANGE EMPIRE RAILWAY MUSEUM
*Train ride, museum, display*
*Standard and narrow gauge*

JIM WALKER, JR.

**Description:** Trains run on 1.5-mile right-of-way, streetcars on 0.7-mile loop within the museum's property.

**Schedule:** Museum grounds–daily: 9 a.m. to 5 p.m., weekends and holidays, 11 a.m. to 5 p.m. Demonstration railroad–year round.

**Admission/Fare:** Free admission. All day ride pass–adults, $8; children 5-11, $6; under age 5 are free. Special events may have additional fees.

**Locomotives/Rolling Stock:** VC Railway 2 Prairie; GF 2 Mogul; UP 2564 Mikado; SP 1474 S4; SP 3100 U25B; UP 942 E8A; and more.

**Special Events:** Rail Festival in April; Railroadiana Swap Meet in March and September; Train Fair in October; Pumpkin Train in October; Santa Train in December.

**Nearby Attractions/Accommodations:** Perris Valley Skydiving Center; Perris Auto Speedway; Lake Perris Recreation Area; March Field Air Museum; Temecula Wineries; Best Western Perris Inn; Mission Inn in Riverside.

**Location/Directions:** I-215, exit west onto Fourth St./Route 74, left on "A" St. to museum.

**Site Address:** 2201 S. "A" St., Perris, CA
**Mailing Address:** PO Box 548, Perris, CA 92570-0548
**Telephone:** (909) 657-2605 and (909) 653-3020
**Fax:** (909) 943-2676
**E-mail:** oerm@juno.com
**Internet:** www.oerm.org

# GOLDEN STATE MODEL RAILROAD
## MUSEUM
*Layout*

GEORGE HALL

**Description:** Three layouts and fixed displays occupying 10,000 square feet.

**Schedule:** May through October, Sundays 1 to 5 p.m.

**Admission/Fare:** Adults, $3; children under 14 and seniors, $2; family, $7.

**Special Events:** Holiday Shows: Sunday after Thanksgiving, Sundays on either side of Christmas.

**Nearby Attractions/Accommodations:** Miller-Knox Regional Park (we are in it), picnics, views of San Francisco, ATSF Railroad Ferry Pier (former), ASTF Richmond yard, USS Red Oak Victory (tours).

**Location/Directions:** Exit I-580 in Richmond at Canal Blvd. from either direction. Turn at signal to Garrard Blvd. (a right from the East Bay, or a left when coming from the San Rafael Bridge). Turn left at the stop sign onto Garrard Blvd. Proceed straight past two stop signs, and the natatorium, and into Ferry Point Tunnel. Dornan Drive is on the other side of the tunnel. We are located about ½ mile past the tunnel on the left across from Miller-Knox Regional Shoreline Park.

*Coupon available, see coupon section.

**Site Address:** 900-A Dornan Dr., Point Richmond, CA
**Mailing Address:** PO Box 1243, El Cerrito, CA 94530
**Telephone:** (510) 234-4884
**Internet:** www.gsmrm.org

# RAILWAY & LOCOMOTIVE HISTORICAL SOCIETY, SOUTHERN CALIFORNIA CHAPTER

*Museum*

*Standard and narrow gauge*

**Description:** Former ATSF Arcadia Depot (1895) houses exhibits and a gift shop. There is an outside display of locomotives and rolling stock, including motor cars; ice refrigerator car; caboose; berth and galley section of business car; horse car showing stable section.

**Schedule:** The second Sunday of every month and the day before, 9 a.m. to 4 p.m. When Easter or Mother's Day falls on the second Sunday, the museum will open on the preceeding weekend, same hours. Daily during the Los Angeles County Fair in September. Other times by request.

**Admission/Fare:** No charge, except during the County Fair which requires a general fair admission.

**Locomotives/Rolling Stock:** Union Pacific/Alco 4-8-8-4 Big Boy, no. 4014 (1941); Atchison Topeka and Santa Fe/Baldwin 4-5-4 Hudson, no. 3450 (1927); Union Pacific DD40X diesel-electric, no. 6915.

**Special Events:** Meetings are held at the Cowan's Room at St. Edmund's Church, 1175 San Gabriel Blvd., San Marino, on the first Tuesday of every month (September-June) at 7:30 p.m.

**Nearby Attractions/Accommodations:** Fairplex R.V. Park; Sheraton Suites Fairplex; NHRA Pomona Drag Strip; NHRA Museum.

**Location/Directions:** Enter the Fairplex at Gate 1, or Main Gate, off Fairplex Dr.

     M

**Site Address:** Los Angeles County Fairplex, Pomona, CA
**Mailing Address:** PO Box 2250, Pomona, CA 91769
**Telephone:** (909) 623-0190
**Internet:** www.trainweb.org/rlhs

**PORTOLA RAILROAD MUSEUM**
*Museum*
*Standard gauge*

NORMAN HOLMES

**Description:** A one-mile ride around a balloon turning track through pine forest. On display are more than 70 freight cars representing nearly every car type of the Western Pacific Railroad; several passenger cars; other rolling stock; railroad artifacts in the diesel shop building.

**Schedule:** Museum–March through mid-December 10 a.m. to 5 p.m. Train–Memorial Day through Sunday after Labor Day: weekends, 11 a.m. to 4 p.m. Grounds open in winter weather permitting.

**Admission/Fare:** Call or write for information.

**Locomotives/Rolling Stock:** Two steam, 1 electric and 32 diesels of all types including 13 former Western Pacific, 6 former Southern Pacific and 3 former Union Pacific. Manufacturers represented: Alco, Baldwin, Electro-Motive, Fairbanks-Morse, General Electric, Ingersol-Rand, and Plymouth. Steam locomotives are former UP 737, an 1887 4-4-0 and former SP 1215, a 1913 0-6-0.

**Special Events:** Feather River Railroad Days, August 18-19. Railfan Photographers Day, September 15.

**Location/Directions:** From State Route 70, travel one mile south on County Road A-15 (Gulling) across the river and through town. Follow signs to the museum.

†See ad on page A-13.

**Site Address:** 700 Western Pacific Way, Portola, CA
**Mailing Address:** PO Box 608, Portola, CA 96122-0608
**Telephone:** (530) 832-4131
**Fax:** (530) 832-1854

51

# POWAY-MIDLAND RAILROAD
*Train ride*
*42" narrow gauge*

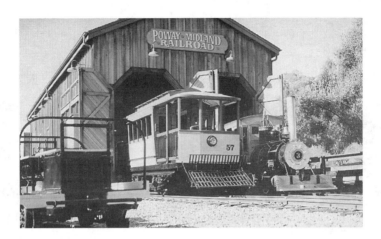

**Description:** Located in Old Poway Park, a place for folks to come and enjoy the Old West. See restored historic buildings and antique rolling stock. Take a ¾-mile train ride around the park.

**Schedule:** Year round. Saturdays 10 a.m. to 4 p.m., Sundays 11 a.m. to 2 p.m. No operation second Sunday of each month. Steam operations first and third weekends only.

**Admission/Fare:** Locomotive, $2; Trolley, $1.50; Speeder, $1; children under age 12, $.50.

**Special Events:** Fourth of July. Train Song Festival, October. Christmas in the Park, second Saturday in December.

**Nearby Attractions/Accommodations:** San Diego, 20 miles. Zoo, Wild Animal Park, Sea World, Legoland, beaches.

**Location/Directions:** I-15 north or south to Poway Rd. exit; 3 miles east to Midland Rd., turn left; 1 mile north to Old Poway Park.

**Site Address:** Old Poway Park, 14134 Midland Rd., Poway, CA
**Mailing Address:** PO Box 1244, Poway, CA 92074-1244
**Telephone:** (858) 486-4063
**Fax:** (858) 513-0745
**E-mail:** pmrrweb@powaymidlandrr.org
**Internet:** www.powaymidlandrr.org

# RIVERSIDE LIVE STEAMERS

*Train ride, layout*
*7½" gauge*

**Description:** One-eighth size trains, all steam, on a 6,800-foot track in Hunter Park.

**Schedule:** Second and fourth Sundays, 10 a.m. to 3 p.m.

**Admission/Fare:** Donation only.

**Special Events:** Spring Meet, April 27-28. Fall Meet, October 26-27.

**Location/Directions:** Corner of Columbia and Iowa, approximately one mile northeast of the junction of California 60/91 and I-215.

**Site Address:** 1496 Columbia Ave., Riverside, CA
**Mailing Address:** PO Box 5512, Riverside, CA 92517
**Telephone:** (909) 779-9024

**CALIFORNIA STATE RAILROAD MUSEUM**
*Museum*
*Standard and 36" gauge*

**Description:** One of the finest interpretive railroad museums in North America, CSRM's 11-acre facilities in Old Sacramento include the 100,000-square-foot museum of railroad history, a reconstructed 1870s Central Pacific passenger station, and an extensive library and archive.

**Schedule:** Year round: daily, 10 a.m to 5 p.m. Closed Thanksgiving, Christmas, New Year's Day.

**Admission/Fare:** Adults, $3; youth and children ages 16 and under, free.

**Locomotives/Rolling Stock:** More than 30 meticulously restored locomotives and cars on display dating from the 1860s to present. Favorites are Pullman-style sleeper, streamlined dining car, 1870s Victorian coaches, and a railway post office.

**Special Events:** Day Out with Thomas, April; Sacramento Jazz Jubilee, Memorial Day weekend; Gold Rush Days, Labor Day weekend; Train Time for Santa, Thanksgiving weekend and December; also regular changing exhibits primarily spring, summer, and fall.

**Nearby Attractions/Accommodations:** Old Sacramento (California's largest concentration of restored 19th century commercial structures), state capitol, Sutter's Fort, Crocker Art Museum, dining, shopping, and lodging.

**Location/Directions:** In Old Sacramento, adjacent to I-5 exit "J" St.

            M

arm  TRAIN  Radio frequencies: 160.335 and 160.440

**Site Address:** Corner of Second and "I" Streets, Old Sacramento, CA
**Mailing Address:** 111 "I" St., Sacramento, CA 95814
**Telephone:** (916) 445-6645
**Fax:** (916) 327-5655
**E-mail:** foundation@californiastaterailroadmuseum.org (general)
**Internet:** www.californiastaterailroadmuseum.org

**CALIFORNIA STATE RAILROAD MUSEUM**
**SACRAMENTO SOUTHERN RAILROAD**
*Train ride*
*Standard gauge*

**Description:** Sacramento Southern is the excursion railroad of the California State Railroad Museum. Built as a subsidiary of the Southern Pacific at the turn of the century, the museum trains have been in regular service since 1984. A 6-mile, 40-minute round trip takes passengers along the Sacramento River on vintage 1920s coaches and open-air excursion cars.

**Schedule:** Steam–April through September: weekends, 11 a.m. to 5 p.m., departing hourly; selected special event weekends, October through December; diesel-powered School Trains–April through June and October through December: Tuesdays and Fridays by reservation.

**Admission/Fare:** Adults, $6; youth 6-12, $3; children under age 6, free.

**Locomotives/Rolling Stock:** No. 10 1942 Porter 0-6-0T, former Granite Rock Company; no. 4466, 1920 Lima 0-6-0, former Union Pacific; more.

**Special Events:** Day Out with Thomas, April; Sacramento Jazz Jubilee, Memorial Day weekend; Gold Rush Days, Labor Day weekend; Train Time for Santa, Thanksgiving weekend and December.

**Nearby Attractions/Accommodations:** Old Sacramento (California's largest concentration of restored 19th century commercial structures), state capitol, Sutter's Fort, Crocker Art Museum, dining, shopping, and lodging.

**Location/Directions:** Northern terminus is the reconstructed Central Pacific Railroad Freight Depot at Front and "K" Streets in Old Sacramento.

Radio frequencies: 160.335 and 160.440

**Site Address:** Front and "K" Streets, Sacramento, CA
**Mailing Address:** 111 "I" St., Sacramento, CA 95814
**Telephone:** (916) 445-6645
**Fax:** (916) 327-5655
**E-mail:** foundation@californiastaterailroadmuseum.org
**Internet:** www.californiastaterailroadmuseum.org

# SAN DIEGO RAILROAD MUSEUM
*Train ride, dinner train, museum, display*
*Standard gauge*

**Description:** Over 80 pieces of railroading equipment is located at the Campo Depot. Tours, steam/diesel train rides, dinners, brunches, wine tours and specialty events available.

**Schedule:** Campo Depot, year round, weekends 10 a.m. to 4 p.m.; Miller Creek, 1½ hour rides, weekends 11 a.m. and 2:30 p.m.; Ticket to Tecate, 6 hr. adventure, selected Saturdays; Dinner Trains and Wine Tours, selected Saturdays; Brunch Trains, selected Sundays.

**Admission/Fare:** Miller Creek Rides–Adults, $12; children, $3. Ticket to Tecate–Adults, $40; children, $20; Dinner, $75; Brunch, $35, Wine Tour, $90.

**Locomotive/Rolling Stock:** Steam and diesel locomotives, passenger cars, boxcars, tank cars, cabooses, speeders, track equipment and more.

**Special Events:** Spring Festival, Santa Trains, Three Kings Train, Boxcar BBQ.

**Nearby Attractions/Accommodations:** Lodging, campgrounds, restaurants, parks, and museums.

**Location/Directions:** I-8 east 50 miles, exit at Buckman Springs Rd., south 10 miles. Road ends at Hwy. 94, turn right. Turn left at Forrest Gate Rd., turn left at second driveway, to the Depot parking lot.

*Coupon available, see coupon section.

**Site Address:** Highway 94 and Campo, San Diego, CA
**Mailing Address:** 1050 Kettner Blvd., San Diego, CA 92101
**Telephone:** (619) 595-3030 days or (619) 478-9937 weekends
**Fax:** (619) 595-3034
**E-mail:** office@sdrm.org
**Internet:** www.sdrm.org

**Description:** Model railroad exhibit with five layouts, toy trains, toy train gallery, 24,000 square feet.

**Schedule:** Tuesdays through Fridays, 11 a.m. to 4 p.m., weekends, 11 a.m. to 5 p.m., Mondays (no holidays).

**Admission/Fare:** Adults, $4; seniors (60+), $3; active duty military and students, $2.50 (must show ID); children under 15 with their family, free.

**Special Events:** Family Days, every other month. Model Railroad Swap Meets, January, May and October. Christmas on the Prado, first full weekend in December (Dec. 7-8).

**Nearby Attractions/Accommodations:** San Diego Zoo, Balboa Park Organ Pavilion, Reuben H. Fleet Science Center, Miniature Train Ride, Natural History Museum, Carousel, Old Globe Theatre.

**Location/Directions:** Hwy. 163 south to Park Blvd. North on Park Blvd. past two traffic signals. Left on Space Theater Way. Straight until dead ends into a parking lot behind museum (Casa de Balboa building).

*Coupon available, see coupon section.

**Site Address:** Balboa Park, 1649 El Prado, San Diego, CA
**Mailing Address:** 1649 El Prado, San Diego, CA 92101
**Telephone:** (619) 696-0199
**Fax:** (619) 696-0239
**E-mail:** sdmodrailm@abac.com
**Internet:** www.sdmodelrailroadm.com

# GOLDEN GATE RAILROAD MUSEUM

*Railway museum*
*Standard gauge*

**Description:** The museum is dedicated to the preservation of vintage steam and diesel locomotives and passenger equipment. It owns and operates many locomotives related to the Bay Area railroads.

**Schedule:** Year round: weekends, 10 a.m. to 4 p.m. Call to confirm.

**Admission/Fare:** Adults, $3; Children, $2.

**Locomotive/Rolling Stock:** SP Baldwin P8 4-6-2 no. 2472; SF Belt Railway Alcos nos. 25 and 49; SF Belt Railway no. 4 0-6-0; SP nos. 3194 and 4450; assorted suburban commuter coaches; daylight cars, other passenger equipment.

**Special Events:** Railroad Retirees Reunion, last weekend in June. Garlic Train to Gilroy Garlic Festival, last weekend in July. Rent-a-Locomotive Program (learn to run steam and diesel locomotives), by appointment. Excursions, other special events as announced.

**Nearby Attractions/Accommodations:** San Francisco Zoo with restored steam train, cable cars, many parks and other attractions.

**Location/Directions:** Highway 101 to Cesar Chavez St. (Army St.) to Evans Ave. to Hunters Point Shipyard, Building 809. Need vehicle registration, proof of insurance, and picture ID for admission to shipyard.

    arm   M

**Site Address:** Bldg. 809, Hunter's Point Naval Shipyard, San Francisco, CA
**Mailing Address:** PO Box 881686, San Francisco, CA 94188-1686
**Telephone:** (415) 822-8728
**Fax:** (415) 822-8739
**E-mail:** info@ggrm.org
**Internet:** www.ggrm.org

## CALIFORNIA TROLLEY AND RAILROAD CORPORATION
*Display*
*Standard gauge*

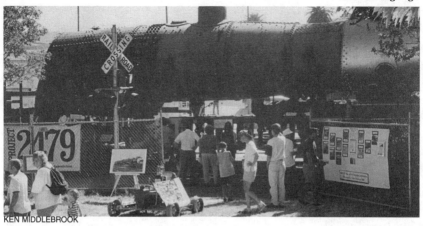

KEN MIDDLEBROOK

**Description:** The non-profit CTRC is developing a railroad museum that will include several relocated railroad structures. Visitors can watch the extensive restoration of steam locomotive no. 2479. A nearby bay window caboose displays the organization's activities and current museum development. The CTRC, in partnership with the History Museums of San Jose, also operates the Trolley Barn in Kelley Park.

**Schedule:** Year round: Saturdays 9 a.m. to 4 p.m. and by appointment.

**Admission/Fare:** Donations appreciated.

**Locomotives/Rolling Stock:** 1923 Baldwin 4-6-2; Southern Pacific no. 2479; 1941 65-ton diesel; Kaiser cement no. 0002; two passenger cars; two cabooses.

**Nearby Attractions/Accommodations:** Kelley Park, Children's Discovery Museum, Tech Museum.

**Location/Directions:** Santa Clara County Fairgrounds, Tully Rd., two miles west of U.S. Highway 101.

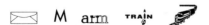

**Site Address:** 344 Tully Rd., San Jose, CA
**Mailing Address:** PO Box 403, Campbell, CA 95009
**Telephone:** (408) 985-2479
**Internet:** www.ctrc.org

# SAN JOSE HISTORICAL MUSEUM
*Museum, layout, trolley car ride*
*Standard gauge*

**Description:** The trolley car operates for rides on ½ mile of track.

**Schedule:** Year round, Saturdays and Sundays. Closed holidays.

**Admission/Fare:** Adults, $6; seniors, $5; youth, $4; under age 5 are free.

**Locomotives/Rolling Stock:** Trolley car no. 124 ex-San Jose; no. 143 Birney; 168 ex-Porto; horse car no. 7 ex-San Francisco.

**Nearby Attractions/Accommodations:** Many attractions within a radius of 40 miles.

**Location/Directions:** Located in Kelley Park, which is a short distance from Highways 280, 680, and 101. Take the no. 73 bus from downtown San Jose.

   arm

**Site Address:** 1650 Senter Rd., San Jose, CA
**Mailing Address:** 1650 Senter Rd., San Jose, CA 95112
**Telephone:** (408) 293-2276
**Fax:** (408) 287-2291

# TRAIN TOWN
*Train ride*
*15" gauge*

**Description:** Train Town is a 10-acre railroad park filled with thousands of trees, animals, lakes, bridges, tunnels, waterfalls, and historic replica structures. Fifteen-inch-gauge live-steam locomotives and diesel replicas pull long passenger trains through the park. Railroad shops and a complete miniature town, built to the same ¼ scale as the railroad. Full-sized rail equipment includes Santa Fe caboose no. 999648; Union Pacific caboose no. 25155; and Southern Pacific's first steel caboose, no. 11.

**Schedule:** June 1 through Labor Day: daily. Year round: Fridays through Sundays. Closed Christmas and Thanksgiving. Call or write for hours.

**Admission/Fare:** Adults, $3.75; seniors and children 15 months to 15, $3.25.

**Locomotives/Rolling Stock:** Replica of no. 5212, 1937 Alco J-1a 4-6-4, former New York Central; no. 1, 1960 Winton Engineering 2-6-0; SW 1200, 1992 custom locomotive; no. 401, 1975 gas-electric motor car.

**Location/Directions:** Sonoma is in wine country, less than an hour north of San Francisco. Train Town is on Broadway (Highway 12), one mile south of the Sonoma Town Square.

**Site Address:** 20264 Broadway, Highway 12, Sonoma, CA
**Mailing Address:** PO Box 656, Sonoma, CA 95476
**Telephone:** (707) 996-2559
**Fax:** (707) 966-6344
**Internet:** www.traintown.com

# WESTERN RAILWAY MUSEUM
*Museum*
*Standard gauge*

BART NADEAU

**Description:** A 9.5-mile interurban round trip over re-electrified Sacramento Northern Railway interurban in rural Solano County. Additional electrification is in progress, planned to open in 2000 and 2001.

**Schedule:** Year round: weekends 11 a.m. to 5 p.m. June through Labor Day: Wednesdays through Sundays 11 a.m. to 5 p.m.

**Admission/Fare:** Adults, $7; seniors (65 and over), $6; children age 14 and under, $4.

**Locomotives/Rolling Stock:** Wood interurbans: Peninsular Railway no. 52; Petaluma & Santa Rosa no. 63; Sacramento Northern no. 1005. Steel interurbans: Napa Valley no. 63; key units 182 and 187. Crandic III steel locomotives: CCT no. 7; SN nos. 652, 654; many streetcars; more.

**Special Events:** Special Montezuma Hills Trains in April, Pumpkin Patch Trains in October, Santa Trains in December.

**Nearby Attractions/Accommodations:** Marine World, Africa USA.

**Location/Directions:** On Highway 12. I-80, 12 miles from the Suisun/Rio Vista exit; or I-5, 23 miles from the Rio Vista/Fairfield exit.

     M arm

**Site Address:** 5848 State Highway 12, Suisun City, CA
**Mailing Address:** 5848 State Highway 12, Suisun City, CA 94585
**Telephone:** (707) 374-2978
**Fax:** (707) 374-6742
**Internet:** www.wrm.org

California, Woodland

*Train ride*
*Standard gauge*

RICHARD JONES

**Description:** A 28-mile, two-hour round trip between Woodland and West Sacramento over former Sacramento Northern Interurban track. Crosses 8,000-foot Fremont Trestle and offers views of the Sacramento River and scenic Yolo County farmlands and wetlands. The railroad also offers specials to Clarksburg.

**Schedule:** Spring Specials: March 18 and 25 and April 22 and 29. Regular season, May through Ocotber: weekends and major holidays. Charters are available year round.

**Admission/Fare:** Adults, $14; seniors, $12; children, $9; family $37; family pizza fare, $52; diesel cab ride, add $10; steam cab ride, add $25.

**Locomotives/Rolling Stock:** No. 1233, former Southern Pacific 0-6-0 switcher; nos. 131, 132, 133 GP-9 EMD diesels, former Southern Pacific.

**Special Events:** Great Train Robberies, Lunch Cruises, Pizza Trains; steam engine runs third weekend every month.

**Nearby Attractions/Accommodations:** Hayes Truck and Tractor Museum, Southern Pacific Depot (under restoration), Woodland Opera House.

**Location/Directions:** I-5 or Highway 113, Main St. exit, one mile west to E. Main and Thomas Streets. Twenty minutes north of Sacramento.

**Radio Frequency:** 160.260

**Site Address:** 341 Industrial Way, Woodland, CA
**Mailing Address:** 341 Industrial Way, Woodland, CA 95776
**Telephone:** (530) 666-9698
**Fax:** (530) 666-2919
**E-mail:** jasdavis@pacbell.net
**Internet:** www.ysrr.com

**CALICO & ODESSA RAILROAD**
*Train ride*

RICHARD JONES

**Description:** 15-minute ride with narration on scenic points.

**Schedule:** Daily, 9 a.m. to 5 p.m.

**Admission/Fare:** Adults, $2.50; children (5-12), $1.25; children under 5, free.

**Special Events:** Calico Civil War, February 16-18; Calico's 29th Annual Spring Festival & Cook-off, May 10-12; Calico Days, October 11-13; Calico Ghost Haunt, October 25-27; Calico Heritage Fest, November 29-30 and December 1; Christmas in Calico, December 14. Please call to verify prices and times of events.

**Nearby Attractions/Accommodations:** Campground, restaurants, gift shops.

**Location/Directions:** Take I-15 to Ghost Town Road exit just 10 minutes north of Barstow, California. Main St. to sign for C.O. Railroad.

**Site Address:** 36600 Ghost Town Road, Yermo, CA
**Mailing Address:** PO Box 638, Yermo, CA 92398
**Telephone:** (760) 254-2122
**Fax:** (760) 254-2005
**E-mail:** calico@mscomm.com
**Internet:** www.calicotown.com

# YREKA WESTERN RAILROAD
*Train ride, museum, layout*
*Standard gauge*

**Description:** Tourist excursion through Shasta Valley to Railroad/Cattle Town of Montague. One hour layover in Montague, 3½ hour tour.

**Schedule:** Summer: June 6 through September 3, Wednesdays through Sundays, 11 a.m. departure returning at 2:30 p.m. Fall: September 8 through October 29, weekends 11 a.m. departure returning at 2:30 p.m.

**Admission/Fare:** Adults, $12.25; seniors (60+) and children (3 through 12), $5.25.

**Locomotives/Rolling Stock:** GM EMD SW-8 no. 21; Baldwin steam locomotive 2-8-2 Mikado no. 19.

**Special Events:** Wild Goose Chase, 10K race, July 14.

**Location/Directions:** I-5 Yreka, CA central off-ramp, east of freeway.

**Site Address:** 300 E. Miner St., Yreka, CA
**Mailing Address:** PO Box 660, Yreka, CA 96097
**Telephone:** (800) 973-5277
**Fax:** (530) 842-4148

**ROYAL GORGE ROUTE RAILROAD**
*Train ride*
*Standard gauge*

RON RUHOFF

**Description:** Experience the grandeur of traveling by train through the spectacular Royal Gorge on the Royal Gorge route. The train operates alongside the Arkansas River from Canon City, traveling over the famous "Hanging Bridge" where the canyon rim towers 1,000 feet above. This is a 24-mile, two-hour round trip ride.

**Schedule:** Mid-May through mid-October: three departures daily. Mid-October through mid-May: every Saturday and Sunday (except Christmas) at 12:30 p.m.

**Admission/Fare:** Round trip: adults, $26.95; children (2-13), $16.50; under 2, no charge if carried on lap.

**Locomotives/Rolling Stock:** FC&NW EMD F7A nos. 402, 403; VIA Rail CC&F passenger car nos. 3225, 5497, 5541, 5562, 5580, 5586, club car 650.

**Nearby Attractions/Accommodations:** Royal Gorge Bridge, rafting, horseback riding, fishing, camping.

**Location/Directions:** Located at the Santa Fe Depot, 401 Water St. (one block south on Third St. off Highway 50). Canon City is 45 miles southwest of Colorado Springs.

**Site Address:** 401 Water St., Canon City, Co 81212
**Mailing Address:** PO Box 859, Georgetown, CO 80444
**Telephone:** (303) 569-2403 and (888) RAILS-4-U
**Fax:** (303) 569-2894
**E-mail:** mark@royalgorgeroute.com
**Internet:** www.royalgorgeroute.com

# DENVER & RIO GRANDE
## U.S. NATIONAL PARK SERVICE
*Display*
*36" gauge*

NPS PHOTO BY LISA LYNCH

**Description:** At Cimarron, 20 miles east of Montrose, a historic narrow gauge railroad exhibit with engine no. 278, its coal tender, a boxcar, and a caboose sit on a stone and steel trestle one mile into the Cimarron River Canyon. At the Cimarron Visitor Center, a cattle car, sheep car, outfit car, hoist car, livestock corral, and interpretive panels illustrate early mountain railroad operations of the Denver & Rio Grande.

**Schedule:** Year round.

**Admission/Fare:** Free.

**Locomotives/Rolling Stock:** Locomotive no. 278, C-16 280, 1882/Baldwin Locomotive Works, Philadelphia, Pennsylvania; tender and D&RGW 0577 caboose.

**Nearby Attractions/Accommodations:** Black Canyon of the Gunnison National Park; Curecanti National Recreation area.

**Location/Directions:** Cimarron is 20 miles east of Montrose on U.S. Highway 50. The exhibit can be seen from the highway. Follow Curecanti National Recreation Area signs.

**Site Address:** U.S. Highway 59, Cimarron, CO
**Mailing Address:** Curecanti NRA, 102 Elk Creek, Gunnison, CO 81230
**Telephone:** (970) 249-1914 ext. 23 and (970) 641-2337 ext. 205
**Fax:** (970) 641-3127
**E-mail:** cure_vis_mail@nps.gov
**Internet:** www.nps.gov/cure

**Colorado, Colorado Springs**

# PIKE'S PEAK HISTORICAL STREET RAILWAY FOUNDATION, INC.
*Ride, museum, display*
*Standard gauge*

**Description:** This interpretive center displays street railway history with a strong emphasis on Colorado Springs street railway history. We also offer a lecture on history and the return of streetcars to Colorado Springs. There are several trips over a 500-foot test track. The operation and history of the car are explained during the ride. You can visit a working car house (former Rock Island Engine House) built in 1888, see cars under restoration, and take a guided tour of the cars on hand and the shop area.

**Schedule:** Year round: Saturdays, 10 a.m. to 4 p.m., closed Thanksgiving, Christmas, and New Year's week. Other times please write or call. Group tours, please call ahead for special showing.

**Admission/Fare:** Adults, $2; children 12 and under, $1.

**Locomotives/Rolling Stock:** Nine Southeastern Pennsylvania Transportation Authority PCCs (Philadelphia) 1947; Los Angeles Railways PCC 1943; Colorado Springs double truck, 1901 Laclede Car Co.; Ft. Collins Municipal Railway, single truck, 1919 Birney, American Car Co.; Colorado Springs double truck, 1901 J. G. Brill Car Co.

**Location/Directions:** I-25, exit Fillmore St. east, south on Tremont St., west on Polk St. When forced to turn south, you will automatically be on Steel Dr. The site is located at the end of Steel Dr.

       arm M

**Site Address:** 2333 Steel Dr., Colorado Springs, CO
**Mailing Address:** PO Box 544, Colorado Springs, CO 80901
**Telephone:** (719) 475-9508 and (719) 471-2619
**Fax:** (719) 475-2814
**Internet:** colospringstrolleys.home.att.net.

# MOFFAT COUNTY VISITOR'S CENTER
*Museum*

PATRICIA STAUFFER

**Description:** Tours of private Pullman railcar of railroad magnate David Moffat. The car was named for his only child, Marcia.

**Schedule:** Memorial Day through Labor Day, Mondays through Fridays, 9 a.m. to 5 p.m.

**Admission/Fare:** Donations accepted.

**Locomotives/Rolling Stock:** Private Pullman car of David Moffat–Moffat Railroad.

**Nearby Attractions/Accommodations:** Adjacent to City Park and the wave pool.

**Location/Directions:** Directly across from Moffat County Visitor's Center.

**Site Address:** 360 E. Victory Way, Craig, CO
**Mailing Address:** 360 E. Victory Way, Craig, CO 81625
**Telephone:** (800) 864-4405
**Fax:** (970) 824-0231
**E-mail:** craigcoc@craig-chamber.com
**Internet:** www.craig-chamber.com

69

# CRIPPLE CREEK AND VICTOR NARROW GAUGE RAILROAD
### Train ride
### Narrow gauge

**Description:** A 4-mile, 45-minute round trip over a portion of the old Midland Terminal Railroad. The train runs south out of Cripple Creek past the old MT wye, over a reconstructed trestle and past many historic mines to the deserted mining town of Anaconda.

**Schedule:** Mid-May through mid-October: daily, 9:30 a.m. to 5:30 p.m., departing every 45 minutes.

**Admission/Fare:** Adults, $9; seniors, $8; children 3-12, $5; under age 3 are free.

**Locomotives/Rolling Stock:** No. 1 1902 Orenstein & Koppel 0-4-4-0; no. 2 1936 Henschel 0-4-0; no. 3 1927 Porter 0-4-0T; no. 13 1946 Bagnall 0-4-0T.

**Nearby Attractions:** Cripple Creek District Museum, Mueller State Park, restaurants, lodging.

**Location/Directions:** From Colorado Springs west on Highway 24 to Highway 67 south to Cripple Creek. Trains leave from former Midland Terminal Railroad Bull Hill Depot.

*Coupon available, see coupon section.

**Site Address:** 520 E. Carr, Cripple Creek, CO
**Mailing Address:** PO Box 459, Cripple Creek, CO 80813
**Telephone:** (719) 689-2640
**Fax:** (719) 689-3256
**Internet:** ccvngrailroad.webjump.com

**Description:** Self-guided museum tours.

**Schedule:** Year round. Mondays through Saturdays, 9 a.m. to 5 p.m.

**Admission/Fare:** Adults, $6; youth 12-18, $3; children 6-11, $3.

**Locomotives/Rolling Stock:** UP Big Boy locomotive 4005 (4-8-8-4); Pikes Peak diner 804; UP rotary snowplow 099-900099; CBQ business car C&S no. 300; CNW locomotive no. 444; Forney locomotive; German locomotive no. 7.

**Nearby Attractions:** Near downtown Denver, the Denver Coliseum, and the National Western Stock Show grounds. Short distance from many attractions.

**Location/Directions:** From I-25 exit on I-70 east, then exit on Brighton Blvd. and go southwest two blocks. Turn right into the museum driveway when you see the sign.

**Site Address:** 4303 Brighton Blvd., Denver, CO
**Mailing Address:** 4303 Brighton Blvd., Denver, CO 80216
**Telephone:** (303) 297-1113
**Fax:** (303) 297-3113
**E-mail:** forney@frii.net
**Internet:** www.forneymuseum.com

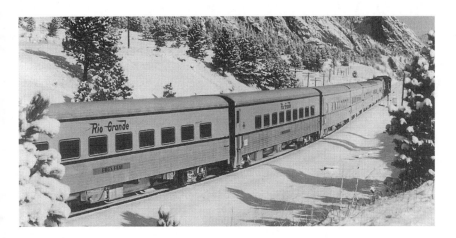

**Description:** A 130-mile round trip on the historic Moffat Line between Denver and Winter Park Resort.

**Schedule:** Weekends, December through April. Saturdays only, June through August.

**Admission/Fare:** $45

**Locomotives/Rolling Stock:** Varies.

**Location/Directions:** Train departs from Denver Union Station.

**Site Address:** Denver Union Station, Denver, CO
**Mailing Address:** 555 17th St., Ste. 2400, Denver, CO 80202
**Telephone:** (303) 296-4754
**Fax:** (303) 298-8881
**Internet:** www.skitrain.com

## GALLOPING GOOSE HISTORICAL
## SOCIETY OF DOLORES, INC.
*Train ride, museum, display, layout*
*36" gauge*

**Description:** The ride is 320 feet; by request, up and back, 640 feet.

**Schedule:** May 15 through October 15, Monday through Saturday, 9 a.m. to 5 p.m.

**Admission/Fare:** Free. Donations accepted.

**Locomotives/Rolling Stock:** RGS motor no. 5 (Galloping Goose).

**Special Events:** Memorial Day, Raft Days, Escalante Days, Railfest.

**Nearby Attractions/Accommodations:** Mesa Verde, Anasazi Heritage Center, McPhee Reservoir.

**Location/Directions:** Southwest Colorado, 45 miles west of Durango Highway 145 north.

**Site Address:** 421 Railroad Ave., Dolores, CO
**Mailing Address:** PO Box 297, Dolores, CO 81323
**Telephone:** (970) 882-7082
**Fax:** (970) 882-2224
**E-mail:** gghs5@fone.net
**Internet:** doloresgallopinggoose@5.org

# DURANGO & SILVERTON NARROW GAUGE RAILROAD
*Train ride, museum*
*Narrow gauge*

ROBERT ROYEM

**Description:** Steam-powered narrow gauge railroad through the scenic San Juan mountains of Colorado. The 90-mile round trip begins in Durango and takes about 9 hours, with a 2¼-hour layover in Silverton for lunch.

**Schedule:** Silverton–May 11 through October 26: daily 8:15 a.m. Additional trains operate at 7:30, 9, and 9:45 a.m. later in the summer. Cascade Canyon Winter Trains–November 20 through May 10: 10 a.m. Closed Christmas. Call for information.

**Admission/Fare:** Silverton round trip–adults, $55-$60; children ages 5-11, $27-$30; parlor car (over 21), $95. Winter Cascade Canyon–adults, $45; children, $22; parlor car (over 21), $75. All tickets include admission to the D&SNGRR Museum. (fares subject to change)

**Locomotives/Rolling Stock:** Locomotives nos. 473, 476, 478, 480, 481, 482, 486, 493, 498, 42; B-2 Cinco Animas, B-3 Nomad, more.

**Special Events:** Narrow Gauge Days, May 10; Iron Horse Bicycle Classic, May 25; Annual Railfest, August 22-25; Photo Special, September 21; Holiday Trains, New Year's Eve Moonlight Train, December.

**Location/Directions:** At the intersection of U.S. Highways 550 and 160 in southwest Colorado. Depot is at the far south end of Main Ave.

†See ad on page A-1.

**Site Address:** 479 Main Ave., Durango, CO
**Mailing Address:** 479 Main Ave., Durango, CO 81301
**Telephone:** (970) 247-2733 and (888) TRAIN-07
**Fax:** (970) 259-9349
**E-mail:** info@durangotrain.com
**Internet:** www.durangotrain.com

**FORT COLLINS
MUNICIPAL RAILWAY**
*Train ride*
*Standard gauge*

**Description:** Trolley ride; 3-mile round trip ride in peaceful residential setting on original right-of-way.

**Schedule:** Weekends and holidays, May through September, noon to 5 p.m.

**Admission/Fare:** Adults, $1; seniors, $.75; children under 12, $.50.

**Locomotives/Rolling Stock:** 1919 Birney single-track streetcar, Ft. Collins car no. 21.

**Special Events:** Mother's Day, Father's Day, Fourth of July.

**Nearby Attractions/Accommodations:** Rocky Mountain National Park, Colorado State University, Poudre Canyon.

**Location/Directions:** From I-25 take exit 269 (Colorado 14, Mulberry St.) west to Jackson St. Right on Jackson St. to Oak St. Left on Oak St. to Depot at Roosevelt St. in City Park.

     M arm

**Site Address:** Roosevelt, Fort Collins, CO
**Mailing Address:** PO Box 635, Fort Collins, CO 80522
**Telephone:** (970) 224-5372
**Internet:** www.fortnet.org/trolley

# GEORGETOWN LOOP RAILROAD
*Train ride*
*Narrow gauge*

RON RUHOFF

**Description:** A 6.5-mile, 70-minute round trip over the right-of-way of the former Colorado & Southern. The train travels through scenic, mountainous terrain and over the reconstructed Devil's Gate Viaduct, a spectacular 96-foot-high curved trestle. The Georgetown Loop Railroad is a project of the Colorado Historical Society.

**Schedule:** Memorial Day weekend through first weekend in October: daily. Silver Plume (exit 226)–9:20 and 10:40 a.m., 12, 1:20, 2:40, and 4 p.m. Devil's Gate (exit 228)–10 and 11:20 a.m., 12:40, 2:00, and 3:20 p.m.

**Admission/Fare:** Adults, $14.50; children (5-15), $9.50. Mine tour–adults, $6; children, $4. Charters and groups rates available. Tickets must be purchased at Old Georgetown Station, 1106 Rose, Georgetown.

**Locomotives/Rolling Stock:** Lima 3-truck Shay, nos. 8, 12, 14; more.

**Nearby Attractions/Accommodations:** Old Georgetown Station, Historic Georgetown, and Silver Plume

**Location/Directions:** I-70 exit 228 for Devil's Gate or exit 226 for Silver Plume. Tickets must be purchased at Old Georgetown Station, 1106 Rose, Georgetown.

      TRAIN

**Radio frequency: 161.115**

**Site Address:** 1106 Rose St., Georgetown, CO
**Mailing Address:** PO Box 217, Georgetown, CO 80444
**Telephone:** (303) 569-2403 and (800) 691-4FUN
**Fax:** (303) 569-2873
**E-mail:** markg@georgetownloop.com
**Internet:** www.georgetownloop.com

# COLORADO RAILROAD MUSEUM
## *Museum*
### *Standard and 36" gauge*

BOB JENSEN

**Description:** An extensive collection of Colorado railroad memorabilia and over 70 historic cars and locomotives, both standard and narrow gauge. It is the home of the Denver HO Model Railroad Club and the Denver Garden Railway Society. "Galloping Goose" motorcars operate on selected weekends.

**Schedule:** Museum–June through August, daily, 9 a.m. to 6 p.m.; September through May, 9 a.m. to 5 p.m. Train–call, fax, or write for schedule. HO model railroad–first Thursday of every month, 7:30 to 9:30 p.m. Richardson Railroad Research Library–Tuesdays through Saturdays, 11 a.m. to 4 p.m.; Thursdays to 9 p.m.

**Admission/Fare:** Adults, $6; seniors, $5; children under age 16, $3; families (parents and children under age 16), $14.50.

**Locomotives/Rolling Stock:** Three RGS "Galloping Geese" motorcars; D&RGW Baldwin 1890 2-8-0 no. 683; Rio Grande Zephyr EMD F9s 5771 and 5762; Chicago Burlington & Quincy 4-8-4 no. 5629; Santa Fe Super Chief 1937 observation car Navajo; more.

**Nearby Attractions/Accommodations:** Coors Brewery, Buffalo Bill Museum, Blackhawk and Central City casinos.

**Location/Directions:** Twelve miles west of downtown Denver. I-70 westbound exit 265 or eastbound exit 266 to W. 44th Ave.

    arm

**Site Address:** 17155 W. 44th Ave., Golden, CO
**Mailing Address:** PO Box 10, Golden, CO 80402
**Telephone:** (303) 279-4591 and (800) 365-6263
**Fax:** (303) 279-4229
**E-mail:** mail@crrm.org
**Internet:** www.crrm.org

# LEADVILLE, COLORADO & SOUTHERN RAILROAD
*Train ride*
*Standard gauge*

BARBARA MALLETTE, THE LEADVILLE PICTURE COMPANY

**Description:** The 22.5-mile, 2.5-hour train trip follows the headwaters of the Arkansas River to an elevation of 11,120 feet, over an old narrow gauge roadbed converted to standard gauge in the 1940s. The train leaves from the restored 1894 railroad depot (formerly Colorado & Southern, built originally for the Denver, South Park & Pacific) in Leadville, the highest incorporated city in the United States. We offer enclosed, open, and sun cars along with snacks, souvenirs, and restrooms in the boxcars.

**Schedule:** Memorial Day weekend through September.

**Admission/Fare:** Adults, $24; children 4-12, $12.50; age 3 and under are free. Group rates available for 20 or more.

**Locomotives/Rolling Stock:** 1955 EMD GP9 no. 1714, former Burlington Northern; EMD GP-9 no. 1918.

**Nearby Attractions/Accommodations:** National Mining Museum, Matchless Mine, Leadville's historic mining district, Tabor Opera House, San Isabel National Forest.

**Location/Directions:** Located 25 miles south of I-70 on Highway 91, Copper Mountain exit. Travel south to Leadville, turn east on E. Seventh St. to depot.

**Site Address:** 327 E. Seventh St., Leadville, CO
**Mailing Address:** Box 916, Leadville, CO 80461
**Telephone:** (719) 486-3936
**Fax:** (719) 486-0671
**E-mail:** info@leadville.train
**Internet:** www.leadville-train.com

**MANITOU & PIKE'S PEAK RAILWAY**
*Train ride*
*Standard gauge (cog)*

**Description:** The M&PP, the highest cog railway in the world, was established in 1889 and has been operating continuously since 1891; it celebrated its centennial of passenger operations in June 1991. A 3¼-hour round trip takes passengers to the summit of Pike's Peak (elevation 14,110 feet) from Manitou Springs (elevation 6,575 feet) and includes a 40-minute stop at the summit.

**Schedule:** Daily; May through mid-June, September and October, 9:20 a.m. and 1:20 p.m.; mid-June through August, every 80 minutes, 8:00 a.m. to 5:20 p.m.

**Admission/Fare:** Adults, $24.50; children 3-11, $13; July through August 15: adults, $25.50; children, $13. Children under 3 free if held on lap. One-way tickets sold on space-available basis.

**Locomotives/Rolling Stock:** Twin-unit diesel hydraulic railcars and single-unit diesel electric railcars.

**Special Events:** Occasional steam-up of former M&PP steam locomotive no. 4, built by Baldwin in 1896.

**Location/Directions:** Six miles west of Colorado Springs.

**Radio frequency: 161.55 and 160.23**

**Site Address:** 515 Ruxton Ave., Manitou Springs, CO
**Mailing Address:** PO Box 351, Manitou Springs, CO 80829
**Telephone:** (719) 685-5401
**Fax:** (719) 685-9033
**E-mail:** cogtrain@iex.net
**Internet:** www.cograilway.com

**TINY TOWN RAILROAD**
*Train ride*
*15" gauge*

**Description:** Tiny Town Railroad, a ¼-scale live-steam railroad, takes passengers from its full-sized station on a one-mile loop around Tiny Town. Started in 1915, Tiny Town is the oldest miniature town in the United States. It features more than 100 handcrafted, ⅙-sized structures laid out in the configuration of a town, rural, and mountainous area.

**Schedule:** Memorial Day through Labor Day: daily. May, September, and October: weekends. 10 a.m. to 5 p.m. Train runs continuously.

**Admission/Fare:** Display–adults, $3; children 3-12, $2; children under age three are free. Train–$1.

**Locomotives/Rolling Stock:** 1970 standard-gauge 4-6-2 "Occasional Rose" propane-fired; 1970 narrow-gauge 2-6-0 "Cinderbell" coal-fired; 1954 F-unit "Molly," gas-powered; 1952 A- and B-unit "Betsy" gas-powered. Open amusement-park-style cars, propane tank car and caboose.

**Nearby Attractions/Accommodations:** Red Rocks Park and Dinosaur Ridge.

**Location/Directions:** Approximately 30 minutes southwest of Denver, off Highway 285.

**Site Address:** 6249 S. Turkey Creek Rd., Morrison, CO
**Mailing Address:** 6249 S. Turkey Creek Rd., Morrison, CO 80465
**Telephone:** (303) 697-6829

# PUEBLO LOCOMOTIVE & RAIL HISTORICAL SOCIETY INC., PUEBLO RAILWAY MUSEUM
### *Museum*
### *Standard and narrow gauge*

RICHARD M. HOLMES

**Description:** Static displays, museum car, and gift shop. Take a motor car or hi-rail ride on the old Pueblo Union Depot passenger tracks on selected weekends. Restoration work is ongoing on former ATSF steam locomotive no. 2912. There is fantastic trainwatching on the BNSF and UP main, adjacent to the museum.

**Schedule:** Museum and gift shop open Fridays and Saturdays or by appointment. Static Displays–year round: daily. Hours are 9:30 a.m. to 4 p.m.

**Admission/Fare:** Free, donations appreciated.

**Locomotives/Rolling Stock:** ATSF Baldwin 4-8-4 Northern no. 2912; Colorado Fuel and Iron, GE 25-ton diesel no. 11; Colorado & Southern caboose no. 10538; Colorado & Wyoming locomotive simulator training car no. 100; Denver & Rio Grande Western caboose no. 01432; Southern Pacific bay window caboose no. 4773; more.

**Special Events:** Open House, weekend following Memorial Day. Pueblo Railfest, September 28-29.

**Nearby Attractions/Accommodations:** Lake Pueblo State Park, Pueblo Weisbrod Aircraft Museum, Union Ave. Historic District.

**Location/Directions:** I-25, exit First St. West to Union Ave., south to "B" St., right turn on "B." Museum is located behind and to the west of the depot. Parking available behind the depot.

**Site Address:** 200 W. "B" St., Pueblo, CO
**Mailing Address:** PO Box 322, Pueblo, CO 81002
**Telephone:** (719) 564-7669
**Fax:** (719) 564-3460
**Internet:** www.pueblorail.com

# OLD HUNDRED GOLD MINE TOUR
*Train ride*
*24" gauge*

W.R. JONES

**Description:** Two-thirds-mile mine train ride and one-hour underground guided mine tour with mining demonstrations. Free gold and silver panning are included. There are mining artifact and rail equipment displays.

**Schedule:** Daily, May 10 through October 20. Tours depart hourly 10 a.m. through 4 p.m.

**Admission/Fare:** Adults, $14.95, children 5-12, $7.95, seniors (60+) $13.95.

**Locomotives/Rolling Stock:** Ex-Campbird, Goodman diesel-mechanical; ex-Sunnyside, Greensburg 4-ton battery electric; ex-N.J. Zinc/Greensburg 6-ton battery electric, various mine cars and rail-mounted mining equipment.

**Special Events:** Hardrockers Holidays mining contests, second weekend in August.

**Nearby Attractions/Accommodations:** Durango & Silverton narrow gauge railroad, Mayflower Gold Mill National Historic landmark.

**Location/Directions:** Five miles east of Silverton on Hwy. 110 and County Road 4-A.

*Coupon available, see coupon section.

**Site Address:** 721 C.R. 4-A Silverton, CO
**Mailing Address:** PO Box 430, Silverton, CO 81433-0430
**Telephone:** (970) 387-5444 and (800) 872-3009
**Fax:** (970) 387-5579
**E-mail:** old100@minetour.com
**Internet:** www.minetour.com

**DANBURY RAILWAY MUSEUM**
*Train ride, museum, display, layout*
*Standard gauge*

RON FREITAG

**Description:** Museum with over 50 pieces of equipment representing ten different railroads. We offer vintage train rides in the yard to the only operable turntable in Connecticut. There is a gift shop, library (by appointment), and displays in the restored 1903 train station seen in Alfred Hitchcock's film *Strangers on a Train.*

**Schedule:** Train rides, Saturdays April through early November. Museum open January through March, Wednesday through Saturday 10 a.m. to 4 p.m., Sunday 12 noon to 4 p.m. April through December, 10 a.m. to 5 p.m., Sunday 12 noon to 5 p.m.

**Admission/Fare:** Adults, $4; children, $2.

**Locomotives/Rolling Stock:** NH 0673 Alco RS-1; B&M 1455 Alco 2-6-0; NYC 4096 EMD E9; NYC 1390 Alco FPA; LIRR 617 (NH 0428) Alco FA; NH 32 Budd RDC-1; GCT-1 dual-ended crane; caboose NH C-627 and PC 23662; many freight and passenger cars.

**Special Events:** Easter Bunny Trains, Haunted Railyard, Holiday Express.

**Nearby Attractions/Accommodations:** Railroad Museum of New England, Valley Railroad, Military Museum, Danbury Fair Mall, many restaurants.

**Location/Directions:** I-84 exit 5, right on Main St., left on White St.

**Site Address:** 120 White St., Danbury, CT
**Mailing Address:** PO Box 90, Danbury, CT 06813-0090
**Telephone:** (203) 778-8337
**Fax:** (203) 778-1836
**Internet:** www.danbury.org/drm

**SHORE LINE TROLLEY MUSEUM**
*Museum*
*Standard gauge*

G. BOUCHER

**Description:** The Shore Line Trolley Museum operates the sole remaining segment of the historic 100-year-old Branford Electric Railway. The 3-mile round trip passes woods, salt marshes, and meadows along the scenic Connecticut shore.

**Schedule:** Memorial Day through Labor Day: daily. May, September, and October: weekends and holidays. April and November: Sundays. Hours 10:30 a.m. to 4:30 p.m. Cars depart every 30 minutes.

**Admission/Fare:** Unlimited rides and guided tours–adults, $6; seniors, $5; children 2-15, $3; under age 2 are free.

**Locomotives/Rolling Stock:** Connecticut Co. suburban no. 775; Montreal no. 2001; Johnstown no. 357; Brooklyn (New York) convertible no. 4573; Third Avenue no. 629.

**Special Events:** Santa Days, Thanksgiving to Christmas on weekends.

**Nearby Attractions/Accommodations:** Holiday Inn Express, East Haven. Yale University. Foxwoods Casino.

**Location/Directions:** I-95 exits 51 north or 52 south and follow signs.

*Coupon available, see coupon section.

**Site Address:** 17 River St., East Haven, CT
**Mailing Address:** 17 River St., East Haven, CT 06512-2519
**Telephone:** (203) 467-6927 and (203) 467-7635 group sales
**Fax:** (203) 467-7635
**E-mail:** BERASLTM@aol.com
**Internet:** www.bera.org

# CONNECTICUT TROLLEY MUSEUM
*Museum*
*Standard gauge*

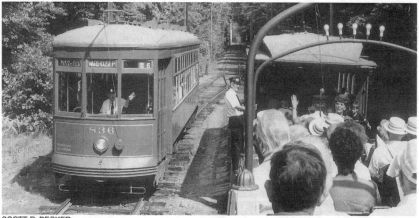

SCOTT R. BECKER

**Description:** A 1.5-mile trolley ride through the countryside.

**Schedule:** April through Memorial Day: Saturday, 10 a.m. to 5 p.m., Sunday, 12 noon to 5 p.m. Memorial Day through Labor Day: Wednesday through Friday, 10 a.m. to 4 p.m., Saturday, 10 a.m. to 5 p.m., Sunday, 12 noon to 5 p.m.; Labor Day through December: Saturday, 10 a.m. to 5 p.m., Sunday, 12 noon to 5 p.m. Closed Thanksgiving, Christmas Eve, and Christmas Day.

**Admission/Fare:** Adults, $6; seniors (62+), $5; youth ages 2-12, $3; under age 2 are free. Group rates are available.

**Trolleys:** Nos. 65, 355, 840, and 1326, former Connecticut Co.; nos. 4, 2056, and 2600, former Montreal Trainways; no. 1850, former Rio de Janeiro; more.

**Special Events:** Halloween program: Little Pumpkin Patch. Trolley rides, games, each child receives a pumpkin. Last three weekends in October, Saturdays 10 a.m. to 4 p.m., Sundays 12 noon to 4 p.m. Winterfest: 1.5-mile trolley ride through tunnel of lights. Day after Thanksgiving through December, Fridays through Sundays, 6 to 9 p.m.

**Location/Directions:** Between Hartford, Connecticut, and Springfield, Massachusetts. I-91, exit 45, ¾ mile east on Route 140.

*Coupon available, see coupon section.

**Site Address:** 58 North Rd. (Route 140), East Windsor, CT
**Mailing Address:** PO Box 360, East Windsor, CT 06088-0360
**Telephone:** (860) 627-6540
**Fax:** (860) 627-6510
**Internet:** www.ceraonline.org

## ESSEX STEAM TRAIN AND RIVERBOAT RIDE
*Train ride, display*
*Standard gauge*

**Description:** A 1.5-hour excursion through the scenic Connecticut River valley with views of the river and wetlands. The passenger trains consist of restored 1920s-era coaches.

**Schedule:** Mid-June through Labor Day, daily. May through mid-June, September, and October: Wednesday through Sunday.

**Admission/Fare:** Train and boat: adults, $18.50; children 3-11, $9.50. Train only: adults, $10.50; children 3-11, $5.50; under age 3 free. Parlor car: extra fare. Open car and caboose (when available): extra fare. Senior discounts. Group rates available. All tickets sold at Essex station only. Essex Clipper dinner train: $52.95 per person, gratuity and beverages extra.

**Locomotives/Rolling Stock:** No. 40, Alco 2-8-2, no. 97, Alco 2-8-0; more.

**Special Events:** "A Day Out with Thomas," Easter Eggspress, Eagle Festival Special, Your Hand on the Throttle, Polar Express Santa Special.

**Nearby Attractions/Accommodations:** Connecticut River Museum, Mystic Seaport, Mystic Aquarium, casinos.

**Location/Directions:** From New York and Boston, I-95 to exit 69 and north on State Route 9 to exit 3. From Hartford, I-91 south to exit 22S and south on State Route 9 to exit 3. Follow signs to Essex Steam Train.

*Coupon available, see coupon section.

**Site Address:** Near junction of State Routes 9 (exit 3) and 154 in Essex, CT
**Mailing Address:** PO Box 452, Essex, CT 06426
**Telephone:** (860) 767-0103
**Fax:** (860) 767-0104
**Internet:** www.essexsteamtrain.com

**CONNECTICUT ANTIQUE
MACHINERY ASSOCIATION, INC.**
*Museum*
*36" gauge*

**Description:** Exhibits show the development of the country's agricultural and industrial technology from the mid-1800s to the present, including a collection of large stationary steam engines in the Industrial Hall; a display of large gas engines; a tractor and farm-implement display in the large tractor barn; the mining museum with its collection of mining artifacts and 18" gauge mining equipment; and the Cream Hill Agricultural School, forerunner of the University of Connecticut.

**Schedule:** Memorial Day through Labor Day: Wednesdays through Sundays, 10 a.m. to 4 p.m.

**Admission/Fare:** Adults, $4; children (5-12), $2; under age 5 are free.

**Locomotives/Rolling Stock:** No. 4 Argent Lumber Co. Porter 2-8-0; no. 5 Hawaii Railway Co. Baldwin 2-4-2; no. 16 Hutton Brick Co. Plymouth 8-ton; no. 18 American Steel & Wire Co. Vulcan 0-4-0-T; no. 111 Tionesta Valley Railway caboose; no. 6 Waynesburg & Washington coach; and various pieces of 18" gauge mining equipment.

**Special Events:** Spring Gas Up, first Sunday in May. Fall Festival, last full weekend in September.

**Nearby Attractions/Accommodations:** Sloane-Stanley Museum.

**Location/Directions:** One mile north of village on Route 7 adjacent to Housatonic Railroad.

          M

**Site Address:** Kent, CT
**Mailing Address:** PO Box 1467, New Milford, CT 06776
**Telephone:** (860) 927-0050
**Internet:** www.ctamachinery.com

# NAUGATUCK RAILROAD/
# RAILROAD MUSEUM OF NEW ENGLAND
*Train ride*
*Standard gauge*

HOWARD PINCUS

**Description:** A 17.5-mile round trip over a former New Haven Railroad line, from the 1881 Thomaston Station along the scenic Naugatuck River and past 100-year-old New England brass mills, on to the face of the Thomaston Dam. The original Naugatuck Railroad opened this route in 1849. The Naugatuck Railroad is operated by the not-for-profit Railroad Museum of New England.

**Schedule:** Starting May 26, weekends, 1 and 3 p.m. Earlier in May, operation for groups of 45 or more. During the fall: 11 a.m., 1 and 3 p.m.

**Admission/Fare:** Adults, $9.95; seniors, $8.95; children 3-12, $6.95. Group rates and charters available.

**Locomotives/Rolling Stock:** New Haven RS-3 no. 529; New Haven U25B no. 2525; Naugatuck GP-9 no. 1732; Canadian National open-window heavyweight coaches from 1920s.

**Special Events:** Occasional excursions over entire 19.6-mile route between Waterbury and Torrington. Also, engineer-for-an-hour program.

**Nearby Attractions/Accommodations:** Amusement parks, vineyards, state parks.

**Location/Directions:** I-84, exit 20 to north on Route 8, exit 38 Thomaston.

†See ad on page A-10.

**Site Address:** E. Main St., Thomaston, CT
**Mailing Address:** PO Box 400, Thomaston, CT 06787-0400
**Telephone:** (860) 283-RAIL
**Fax:** (203) 269-3364
**E-mail:** rrexc@snet.net
**Internet:** www.rmne.org

# CONNECTICUT EASTERN RAILROAD MUSEUM
*Museum, display*
*Standard gauge*

ROBERT A. LA MAY

**Description:** The museum is gradually restoring trackage (approximately 1.2 miles) and a small yard on the New Haven Railroad (Air Line). Columbia Junction six-stall roundhouse and turntable are being restored, complete with wye track. Smaller buildings and rolling stock are also being restored.

**Schedule:** May 4-5 through November 2-3: Saturday and Sunday, 10 a.m. to 4 p.m.; Fourth of July, 1 to 5 p.m.

**Admission/Fare:** Adults and seniors, $3; children 12 and under are free.

**Locomotives/Rolling Stock:** Alco S-4 K&L no. 1, former CV no. 8081; GE 44-ton Valley Railroad no. 0800, former LIRR; GE 25-ton Northeast Utilities; Alco RS-11 Lamoille Valley no. 3608, former CV no. 3608. New Haven coaches nos. 8673 and 8695; NH wooden boxcar no. 171568; other freight and passenger cars.

**Special Events:** April and October: train shows with open house at the museum.

**Nearby Attractions/Accommodations:** Windham Textile and History Museum, Jillson House Museum, bed and breakfasts.

**Location/Directions:** Follow Main St. (Route 66) in Willimantic to Bridge St. (Route 32 south). Cross railroad tracks, turn right at museum sign and continue to museum.

     M TRAIN

**Site Address:** 55 Bridge St. (Rt. 32), Willimantic, CT
**Mailing Address:** PO Box 665, Willimantic, CT 06226
**Telephone:** (860) 228-9671
**E-mail:** rr_webma@cteastrrmuseum.org
**Internet:** www.cteastrrmuseum.org

# WILMINGTON & WESTERN RAILROAD
*Train ride, dinner train*
*Standard gauge*

SETH JACKSON

**Description:** A ten-mile, 1¼-hour round trip over a portion of former Baltimore & Ohio Landenberg Branch from Greenbank Station to Mt. Cuba. Occasional trips to Yorklyn and Hockessin are also offered.

**Schedule:** April through December: Saturdays and/or Sundays, one- and two-hour excursions along the Red Clay Valley. Call or write for timetable.

**Admission/Fare:** Varies, please call or write for information. Caboose rentals, group rates, and private charters are available.

**Locomotives/Rolling Stock:** Two SW-1 EMD switchers; 1909 Alco steam 4-4-0; 1907 Baldwin 0-6-0; 1910 Canadian Locomotive Co. 2-6-0; 1929 PRR railcar.

**Special Events:** Easter Bunny Special, Santa Claus Express, Dinner and/or Murder Mystery Trains, Civil War Weekend.

**Nearby Attractions/Accommodations:** Longwood Gardens, Hagley Museum, Kalmar Nyckel, Winterthur Museum.

**Location/Directions:** I-95, exit 5, follow Route 141 north to Route 2 west, then follow Route 41 north. Greenbank Station is on Route 41 just north of Route 2, 4 miles southwest of Wilmington.

**Radio frequency: 160.755**

**Site Address:** 2201 Newport-Gap Pike, Route 41, Wilmington, DE
**Mailing Address:** PO Box 5787, Wilmington, DE 19808
**Telephone:** (302) 998-1930
**Fax:** (302) 998-7408
**E-mail:** schedule@wwrr.com
**Internet:** www.wwrr.com

**Description:** Guided tours of a 1929 private Pullman car.

**Schedule:** Tuesdays through Saturdays, 9 a.m. to 4 p.m.

**Admission/Fare:** Adults, $6; seniors, $5.50; children, $3.

**Locomotives/Rolling Stock:** Pullman Standard Car & Manufacturing Co. 1929/30 "Esperanza" no. 6242

**Nearby Attractions/Accommodations:** Thomas A. Edison winter home, baseball spring training camps for Boston Red Sox and Minnesota Twins, Sanibel Island, beaches.

**Location/Directions:** I-75, exit 23, drive 5 miles west to downtown Ft. Myers. Peck St. is one block south of Dr. Martin Luther King Jr. Blvd.

      M

**Site Address:** 2300 Peck St., Ft. Myers, FL
**Mailing Address:** 2300 Peck St., Ft. Myers, FL 33901
**Telephone:** (941) 332-5955
**Fax:** (941) 332-6637
**E-mail:** msantiago@cityftmyers.com

# MURDER MYSTERY DINNER TRAIN
# ON THE SEMINOLE GULF RAILWAY
*Train ride, dinner train*
*Standard gauge*

**Description:** A working railroad with daytime excursion trains, which can be boarded at Colonial Station for a 1½-hour round trip or for trips that include the scenic Caloosahatchee River bridge crossing. Dinner theater trains depart for a 3½-hour round trip from Colonial Station in Fort Myers. They stop on the Caloosahatchee Bridge for the scenic view before continuing the ride north. Special holiday trains include the Rail/Boat Christmas train to Punta Gorda featuring a tour by boat, viewing decorated homes and boats along the canals of Punta Gorda Isles.

**Schedule:** Excursion trains–year round: Wednesdays and weekends. Murder mystery dinner train, five nights a week. Wednesday through Saturday, 6:30 p.m., Sunday, 5:30 p.m.

**Admission/Fare:** Excursion train–adults, $7 and up; children 3-12, $4 and up. Dinner train theater, $47.98 and up.

**Locomotives/Rolling Stock:** Eight GP9s; three RDCs; four dining cars; Sanibel and Captiva, former CN, Marco, and Gasparillo; kitchen; more.

**Special Events:** Easter, Mother's Day, Father's Day, Thanksgiving, Christmas rail/boat dinner trains in December and New Year's Eve party dinner trip.

**Location/Directions:** Excursion and dinner trains depart from Colonial Station near the Colonial Blvd. (State Route 884) and Metro Parkway intersection in Fort Myers, 3 miles west of I-75 exit 22.

**Site Address:** Fort Myers, FL
**Mailing Address:** 4410 Centerpointe Dr., Ste. 207, Fort Myers, FL 33916
**Telephone:** (941) 275-8487, (800) SEM-GULF, and (800) 736-4853
**Fax:** (941) 275-0581
**E-mail:** appelberg@semgulf.com
**Internet:** www.semgulf.com

## RAILROAD MUSEUM OF SOUTH FLORIDA'S TRAIN VILLAGE
*Train ride, display*
*7½" gauge*

MICHAEL MULLIGAN

**Description:** A 15-minute, 1⅛-mile ride in county park with tunnel, bridges, gardens, and miniature villages along the right-of-way.

**Schedule:** Year round: daily, Mondays through Fridays, 10 a.m. to 2 p.m. Saturdays and holidays, 10 a.m. to 4 p.m. Sundays, 12 to 4 p.m. Weekends only August and September. Closed Thanksgiving and Christmas.

**Admission/Fare:** $2.50; children under age 5, $.50. Park charges for parking–$.75 per hour with $3 maximum per day.

**Locomotives/Rolling Stock:** Miniature scale 7½" locomotives include: FP7A diesels nos. 1994, 1996 and 2000; GP50 0-6-0 no. 143 gasoline with steam sound; units pull 3 to 5 rider cars; Atlantic Coast Line standard gauge no. 143 0-6-0 on display.

**Special Events:** Easter Bunny Express–Good Friday, Saturday, Easter Sunday. Halloween Express and Christmas Holiday Express with night rides (extra fare). Call or write for information.

**Nearby Attractions/Accommodations:** Sanibel Island, Shell Factory, Edison and Ford winter estates, many motels, hotels, and campgrounds.

**Location/Directions:** Located in Lakes Regional Park/Lee County facility, which is ⅛ mile west of U.S. 41 and Gladiolus Dr.

**Site Address:** 7330 Gladiolus Dr., Fort Myers, FL
**Mailing Address:** PO Box 7372, Fort Myers, FL 33911-7372
**Telephone:** (941) 267-1905

# GOLD COAST RAILROAD MUSEUM
*Train ride, museum, display, layout*
*24" gauge*

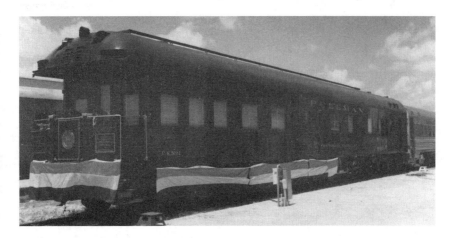

**Description:** Two-foot equipment operates Saturday and Sunday at 1 p.m. and 3 p.m. We offer a 15- to 20-minute ride on the property.

**Admission/Fare:** Adults, $5; children (12 and under), $3; under 3 free. Train ride: $2 per person.

**Locomotives/Rolling Stock:** Presidential Pullman "Ferdinand Magallan"; *California Zephyr* "Silver Crescent"; FEC no. 136 coach, assortment of stainless sleepers, coach, and diners; FEC "Wreck Train."

**Nearby Attractions:** Penny Thompson camping grounds, Monkey Jungle, Miami Metro Zoo, Everglades, Florida Keys within easy drive. Hotels, shopping centers, restaurants.

**Location/Directions:** Florida Turnpike south to exit 16, SW 152nd St. Follow signs to Metro Zoo. Turn left onto property, and museum is the first right off access road.

**Site Address:** 12450 SW 152nd St., Miami, FL
**Mailing Address:** 12450 SW 152nd St., Miami, FL 33177
**Telephone:** (305) 253-0063
**Fax:** (305) 233-4641
**E-mail:** lclltd@gate.net
**Internet:** www.goldcoast-railroad.org

# MOUNT DORA, TAVARES & EUSTIS RAILROAD
*Train ride*
*Standard gauge*

**Description:** Operates on the 11-mile Sorrento Branch of the Florida Central Railroad. The route travels through orange groves, rural Florida, and skirts around Lake Dora. One-hour ride on 1928 "Dora Doodlebug" motor car, 75-minute ride on Mount Dora Cannonball steam train, and 2½ hour Orange Blossom Dinner Train.

**Schedule:** Year round. Motor car operates weekdays, steam train operates on Saturdays and Sundays.

**Admission/Fare:** Doodlebug–adults, $8.50; seniors, $9.00; children (under 12), $6.00. Steam–adults, $16; seniors, $15; children (under 12), $8. Dinner train–$30.00 per person.

**Locomotives/Rolling Stock:** 1928 Brill Interurban converted to Edwards gas-mechanical M-201; no. 4 Baldwin 2-6-2, Reader Railroad; two coaches, combine, and open-air gondola car, 1928 Brill gas-mechanical M-55.

**Special Events:** Art Festival, Craft Fair, Pumpkin Train, Santa Express, antique car fest, antique boat show, 76-mile round-trip excursions to Orlando on steam train.

**Location/Directions:** Located 30 minutes north of Orlando, Hwy. 441 north, left on Donelly St., on the corner of Alexander St. and Third Ave.

**Site Address:** 150 W. Third Ave., Mount Dora, FL
**Mailing Address:** PO Box 641, Mount Dora, FL 32756
**Telephone:** (352) 383-4368
**Fax:** (352) 383-9360
**Internet:** www.doradoodlebug.com

© FLAGLER MUSEUM

**Description:** Whitehall, a 55-room Gilded Age estate and National Historic Landmark, was the winter home of Henry M. Flagler, developer of the Florida East Coast Railway that linked the east coast of Florida. Experience life during America's Gilded Age through the eyes of one of its most important citizens, Henry Flagler. Flagler, with partners John D. Rockefeller and Samuel Andrews, founded Standard Oil. Displays and exhibits focus on the contributions Flagler made to the state of Florida by building the Florida East Coast Railway and developing tourism and agriculture as the state's major industries.

**Schedule:** Year round: Tuesdays through Saturdays, 10 a.m. to 5 p.m. Sundays, noon to 5 p.m. Closed Thanksgiving, Christmas Day, and New Year's Day.

**Admission/Fare:** Adults, $8; children 6-12, $3. Free on Founders Day.

**Locomotives/Rolling Stock:** FEC Car no. 91, Henry Flagler's private railcar, built in 1886.

**Special Events:** Whitehall Lecture Series, February. Founders Day, June 5. Flagler Museum Music Series, November through March. Holiday tours, December.

**Nearby Attractions/Accommodations:** Museums, zoo, Atlantic Ocean.

**Location/Directions:** I-95 to exit 52 (Okeechobee Blvd.). Travel 3 miles across Intracoastal Waterway, left on Cocoanut Row. Museum is ¾ mile on left.

**Site Address:** Cocoanut Row and Whitehall Way, Palm Beach, FL
**Mailing Address:** PO Box 969, Palm Beach, FL 33480
**Telephone:** (561) 655-2833
**Fax:** (561) 655-2826
**E-mail:** flagler@emi.net
**Internet:** www.flagler.org

**Florida, Parrish**

**FLORIDA GULF COAST
RAILROAD MUSEUM, INC.**
*Train ride, museum*
*Standard gauge*

GLENN MILEY

**Description:** A 1½-hour train ride with some exhibits.

**Schedule:** May through September, Sundays 1 and 3 p.m. October through April, Saturdays 11 a.m. and 1 p.m. and Sundays 1 and 3 p.m.

**Admission/Fare:** Adults, $10; children ages 3-11, $6.

**Locomotives/Rolling Stock:** EMD GP7 no. 1835; Alco RS3 No. 1633; GE 44-ton no. 100; passenger coach no. 2002; tavern lounge "Kentucky Club" no. 3251; Pullman MU car no. 3518; caboose no. 518415; caboose no. 12070; Pullman sleeper "Short Leaf Pine," no. 3464; more.

**Special Events:** Civil War weekends and Wild West Tin Robbery weekends, spring and fall; Christmas Santa Train.

**Nearby Attractions/Accommodations:** Busch Gardens, Manatee River State Recreational area, Roaring 20's Pizza & Pipes, J.P. Igloos Ice Rink , Ellenton Outlet Mall, Tampa Union Station (Amtrak).

**Location/Directions:** I-75 exit 45, east 5 miles to U.S. 301, south ¼ mile to 83rd St. E., left into parking.

*Coupon available, see coupon section.

**Radio Frequency: Family Blue**

**Site Address:** 12210 83 St. E., Parrish, FL
**Mailing Address:** PO Box 355, Parrish, FL 34219
**Telephone:** (941) 776-0906
**Fax:** (941) 917-0081
**E-mail:** traininfo@fgcrrm.org
**Internet:** www.fgcrrm.org

# CENTRAL FLORIDA RAILROAD MUSEUM
*Museum, display, layout*

**Description:** A large museum emphasizing the history of Florida railroads. (Operated by Central Florida Chapter, NRHS.)

**Schedule:** Sundays, 2 to 5 p.m. Closed major holidays.

**Admission/Fare:** Free.

**Locomotives/Rolling Stock:** Clinchfield caboose.

**Special Events:** Railroad Show in November and May.

**Nearby Attractions/Accommodations:** Winter Garden Heritage Museum, Orlando attractions, West Orange Trail (built on ex-Orange Belt, ex-Plant System, ex-ACL line.)

**Location/Directions:** Turnpike to Winter Garden exit, east on State Route 50 to Dillard St., left on Dillard, left on Plant, left on Lakeview, left on Plant, right on Boyd St.

**Site Address:** 101 S. Boyd St., Winter Garden, FL
**Mailing Address:** 101 S. Boyd St., Winter Garden, FL 34787
**Telephone:** (407) 656-8749
**E-mail:** irvl@peoplepc.com

**Description:** This tropical showplace includes Cypress Junction, where ten high-speed model trains tour tiny replicas of U.S. landmarks–Miami, New Orleans, Mt. Rushmore–on 1,100 feet of track.

**Schedule:** Year round: daily, 10:30 a.m. to 5 p.m. Extended hours during special seasons.

**Admission/Fare:** Entrance price to theme park: adults, $32.95 plus tax; children (6-12), $16.95 plus tax; kids free.

**Locomotives/Rolling Stock:** Santa Fe no. 3571; B&O or Chessie System BTO no. 3597; Seaboard System no. 6378; Lehigh Valley no. 211; Atlantic Coast Line C-O no. 47124.

**Nearby Attractions/Accommodations:** Bok Tower, Fantasy of Flight, and all Orlando attractions.

**Location/Directions:** I-4 to U.S. 27 south to 540 west. Located in central Florida.

**Site Address:** 2641 S. Lake Summit, Winter Haven, FL
**Mailing Address:** PO Box 1, Cypress Gardens, FL 33884
**Telephone:** (863) 324-2111 and (800) 282-2123
**Fax:** (863) 324-7946
**E-mail:** rderidder@cypressgardens.com
**Internet:** www.cypressgardens.com

# BLUE RIDGE SCENIC RAILWAY
## Train ride, display, layout

DICK HILLMAN

**Description:** A 3-hour round trip (includes layover) along the Toccoa River to McCaysville, Georgia, on the old L&N Hook and Eye Division. There is a large gift shop and tourist information area.

**Schedule:** April through mid-December: Friday, Saturday, and Sunday departures.

**Admission/Fare:** Adults, $24; children, $12.

**Locomotives/Rolling Stock:** Various diesel locomotives available to us through our parent company, Georgia Northeastern Railroad. GP7 no. 2097; GP9 no. 6576; GP10 no. 7529; GP10 no. 7562; GP18 no. 8704; GP18 no. 8705; GP20 no. 316; GP20 no. 4125; SW1 no. 77, 1947; NW1 no. 81, 1948.

**Nearby Attractions/Accommodations:** Amicalola Falls State Park; Helen, Georgia (alpine village), surrounded by national forests, hiking and biking trails; Ocoee Whitewater Center.

**Location/Directions:** Ninety miles north of Atlanta, Georgia and 85 miles southeast of Chattanooga, Tennessee.

**Site Address:** 241 Depot St., Blue Ridge, GA
**Mailing Address:** 241 Depot St., Blue Ridge, GA, 30513
**Telephone:** (706) 632-9833
**Fax:** (706) 258-2756
**Internet:** www.brscenic.com

**Description:** Visitors meet rail history "hands on" through the display of over 90 pieces of retired railway rolling stock, including a World War II troop kitchen, railway post office, the 1911 Pullman "Superb" used by President Warren Harding, a modern office car, vintage steam locomotives, restored wooden cabooses. Short on-site train ride aboard vintage cabooses.

**Schedule:** April through November: Thursday, Friday, Saturday, 10 a.m. to 5 p.m. December through March: Saturdays, 10 a.m. to 5 p.m. Train rides complimentary with admission.

**Admission/Fare:** Adults, $6; seniors and children 2-12, $4; under age 2 are free.

**Locomotives/Rolling Stock:** 1950 and 1941 HRT GE 44-ton nos. 2 and 5; 1943 Georgia Power Porter 0-6-0T no. 97; 1954 CRR caboose no. 1064; SOU caboose XC7871; SCL caboose no. 01077.

**Location/Directions:** I-85 northwest of Atlanta to west on exit 104 (Pleasant Hill Rd.) for 3.5 miles to U.S. 23 (Buford Highway). North ¼ mile to Peachtree Rd., turn west to museum entrance.

**Site Address:** 3595 Peachtree Rd., Duluth, GA
**Mailing Address:** PO Box 1267, Duluth, GA 30096
**Telephone:** (770) 476-2013
**Fax:** (770) 926-6095
**E-mail:** admin@srmduluth.org
**Internet:** www.srmduluth.org

**KENNESAW CIVIL WAR MUSEUM**
*Museum*
*Standard gauge*

**Description:** The Andrews Raid and the Great Locomotive Chase, one of the unusual episodes of the Civil War, has been much publicized over the years. The "General," now one of the most famous locomotives in American history, is enshrined in a museum within 100 yards of the spot where it was stolen on April 12, 1862. The old engine, still operable, last ran in 1962. The Kennesaw Civil War Museum was officially opened on April 12, 1972, 110 years after the historic seizure of the "General."

**Schedule:** Undergoing renovation October 2001 through October 2002. Please call for hours.

**Admission/Fare:** Adults, $3; seniors, $2.50; children 7-15, $1.50; age 6 and under are free.

**Locomotives/Rolling Stock:** Rodgers Ketchum & Grosvenor 4-4-0 no. 3; Western & Atlantic "General."

**Special Events:** Big Shanty Festival, April. Kennesaw Antique Fair, fall.

**Nearby Attractions/Accommodations:** Kennesaw Mountain Park; more.

**Location/Directions:** I-75 north (from Atlanta) exit 273 (Wade Green Rd.), west 2.3 miles. Museum is on right.

*Coupon available, see coupon section.

**Site Address:** 2829 Cherokee St., Kennesaw, GA
**Mailing Address:** 2829 Cherokee St., Kennesaw, GA 30144
**Telephone:** (770) 427-2117 and (800) 742-6897
**Fax:** (770) 429-4538
**E-mail:** kcwm@juno.com
**Internet:** www.thegeneral.org

# ROUNDHOUSE RAILROAD MUSEUM
*Museum, display, layout*

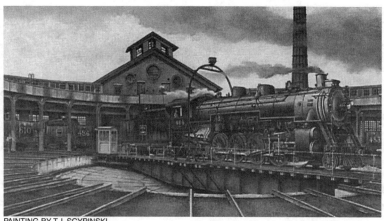

PAINTING BY T.J. SCYPINSKI

**Description:** Savannah's Roundhouse Railroad Museum is the oldest and most complete antebellum railroad manufacturing and repair facility still standing in the U.S. and is a National Historic Landmark. Construction of the site began in 1845 and 13 of the original structures are still standing, including the massive roundhouse and operating turntable and the 125-foot smokestack. There are permanent exhibits in five of the structures on site.

**Schedule:** Year round. Daily. Self-guided tours, 9 a.m. to 4 p.m.

**Admission/Fare:** Adults, $4; AARP, AAA, students, and military, $3.50; children 5 and under, free

**Locomotives/rolling stock:** Steam locomotive no. 223; 1886 steam locomotive; 1913 steam locomotive goat; GP 35 no. 2715; Central of Georgia inspection car no. 2; officer's car "Columbus."

**Nearby Attractions/Accommodations:** Savannah History Museum and Savannah's Historic District of Homes and Museums. Located across the street from the Courtyard by Marriott Hotel.

**Location/Directions:** I-16 east to Martin Luther King Jr. Blvd. exit. Left on Martin Luther King Jr. Blvd., and then left on Harris St.

*Coupon available, see coupon section. †See ad on page A-3.

**Site Address:** 601 W. Harris St., Savannah, GA
**Mailing Address:** 601 W. Harris St., Savannah, GA 31401
**Telephone:** (912) 651-6823
**Fax:** (921) 651-3194
**E-mail:** hrs@chsgeorgia.org
**Internet:** www.chsgeorgia.org

# HAWAIIAN RAILWAY SOCIETY
*Train ride, museum, display*
*36" gauge*

MARK D. BRUESHABER

**Description:** A 6½-mile, 90-minute ride along OR&L track from Ewa to Kahe Point, where passengers can witness the surf crashing against the rocks. The train passes former Barbers Point Naval Air Station, Ko'Olina Golf Course, and more. Fully narrated trip provides railroading history of the area.

**Schedule:** Sunday, 12:30 and 2:30 p.m. (weather permitting). Call for information.

**Admission/Fare:** Adults, $8; seniors and children ages 2-12, $5; under age 2 are free.

**Locomotives/Rolling Stock:** Two Whitcomb diesel-electrics, nos. 302 and 423; converted U.S. Army flatcars; parlor car no. 64.

**Special Events:** Halloween rides. Call or write for information.

**Nearby Attractions/Accommodations:** Ihilani Resort; Ko'Olina Golf Course; Paradise Cover Luau.

**Location/Directions:** Freeway H-1, exit 5A, continue on 76 (Fort Weaver Rd.) south to Renton Rd., take a right on Renton Rd., and left on Fleming Rd.

        arm TRAIN M

**Site Address:** 91-1001 Renton Rd., Ewa Town, HI
**Mailing Address:** PO Box 60369, Ewa Station, Ewa, HI 96706
**Telephone:** (808) 681-5461
**Fax:** (808) 681-4860
**E-mail:** hirailway@aol.com
**Internet:** hometown.aol.com/hawaiianrailway/index.html

# LAHAINA, KAANAPALI & PACIFIC RAILROAD
*Train ride, dinner train*
*36" gauge*

**Description:** The "Sugar Cane Train" chugs its way through the colorful history and breath-taking scenes of Maui by bringing back memories, sounds, and experiences of turn-of-the-century sugar plantation life. The sugar trains of the past were used to transport sugar cane from the fields to the mills and were a popular means of transportation for sugar workers in the early 1900s. Passengers are taken on an entertaining and historical tour by one of our singing conductors. The train stations are designed to resemble turn-of-the-century boarding platforms and are a delightful glimpse at Hawaii's historical and cultural past.

**Schedule:** Year round: Call or write for information.

**Admission/Fare:** Call or write for information.

**Locomotives/Rolling Stock:** No. 1, "Anaka," 1943 Porter 2-4-0 and no. 3, "Myrtle," 1943 Porter 2-4-0, both former Carbon Limestone Co.; no. 45, "Oahu," 1959 Plymouth diesel, former Oahu Railway; nine 19th century King Kalakaua replica nostalgic coaches; two non-operational displays of Oahu 5 and Oahu 86 from Oahu Railway; more.

**Nearby Attractions/Accommodations:** Historic town of Lahaina, Maui, and resort area of Kaanapali.

**Location/Directions:** Lahaina Station located near Pioneer Mill, turn off Highway 30 at Hinau St., turn right at Limahana St.

**Site Address:** 975 Limahana Pl., Ste. 203, Lahaina, Maui, HI
**Mailing Address:** 975 Limahana Pl., Ste. 203, Lahaina, Maui, HI 96761
**Telephone:** (800) 499-2307, (888) LKP-MAUI, and (808) 661-0089 (recording)
**Fax:** (808) 661-8389

# AMERICAN FREEDOM
# DINNER TRAIN
*Dinner train*
*Standard gauge*

GEO. BROCKMAN

**Description:** Fabulous scenic five-hour dinner train on the famous and historic Camas Prairie Railroad along the Clearwater River out of Lewiston, Idaho, featuring cars from the American Freedom Train.

**Schedule:** Operating 52 weeks per year. Call 1-888-RR-DINER for information and reservations.

**Admission/Fare:** $85 per person.

**Locomotives/Rolling Stock:** American Freedom Train cars; using Camas Prairie Road locomotives for motive power; locomotives are GE B-23-7.

**Special Events:** Anniversaries, birthdays, class and family reunions, office parties and seminars, weddings, community celebrations and events, as well as holiday events and special trains.

**Nearby Attractions/Accommodations:** Lewiston, Idaho, and the surrounding region is a year-round recreational paradise with a variety of fine lodging facilities.

**Location/Directions:** Located on U.S. Highway 12, known as the official Lewis and Clark Bicentennial Trail Highway system. Lewiston, Idaho, is directly south of Spokane, Washington, traveling on Highway 95. Contact the Lewiston, Idaho, Chamber of Commerce (208) 743-3531.

**Site Address:** Fifth and Railroad, Lewiston, ID
**Mailing Address:** 610½ Main St., Lewiston, ID 83501
**Telephone:** (208) 743-2233 and (888) RR-DINER
**Fax:** (208) 746-8306 (auto)
**E-mail:** americanfreedomdinnertrain@lewiston.com
**Internet:** www.americanfreedomdinnertrain.com

**Description:** Built in 1903, this train depot is now the home of the Canyon County Museum. Used as a depot until 1926, and then as offices for the Union Pacific Railroad, the building now houses displays of both Canyon County and Union Pacific memorabilia.

**Schedule:** Year round, Tuesday through Saturday, 1 to 5 p.m.

**Admission/Fare:** Free. Suggested donation: Adults, $1, children $.50.

**Locomotives/Rolling Stock:** Union Pacific Caboose no. 25076, can be toured; steam crane circa 1917.

**Special Events:** Snake River Stampede, Good Old Dayz Celebration, starts second weekend in July, includes rodeo, entertainment, lots of family activities, parade.

**Nearby Attractions/Accommodations:** War Hawk Air Museum, WWII memorabilia; Celebration Park, petroglyphs and interpretive center; Oregon trail sites, several throughout Treasure Valley area; Old Fort Boise, replica of old fort.

**Location/Directions:** I-84 take Garrity exit, turn left on Garrity Rd. to 16th Ave., then turn left at Lakeview Park. Go over overpass and turn right on first street. Turn right on 12th Ave., and go one block to Front St. to Depot museum.

       M

**Site Address:** 1200 Front St., Nampa, ID
**Mailing Address:** 1200 Front St., Nampa, ID
**Telephone:** (208) 467-7611
**E-mail:** canyondepomuseum@aol.com

**Description:** The museum offers pictorial exhibits and railroad artifacts.

**Schedule:** April, 9 a.m. to 5 p.m. Monday through Saturday; May, 9 a.m. to 5 p.m. daily; June through August, 9 a.m. to 7 p.m. daily; September, 9 a.m. to 5 p.m. daily; October, 9 a.m. to 3 p.m. Closed October 15 for season.

**Admission/Fare:** Adults, $2; seniors, $1.50; children 6-16, $1; under 6 are free; family, $6. For tour information, please call.

**Special Events:** Depot Day Festival and Car Show, Saturday before Mother's Day.

**Nearby Attractions/Accommodations:** Mine Tour, Mining Museum, Oasis Bordello Museum.

**Location/Directions:** I-90, exit 62, Wallace, Idaho.

*Coupon available, see coupon section.

**Site Address:** 219 Sixth St., Wallace, ID
**Mailing Address:** PO Box 469, Wallace, ID 83873
**Telephone:** (208) 752-0111
**Fax:** (208) 753-9361

# HISTORIC PULLMAN FOUNDATION
*Museum*

**Description:** The Historic Pullman Foundation operates the Pullman Visitor Center, which gives an overview of George Pullman, the Pullman Company, and Mr. Pullman's town built in the 1880s, which still exits.

**Schedule:** Year round. Monday through Friday, 11 a.m. to 2 p.m.; Saturday, 10 a.m. to 2 p.m.; Sunday, 10 a.m. to 3 p.m.

**Admission/Fare:** Adults, $3; students, $2 suggested donation; group tours available.

**Special Events:** Annual Pullman House Tour, second weekend in October, 11 a.m. to 5 p.m. First Sunday guided walking tours, 12:30 and 1:30 p.m., May through October.

**Nearby Attractions/Accommodations:** Museum of Science and Industry, Downtown Chicago, riverboat casinos, Sandridge Nature Center, South Suburban Geneology Society, Ridge Historic District, International Harborside Golf Course, River Oaks Mill, Calumet Park Beach, East Side Historical Society, Wolf Lake.

**Location/Directions:** I-94 to 111th St. (exit 66A), travel west four blocks. Metra Electric stops at 111th St./Pullman, 115th St./Kensington, and downtown Chicago.

*Coupon available, see coupon section.

**Site Address:** 11141 S. Cottage Grove Ave., Chicago, IL
**Mailing Address:** 1000 E. 111th St., 10th Floor, Chicago, IL 60628-4697
**Telephone:** (773) 785-3828
**Fax:** (773) 785-8182
**E-mail:** PullmanHPF@aol.com
**Internet:** www.pullmanil.org

**Description:** The Museum of Science and Industry is one of the nation's preeminent centers for informal science and technology education. The model railroad exhibit was originally installed in 1941. The layout is approximately 3,000 square feet. Features include an O gauge track that is $\frac{1}{48}$ actual size, totaling 1,200 feet, in addition to 10,000 feet of switchboard wire, 350 relays, 5,500 trees, 150 telegraph poles, as well as a host of freight cars.

**Schedule:** Labor Day through Memorial Day: weekdays, 9:30 a.m. to 4 p.m.; weekends and holidays, till 5:30 p.m. Memorial Day through Labor Day: daily, 9:30 a.m. to 5:30 p.m. Closed December 25.

**Admission/Fare:** Adults, $9; seniors, $7.50; children 3-11, $5. Chicago residents receive a discount. General admission is free on Thursdays.

**Locomotives/Rolling Stock:** Engine 999 was the first vehicle to go over 100 mph. The *Pioneer Zephyr* was the first streamlined diesel-electric train.

**Nearby Attractions/Accommodations:** Hyde Park, University of Chicago, Shedd Aquarium, Field Museum, Planetarium, Art Institute, Navy Pier.

**Location/Directions:** Lake Shore Dr. south to 57th St.

**Site Address:** 57th St. and Lake Shore Dr., Chicago, IL
**Mailing Address:** 57th St. and Lake Shore Dr., Chicago, IL 60637
**Telephone:** (773) 684-1414
**Fax:** (773) 684-2907
**Internet:** www.msichicago.org

# AMERICAN ORIENT EXPRESS
*Train ride*
*Standard gauge*

**Description:** Luxury rail vacations across the U.S., Canada, and Mexico by vintage streamliner train. Eight- to eleven-day programs.

**Schedule:** Operating season, February through November.

**Admission/Fare:** Prices based on tour and accommodations. Fares start at $2,890 per person. Vintage Pullman based on double occupancy.

**Nearby Attractions/Accommodations:** Tours include Antebellum South; Transcontinental Journey; Pacific Coast Explorer; Great Trans-Canada; Autumn in New England and Quebec; Southwest and Mexico's Copper Canyon; Rail Journey; Great Northwest and Rockies; National Parks of the West.

**Site Address:** Varies.
**Mailing Address:** 5100 Main St., Suite 300, Downers Grove, IL 60515
**Telephone:** (800) 320-4206 or (630) 663-4550
**Fax:** (630) 663-1595
**Internet:** www.americanorientexpress.com

**ELIZABETH DEPOT MUSEUM**
*Museum*

**Description:** Depot museum displaying artifacts of the Chicago Great Western Railroad. This depot serviced the nearby Winston Tunnel, the longest railroad tunnel in Illinois. The museum features a model of the tunnel.

**Schedule:** May through October: weekends 1 to 4 p.m.

**Admission/Fare:** Free

**Special Events:** Great Western Day, first Saturday in May, and Hobo Hap'nin', first Saturday after Labor Day, both featuring additional displays and activities relating to the railroad.

**Nearby Attractions/Accommodations:** Apple River Fort, also in downtown Elizabeth; Mississippi Palisades State Park, Apple River Canyon State Park.

**Location/Directions:** Three miles east of the Great River Road on U.S. Highway 20; turn right on Myrtle St. at the Veterans' Monument in downtown Elizabeth.

**Site Address:** Myrtle St., Elizabeth, IL
**Mailing Address:** PO Box 353, Elizabeth, IL 61028-0353
**Telephone:** (815) 858-2098
**E-mail:** elizabethdepot@yahoo.com

**SILVER CREEK & STEPHENSON RAILROAD**

*Train ride, display*
*Standard gauge*

STEVE SNYDER

**Description:** The turn-of-the-century Silver Creek Depot is a tribute to an important part of our country's transportation history. On display are lanterns, locks and keys, whistles, sounders, tickets, couplers, and more, representing railroads from across the country. The 4-mile train trip travels through Illinois farmland and stands of virgin timber known as "Indian Gardens," crossing Yellow Creek on a 30-foot-high cement and stone pier bridge.

**Schedule:** May 26-27; June 15-16; July 4, 26-28; Sept. 2, 28-29; Oct. 12-13, 26-27; 11 a.m. to 5 p.m.

**Admission/Fare:** Adults, $4; children (under 12), $2.

**Locomotives/Rolling Stock:** 1912, 36-ton Heisler; 1941 bay-window caboose, former Chicago, Milwaukee, St. Paul & Pacific; 1889 wooden caboose with cupola, former Hannibal & St. Joseph, reported to be the oldest running caboose in Illinois; 1948 caboose, former Illinois Central Gulf; covered flatcar; 14-ton Brookville switch engine; 12-ton Plymouth switch engine; and work cars.

**Location/Directions:** Intersection of Walnut and Lamm Roads, ½ mile south of Stephenson County Fairgrounds.

        M

**Site Address:** 2954 W. Walnut Rd., Freeport, IL
**Mailing Address:** PO Box 255, Freeport, IL 61032
**Telephone:** (815) 232-2306
**E-mail:** peggy1@mwci.net

113

# HISTORIC GREENUP DEPOT
*Museum, display*

**Schedule:** Daily, 10 a.m. to 4 p.m.

**Admission/Fare:** Free.

**Special Events:** Cumberland County Fair, third week in August. Fall Festival, first Saturday in October.

**Nearby Attractions/Accommodations:** Greenup is the town of covered porches; a covered bridge; restored Johnson Building.

**Location/Directions:** I-70, 34 miles west of Terre Haute, Indiana. The Old National Trail or Cumberland Road runs through Greenup.

**Site Address:** 204 W. Cumberland St., Greenup IL
**Mailing Address:** 204 W. Cumberland St., Greenup, IL 62428

# KANKAKEE MODEL RAILROAD CLUB AND MUSEUM
*Museum, display, layout*

GLENN JOHNSON

**Description:** Full-size 85-foot Pullman standard coach on display outside.

**Schedule:** Weekends, 12 to 4 p.m.

**Admission/Fare:** Free.

**Special Events:** October 18th and March Swap Meets.

**Nearby Attractions/Accommodations:** Kankakee River State Park, Hampton Inn, Holiday Inn, Quality Inn, Kankakee Historical Museum, Frank Lloyd Wright homes.

**Location/Directions:** I-57 south to exit 312, I-57 north to exit 312. West to East Avenue, downtown Kankakee. Located in Illinois Central depot.

**Site Address:** 197 S. East Ave., Kankakee, IL
**Mailing Address:** 197 S. East Ave., Kankakee, IL 60901
**Telephone:** (815) 929-9320
**Fax:** (815) 933-8611

115

RITA HATCH

**Description:** Trackside B&B 100 feet from double main line of BNSF, former SF. Sixty to 70 trains daily in 20 different paint schemes. Three rooms, one trackside. Galesburg has classifications yards with a bridge over the yards with parking on bridge.

**Admission/Fare:** Room rate: double, $75, plux tax; single $60, plus tax.

**Special Events:** Galesburg Railroad Days, fourth weekend in June.

**Nearby Attractions/Accommodations:** Classification yards.

**Site Address:** 976 Mine Rd., Knoxville, IL
**Mailing Address:** 976 Mine Rd., Knoxville, IL 61448
**Telephone:** (877) 570-5042
**E-mail:** knoxsta@galesburg.net
**Internet:** www.rrhistorical.com/knox

116

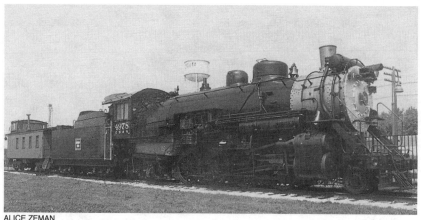

ALICE ZEMAN

**Description:** The restored 1940s station features an operating HO layout replica of downtown Mendota in the 1940s during its heyday as a railroad center with the Milwaukee, Illinois Central, and Burlington Railroads. Also see the old-time telegraphy office, railroad memorabilia, and more. One-mile motor car rides on selected dates and times. Live web cam of railroad depot and tracks 24/7.

**Schedule:** June through August: daily except Mondays and Tuesdays, 12 to 5 p.m. September through May: Saturdays and Sundays, 12 to 5 p.m.

**Admission/Fare:** $2; children under age 12, $1; members are free. Tours available.

**Locomotives/Rolling Stock:** Burlington O-1A Mikado-type locomotive 2-8-2 no. 4978; tender; Burlington waycar no. 14451; Milwaukee Road combine car no. 2713; more.

**Special Events:** Railroad Crossing Days, June 15-16, third weekend of June. Mendota Sweet Corn Festival, second weekend of August.

**Nearby Attractions/Accommodations:** Hume-Carnegie Historical Museum, Breaking the Prairie Agricultural Museum, restaurants, lodging, campgrounds.

**Location/Directions:** I-39/51 and Route 34, approximately 100 miles west of Chicago and 50 miles south of Rockford.

**Site Address:** 783 Main St., Mendota, IL
**Mailing Address:** PO Box 433, Mendota, IL 61342
**Telephone:** (815) 538-3800
**Internet:** www.mendotamuseums.org

# MONTICELLO RAILWAY MUSEUM
*Train ride, museum*
*Standard gauge*

DAVID MARSHALL

**Description:** A 7-mile round trip on former Illinois Central and Illinois Terminal trackage. Passengers board at either the Illinois Central depot at the museum or the 1899 Wabash depot downtown Monticello. Visitors view displays located both inside and outside railcars.

**Schedule:** May through October: weekends and holidays. Museum site departures: Saturdays, 11 a.m., 12:30, 2, and 3:30 p.m.; Sundays, 12:30, 2, and 3:30 p.m. Wabash depot departures: Saturdays, 11:30 a.m., 1 and 2:30 p.m.; Sundays, 1 and 2:30 p.m. Charters, private cars, on request.

**Locomotives/Rolling Stock:** 1907 Southern Railway Baldwin 2-8-0 no. 401; 1916 Mississippi Eastern Baldwin 4-6-0 no. 303; 1953 Wabash EMD F-7A no. 1189; 1959 CN MLW FPA-4 no. 6789; 1955 LIRR Alco RS-3 no. 301; more.

**Special Events:** Throttle Times; Caboose Days, August. Railroad Days, September. Ghost Train, October. Lunch with Santa, December.

**Nearby Attractions/Accommodations:** Rayville Railroad Museum, Allerton Park, nearby Amish and Lincoln sites, Best Western, Foster Inn.

**Location/Directions:** I-72 exit 166, Market St. Turn onto Iron Horse Pl. at traffic light, go past Best Western to museum.

**Site Address:** 993 Iron Horse Pl., Monticello, IL
**Mailing Address:** PO Box 401, Monticello, IL 61856-0401
**Telephone:** (217) 762-9011 (weekends) and (800) 952-3396 (weekdays)
**E-mail:** mrm@prairienet.org
**Internet:** www.prairienet.org/mrm

**WHEELS O' TIME MUSEUM**
*Museum*

TOM MITCHELL

**Description:** Steam locomotive, combine car, caboose, and switcher, plus three buildings displaying antique autos, fire trucks, tractors, clocks, musical devices, toys, clothing, and much more.

**Schedule:** May through October: Wednesdays through Sundays, 12 to 5 p.m. Summer holidays.

**Admission/Fare:** Adults, $4.50; children, $2.00. Under 3 free.

**Locomotives/Rolling Stock:** Rock Island Pacific no. 886; Milwaukee Road combine car; TP&W caboose.

**Nearby Attractions/Accommodations:** Wildlife Prairie Park, Lakeview Museum.

**Location/Directions:** On Route 40, north of Peoria, 2 miles north of the Route 6 intersection.

**Site Address:** 11923 N. Knoxville, Peoria, IL
**Mailing Address:** PO Box 9636, Peoria, IL 61612-9636
**Telephone:** (309) 243-9020
**E-mail:** wotmuseum@aol.com
**Internet:** wheelsotime.org

**Description:** Rochelle provides an area for train watching for everyone. Two busy mainline railroads (UP and BNSF) cross on the diamonds, averaging 80 to 90 trains in a 24-hour period. Gift shop and heated restrooms are available for all your needs.

**Schedule:** Park open 365 days a year. Gift shop open every day, except Tuesdays, year round.

**Admission/Fare:** Free.

**Locomotives/Rolling Stock:** Whitcomb locomotive on display for the children's enjoyment.

**Nearby Attractions/Accommodations:** Motels and restaurants nearby with Magic Waters only ½-hour drive away in Rockford, Illinois.

**Location/Directions:** From north and south, take I-39 to Illinois 38 exit west. From east and west, take I-88 to Illinois 251 north.

**Site Address:** 124 N. Ninth St., Rochelle, IL
**Mailing Address:** 124 N. Ninth St., Rochelle, IL 61068
**Telephone:** (815) 562-8107
**E-mail:** atsf525@aol.com
**Internet:** www.foxdir.net/rrpark

RICHARD M. SCHROEDER

**Description:** Displays show the history of the former Chicago & Eastern Illinois and other area railroads. The Baggage Room contains an HO model railroad. The Depot Museum preserves the railroads' history in east central Illinois and western Indiana in a former C&EI Railroad Depot.

**Schedule:** Memorial Day weekend through last Sunday in September: weekends, noon to 4 p.m. and by appointment.

**Admission/Fare:** Free. Donations are appreciated.

**Nearby Attractions/Accommodations:** Rossville Historical Society Museum, Mann's Chapel, Vermilion County Museum, 15 antique shops in downtown area.

**Location/Directions:** In Rossville, one block north on Illinois Route 1 to Benton St., east three blocks to CSX transportation tracks.

    M

**Site Address:** E. Benton St., Rossville, IL
**Mailing Address:** PO Box 1013, Danville, IL 61834-1013
**Telephone:** (217) 748-6615
**E-mail:** djcnrhs@prairienet.org or rickshro@aol.com
**Internet:** http://www.prairienet.org/djc-nrhs/

# FOX RIVER TROLLEY MUSEUM
*Train ride, museum*
*Standard gauge*

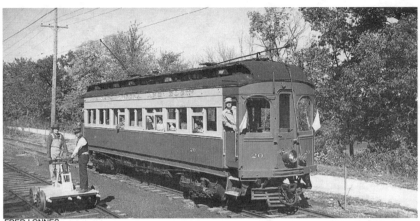
FRED LONNES

**Description:** Ride the historic 105-year-old remnant of an interurban railroad aboard Chicago-area interurban and "L" equipment.

**Schedule:** Sundays and holidays (Memorial Day, July 4, and Labor Day), May 12 through November 3. Saturdays, June 29 through Labor Day and October 19 and 26. 11 a.m. to 5 p.m.

**Admission/Fare:** Adults, $2.50; seniors, $2; children (3-11), $1.50; under age 3, free. Second ride, $.50.

**Locomotives/Rolling Stock:** Historic Chicago interurban and "L" equipment including CA&E no. 20; North Shore nos. 715 and 756; more.

**Special Events:** Mother's Day; Spring Caboose Day, June 2; Father's Day; Red, White and Blue Day, July 4; Trolley Fest and Riverfest, August 17-18; Fall Foliage/Caboose Days October 6 and 13; Pumpkin Trolley, October 19-20 and 26-27.

**Nearby Attractions/Accommodations:** Grand Victoria Casino, Elgin Area Museum, Elgin, Batavia Depot Museum (CB&Q), Blackhawk Forest Preserve, South Elgin; historic towns of St. Charles, Geneva, and Batavia. Major motel/hotel accommodations available in the area.

**Location/Directions:** Illinois 31 south from I-90 or U.S. 20, or north from I-88. Site is three blocks south of State St. stoplight in South Elgin.

**Site Address:** 365 S. LaFox St. (Illinois 31), South Elgin, IL
**Mailing Address:** PO Box 315, South Elgin, IL 60177-0315
**Telephone:** (847) 697-4676
**E-mail:** info@foxtrolley.org
**Internet:** www.foxtrolley.org

# ILLINOIS RAILWAY MUSEUM
### *Train ride, museum, display*
### *Standard gauge*

**Description:** A collection of more than 400 pieces of equipment and artifacts, operating and/or on display in car barns and open railyards, including steam, diesel, and electric locomotives; electric interurbans, elevated cars, and streetcars; trolley buses and motor buses, as well as passenger and freight equipment; a C&NW depot built in 1851, a signal tower, and a restored Chicago "L" station. A 9.5-mile round trip over our 4.8-mile reconstructed Elgin & Belvedere right-of-way is offered, featuring steam and/or diesel trains and electric interurbans on weekends and streetcars on weekdays.

**Schedule:** Weekdays, Memorial Day through Labor Day; Saturdays, May through October; Sundays, April through October.

**Admission/Fare:** Weekends: adults, $8; children 5-11/seniors 62+, $6. Weekdays: adults, $6; children 5-11, $4. Maximum family admission, $35. Higher fares for some special events.

**Locomotives/Rolling Stock:** No. 2903 Santa Fe 4-8-4; no. 2050 N&W 2-8-8-2; no. 9911A CB&Q EMC E5; no. 6930 UP DDA 40X; Electroliner; many more.

**Special Events:** Chicago Weekend, June; 4th of July Trolley Pageant; Vintage Transport Day, August; Thomas the Tank Engine, call for details..

**Location/Directions:** One mile east of Union off U.S. Route 20.

*Coupon available, see coupon section. †See ad on page A-19.

**Site Address:** 7000 Olson Rd., Union, IL
**Mailing Address:** PO Box 427, Union, IL 60180
**Telephone:** (815) 923-4391 or (815) 923-4000 recorded message
**Fax:** (815) 923-2006
**Internet:** www.irm.org

## VALLEY VIEW
## MODEL RAILROAD
### *Layout*

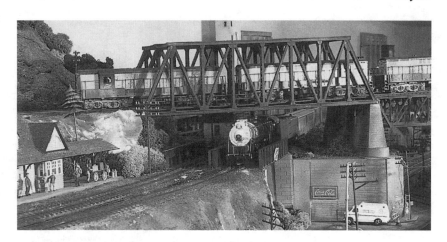

**Description:** This display is modeled after the Chicago & North Western's Northwest line, with accurate track layouts of some of the towns modeled. Three to four trains operate simultaneously over the railroad, which has eight scale miles of track, 20 ever-changing trains, 300 buildings, 64 turnouts, 700 vehicles, 900 people, 84 operating signal lights, 350 pieces of rolling stock, and operating grade crossings with flashers and gates. Extra equipment is on static display in the gift shop.

**Schedule:** Memorial Day through Labor Day: Wednesdays, Saturdays, and Sundays.

**Admission/Fare:** Adults, $5; seniors, $4; children, $2.50; age 5 and under are free.

**Nearby Attractions/Accommodations:** Illinois Railway Museum, Wild West Town, McHenry County Museum.

**Location/Directions:** From Illinois Railway Museum, travel north ¾ mile on Olson Rd. to Highbridge.

*Coupon available, see coupon section.

**Site Address:** 17108 Highbridge Rd., Union, IL
**Mailing Address:** 17108 Highbridge Rd., Union, IL 60180
**Telephone:** (815) 923-4135

**Indiana, Connersville**

# WHITEWATER VALLEY RAILROAD
*Train ride*
*Standard gauge*

JOHN R. HILLMAN

**Description:** This line offers a 32-mile, five-hour round trip to Metamora, Indiana, a restored canal town with shops and a working grist mill. A two-hour stopover at Metamora gives passengers a chance to tour the town.

**Schedule:** May through October: weekends and holidays, 12:01 p.m. May: Wednesday through Friday, 10 a.m.; October: Thursday and Friday, 10 a.m.

**Admission/Fare:** Adults, $14; children 2-12, $7; under age 2 are free. One-way and group rates available.

**Locomotives/Rolling Stock:** No. 6, 1907 Baldwin 0-6-0, former East Broad Top; no. 8, 1946 General Electric, former Muncie & Western; no. 11, 1924 Vulcan 0-4-0T; no. 100, 1919 Baldwin 2-6-2; no. 25, 1951 Lima SW7.5; no. 210, 1946 General Electric 70-ton; no. 709, 1950 Lima SW10; no. 2561, 1931 Plymouth 32-ton gas engine; no. 9339, 1948 Alco S1; no. 9376, 1950 Lima SW12, former Baltimore & Ohio; more.

**Special Events:** Metamora Canal Days, first weekend in October; Christmas Trains, November and December. Train-to-Dinner, first and third Fridays of each month May through October.

**Nearby Attractions/Accommodations:** Whitewater State Park, Brookville Lake, Mary Gray Bird Sanctuary.

**Location/Directions:** Corner of Fifth and Grand in downtown Connersville (Market St.).

Radio Frequency: 160.650

**Site Address:** 455 Market St., Connersville, IN
**Mailing Address:** PO Box 406, Connersville, IN 47331
**Telephone:** (765) 825-2054
**Fax:** (765) 825-4550
**Internet:** www.whitewatervalleyrr.org

**CORYDON SCENIC RAILROAD**
*Train ride*
*Standard gauge*

RICHARD PEARSON

**Description:** A 16-mile train ride through Southern Indiana Hills on air-conditioned Silverliner cars; live entertainment and guide.

**Schedule:** May through October; schedule varies.

**Admission/Fare:** Adults, $9; children, $5.

**Nearby Attractions/Accommodations:** First state capitol building.

**Location/Directions:** I-64, exit 105 to train station in downtown Corydon.

**Site Address:** 210 W. Walnut St., Corydon, IN
**Mailing Address:** PO Box 10, Corydon, IN 47112
**Telephone:** (812) 738-8000
**Fax:** (812) 738-3101

# NATIONAL NEW YORK CENTRAL RAILROAD MUSEUM
*Museum*

TAIGMARTIN INC.

**Description:** The museum traces the rich history of the New York Central and its impact on Elkhart and the nation. Extensive hands-on exhibits bring railroading alive.

**Schedule:** Year round: Tuesdays through Fridays, 10 a.m. to 2 p.m.; Saturdays 10 a.m. to 4 p.m.; Sundays 12 to 4 p.m. Closed Mondays and major holidays.

**Admission/Fare:** Adults, $2; seniors (62+) and students 6-12, $1; children age 5 and under are free.

**Locomotives/Rolling Stock:** NYC 3001 L3a Mohawk Alco 1940; NYC 4085 E8 EMD 1953; PRR 4882 GG1; six passenger cars; seven freight cars, seven cabooses; six non-revenue.

**Nearby Attractions/Accommodations:** Northern Indiana Amish Country, Midwest Museum of American Art, Time Was Museum, S. Ray Miller Auto Museum, Woodlawn Nature Center, Ruthmere, RV/MH Museum, Elkhart County Historical Museum.

**Location/Directions:** Indiana Toll Road (I-80/90) exit 92. Main St. in downtown Elkhart. The museum is in the historic freighthouses next to the Norfolk Southern main line.

             Elkhart

**Site Address:** 721 S. Main St., Elkhart, IN
**Mailing Address:** PO Box 1708, Elkhart, IN 46515
**Telephone:** (219) 294-3001
**Fax:** (219) 295-9434
**E-mail:** artscul@michiana.org
**Internet:** www.nycrrmuseum.org

**FORT WAYNE RAILROAD
HISTORICAL SOCIETY**
*Train ride, museum*
*Standard gauge*

TOM NITZA

**Description:** The Fort Wayne Railroad Historical Society is home to steam locomotive 765, which has operated excursions throughout the Midwest. The society also has other historic railroad equipment. You can tour the facility, talk to the people who maintain and operate this historic rail equipment, sit in the engineer's seat of a 400-ton iron horse and get a conductor's eye view from a 100-year-old caboose. For the ultimate railfan experience, the society offers an Engineer for an Hour program on our diesel locomotive. Several times each year, the society has operating days when you can see railroad equipment in action and ride a vintage caboose.

**Schedule:** Call for a recorded message or write for information.

**Admission/Fare:** No admission charge for museum/self-guided tour.

**Locomotives/Rolling Stock:** NKP 2-8-4 Berkshire steam locomotive no. 765; Lake Erie & Fort Wayne 0-6-0 no. 1; NKP wooden caboose no. 141; Wabash wooden caboose no. 2543; N&W wrecker no. 540019; 44-ton Davenport diesel no. 1231; NKP wooden boxcar no. 83047.

**Special Events:** Caboose rides, tours, and annual open house in August; write for details.

**Location/Directions:** From New Haven take Dawkins Rd. east to Ryan Rd., left to Edgerton Rd., turn right and site is 1.5 miles on the right.

**Site Address:** 15808 Edgerton Rd., New Haven, IN
**Mailing Address:** PO Box 11017, Fort Wayne, IN 46855
**Telephone:** (219) 493-0765
**E-mail:** info@765.org
**Internet:** www.765.org

**Indiana, French Lick**

**FRENCH LICK, WEST BADEN & SOUTHERN RAILWAY**
*Train ride*
*Standard gauge*

ALAN BARNETT

**Description:** A round trip between the resort town of French Lick and Cuzco, site of Patoka Lake. The train traverses wooded Indiana limestone country and passes through one of the state's longest railroad tunnels.

**Schedule:** April through October: weekends and May 29 and September 4: 10 a.m., 1 and 4 p.m. November: 1 p.m. June through October: Tuesdays, 1 p.m.

**Admission/Fare:** Please call for information.

**Locomotives/Rolling Stock:** 1947 General Electric 80-ton diesel no. 3; 1947 Alco RS-1 no. 4; open-window Rock Island coaches.

**Special Events:** Wild West holdups are scheduled for many holiday weekends. Call or write for dates and times.

**Nearby Attractions/Accommodations:** French Lick Springs Resort.

**Location/Directions:** Trains depart the old Monon Passenger Depot on Highway 56 in French Lick.

**Site Address:** 1 Monon St., French Lick, IN
**Mailing Address:** 1 Monon St., French Lick, IN 47432
**Telephone:** (812) 936-2405 and (800) 74-TRAIN
**Fax:** (812) 936-2904

129

**HESSTON STEAM MUSEUM**
*Train ride, museum*
*Various gauges*

RON STAHOUIAK

**Description:** Train rides from full scale to amusement-park size to hobby scale. Each railroad has 2 to 2.5 miles of mainline trackage, all live-steam operation. Operational steam sawmill, steam light plant, more.

**Schedule:** Memorial Day weekend through Labor Day: Saturdays and Sundays. September through October: Sundays. Noon to 5 p.m.

**Admission/Fare:** Free admission except Labor Day weekend. Train rides, adults, $3; children, $2.

**Locomotives/Rolling Stock:** Darjeeling & Himalayan built by Atlas Works; New Mexico Lumber Shay built by Lima Locomotive; Orenstein and Koppel no. 080, German-built in 1938; Koblen Danake Werke no. 040, built in Czechoslovakia 1939; Porter Mogul no. 17 built in 1923.

**Special Events:** Whistle-Stop Days, Memorial Day weekend; Whistle Fest, July 4; Annual Steam Show, Labor Day weekend.

**Nearby Attractions/Accommodations:** Lighthouse Mall, Dunes National Lakeshore, Washington Park Beach/Zoo, Blue Chip Casino, charter boat fishing, Door Prairie Auto Museum, motels.

**Location/Directions:** South of Indiana-Michigan state line. Four miles east of State Road 39 north of LaPorte or south of New Buffalo to 1000 North, turn east, traveling for about 3 miles.

*Coupon available, see coupon section.

**Site Address:** LaPorte County Rd. 1000 North, Hesston, IN
**Mailing Address:** 2946 Mt. Clair Way, Michigan City, IN 46360
**Telephone:** (219) 872-5055
**Fax:** (219) 874-8239
**Internet:** www.hesston.org

# CARTHAGE, KNIGHTSTOWN & SHIRLEY RAILROAD
*Train ride*
*Standard gauge*

**Description:** A 10-mile, one-hour round trip from Knightstown to Carthage, Indiana.

**Schedule:** May through October: weekends, 11 a.m., 1 and 3 p.m. Fridays, 11 a.m.

**Admission/Fare:** Adults, $7; children 3-11, $5; under age 3 ride free. Group rates available.

**Locomotives/Rolling Stock:** No. 215 44-ton GE, miscellaneous coaches and cabooses.

**Location/Directions:** Thirty miles east of Indianapolis on U.S. 40; three miles out of I-70 on State Route 109.

**Site Address:** 112 W. Carey St., Knightstown, IN
**Mailing Address:** 112 W. Carey St., Knightstown, IN 46148
**Telephone:** (765) 345-5561 or 800-345-2704 (Indiana only)

131

# LINDEN RAILROAD MUSEUM
*Museum*

**Description:** Operated by the Linden-Madison Township Historical Society, this museum is housed in the former Linden depot built by the Chicago, Indianapolis & Louisville Railway and the Toledo, St. Louis & Western Railroad in 1908. Restored to its 1950s appearance, the depot houses a collection of railroadiana from the Nickel Plate and Monon railroads. An HO model railroad club operates a 1950s depiction of Linden in the Monon baggage room. Both O and N gauge layouts are featured in the NKP baggage room.

**Schedule:** May through September: Friday through Sunday, 1 to 5 p.m. Group tours by appointment.

**Admission/Fare:** Adults, $2; teens 13-17, $1; children 6-12, $.50; under age 6 are free.

**Locomotives/Rolling Stock:** Former Nickel Plate caboose no. 497; Fairmont A-3 motor car; Monon boxcar no. 1620; Monon caboose no. 283.

**Nearby Attractions/Accommodations:** Old jail museum, Crawfordsville, Indiana.

**Location/Directions:** South of Lafayette on U.S. 231 and 7.9 miles north of the Crawfordsville exit off I-74. The depot museum is across from Jane Stoddard Park in Linden.

          M

**Site Address:** 520 N. Main St., Linden, IN
**Mailing Address:** PO Box 154, Linden, IN 47955
**Telephone:** (765) 339-7245 or (800) 866-3973
**E-mail:** weaver@tctc.com
**Internet:** http://www.tctc.com/~weaver/depot.htm

# JEFFERSON COUNTY HISTORICAL SOCIETY RAILROAD MUSEUM
*Museum*

© Jefferson County Historical Society 1992

Madison Railroad Station
Built 1895

**Description:** Restored 1895 Pennsylvania Railroad station known for its 2½-story octagon waiting room topped by stained glass windows. View other local railroad memorabilia, civil war and steam boat displays.

**Schedule:** May 1 through October 31: Mondays through Saturdays 10 a.m. to 4:30 p.m., Sundays 1 to 4 p.m. November through April, weekdays only.

**Admission/Fare:** $3; youth 16 and under are free.

**Locomotives/Rolling Stock:** 1920 L&N caboose.

**Special Events:** Madison in Bloom, last weekend in April and first weekend in May.

**Nearby Attractions/Accommodations:** Clifty Falls State Park, Lanier Mansion, antique shops, wineries, bed and breakfast, Ohio River.

**Location/Directions:** Highways 56 and 421, located in downtown historic Madison.

        M

**Site Address:** 615 W. First St., Madison, IN
**Mailing Address:** 615 W. First St., Madison, IN 47250
**Telephone:** (812) 265-2335
**Fax:** (812) 273-5023
**E-mail:** jchs@seidata.com
**Internet:** www.seidata.com/~jchs

# HOOSIER VALLEY RAILROAD MUSEUM, INC.
*Train ride, museum*
*Standard gauge*

M.W. KNEBEL

**Description:** Established in North Judson since 1988, the organization has been in the process of building the physical plant for a working railroad museum. The collection today consists of 30 pieces of railroad rolling stock. This includes the former 2-8-4 Chesapeake & Ohio steam locomotive no. 2789, which is under roof. We offer short caboose rides May through September. Wheelchair lift equipped.

**Schedule:** Year round: Saturdays, 8 a.m. to 5 p.m.

**Admission/Fare:** No admission fee.

**Locomotives/Rolling Stock:** C&O 1947 Alco K-4 2-8-4 no. 2789; Erie 1947 Alco S-1 switcher no. 310; EL caboose no. C345; 30 pieces rolling stock.

**Nearby Attractions/Accommodations:** Tippecanoe River State Park, Bass Lake State Beach, Kersting's Cycle Center & Museum, Oak View Motel.

**Location/Directions:** Seventy miles southeast of downtown Chicago, Indiana 10 and 39.

       TRAIN M

**Site Address:** 507 Mulberry St., North Judson, IN
**Mailing Address:** PO Box 75, North Judson, IN 46366
**Telephone:** (574) 223-3834 (treas.), (574) 946-6499 (sec.), 574) 896-3950 (museum)
**E-mail:** hvrm@yahoo.com
**Internet:** http://hvrm.railfan.net

# BOONE & SCENIC VALLEY RAILROAD
*Train ride, dinner train, museum, display*
*Standard gauge*

**Description:** Operating railroad museum. Also, dinner and dessert trains, museum and gift shop.

**Schedule:** Saturdays in May; Memorial Day through October, daily.

**Admission/Fare:** Regular trains: adults, $12, children 3-12, $5. Dinner trains, $50, dessert train, $25.

**Special Events:** Pufferbilly Days, second weekend in September; Civil War re-enactment, end of July.

**Nearby Attractions/Accommodations:** Birthplace of Mamie Doud Eisenhower, Country Relics Village.

**Location/Directions:** Forty-five miles northwest of Des Moines on Hwy. 30.

          arm TRAIN

**Site Address:** 225 Tenth St., Boone, IA
**Mailing Address:** PO Box 603, Boone, IA 50036
**Telephone:** (800) 626-0319
**Fax:** (515) 432-4253
**E-mail:** b&svrr@tdsi.net
**Internet:** www.scenic-valleyrr.com

**Description:** Trainland U.S.A. is an operating toy train museum featuring Lionel trans and accessories. This exhibit represents three eras of time: frontier, steam, and diesel.

**Schedule:** Memorial Day weekend through Labor Day, 10 a.m. to 6 p.m.

**Nearby Attractions/Accommodations:** International Wrestling Institute and Museum, Newton Jasper County Historical Museum, Newton, Living History farms, Des Moines.

**Location/Directions:** Exit 155 off I-80, 2½ miles north on Hwy. 117.

*Coupon available, see coupon section.

**Site Address:** 3135 Hwy. 117 N., Colfax, IA
**Mailing Address:** 3135 Hwy. 117 N., Colfax, IA 50054-7534
**Telephone:** (515) 674-3813
**Fax:** (515) 674-3813
**E-mail:** trainsjudy@aol.com

**RAILSWEST RAILROAD MUSEUM**
*Museum, display, layout*

ROBERT HASTINGS

**Description:** The RailsWest Railroad Museum and HO model railroad are housed in an 1899 former Rock Island depot. The museum contains displays of historic photos, dining car memorabilia, uniforms, and many other interesting items used during the steam era. The 22 x 33-foot model railroad depicts scenery of the Council Bluffs/Omaha area, featuring train lines that served the heartland: Union Pacific; Chicago & Northwestern; Wabash; Chicago Great Western; Wabash, Rock Island; Milwaukee Road; Chicago, Burlington & Quincy.

**Schedule:** May: weekends, 1 to 5 p.m. Memorial Day through Labor Day: Tuesdays through Saturdays, 10 a.m. to 4 p.m. and Sundays, 1 to 5 p.m. December: weekends, 1 to 5 p.m. Closed major holidays.

**Locomotives/Rolling Stock:** UP steam locomotive no. 814; CB&Q steam engine no. 915; CB&Q waycar no. 13855; CB&Q Omaha club car; Budd RPO former UP no. 5908; 1967 Rock Island caboose 17130; UP boxcar no. 462536.

**Special Events:** Depot Days, last weekend in September. Christmas at the Depot, weekends in December

**Location/Directions:** I-80 exit 3, travel north one mile or I-29 exit Lake Manawa.

*Coupon available, see coupon section.

**Site Address:** 1512 S. Main St., Council Bluffs, IA
**Mailing Address:** PO Box 2, Council Bluffs, IA 51502
**Telephone:** (712) 323-5182

# FORT MADISON, FARMINGTON & WESTERN RAILROAD

*Train ride, museum*
*Standard gauge*

**Description:** An authentic re-creation of a pre-World War II branchline terminus. A country village, roundhouse with displays, an extensive collection of hand and motor cars, and the yard are on display. A wye is demonstrated and there are many restored pieces of rolling stock. The ride is two miles through woods, up grade, and over a trestle.

**Schedule:** Please call for recorded event schedule.

**Admission/Fare:** Adults, $5; students, $4; under age 5 are free. Price includes admission and ride.

**Locomotives/Rolling Stock:** Plymouth 35-ton; 8-ton Vulcan no. 1; 1913 Baldwin no. 4; Edwards Doodlebug no. 507; 30-ton steam crane no. 3; more.

**Special Events:** Railroad Days, September. Santa Train, December. Please call for dates.

**Nearby Attractions/Accommodations:** Old Fort Madison, Midwest Old Threshers Heritage Museums.

**Location/Directions:** Off Highway 2 between Fort Madison and Donnellson in southeast Iowa.

**Radio frequency:** 464.9750

**Site Address:** 2208 220th St., Donnellson, IA
**Mailing Address:** 2208 220th St., Donnellson, IA 52625
**Telephone:** (319) 837-6689
**Fax:** (319) 837-6080
**E-mail:** dminer@minermfgco.com
**Internet:** www.minermfgco.com/Minerville/Railroad.htm

# KEOKUK SCENIC RAILWAY
*Train ride, museum*
*Standard gauge*

**Description:** A 2-hour trip to Elvaston, Illinois; a 3-hour trip to McCall, Illinois; and a 4-hour charter only trip to Burnside, Illinois. All trips depart from and return to Keokuk Union Station and travel over the Mississippi River bridge into Illinois. Each train has a special theme.

**Schedule:** Theme trains run throughout the year and require reservations. Call for scheduling information or visit our website.

**Admission/Fare:** Adults, $15; children 4-15, $8; 3 and under, free on parent's lap. First-class accomodations aboard "Chief Keokuck" Lounge-Observation Car, $10 extra per person. Special rates for charter trains.

**Locomotives/Rolling Stock:** Two Vintage Alco RS-3 locomotives; lounge-observation car "Chief Keokuck"; vintage chair cars.

**Special Events:** Eagle Days Train, January 19-20. Easter Bunny Train, April 13. Civil War re-enactment, April 28. Classic Cars/Train, May 25. Father and Son train ride, June 15. Liberty specials, July 4. Navoo Grape Festival, September 2. Ghost Train, October 26. Santa Claus specials, December 7.

**Nearby Attractions/Accommodations:** George M. Verity Riverboat Museum, Mississippi River Observation Decks, Lock & Dam no. 19 Hydro-electric Plant, National Cemetary, antiques, historic homes, more.

**Location/Directions:** Located in the historic Union Depot at Keokuk's riverfront.

**Radio Frequency:** 160.395

**Site Address:** 200 S. Water St., Keokuk, IA
**Mailing Address:** 1318 South Johanson Rd., Peoria, IL 61607
**Telephone:** (309) 697-1400
**Fax:** (309) 697-5387
**E-mail:** tickets@keokuktrainride.com
**Internet:** www.keokuktrainride.com

# ABILENE & SMOKY VALLEY RAILROAD
*Train ride*
*Standard gauge*

**Description:** A 1½-hour, 10-mile round trip through the Smoky Hill River Valley from historic Abilene to Enterprise, Kansas. The track crosses the Smoky Hill River on a high steel span bridge.

**Schedule:** Memorial Day through Labor Day: Tuesdays through Sundays. May, September through October: weekends. Dinner train specials. Call or write for more information.

**Admission/Fare:** Adults, $8.50; children 3-11, $5.50. Dinner train prices vary. All prices subject to change without notice.

**Locomotives/Rolling Stock:** 1945 Alco S1; 1945 GE 44-ton; 1945 Whitcomb 45-ton side-rod; more.

**Special Events:** Abilene–Chisholm Trail Day, Saturday of first full weekend in October. Easter Bunny Train. Santa Claus Train. Call or write for details.

**Nearby Attractions/Accommodations:** Eisenhower Center, Dickinson County Heritage Center, C.W. Parker Carousel, Greyhound Hall of Fame, Great Plains Theater Festival, Abilene Community Theater.

**Location/Directions:** I-70 exit 275, south 2 miles on K-15 (Buckeye St.). Park in lot west of Eisenhower Center (shared lot with Greyhound Hall of Fame).

**Site Address:** 417 S. Buckeye, Abilene, KS
**Mailing Address:** PO Box 744, Abilene, KS 67410
**Telephone:** (785) 263-1077, (888) 426-6687 and (888) 426-6689 (reservations)
**Fax:** (785) 263-1066
**Internet:** www.asvrr.org

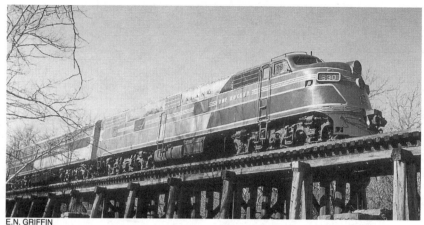
E.N. GRIFFIN

**Description:** This line was constructed in 1867 as the Leavenworth, Lawrence & Galveston, the first railroad south of the Kansas River. The Midland Railway is a volunteer-operated intrastate common-carrier passenger railroad. Trains operate to the former town site of Norwood for an 11-mile round trip through scenic eastern Kansas farmland and woods.

**Schedule:** Departure times: Memorial Day weekend through October: weekends, 11:30 a.m., 1:30 and 3:30 p.m. and Thursdays, 10:30 a.m..

**Fare/Admission:** Adults, $8; children ages 4-12, $4; under age 4 ride free. All-day fare (all ages), $15. Discounts for groups of 25 or more.

**Locomotive/Rolling Stock:** No. 524, 1946 EMD NW2, former Chicago, Burlington & Quincy; no. 142 RS-3M, former Missouri-Kansas-Texas; no. 652 E8, former CRI&P; 8255 RS-3, former NYC-630 and CR&IP E6 no. 630.

**Special Events:** Maple Leaf Festival, third weekend in October; Halloween Trains, last weekend in October. Railfans Weekend, date to be announced (call for information).

**Location/Directions:** About 30 miles southwest of Kansas City on U.S. 56 at the 1906 former AT&SF depot, seven blocks west of downtown.

**Radio Frequency:** 161.055

**Site Address:** 1515 High St., Baldwin City, Kansas
**Mailing Address:** PO Box 412, Baldwin City, KS 66006
**Telephone:** (785) 594-6982 and (800) 651-0388
**Fax:** (816) 873-3387
**Internet:** www.midland-ry.org

**ELLIS RAILROAD MUSEUM**
*Museum, display, layout*
*24" gauge*

**Schedule:** Daily.

**Admission/Fare:** Museum: $2; children 1-12, $1. Train ride: $2; children 1-12, $1.

**Nearby Attractions/Accommodations:** Campgrounds.

**Location/Directions:** Exit off I-70 at Ellis, south 8 blocks.

**Site Address:** 911 S. Washington, Ellis, KS
**Mailing Address:** Box 84, Plainville, KS 67663
**Telephone:** (785) 726-4493

# GREAT PLAINS TRANSPORTATION MUSEUM, INC.
*Museum*
*Standard*

J. HARVEY KOEHN

**Description:** Museum with outdoor displays of locomotives, cabooses, and cars; indoor displays of artifacts and memorabilia.

Schedule: Year round, Saturdays, 9 a.m. to 4 p.m., April through October, Sundays, 1 to 4 p.m.

**Admission/Fare:** Adults, $3.50; children 3-12, $2.50.

**Locomotives/Rolling Stock:** ATSF 4-8-4 no. 3768; ATSF SDFP45 no. 93; BN NW2 no. 421; Whitcomb GM-2; Plymouth industrial locomotive; Frisco caboose 876; Central Kansas Railway caboose 1959; CB&Q caboose 13519; ATSF coach, baggage caboose 2312; MoPac caboose 13495; UP caboose no. 24538; ATSF baggage car 190006.

**Nearby Attractions/Accommodations:** In the heart of historic Old Town.

**Location/Directions:** Across from Wichita Union Station.

*Coupon available, see coupon section.

**Site Address:** 700 E. Douglas Ave., Wichita, KS
**Mailing Address:** 700 E. Douglas Ave., Wichita, KS 67202
**Telephone:** (316) 263-0944

# MY OLD KENTUCKY DINNER TRAIN
*Dinner train*

**Description:** Thirty-five-mile round trip through the Kentucky countryside. Fine dining and whisper-perfect service aboard vintage 1940s dinner train.

**Schedule:** Year-round operation. Lunch on Saturdays, 12 noon; dinner, Tuesday through Saturday, 5 p.m. Schedule subject to change.

**Admission/Fare:** Lunch, $42.95 plus tax, per person; dinner, $59.95 plus tax, per person.

**Locomotives/Rolling Stock:** Two FP7A units nos. 1940 and 1941; Budd diner 1940 era, nos. 011 (formerly Eisenhower family car), 007, 777 and 021.

**Special Events:** Bourbon Festival, September. Murder Mysteries, fall and spring.

**Nearby Attractions/Accommodations:** Bardstown is a major historical site with many attractions; most major chain hotels; home to "My Old Kentucky Home."

**Location/Directions:** Forty-five minutes south of Louisville, Kentucky, on Highway 31E.

**Site Address:** 602 N. Third St., Bardstown, KY
**Mailing Address:** PO Box 279, Bardstown, KY 40004
**Telephone:** (502) 348-7300
**Fax:** (502) 348-7780
**E-mail:** info@rjcorman.com
**Internet:** www.kydinnertrain.com

# HARDIN SOUTHERN RAILROAD
*Train ride, display*
*Standard gauge*

**Description:** This line is a working common-carrier railroad offering seasonal Nostalgia Train passenger service for a two-hour, 18-mile journey to the past. Built in 1890, the railroad was once a portion of the Nashville, Chattanooga & St. Louis Railway's Paducah main line through the Jackson Purchase in western Kentucky. The railroad is a designated Kentucky State Landmark. Today's trip features the rural farms and lush forests of the Clarks River Valley.

**Schedule:** May 25 through October 31: weekends, mid-day and late afternoon.

**Admission/Fare:** Adults, $10.25; children 3-12, $6.50. Tour, group, and charter rates available.

**Locomotives/Rolling Stock:** No. 863, 1940 Electro-Motive Corporation SW1, former Milwaukee Road; no. 4 Baldwin 1914 2-6-2 steam locomotive; air-conditioned coaches.

**Special Events:** Easter, Mother's Day, Halloween, Christmas.

**Nearby Attractions/Accommodations:** Land Between the Lakes National Recreation Area. Hardin's Railroad Restaurant.

**Location/Directions:** In western Kentucky, southeast of Paducah via I-24 and State Route 641; 6 miles from the Tennessee Valley Authority's Land Between the Lakes National Recreation Area. Hardin is located at junction of Routes 641/80. Depot is on Route 80 in the center of town.

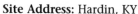

**Site Address:** Hardin, KY
**Mailing Address:** PO Box 20, Hardin, KY 42048
**Telephone:** (270) 437-4555
**Fax:** (270) 753-7006
**E-mail:** office@hsrr.com
**Internet:** www.hsrr.com

# KENTUCKY RAILWAY MUSEUM
*Train ride, dinner train, museum, display, layout*
Standard gauge

ELMER KAPPELL

**Description:** Twenty-two-mile round trip through Rolling Fork River valley.

**Schedule:** March through May, weekends; June through September, Tuesday through Sunday; October through December, weekends. Call for trip times.

**Admission/Fare:** Adults and teens, $12.50; children 3-12, $8; under 3, free; cab rides, $25. Steam weekends, adults and teens, $15; children 3-12, $8; under 3, free; cab rides, $35.

**Locomotives/Rolling Stock:** L&N 4-6-2 no. 152; Monon BL-2 no. 32; SF CF-7 no. 2546; USA F-M H-12-44 no. 1846; L&N 2554; L&N 2572; SAL 821; MKT 884; TC 8038 (diner); other locomotives and rolling stock on display.

**Nearby Attractions/Accommodations:** My Old Kentucky Home State Park, Historic Bardstown, Mammoth Cave National Park, Lincoln birthplace (national historic site), Lincoln boyhood home, Maker's Mark Distillery (national landmark), Bernheim Forest.

**Location/Directions:** Three-and-one-half miles east of I-65 at exit 105 (Boston exit); 12 miles south of Bluegrass Parkway at exit 21 (New Haven exit).

*Coupon available, see coupon section.

Radio Frequency: 160.545

**Site Address:** 136 S. Main St., New Haven, KY
**Mailing Address:** PO Box 240, New Haven, KY 40051
**Telephone:** (502) 549-5470 and (800) 272-0152
**Fax:** (502) 549-5472
**E-mail:** kyrail@bardstown.com
**Internet:** www.kyrail.org

# KENTUCKY CENTRAL RAILWAY
*Museum*
*Standard gauge*

RUTH ANN COMBS

**Description:** Excursions pending reinstatement.

**Schedule:** By appointment.

**Admission/Fare:** Free.

**Locomotives/Rolling Stock:** 1925 Baldwin 2-6-2, former Reader no. 11; no. 9, VO, 1000 Baldwin diesel, former LaSalle & Bureau County Railroad; three coaches, former Erie Lackawanna; KCR no. 1, former Southern Railway concession/observation car; bay-window caboose no. X225, former Southern Railway; caboose no. 904055, former Baltimore & Ohio.

**Location/Directions:** U.S. 460 E (North Middletown Rd.).

     TRAIN

**Site Address:** U.S. 460 East, Paris, KY
**Mailing Address:** 1749 Bahama Rd., Lexington, KY 40509
**Telephone:** (859) 293-0807

**BIG SOUTH FORK SCENIC RAILWAY**
*Train ride*
*Standard gauge*

**Description:** Three- and four-hour trips into the remote beautiful Big South Fork National Park. Each trip includes stopovers at restored Blue Heron and Barthell Mining Camps. Included in the ticket price is admission to the McCreary County Museum.

**Schedule:** May 1 through September 30: Wednesday through Saturday, 10 a.m.; Wednesday through Sunday and Memorial Day and Labor Day, 11 a.m.; weekends, 2:30 p.m. October 1 through October 31: Tuesday through Saturday, 10 a.m.; Tuesday through Sunday, 11 a.m.; weekends, 2:30 p.m.

**Admission/Fare:** Adults, $15; seniors, $14; children, $7.50. Group rates available.

**Locomotives/Rolling Stock:** Nos. 102 and 105, 1942 Alcos; open cars; caboose.

**Special Events:** Haunted Halloween Train, last three Fridays in October. Cumberland Heritage Day, middle of October (call).

**Nearby Attractions/Accommodations:** Cumberland Falls State Park, Big South Fork National River and Recreation Area.

**Location/Directions:** Kentucky 92, one mile west of U.S. 27 on State Route 92 and 33 miles south of Somerset, Kentucky.

**Site Address:** 21 Henderson St., Stearns, KY
**Mailing Address:** Box 368, Stearns, KY 42647
**Telephone:** (800) GO-ALONG
**Fax:** (606) 376-5332
**Internet:** www.bsfsry.com

**BLUEGRASS RAILROAD MUSEUM**
*Train ride*
*Standard gauge*

**Description:** The Bluegrass Railroad Museum offers a 1½-hour, 11½-mile round trip train ride through horse, cattle, and tobacco farms, over an ex-Southern Railway branch line that was built by the Louisville Southern Railroad in 1889. (For the year 2002, the train will not run to the Kentucky River, but will stop ½ mile short of the river. We will be replacing the trestle at milepost 3.7. We plan to return to the Kentucky River in 2003.)

**Schedule:** May 27, 2002, to October 28, 2002, open weekends only. Saturdays, 1:30 and 3:30 p.m.; Sundays, 1:30 p.m.

**Admission/Fare:** Adults, $8; seniors, $7; children under 12, $6. Special events: Adults, $10; seniors, $9; children, $8.

**Locomotives/Rolling Stock:** Alco MRS1s nos. 2043 and 2086; Fairbanks Morse H12-44 1849, former U.S Army; L&N caboose no. 1086; Southern caboose X741.

**Special Events:** Book Bandits Robbery, June 1, 2; Wild West Train Robbery, June 22, 23; Civil War Train Robbery, August 7, 8; Clown Daze, October 5, 6; Halloween, October 18, 19, 25, 26; Santa Train, December 7, 8, 14, 15. (Special events have special hours; please call for information.)

**Location/Directions:** Woodford County Park off U.S. 62 (Tyrone Pike).

Radio frequency: 160.275, 161.160, 160.500, 161.190

**Site Address:** Versailles, Kentucky
**Mailing Address:** PO Box 27, Versailles, KY 40383-0027
**Telephone:** (859) 873-2476 or (800) 755-2476
**Internet:** www.bgrm.org

# DEQUINCY RAILROAD MUSEUM
*Museum*

**Description:** Nestled among tall pines at the beginning of Louisiana's foothills in north Calcasieu County, the city of DeQuincy was at the intersection of two major railroads in 1895. Its turn-of-the-century beginnings have been preserved, including two major historical landmarks–the All Saints Episcopal Church and the Kansas City Southern Railroad Depot. Both structures are on the National Register of Historic Places, and the depot now houses the railroad museum. There are a vintage caboose, a passenger coach, and a host of railroad artifacts.

**Schedule:** Mondays through Fridays, 9 a.m. to 4 p.m. and weekends, 12:00 to 4 p.m.

**Admission/Fare:** Free, donations appreciated.

**Locomotives/Rolling Stock:** No. 124 0-6-0 steam engine, built 1913 by America Locomotive Co.; Pullman railcar no. 4472, 85 feet in length; MP caboose no. 13487, built 1929.

**Special Events:** Louisiana Railroad Days Festival, second weekend in April.

**Nearby Attractions/Accommodations:** Gambling boats in Lake Charles, Acadian Trails.

**Location/Directions:** On Highway 12.

         Lake Charles, LA

**Site Address:** 400 Lake Charles Ave., DeQuincy, LA
**Mailing Address:** PO Box 997, DeQuincy, LA 70633
**Telephone:** (337) 786-2823 and (337) 786-7113

# Louisiana, Long Leaf

SOUTHERN FOREST
HERITAGE MUSEUM
*Train ride, museum*
*Standard gauge*

HENRY TAVES

**Description:** Guided tours of a historic sawmill complex. The commissary offers exhibits and a gift shop. The motor car ride is ⁹⁄₁₀ mile.

**Schedule:** Year round, 9 a.m. to 5 p.m., except Thanksgiving and Christmas.

**Admission/Fare:** Admission is charged.

**Locomotives/Rolling Stock:** 4-6-0 Red River & Gulf no. 106; 2-6-0 Meridian Lumber co. no. 202; 4-6-0 Crowell Long Leaf Lumber Co. no. 400

**Nearby Attractions/Accommodations:** Alexander State Forest (camping), 11 miles; restaurants, 3 miles.

**Location/Directions:** From I-49 take exit 66 and travel west on State Route 112 to Forest Hill; follow signs 3.3 miles south on State Route 497. The site is halfway between Forest Hill and Glenmora on State Route 497.

*Coupon available, see coupon section.

          M

**Site Address:** 77 Long Leaf Rd., Long Leaf, LA
**Mailing Address:** PO Box 101, Long Leaf, LA 71448-0101
**Telephone:** (318) 748-8404
**Fax:** (318) 748-8404

151

**Maine, Alna**
**(Sheepscot Station)**

## WISCASSET, WATERVILLE & FARMINGTON RAILWAY MUSEUM
*Train ride, museum, display*
*24" gauge*

JOHN MCNAMARA

**Description:** Ride on 1-mile mainline track on original roadbed in coach or caboose behind 12-ton diesel or steam locomotive.

**Schedule:** Memorial Day through Columbus Day: weekends, 10 a.m. to 5 p.m. Columbus Day through Christmas: Saturdays 9 a.m. to 5 p.m. Year round, workdays, Saturday 7 a.m. to sundown. Steam, May 4 and 5, June 15 and 16, August 10 and 11. Others to be scheduled.

**Admission/Fare:** Train ride–adults, $4; children, $2. Diesel–adults, $3; children, $1.50. Museum–free.

**Locomotives/Rolling Stock:** WW&F no. 9 Portland Co. Forney 044; WW&F no. 10 Vulcan Forney 044; W&Q no. 3 coach Jackson & Sharp; W&Q boxcar Portland Co.; WW&F flatcar no. 118 Portland Co., WW&F caboose 320 museum-built.

**Special Events:** Annual meeting, May 4; annual picnic, August 10 and 11.

**Nearby Attractions/Accommodations:** Alna Center School (one-room schoolhouse), Alna Meeting House (1789), Head Tide Church.

**Location/Directions:** Four and a half miles north of Wiscasset on Route 218, left on Cross Rd.

**Site Address:** 97 Cross Rd., Alna, ME
**Mailing Address:** PO Box 242, Alna, ME 04535-0242
**Telephone:** (207) 882-4193
**E-mail:** webmaster@wwwfry.org
**Internet:** www.wwfry.org

152

# COLE LAND TRANSPORTATION MUSEUM
*Museum*
*Standard gauge*

**Description:** Two hundred Maine antique land transportation vehicles, as well as 2,000 photographs of life in early Maine communities, enlarged, displayed, and captioned. Home of the Maine State World War II veterans memorial.

**Schedule:** May 1 through November 11: daily, 9 a.m. to 5 p.m.

**Admission/Fare:** Adults, $5; seniors, $3; under 19, free.

**Location/Directions:** From I-95, take exit 45B. Turn left at the traffic light and follow the signs.

**Site Address:** 405 Perry Rd., Bangor, ME
**Mailing Address:** 405 Perry Rd., Bangor, ME 04401
**Telephone:** (207) 990-3600
**Fax:** (207) 990-2653
**E-mail:** mail@colemuseum.com
**Internet:** www.colemuseum.org

## BIDDEFORD STATION GREAT NORTHERN NARROW GAUGE RAILROAD

*Train ride, dining car, museum, display*
*Standard and 24" gauge*

R. DAY

**Description:** Narrow gauge train ride of 1 kilometer, Great Northern Railway Museum, dining car operation. We also have a gift shop, antiques, and crafts.

**Schedule:** May to December: Saturdays and Sundays, 11 a.m. to 4 p.m. Daily, 11 a.m. to 4 p.m. by chance.

**Admission/Fare:** Train ride–adults, $3; seniors and children under 12, $2.

**Locomotives/Rolling Stock:** Plymouth narrow gauge diesel no. 690; GN narrow gauge diesel no. 12; GN Shay no. 1; GN caboose X256; GN ranch car no. 1244; narrow gauge Fairmont cars and trailers; standard gauge Fairmont cars and trailers.

**Nearby Attractions/Accommodations:** Greater Portland area, Funtown USA, Old Orchard Beach Amusements, summer theaters, Seashore Trolley Museum, Maine coastal attractions, hotels.

**Location/Directions:** Maine Turnpike, exit Biddeford to U.S. Route 1, turn south (right) ¾ mile to Biddeford Station, which is on the left. A Shay locomotive is parked at the entrance.

            M

**Site Address:** Route 1, south at Biddeford city line, Biddeford, ME
**Mailing Address:** PO Box 661, Biddeford, ME 04005-0661
**Telephone:** (207) 282-9255
**Fax:** (207) 967-5880

**BOOTHBAY RAILWAY VILLAGE**
*Train ride, museum, display*
*24" gauge*

**Description:** Ride a coal-fired, narrow gauge train through woods and a covered bridge, around a re-created historic village. View an exceptional display of antique autos and restored railroad buildings and other historic structures

**Schedule:** Memorial Day through Columbus Day, 9:30 a.m. to 5 p.m. Call to confirm.

**Admission/Fare:** Adults, $7; children (3-12), $3. Memberships available.

**Locomotives/Rolling Stock:** Three Henschel coal-fired locomotives, 1913, 1936, 1938; two Baldwin saddle tank locomotives 1882; Plymouth Gas locomotive; Model T Ford Inspection 1923; closed coach; open coach; caboose; three boxcars ca. 1910; combine Laconia 1884; and handcar.

**Special Events:** Father's Day, June 16; Antique Engine Meet, July 5 and 6; Antique Auto Days, July 20 and 21; Children's Day, August 18; Maine Narrow Gauge Railroad Day, September 15; Fall Foliage Craft Fair, October 12 and 13.

**Nearby Attractions/Accommodations:** The Boothbay Region is a vital tourist area in midcoast Maine, with a variety of shops, restaurants and accommodations.

**Location/Directions:** Take Coastal Route 1 to the midcoast region, then take Route 27 south for 8 miles to the museum.

         M arm TRA͡IN

**Site Address:** Route 27, Boothbay, ME
**Mailing Address:** PO Box 123, Boothbay, ME 04537
**Telephone:** (207) 633-4727
**Fax:** (207) 633-4733
**E-mail:** staff@railwayvillage.org
**Internet:** www.railwayvillage.org

155

**SEASHORE TROLLEY MUSEUM**
*Train ride*
*Standard gauge*

**Description:** A 25-minute, 3.5-mile trolley ride. Fifty-four streetcars on display in three car barns and Restoration Shop.

**,Schedule:** Daily, June 17 through October 8, 10 a.m. to 5 p.m. Weekends, May 5 through June 17 and October 8 through October 28.

**Admission/Fare:** Adults, $7.50; seniors, $5.50; children (6-16), $5.00; 5 and under, free.

**Locomotives/Rolling Stock:** Restored streetcars, interurbans, subways, buses, PCC cars.

**Special Events:** Mother's Day, May 12. Father's Day, June 16. Trolley Parade, July 4. Trolley Birthday Celebration, August 10 and 11. Pumpkin Patch weekend, September 28 and 29.

**Nearby Attractions/Accommodations:** Downtown Kennebunkport and several beautiful beaches.

**Location/Directions:** Maine Turnpike, Kennebunkport exit. Left onto Route 35 to downtown Kennebunkport. Left on Route 1, north for 2.8 miles. Right at traffic light onto Log Cabin Rd. Museum is 1.7 miles on left.

Radio frequency: 160.470

**Site Address:** 195 Log Cabin Rd., Kennebunkport, ME
**Mailing Address:** PO Box A, Kennebunkport, ME 04046
**Telephone:** (207) 967-2800
**Fax:** (207) 967-0867
**E-mail:** carshop@gwi.net
**Internet:** www.trolleymuseum.org

**Description:** Oakfield Station has been restored to its original condition. Exhibits included hundreds of photographs dating back to the beginning of the Bangor & Aroostook Railroad in 1891. You'll see the building of this epic rail line through some of the most rugged terrain in the East. Other memorabilia include vintage signs and advertising pieces, signal lanterns, original railroad maps, telegraph equipment, newspapers chronicling the area's history, restored mail cars, and a rejuvenated C-66 caboose. Railroad history lives at Oakfield Station.

**Schedule:** Memorial Day weekend through Labor Day: Saturdays 12 to 4 p.m. and Sundays 1 to 4 p.m.

**Admission/Fare:** Donations appreciated.

**Locomotives/Rolling Stock:** BAR C-66 caboose.

**Nearby Attractions/Accommodations:** Restaurants and lodging.

**Location/Directions:** I-95 exit 60, turn right for 1 mile, turn left at hardware store, cross bridge, turn right to end of street.

**Site Address:** Station St., Oakfield, ME
**Mailing Address:** PO Box 62, Oakfield, ME 04763
**Telephone:** (207) 757-8575
**E-mail:** oakfield.rr.museum@ainop.com
**Internet:** www.ainop.com/users/oakfield.rr/

**SANDY RIVER & RANGELEY LAKES RAILROAD DIVISION OF PHILLIPS HISTORICAL SOCIETY**

*Train ride, museum, display*
*24" gauge*

KEN TEELE

**Description:** Ride on the original roadbed of the SR&RL Railroad in 1884 Laconia Coach no. 18 powered by a replica of SR&RL no. 4. Take a trip back in time as you visit our roundhouse. See the ongoing restoration of SR&RL Coach no. 18, and view our roster.

**Schedule:** June 2 and 16; July 7, 20, and 21; August 4, 16, 17, 18, and 31; September 1, 2, 15, 28, and 29; October 5, 6, 12, and 13: hours are 11 a.m. to 3 p.m. Special 8:30 p.m. night trains on August 16 and 17.

**Admission/Fare:** Train–$3; children under age 13 are free.

**Locomotives/Rolling Stock:** SR&RL no. 4 replica; coaches nos. 17 and 18; cabooses nos. 556 and 559 (a replica of no. 556); flangers nos. 503 and 505; toolcar; flatcar; handcars; two Brookvilles; a Plymouth; MEC coach no. 170; Concord & Montreal coach no. 77.

**Special Events:** Phillips Old Home Days, August 16-18.

**Nearby Attractions/Accommodations:** Stanley Museum, Nordica Homestead, logging museum in Rangeley, Small Falls, Mt. Blue State Park, the Elcourt Bed and Breakfast, the Herbert Hotel. Several motels and restaurants in Farmington.

**Location/Directions:** Eighteen miles north of Farmington on State Route 4. Cross the bridge in downtown Phillips and up the hill ½ mile.

*Coupon available, see coupon section.

        M

**Site Address:** Bridge Hill Rd., Phillips, ME
**Mailing Address:** PO Box B, Phillips, ME 04966
**Telephone:** (207) 778-3621
**Fax:** (207) 779-1901
**E-mail:** awb@ime.net
**Internet:** www.srrl-rr.org

**MAINE NARROW GAUGE RAILROAD COMPANY AND MUSEUM**
*Train ride, museum, display*
*24" gauge*

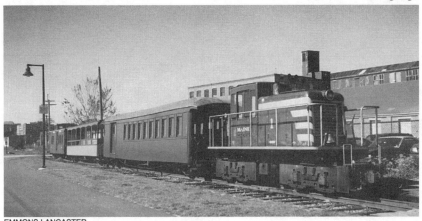

EMMONS LANCASTER

**Description:** A 3-mile round trip along the edge of Casco Bay.

**Schedule:** Museum, seven days a week. Closed Thanksgiving and Christmas.

**Admission/Fare:** Museum: free, donations accepted. Rides: adults, $5; children, $3.

**Locomotives/Rolling Stock:** No. 8 Bridgton steam locomotive; nos. 3 and 4 Monson steam locomotives; no. 1 Edaville diesel; coaches from Bridgton/Harrison; Sandy River Railroad; Edaville.

**Special Events:** Flower Show Steam Trains, March; Boat Show Steam Trains, March; Memorial Day weekend, July 4th, and Steamfest, September.

**Nearby Attractions/Accommodations:** Portland's "Old Port" shopping area, walking trail, children's museum, many restaurants.

**Location/Directions:** Old Portland Co. site Hwy. 295 to exit 7, Franklin St. Turn left on Fore St.

Radio frequency: 160.245

**Site Address:** 58 Fore St., Building 6, Portland, ME
**Mailing Address:** 58 Fore St., Building 6, Portland, ME 04101-4842
**Telephone:** (207) 828-0814
**Fax:** (207) 879-6132
**E-mail:** mngrr@clinic.net
**Internet:** www.mngrr.rails.net

**Description:** 1½-hour and 2-hour excursions aboard our historic 1913 Swedish steam locomotive and self-propelled Budd rail diesel car, along scenic countryside and coast. Please call for more information.

**Schedule:** Please call for information.

**Admission/Fare:** Please call for information.

**Special Events:** Mother's Day; Family Day; Father's Day; Independence Day; Family Day II; Common Ground Fair Shuttle from Belfast, Brooks, and Unity; Fall Foliage; Halloween Train; Thanksgiving Dinner Train; Santa Charity Express; Locomotion! Ultimate Rail Fantasy.

**Nearby Attractions/Accommodations:** Field of Dreams Recreational Park, Common Ground Fairgrounds, Copper Heron Bed and Breakfast, coastal picnic areas.

**Location/Directions:** Located in the heart of Unity, Maine, and the waterfront in Belfast, Maine.

**Site Address:** One Depot St., Unity, ME; and Front St., Belfast, ME
**Mailing Address:** PO Box 555, Unity, ME 04988
**Telephone:** (800) 392-5500
**Fax:** (207) 948-5903
**E-mail:** bmlrr@uninets.net
**Internet:** www.belfastrailroad.com

**Description:** The birthplace of American railroading, offering a nostalgic journey into America's railroading past.

**Schedule:** Daily, 10 a.m. to 5 p.m. Closed major holidays.

**Admission/Fare:** Adults, $8; seniors (60+), $7; children 2 through 12, $5.

**Locomotives/Rolling Stock:** 250 pieces of rolling stock.

**Special Events:** Call for dates and times.

**Nearby Attractions/Accommodations:** Camden Yards, PSI Net Stadium, Babe Ruth Museum, ten blocks from the Inner Harbor.

**Location/Directions:** 95 to 395 to Martin Luther King Blvd. Follow signs to museum.

*Coupon available, see coupon section. †See ad on page A-19.

       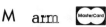   

**Site Address:** 901 W. Pratt St., Baltimore, MD
**Mailing Address:** 901 W. Pratt St., Baltimore, MD 21223
**Telephone:** (410) 752-2490
**Fax:** (410) 752-2499
**E-mail:** boinfo@mindspring.com
**Internet:** www.borail.org

# BALTIMORE STREETCAR MUSEUM
*Train ride*
*5'4½" gauge*

ANDREW S. BLUMBERG

**Description:** Relive rail transit in the city of Baltimore from 1859 to 1963 through a 15-car collection (13 electric, 2 horse-drawn). Cars operate over 1¼-mile round trip trackage. The Visitors' Center contains displays and the Trolley Theatre, a streetcar mockup and video presentation.

**Schedule:** June 1 through October 31: weekends. November 1 through May 31: Sundays. Hours are noon to 5 p.m.

**Admission/Fare:** Adults, $56; seniors and children 4-11, $3; family, $24.

**Locomotives/Rolling Stock:** No. 417, circa 1888 single-truck closed car; no. 554, 1896 single-truck summer car, no. 1050, 1898 single-truck closed car and no. 264, 1900 double-truck convertible car, all Brownell Car Co.; no. 1164, 1902 double-truck summer car, no. 3828, 1902 double-truck closed car; no. 4533, 1904 single-truck closed car; and no. 6119, 1930 Peter Witt car, all J.G. Brill Co.; no. 3715, 1913 double-truck crane; no. 7407, 1944 Pullman-Standard PCC car; more.

**Special Events:** Mother's, Father's, and Grandparent's Days. Museum Birthday Celebration. Pumpkin Junction, October. Tinsel Trolley, December; more. Call, write, or check website for more information.

**Nearby Attractions/Accommodations:** B&O Railroad Museum.

**Location/Directions:** One block west on Lafayette Ave. to Falls Rd.

*Coupon available, see coupon section.

         M arm

**Site Address:** 1901 Falls Rd., Baltimore, MD
**Mailing Address:** PO Box 4881, Baltimore, MD 21211
**Telephone:** (410) 547-0264
**Fax:** (410) 547-0264
**Internet:** www.baltimoremd.com/streetcar/

# CHESAPEAKE & ALLEGHENY STEAM PRESERVATION SOCIETY

*Train ride*
*7½", 4¾", 3½"*

PAUL SEYFRIT

**Description:** A 6- to 8-minute ride using live-steam engines on the 7½" gauge 1/8 scale trains on about 3,400 feet of track.

**Schedule:** April through November: second Sunday, 11 a.m. to 3:30 p.m.

**Admission/Fare:** Free, donations accepted.

**Locomotives/Rolling Stock:** Depends on what owners bring. We have 4-4-0, 4-4-2, 4-6-2, 4-6-4, 4-8-4, and others.

**Nearby Attractions/Accommodations:** Baltimore & Ohio Museum, Baltimore Inner Harbor.

**Location/Directions:** From the west–take I-70 east, go across the Baltimore Beltway I-695, exit to the right onto Security Blvd.; turn right at the first light onto Forest Park Ave.; turn right at the next light onto Windsor Mill Rd.; the park will be on the right. From the south–take I-695 to exit 16, stay in the right lane for Security Blvd.; follow above directions. From the north–take I-695, follow signs to I-70; once on exit ramp stay to the left for Security Blvd.; follow above directions.

**Site Address:** Leakin Park, Windsor Mill Rd., Baltimore, MD
**Mailing Address:** 10121 Durango Dr., Damascus, MD 20872
**Telephone:** (301) 253-6309 and (410) 448-0730 (recording)
**E-mail:** seyfritp@erols.com
**Internet:** http://calslivesteam.org

# BOWIE RAILROAD
## STATION MUSEUM
### *Museum*

**Description:** 1910 restored Pennsylvania Railroad depot, interlocking tower, caboose, and model trains. Collections illustrate local rail history, 1870 to today, alongside Amtrak/MARC corridor.

**Schedule:** Saturdays and Sundays, 12 to 4 p.m.

**Admission/Fare:** Free.

**Locomotives/Rolling Stock:** N&W caboose no. 518303, built 1922.

**Special Events:** Spring Fling, last Sunday in April; Fall Fest, last Sunday in September; Train Spotting Day, Sunday of Thanksgiving weekend.

**Nearby Attractions/Accommodations:** Five sites in City of Bowie Museums and near National Capital Trolley Museum and B&O Railroad Museum. Close to Patuxent State Park. Enjoy dinner at the Railroad Inn.

**Location/Directions:** U.S. 50 or U.S. 295 to Maryland Route 197 for Bowie. Route 564 to Old Bowie. Route 564 becomes Eleventh St. The museum is at Eleventh and Chestnut on the south side of the rail line.

        M arm

**Site Address:** 8614 Chestnut Ave., Bowie MD
**Mailing Address:** 12207 Tulip Grove Dr., Bowie MD 20715
**Telephone:** (301) 809-3088
**Fax:** (301) 809-2308
**E-mail:** museums@cityofbowie.org
**Internet:** www.cityofbowie.org/comserv/museums.htm

**Description:** Brunswick yards handled all B&O passenger and freight on the east-west main line. The 863 feet of track in an interactive HO layout traces the route from Washington, D.C., to Brunswick. Railroad artifacts include numerous historic photographs, tools, signals, equipment, and uniforms. Exhibitions of circa 1900 life in a railroad town; women's and labor history. At the same site is the National Park Service C&O Canal Historical Park Visitor Center.

**Schedule:** All year: Saturdays, 10 a.m. to 4 p.m.; Sundays, 1 to 4 p.m.; April through September additional Thursdays and Fridays, 10 a.m. to 2 p.m.

**Admission/Fare:** Adults, $5; seniors, $4; children age 6 and up, $2.50.

**Special Events:** Railroad History Days, first full weekend in April. Railroad Days, first full weekend in October. Victorian Christmas, weekend after Thanksgiving.

**Nearby Attractions/Accommodations:** Harper's Ferry Toy Train Museum, Walkersville Southern Railroad, River and Trail Outfitters, Potomac and Shenandoah expeditions and ski tours.

**Location/Directions:** From Washington, D.C.–I-270 north to U.S. 340 west to Brunswick. From Baltimore–I-70 west to I-340 west to Brunswick. From Leesburg, Virginia, U.S. 15 north to U.S. 340 west.

*Coupon available, see coupon section.

**Site Address:** 40 W. Potomac St., Brunswick, MD
**Mailing Address:** 40 W. Potomac St., Brunswick, MD 21716
**Telephone:** (301) 834-7100
**Fax:** (301) 834-4101
**E-mail:** rebeccatrussell@earthlink.net
**Internet:** www.brrm.org

**Description:** The CBRM preserves and interprets the history of the Chesapeake Beach Railway, which brought people from Washington, D.C., to the resorts of Chesapeake Beach and North Beach from 1900 until 1935. The museum exhibits photographs and artifacts of the railroad and resort.

**Schedule:** May 1 through September 30: daily, 1 to 4 p.m. April and October: weekends only. By appointment at all other times.

**Admission/Fare:** Free.

**Locomotives/Rolling Stock:** The CBR chair car "Dolores" is undergoing restoration by the museum staff and volunteers. Only one half of "Dolores" survives; it is the only known CBR rolling stock to survive.

**Special Events:** Right of Way Hike, April 6 (rain date April 13); Antique Car Show, May 19; Bay Breeze Summer Concerts, June 13, July 11, August 8, September 12, 7:30 p.m; summer children's programs, mid-June through mid-August, Thursdays, 10 a.m.; Holiday Open House, December 1.

**Nearby Attractions/Accommodations:** Chesapeake Beach Water Park, Bayfront Park, Breezy Point Beach and Campground.

**Location/Directions:** From Washington's Capital Beltway–I-95 to Route 4 south. From Baltimore Beltway–I-695 to Route 301 south to Route 4 south. Left on Route 260, right on Route 261 to museum.

      M

**Site Address:** 4155 Mears Ave., Chesapeake Beach, MD
**Mailing Address:** PO Box 1227, Chesapeake Beach, MD 20732
**Telephone:** (410) 257-3892

**Maryland, Colesville**

# NATIONAL CAPITAL TROLLEY MUSEUM
*Streetcar ride, museum*
*Standard gauge*

KEN RUCKER

**Description:** Visit "From Streetcars to Light Rail," a computer-based exhibit, view an O gauge model of the trolley line from Rock Creek Loop to Chevy Chase Lake. Enjoy a 1¾-mile, 20-minute round trip in Northwest Branch Park on cars selected from the museum's collection of 15 streetcars.

**Schedule:** January 2 through November 30: weekends, 12 to 5 p.m. June 15 to August 15: Thursdays and Fridays, 11 a.m. to 3 p.m. October 1 to November 15 and March 15 to May 15: Thursdays and Fridays, 10 a.m. to 2 p.m. December: weekends, 5 to 9 p.m.

**Admission/Fare:** Adults, $2.50 (5 rides for $6.25); children 2-17, $2 (5 rides for $5); under age 2 are free.

**Locomotives/Rolling Stock:** DCTS 1101; CTCo 1053; TTC 4603; European trams; Washington work cars.

**Special Events:** Snow Sweeper Day, March 24. Cavalcade of Street Cars, April 22. Montgomery County History Day, July 8. Fall Open House, October 21. Holly Trolley Fest, December.

**Nearby Attractions/Accommodations:** Brookside Gardens, Sandy Spring Museum, Montgomery County Historical Society, nation's capital.

**Location/Directions:** On Bonifant Rd. between Layhill Rd. (Route 182) and New Hampshire Ave. (Route 650), north of Wheaton.

*Coupon available, see coupon section.

      M arm

**Site Address:** 1313 Bonifant Rd., Colesville, MD
**Mailing Address:** 1313 Bonifant Rd., Colesville, MD 20905
**Telephone:** (301) 384-6088
**Fax:** (301) 384-2865
**E-mail:** nctm@dctrolley.org
**Internet:** www.dctrolley.org

# ELLICOTT CITY B&O RAILROAD STATION MUSEUM
*Museum, layout*

**Description:** Oldest railroad station in America. Forty layouts of the first 13 miles of the B&O.

**Schedule:** Fridays, Saturdays, Mondays, 11 a.m. to 4 p.m. Sundays, 12 to 5 p.m. Closed Mondays after Labor Day. Call for hours.

**Admission/Fare:** Adults, $4; seniors and students, $3; children 12 and under, $2.

**Locomotives/Rolling Stock:** 1927 Class I-50 caboose; Speeder car; hand car.

**Special Events:** Seasonal programs.

**Location/Directions:** Corner of Maryland Ave. and Main St. in historic Ellicott City.

**Site Address:** 2711 Maryland Ave., Ellicott City, MD
**Mailing Address:** 2711 Maryland Ave., Ellicott City, MD 21043
**Telephone:** (410) 461-1944
**Fax:** (410) 461-1944
**E-mail:** ecbostation@aol.com
**Internet:** www.b-orrstationmuseum.org

# GAITHERSBURG RAILWAY MUSEUM
### *Museum, display, layout*

GERALD A. HOTT

**Description:** Outdoor display of steam locomotives, Army kitchen car/ Western Maryland Railway M of W car K3008, B&O caboose and baggage wagons. Historic railroad photos on display in restored brick B&O freight house. Model railroad display (operating).

**Schedule:** Thursdays through Saturdays, 10 a.m. to 2 p.m. except February. Tours by prior arrangement.

**Admission/Fare:** Free. Donations appreciated.

**Locomotives/Rolling Stock:** Buffalo Creek & Gauley Alco Consolidation steam locomotive no. 14; Defense Transp. Corps troop kitchen car, Western Maryland Railway M of W car K3008; Baltimore & Ohio Railroad, Keyser WV shops, I12 wagontop bay window caboose C2490; baggage wagons (restored and unrestored).

**Special Events:** Gaithersburg Olde Towne Day, fourth Sunday in September.

**Nearby Attractions/Accommodations:** Restaurants, antique shops in Olde Towne Gaithersburg. Large HO layout under construction by Gaithersburg Model Railroad Society.

**Location/Directions:** Maryland Route 355 (Frederick Ave.) to S. Summit Ave.; north on S. Summit three blocks to B&O (now CSX) passenger station and freight house.

     Rockville, Maryland

**Site Address:** 5 S. Summit Ave., Gaithersburg, MD
**Mailing Address:** c/o 19 Brighton Dr., Gaithersburg, MD 20877-1809
**Telephone:** (301) 926-4660 and (301) 258-6160

CRYSTAL SPRECHER

**Description:** Memories of the Western Maryland Railway Roundhouse Complex, artifacts, photos, and displays. Outdoor display of Western Maryland Railway Baldwin Diesel Locomotive V01000, no. 132 and Hagerstown & Frederick Railway Trolley no. 168.

**Schedule:** Year round: Friday through Sundays, 1 to 5 p.m.

**Admission/Fare:** Adults, $3; children age 12 and under, $.50.

**Locomotives/Rolling Stock:** EMD Model 40 switcher; Alco MRS-1s; N&W and Reading cabooses; C&O Derby Club passenger car; PRR B-60 baggage car; B&O X-29 boxcar.

**Special Events:** Railroad Heritage Days, June. Autumn Leaf Excursions, October. The Trains of Christmas Display, December-January.

**Nearby Attractions/Accommodations:** Antietam National Battlefield, Hagerstown City Park, Hager House, Museum of Fine Arts.

**Location/Directions:** I-81 to exit 2, U.S. 11 north to museum; I-70 to exit 32; U.S. 40 west to U.S. 11, south to museum.

**Site Address:** 300 S. Burhans Blvd. (U.S. 11), Hagerstown, MD
**Mailing Address:** PO Box 2858, Hagerstown, MD 21741-2858
**Telephone:** (301) 739-4665
**Fax:** (301) 739-5598
**Internet:** www.roundhouse.org

# WALKERSVILLE SOUTHERN RAILROAD
*Train ride*
*Standard gauge*

PAUL J. BERGDOLT

**Description:** An 8-mile, one-hour round trip through the woods and rural farm country north of Frederick, Maryland.

**Schedule:** May through October: Saturdays and Sundays, departs at 11 a.m., 1 and 3 p.m.

**Admission/Fare:** Adults, $7; children 3-12, $3.50; under age 3 ride free unless occupying a seat.

**Locomotives/Rolling Stock:** Plymouth 0-4-0 no. 1; Davenport 0-4-0 no. 2; converted flatcar no. 11; coach no. 12, former troop sleeper; caboose no. 2827, former Wabash; former PRR N5 cabin car no. 477532.

**Special Events:** Saturday Evening Mystery Dinner Trains, Father's and Mother's Day special, Track Car Days, Nature Trains, Civil War Days, Circus Days, Heritage Days, Ghost Trains, Santa Claus Specials. Call for details.

**Nearby Attractions/Accommodations:** Heritage Farm Park, Walkersville, Maryland. Catoctin Mountain Zoological Park, Thurmont, Maryland.

**Location/Directions:** Two miles east on Biggs Ford Rd., off U.S. Route 15, 3 miles north of Frederick. Located 50 miles west of Baltimore and 50 miles northwest of Washington, D.C.

**Radio frequency:** 160.6500 and 160.7250

**Site Address:** 34 W. Pennsylvania Ave., Walkersville, MD
**Mailing Address:** PO Box 651, Walkersville, MD 21793-0651
**Telephone:** (301) 877-363-WSRR
**Fax:** (301) 898-0899
**E-mail:** grtucker@erols.com
**Internet:** www.wsrr.org

**WALKER TRANSPORTATION COLLECTION**
**BEVERLY HISTORICAL SOCIETY**
**& MUSEUM**
*Display*

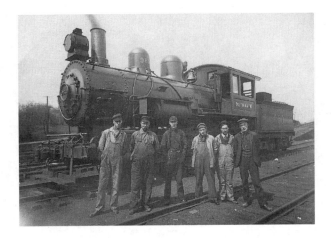

**Description:** Repository of photos/negatives, slides, maps, documents, artifacts, some models relating to most modes of transportation in
Massachusetts/Eastern New England.

**Admission/Fare:** Free. Donations requested. Annual supporter: $25.

**Nearby Attractions/Accommodations:** Historic Salem, Massachusetts, and
renowned Peabody-Essex Museum. John Hale Farm and historic Balch
House are located in Beverly.

**Location/Directions:** U.S. Route 1A, North; WTC at Beverly Historical
Socity & Museum in Beverly, Massachusetts. Housed in historic John
Cabot house.

    M

**Site Address:** 117 Cabot St., Beverly, MA
**Mailing Address:** 117 Cabot St., Beverly, MA 01915
**Telephone:** (978) 922-1186 (weekdays and Wednesday nights)
**E-mail:** info@beverlyhistory.org

# EDAVILLE RAILROAD
*Train ride*
*24" narrow gauge*

**Description:** Five-and-a-half-mile train ride around a 1,500-acre cranberry plantation, museum, rides, etc.

**Schedule:** July through August, Friday through Monday. October, November, May and June, weekends. November 9 through January 5, daily.

**Admission/Fare:** Adults, $12.50; seniors, $11.50; children (3-12), $8.50; under 3 are free.

**Locomotives/Rolling Stock:** 1949 GE diesel; 1951 Whitcomb diesel; 1938 Hudswell-Clark steam; no. 11 combine 1900; no. 21 coach 1901; no. 26 coach 1986.

**Nearby Attractions/Accommodations:** Myles Standish State Forest, Plymouth Plantation.

**Location/Directions:** Route 495, exit 2 to Route 58, 4 miles on left.

**Site Address:** 7 Eda Ave., South Carver, MA
**Mailing Address:** PO Box 825, Carver, MA 02330
**Telephone:** (508) 866-8190
**Fax:** (508) 866-7921
**E-mail:** bjohnson@edaville.org

# OLD COLONY AND FALL RIVER RAILROAD MUSEUM
### *Museum*

JACK DARMODY

**Description:** The museum, located in railroad cars that include a renovated Pennsylvania Railroad coach, features artifacts of the New Haven, Penn Central, Conrail, Amtrak, and other New England railroads.

**Schedule:** April 20 through June 30 and September through November 17: Saturdays 12 to 4 p.m. and Sundays 10 a.m. to 2 p.m. July 1 through September 2: Thursdays through Sundays 12 to 5 p.m.

**Admission/Fare:** Adults, $2; seniors, $1.50; children 5-12, $1; under age 5 are free. Group rates available.

**Rolling Stock:** Pennsylvania P-70 coach; no. 42 New Haven R.D.C. "Firestone"; New Haven 40-foot boxcar no. 33401; New York Central N7B caboose no. 21052.

**Special Events:** Annual Railroad Show, third weekend in January. Fall River Celebrates America waterfront festival, mid-August.

**Nearby Attractions/Accommodations:** Battleship Cove (six warships on display), Marine Museum at Fall River, Heritage State Park, Fall River Carousel.

**Location/Directions:** The museum is located in a railroad yard at the corner of Central and Water Streets, across from the entrance to Battleship Cove.

*Coupon available, see coupon section.

      M

**Site Address:** 2 Water St., Fall River, MA
**Mailing Address:** PO Box 3455, Fall River, MA 02722-3455
**Telephone:** (508) 674-9340
**E-mail:** railroadjc@aol.com
**Internet:** www.ocandfrrailroadmuseum.com

# BERKSHIRE SCENIC RAILWAY
*Train ride, museum, display, layout*
*Standard gauge*

**Description:** Fifteen-minute short shuttle train ride within Lenox Station yard, with narrative of Berkshire railroading and Lenox Station history. Locomotive cab tours for youngsters. The museum is in the restored Lenox station. Restored former New York, New Haven & Hartford NE-5 caboose; Fairmont speeder and track-gang train; displays about Berkshire railroading history; railroad videos; exhibit of photos of Gilded-Age Berkshire "Cottages"; two model railroads.

**Schedule:** May through October: weekends and holidays, 10 a.m. to 4 p.m. Lenox local shuttle trains operate half-hourly.

**Admission/Fare:** Adults, $2; children under age 14, $1.

**Locomotives/Rolling Stock:** GE 50-ton switcher no. 67; Maine Central Alco S-1 no. 954; New York Central EMD SW8 no. 8619.

**Special Events:** Fire Apparatus Display, Gas Engine Show, Circus Day, Halloween Special, Santa Special. Call or write for information.

**Nearby Attractions/Accommodations:** Tanglewood, summer home of the Boston Symphony Orchestra. The Norman Rockwell Museum.

**Location/Directions:** U.S. 7/20 to Housatonic St., travel east 1.5 miles.

**Radio frequency: 161.400**

**Site Address:** Willow Creek Rd., Lenox, MA
**Mailing Address:** PO Box 2195, Lenox, MA 01240
**Telephone:** (413) 637-2210
**Fax:** (518) 392-2225
**E-mail:** wordworks@taconic.net
**Internet:** www.regionnet.com/colberk/berkshirerailway.html

175

# SHELBURNE FALLS TROLLEY MUSEUM
*Train ride, museum, display, layout*

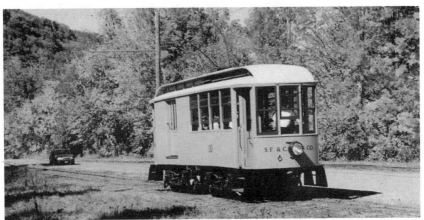

DAVID C. BARTLETT

**Description:** Museum with caboose, 15-minute trolley ride with interpretive talk by motormen/conductors; locomotive, trolley, and railroad displays.

**Schedule:** Memorial Day to November, weekends and holidays, 12 to 5 p.m.

**Admission/Fare:** Museum, free. Trolley, adults, $2; children under 6, free.

**Locomotives/Rolling Stock:** 1896 Wason trolley car no. 10; 1934 Baldwin saddle tank steam locomotive no. 110; 1910 Central Vermont caboose no. 4015; Bangor & Aroostook "American Flyer" coach.

**Special Events:** Trolleyfest Day, Amherst Railway Society Appreciation Day.

**Nearby Attractions/Accommodations:** Shelburne Falls: Bridge of Flowers, Glacial Potholes, several restaurants, bed and breakfasts, campgrounds, artisan's studios, craft shops.

**Location/Directions:** Next to the Boston & Maine tracks in Shelburne Falls; Route 91 or Route 2 to Greenfield, west on Route 2 approximately 8 miles to the Buckland side of Shelburne Falls. Take Depot St. to Rail Yard.

*Coupon available, see coupon section.

      M arm

**Site Address:** 14 Depot St., Buckland, MA
**Mailing Address:** PO Box 272, Shelburne Falls, MA 01370
**Telephone:** (413) 625-9443 and (413) 624-0192
**E-mail:** trolley@sftm.org
**Internet:** www.sftm.org

**Description:** Model train room with seven operating layouts and railroad artifacts.

**Schedule:** Tuesdays through Sundays, 10 a.m. to 4 p.m. Closed Mondays and major holidays.

**Admission/Fare:** Adults, $5; seniors (65+), $4; children (2-16), $3.

**Locomotives/Rolling Stock:** Models only.

**Special Events:** "Train Time" exhibit, November 2002 through January 2003 (bi-annual). Annual Railroad Hobby Show, first weekend in January.

**Nearby Attractions/Accommodations:** Wenham Tea House and shops, numerous historical sites and museums in region. Beautiful beaches, scenic drives, quaint towns.

**Location/Directions:** Route 128 north to exit 20A (Route 1A north). Follow Route 1A north for 2.3 miles. The museum is on the right next to Town Hall.

*Coupon available, see coupon section.

         M

**Site Address:** 132 Main St., Wenham, MA
**Mailing Address:** 132 Main St., Wenham, MA 01984
**Telephone:** (978) 468-2377
**Fax:** (978) 468-1763
**E-mail:** info@wenhammuseum.org
**Internet:** www.wenhammuseum.org

# ADRIAN & BLISSFIELD RAILROAD COMPANY
*Dinner train, train ride*
*Standard gauge*

**Description:** This working, common-carrier freight and passenger railroad offers 14-mile, 1½-hour round trips from Blissfield to Lenawee Junction over a former New York Central line. The train travels through the village of Blissfield, crosses the River Raisin, and runs through Lenawee County farmland to Lenawee Junction. The Old Road Dinner Train is a two- to three-hour round trip featuring traditional, impeccable dining-car service including an elegant four-course dinner and a murder mystery.

**Schedule:** Call for schedule.

**Locomotives/Rolling Stock:** Nos. 1751 and 1752, 1957 EMD GP9s, former Grand Trunk Western/Central Vermont; dining cars "Columbia River" (former Union Pacific, 1949) and "River Raisin" (former Canadian National, 1937).

**Special Events:** Santa Trains and New Year's Eve dinner train.

**Location/Directions:** U.S. 223 and Depot St. Ten miles west of exit 5 off U.S. 23 and 20 miles northwest of Toledo.

**Site Address:** 301 E. Adrian St., Blissfield, MI
**Mailing Address:** PO Box 95, Blissfield, MI 49228
**Telephone:** (517) 265-3626
**Internet:** www.murdermysterytrain.com

**JUNCTION VALLEY RAILROAD**
*Train ride*
*14⅛" gauge*

**Description:** The ride, more than 2 miles long, travels 22 feet down into a valley, around a lake, over 865 feet of bridges and trestles, and through a 100-foot tunnel, playground, and picnic area. We have a 10-stall roundhouse with turntable, five-track switchyard, railroad shops, and railroad hobby shop.

**Schedule:** Train rides–Mid-May through Labor Day: Mondays through Saturdays, 10 a.m. to 6 p.m.; Sundays, 1 to 6 p.m. September through October 7: weekends, 1 to 5 p.m. Railroad hobby shop open year round.

**Admission/Fare:** Adults, $5; seniors, $4.75; children, $4.25. Special events fares are higher. Group rates available.

**Locomotives/Rolling Stock:** No. 1177 GP45; no. 333 SW1500; no. 4 Plymouth; no. 300 SW1500 booster unit; no. 5000 WS4A; no. 7000 WS4A; no. 6000 WS4B; no. 555 MP15. Sixty-five railroad cars of all types. All are built ¼ the size of their prototype.

**Special Events:** Opening Day balloon launch. Valley of Flags, July 4. Railroad Days, June 22-23, July 20-21, August 17-18. Halloween Spook Ride, October, and more.

**Location/Directions:** I-75, Bridgeport exit, head south for 2 miles. Located 5 miles west of historic Frankenmuth.

*Coupon available, see coupon section.

**Site Address:** 7065 Dixie Highway, Bridgeport, MI
**Mailing Address:** 7065 Dixie Highway, Bridgeport, MI 48722
**Telephone:** (517) 777-3480
**Fax:** (517) 777-4070
**Internet:** http://gtesupersite.com/jvrailroad

KEMPF MODEL CITY

**Description:** 1912 Grand Trunk Depot Museum with railroad and other historical artifacts from around the area. We also have the Kempf Model City and a Grand Trunk Western caboose

**Schedule:** May through September, Saturdays and Sundays, 1 to 4 p.m.

**Admission/Fare:** Donations.

**Locomotives/Rolling Stock:** GTW caboose no. 78899; C&O speeder.

**Nearby Attractions/Accommodations:** Motels in Imlay City; campground on Beech Grove Road in Emmett; ½ hour away from Pt. Huron, Michigan, and Canada.

**Location/Directions:** ¼ mile east of the Village of Capac off Capac Rd. on south side of Downey Rd. (M-21).

**Site Address:** 401 E. Kempf Ct., Capac, MI
**Mailing Address:** 401 E. Kempf Ct., Capac, MI 48014
**Telephone:** (810) 395-2859

# CHARLOTTE SOUTHERN RAILROAD
# OLD ROAD DINNER TRAIN
*Train ride, dinner train*
*Standard gauge*

**Description:** This working, common-carrier freight and passenger railroad offers 7-mile, 2½-hour round trips from downtown Charlotte over a former New York Central line. The Old Road Dinner Train features traditional impeccable dining-car service, including an elegant five-course dinner and cash bar, and murder mystery.

**Schedule:** Year round: call for information; charters anytime.

**Admission/Fare:** Dinner train fares vary; call for current pricing.

**Locomotives/Rolling Stock:** GE 44-tonner no. 3, 1956, the last one built, former Dansville & Mt. Morris Railroad; Dining cars "Butternut Creek" and "Battle Creek," both former Canadian National, nos. 5208 and 2502, built 1937 and 1954; baggage-generator car no. 5674, former Union Pacific, 1958; RPO no. 105, former Canadian National, 1924; coaches nos. 2957 and 2959, former Long Island 1956.

**Special Events:** Frontier Days, September. Santa Train. Special trips, senior charters, and bus tour group charters with or without meals.

**Nearby Attractions/Accommodations:** Michigan State Historical Museum in Lansing.

**Location/Directions:** 451 N. Cochrane St. is at the north end of downtown Charlotte's main street. Charlotte is 15 miles southwest of Lansing, just off I-69 exit 61.

         Lansing

**Site Address:** 451 N. Cochrane St., Charlotte, MI
**Mailing Address:** PO Box 265, Charlotte, MI 48813
**Telephone:** (888) 726-8277
**Fax:** (248) 583-3194
**E-mail:** ihswabash@msn.com
**Internet:** www.murdermysterytrain.com

**Michigan, Clinton**

E. JESCHKE

**Description:** The Southern Michigan Railroad Society offers train rides: 6 miles or 12 miles, one way; 12 miles or 24 miles, round trip.

**Schedule:** May through September: Sundays, 11 a.m. and 2 p.m.; October: Saturdays and Sundays, 11 a.m., 1:30 and 4 p.m.

**Admission/Fare:** May through September: adults, $8; seniors, $7; children (2-12), $5. October: adults, $15; seniors, $10; children (2-12), $8.

**Locomotives/Rolling Stock:** 1943 GE 44-ton diesel no. 75; 1938 Plymouth no. 1; Alco RS-1 diesel; GMDH (prototype); South Shore & South Bend commuter car; 1950 caboose no. 21692, former New York Central; 1944 caboose no. 19882, former New Haven; 1949 gondola no. 726456, former New York Central.

**Special Events:** Clinton Fall Festival, September 29-30. Fall Color Tours, October weekends.

**Nearby Attractions/Accommodations:** Less than 10 miles from Irish Hills, which has many tourist accommodations. Tecumseh and Clinton have many parks and restaurants.

**Location/Directions:** Twenty-five miles southwest of Ann Arbor, Michigan, and 54 miles northwest of Toledo, Ohio.

P 🚌 ✳ M

**Site Address:** 320 S. Division St. Clinton, MI
**Mailing Address:** PO Box K, Clinton, MI 49236
**Telephone:** (517) 456-7677
**Fax:** (517) 456-7677
**Internet:** www.railfanhomepage.com/smrs

# COOPERSVILLE & MARNE RAILWAY
*Train ride, dinner train, display*
*Standard gauge*

THOMAS L. CHUBINSKI

**Description:** Fourteen-mile trip. Murder mystery dinner train, spring and fall.

**Schedule:** June through October: Saturdays, 1 and 3 p.m. Closed holiday weekends.

**Admission/Fare:** Adults, $11; seniors, $9; children, $7. Great Train Robbery and Pumpkin Trains: Adults, $13.50; seniors, $11.50; children, $9.50.

**Locomotives/Rolling Stock:** Former GTW SW9 7014; two former Lackawanna commuter cars; two former CN commuter cars; former GTW caboose; former Dupont/Standard Oil 50-ton GE center cab; former C&O 250-ton wreck crane; former Lansing W&L.

**Special Events:** Great Train Robbery, September 22 and 29; Pumpkin Trains, October 6, 13, 20 and 27; Summerfest/Railroad Days, August 11.

**Nearby Attractions/Accommodations:** Coopersville Area Farm Museum and the Coopersville Historical Museum in the Coopersville Interurban Station, Lake Michigan at Grand Haven, Michigan Adventure Land, USS Siversides submarine in Muskegon, John Ball Zoo and Frederick Meijer Garden in Grand Rapids.

**Location/Directions:** I-96 to exit 16 or 19, then follow signs to downtown Coopersville (halfway between Grand Rapids and Muskegon.)

      **Radio frequency:** 160.695

**Site Address:** 311 Danforth, Coopersville, MI
**Mailing Address:** PO Box 55, Coopersville, MI 49404
**Telephone:** (616) 997-7000
**Internet:** www.coopersville.org

**LAKE CENTRAL RAIL TOURS**
*Train ride*
*Standard gauge*

RAY KAMMER

**Description:** Festival shuttle trips; long-distance fall color trips; steam excursions. Departure points vary.

**Schedule:** Varies.

**Admission/Fare:** Varies per trip.

**Locomotives/Rolling Stock:** EMD GP-35s; PM 2-8-4 no. 1225; 1950s era passenger train, open-window and air-conditioned consist varies.

**Special Events:** Durand Railroad Days, May; Howell Melon Fest, August, more.

**Attractions/Accommodations:** Birch Run, Frankenmuth.

**Site Address:** Corunna, MI
**Mailing Address:** PO Box 221, Corunna, MI 48817
**Telephone:** (810) 638-7248
**E-mail:** ra1508vh@cs.com
**Internet:** www.lakecentralrailtours.com

**Michigan, Dearborn**

HENRY FORD MUSEUM AND
GREENFIELD VILLAGE RAILROAD

*Train ride*
*Standard gauge*

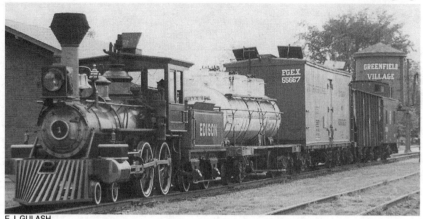

E.J. GULASH

**Description:** The Greenfield Village Railroad offers a 2½-mile, 35-minute narrated circuit of the world-famous Greenfield Village in open-air passenger cars. While riding you will hear interpretations of the history of the village, its occupants and the railroad. The Henry Ford Museum, a general museum of American history occupying about 12 acres under one roof, contains a huge transportation collection, including the widely acclaimed "Automobile in American Life" exhibit. Greenfield Village is an 81-acre outdoor museum comprising more than 80 historic structures. A new visitor experience is a recreation of the Detroit, Toledo & Milwaukee roundhouse; a six stall repair facility from 1884. Visitors can get an up close look at repairs taking place on the trains of Greenfield Village. Also at the site are 1941 Lima 2-6-6-6 no. 1601; a 1902 Schenectady 4-4-2; an 1858 Rogers 4-4-0; an 1893 replica of the "DeWitt Clinton"; 1909 Baldwin 2-8-0, former Bessemer & Lake Erie no. 154.

**Schedule:** Call or write for information.

**Admission/Fare:** Call or write for information.

**Locomotives/Rolling Stock:** No. 1, 1876 Ford Motor Co. 4-4-0 (rebuilt 1920s); no. 3, 1873 Mason-Fairlie 0-6-4T, former Calumet & Hecla Mining; no. 8, 1914 Baldwin 0-6-0, former Michigan Alkali Co.

**Location/Directions:** One-half mile south of U.S. 12 (Michigan Ave.) between Southfield and Oakwood Blvd. (freeway M39).

P  🚌  ✳  🍺  ⛩  🎨  ⛪  ✉  M  TRAIN

Dearborn

**Site Address:** 20900 Oakland Blvd., Dearborn, MI
**Mailing Address:** PO Box 1970, Dearborn, MI 48121
**Telephone:** (313) 271-1620
**Internet:** www.hfmgv.org

185

**MICHIGAN AUSABLE VALLEY RAILROAD**
*Train ride*
*16" gauge*

**Description:** A 1½-mile, 18-minute scenic ride on a ¼ scale passenger train that runs through part of the Huron National Forest, and overlooks beautiful AuSable Valley. You will pass through a 115-foot wooden tunnel and over two wooden trestles, one over 220 feet long, to view the wooded valley below. The MAV Railroad is also home to Schrader's Railroad Gift Catalog. You will find one-of-a-kind items in the quaintly designed Railroad Depot Gift Shop from past and present catalogs.

**Schedule:** Weekends and holidays *only,* Memorial Day weekend through Labor Day: 10 a.m. to 5 p.m. First two weekends in October: fall color.

**Admission/Fare:** $3; children under age 2 are free.

**Locomotives/Rolling Stock:** ¼ scale 16-inch Hudson steam locomotive 4-6-4 no. 5661, built by E.C. Eddy of Fairview and formerly run on the Pinconning & Blind River Railroad; two F7 diesel hydraulic locomotives built by Custom Locomotive, Chicago, Illinois; nine ¼ scale passenger streamline coaches.

**Nearby Attractions/Accommodations:** Huron National Forest, canoe ride National Scenic AuSable River, campgrounds, nature hikes.

**Location/Directions:** North on I-75 exit 202 onto M-33, north to Fairview. Turn south at blinker light in Fairview and go 3.5 miles south on Abbe Rd.

*Coupon available, see coupon section.

**Site Address:** 230 S. Abbe Rd., Fairview, MI
**Mailing Address:** 230 S. Abbe Rd., Fairview, MI 48621
**Telephone:** (989) 848-2229
**Fax:** (989) 848-2240

**HUCKLEBERRY RAILROAD**
*Train ride*
*Narrow gauge*

**Description:** Steam locomotive and historic wooden coaches depart from 1860s Crossroads Depot for 8-mile excursion. Route borders Mott Lake and crosses 26-foot trestle. Operated in conjunction with Crossroads Village, living history museum of 33 buildings and paddle wheel riverboat.

**Schedule:** Mid-May through August, Tuesdays through Sundays. September, weekends. Weekdays, 10 a.m. to 5 p.m., weekends and holidays 11 a.m. to 5:30 p.m. Call for October through November dates and hours.

**Admission/Fare:** Village, train, and boat: adults (13-59), $13; seniors (60+), $12; children (3-12), $8.25; age 2 and under free.

**Locomotives/Rolling Stock:** Baldwin 4-6-0 HRR no. 2; Baldwin 2-8-2 HRR no. 464; Plymouth diesel HRR no. 5; caboose and 14 historic coaches.

**Special Events:** Weekend events throughout summer, Halloween and Christmas trains. Railfans weekend, August.

**Nearby Attractions/Accommodations:** Timber Wolf Campground, Stepping Stone Falls, outlet shopping, dinner cruises, numerous restaurants and motels.

**Location/Directions:** Just north of Flint, Michigan. I-475 off either I-75 or I-69 to exit 11, follow signs to railroad and Crossroads Village.

*Coupon available, see coupon section.

**Site Address:** 6140 Bray Rd., Flint, MI
**Mailing Address:** 5045 Stanley Rd., Flint, MI 48506
**Telephone:** (810) 736-7100 and (800) 648-7275
**Fax:** (810) 736-7220
**E-mail:** gencopks@concentric.net
**Internet:** geneseecountyparks.org

# FLUSHING AREA HISTORICAL SOCIETY & CULTURAL CENTER
*Museum*
*Narrow gauge*

**Description:** The collection includes items of the area's historical past, including permanent displays of railroad items. Other displays change periodically.

**Schedule:** May through first Sunday in December, open Sundays. Closed holiday weekends.

**Admission/Fare:** Free.

**Nearby Attractions/Accommodations:** There are several antique shops in the area.

**Location/Directions:** Take I-75 to exit 122 (Pierson Rd.) and go west approximately five miles. Pierson Rd. becomes Main St. in Flushing.

    M

**Site Address:** 431 W. Main St., Flushing, MI
**Mailing Address:** PO Box 87, Flushing, MI 48433
**Telephone:** (810) 487-0814 (recording)

**Description:** On display: Pere Marquette 2-8-4 no. 1223, PM boxcar 72222, PM caboose A-986, Grand Trunk wood caboose 77915.

**Schedule:** Year round outdoor display.

**Admission/Fare:** Free.

**Special Events:** Ice Cream Social annual in August.

**Nearby Attractions/Accommodations:** Tri-Cities Historical Museum, Grand Haven State Park.

**Location/Directions:** Downtown Grand Haven.

**Site Address:** Chinook Pier Park, Grand Haven, MI
**Mailing Address:** 1 N. Harbor, Grand Haven, MI 49417
**Telephone:** (616) 842-0700
**Fax:** (616) 842-3698
**E-mail:** tcmuseum@grandhaven.com

# IRON MOUNTAIN IRON MINE
*Train ride*
*24" gauge*

**Description:** Designated a Michigan Historical Site, the Iron Mountain Iron Mine offers guided underground tours by mine train. Visitors travel 2,600 feet into the mine to see mining demonstrations and the history of iron mining in Michigan's Upper Peninsula. Mining equipment dating from the 1870s is shown and explained.

**Schedule:** June 1 through October 15: daily, 9 a.m. to 5 p.m.

**Admission/Fare:** Adults, $7; children 6-12, $6; children under 6 are free. School and group rates available.

**Locomotives/Rolling Stock:** Electric locomotive and five cars.

**Location/Directions:** Nine miles east of Iron Mountain on U.S. 2.

*Coupon available, see coupon section.

**Site Address:** Iron Mountain, MI
**Mailing Address:** PO Box 177, Iron Mountain, MI 49801
**Telephone:** (906) 563-8077
**E-mail:** ironmine@uplogon.com
**Internet:** www.ironmountainironmine.com

**Michigan, Lake Linden**

# COPPER COUNTRY RAILROAD
# HERITAGE CENTER
*Train ride, museum, display, layout*
*36" gauge*

**Description:** The line is currently under construction. Total length, 1.4 miles, including interpretative program on copper milling.

**Schedule:** May 31 through October 15, 10 a.m. to 5 p.m.; tours in off-season for groups only until December 13 or after April 1.

**Admission/Fare:** Adults, $5; children/seniors, $2; train fare: Adults, $5; children/seniors, $2 (August 2001).

**Locomotives/Rolling Stock:** 1915 Porter 0-4-0 tank engine used by Calumet & Hecla; caboose Soo Line no. 261; C&H plow/flanger no. 2; C&H flanger (both constructed by C&H Mining) offsite exhibits; Q&TL RR 2-6-0 and 2-8-0; various other 36" gauge equipment, Russell snowplow C&H.

**Special Events:** Railroad Days, third weekend in August.

**Nearby Attractions/Accommodations:** Lake Linden Village campground (hook-ups, swimming beach, boat launch), Quincy Mine Hoist, McClain and Port Wilkens State Parks, Keweenaw National Historical Park, 40 miles by boat to Isle Royale National Park.

**Location/Directions:** Take U.S. 41 or M-26 to Houghton, cross Portage Lift Bridge to M-26 (right), 10 miles on southwest side of Lake Linden.

**Site Address:** 5500 Highway M-26, Lake Linden, MI
**Mailing Address:** PO Box 127, Lake Linden, MI 49945
**Telephone:** (906) 296-4121
**Fax:** (906) 296-0862
**E-mail:** richard@raildreams.com

# MICHIGAN TRANSIT MUSEUM
*Train ride, museum*
*Standard gauge*

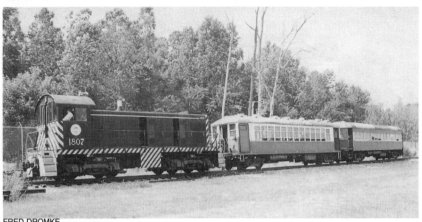

FRED DROMKE

**Description:** Train ride to military air museum and 1859 Depot Museum.

**Schedule:** End of May through October, Sundays. Depot Museum year round, Saturdays and Sundays, 1 to 4 p.m.

**Admission/Fare:** Adults, $6; children 4-12, $3.

**Locomotives/Rolling Stock:** Alco S-1 no. 1807 diesel switch engine; two Chicago "L" cars, series 4000; and an interurban.

**Nearby Attractions/Accommodations:** Selfridge Military Air Museum, Sunday afternoons.

**Location/Directions:** Train rides from Joy Rd. Park, east of Gratiot, one mile north of Mt. Clemens.

    M arm

**Site Address:** Depot Museum, 200 Grand Ave., Mt. Clemens, MI
**Mailing Address:** PO Box 12, Mt. Clemens, MI 48046
**Telephone:** (810) 463-1863
**Fax:** (810) 463-9814
**Internet:** www.mtmrail.com

# Michigan, Mt. Pleasant

## LAKE CENTRAL RAIL TOURS, THE MOUNTAINTOWN LIMITED

*Dinner train*
*Standard gauge*

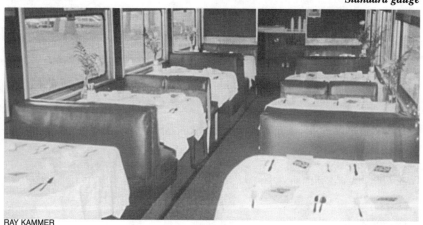

RAY KAMMER

**Description:** Dinner train ride of varying lengths.
**Schedule:** Schedule varies; call for information.
**Admission/Fare:** Fares vary.
**Locomotives/Rolling Stock:** EMD GP-35s; 1950s era dining cars
**Nearby Attractions/Accommodations:** Soaring Eagle Casino
**Location/Directions:** Mid-Michigan, off Route 23.

**Site Address:** Mountaintown Station, 506 W. Broadway, Mt. Pleasant, MI
**Mailing Address:** 506 W. Broadway, Mt. Pleasant, MI 48858
**Telephone:** (517) 775-2337
**E-mail:** ra1508vh@cs.com
**Internet:** www.mountaintown.com or www.lakecentralrailtours.com

193

# MICHIGAN STATE TRUST FOR RAILWAY PRESERVATION, INC.
*Train ride*
*Standard gauge*

STEAM RAILROADING INSTITUTE

**Description:** A 1941 steam locomotive. Occasional events, exhibits, and excursions.

**Schedule:** Saturdays, 10 a.m. to 5 p.m. Occasional events as announced. Weekdays and Sundays by appointment.

**Admission/Fare:** Free. Event prices as announced. Mailing list members receive updates, $25 annually.

**Locomotives/Rolling Stock:** Pere Marquette 2-8-4 no. 1225 (Lima, 1941); 1919 PM turntable; Flagg Coal Co. 040T no. 75 (Vulcan, 1939).

**Special Events:** Engineer-for-an-Hour program permits MSTRP members to operate Locomotive 1225. Also, other interactive railroading programs. Coming for 2002: Steam Railroading Institute–an 11-stall roundhouse with steam locomotive service and museum; Railroad History Train–a mobile railcar with classroom and museum to extend our base in Shiawassee County.

**Nearby Attractions/Accommodations:** Durand Depot Museum, Historic Crossroads Village. Call, fax or e-mail for local accommodations.

**Location/Directions:** Located in Tuscola and Saginaw Bay Railway Yard on S. Oakwood St., off Highway M-71 in southeast Owosso.

**Site Address:** 600 S. Oakwood St., Owosso, MI
**Mailing Address:** PO Box 665, Owosso, MI 48867-0665
**Telephone:** (989) 725-9464
**Fax:** (989) 723-1225
**Internet:** www.mstrp.com

HERB MCCULLAGH

**Description:** An educational and research facility dedicated to the preservation and enhancement of railroad technology and lore. Operating diesel locomotives, caboose(s), Armstrong interlocking tower, combine coach (under restoration) 1907 Pere Marquette depot, HO model train.

**Schedule:** Second and fourth Sunday of each month, 1 to 5 p.m. Also open by appointment for groups or individuals. Guided tour every hour on the half.

**Admission/Fare:** General Admission, $1; family rate, $3.

**Locomotives/Rolling Stock:** GP-9 locomotives (operable) GTW 4428 and GTW 4433; C&O cabooses 903577, 900342, 900977 (latter two under restoration); combine C&O 911245 (under restoration) converted to MW cook car by C&O.

**Nearby Attractions/Accommodations:** Frankenmuth; Junction Valley ¼ scale railroad; Japanese gardens, children's zoo; waterslide and wave pool; many motels along I-675 and fine hotel downtown.

**Location/Directions:** I-75 to exit 149 (M-46 West–Holland Ave.) Follow through city and across river. Left at first traffic light (Michigan Ave.) and follow across tracks. Turn right at museum sign. Follow to Maple and turn right.

        M

**Site Address:** 900 Maple St., Saginaw, MI
**Mailing Address:** 900 Maple St., Saginaw, MI 48602
**Telephone:** (517) 790-7994

# TOONERVILLE TROLLEY, TRAIN AND BOAT TOURS
*Train ride*
*24" gauge*

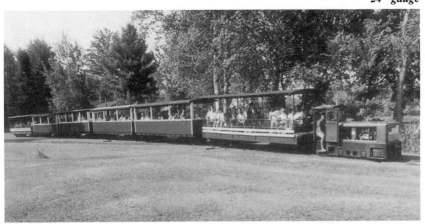

**Description:** Enjoy a 6½-hour train and boat tour to Tahquamenon Falls or 1¾-hour wilderness train ride, 5½ miles one way. Longest 24" rail in the country.

**Schedule:** June 15 through October 6. Please call for schedule.

**Admission/Fare:** Six-and-a-half-hour trip to falls: adults, $25; children 6-15, $12.50; under 6, free; 1¾-hour train ride: adults, $12; children 6-15, $6; under 6 free.

**Locomotives/Rolling Stock:** Two 1964 Plymouth 5-ton diesels; 1957 Plymouth 5-ton gas; 11 passenger cars.

**Nearby Attractions/Accommodations:** 20 minutes from Newberry, Michigan; many motels, restaurants, and campsites. Nearby attractions: Oswald's Bear Ranch, Whitefish Point lighthouse, logging museum.

**Location/Directions:** East of Newberry, Michigan, just off M-28 at Soo Junction. One hour from Mackinac Bridge or Sault Ste. Marie.

*Coupon available, see coupon section.

**Site Address:** Soo Junction, MI
**Mailing Address:** 5883 County Road 441, Newberry, MI 49868
**Telephone:** (888) 77-TRAIN or (906) 293-3806
**E-mail:** soojunction@portup.com
**Internet:** www.destinationmichigan.com/toonerville-trolley.html

**THE GRAND TRAVERSE
DINNER TRAIN**
*Dinner train*

GLEN RAUTH

**Description:** Elegant gourmet rail dining excursions from Traverse City, Michigan, aboard Grand Traverse Dinner Train.

**Schedule:** Mondays through Saturdays, 9 a.m. to 6 p.m.

**Admission/Fare:** Seasonal rates.

**Locomotives/Rolling Stock:** EMD 16-567B engines; F7 locomotives; GTDR 1950; F7 locomotives GTDR 1951; baggage coach converted to galley; two articulated dining coaches circa 1930s.

**Special Events:** Mother's Day; Father's Day; Valentines; Halloween; Thanksgiving; Victorian Christmas; New Year's Eve; kiddie Santa rides; bunny rides.

**Location/Directions:** Corner of 8th and Woodmere Ave.

**Site Address:** 642 Railroad Place, Traverse City, MI
**Mailing Address:** 642 Railroad Place, Traverse City, MI 49686
**Telephone:** (231) 933-3768
**Fax:** (231) 933-5400
**E-mail:** gtdt@dinnertrain.com
**Internet:** www.dinnertrain.com

## MICHIGAN STAR CLIPPER DINNER TRAIN/COE RAIL
*Dinner train, train ride*
*Standard gauge*

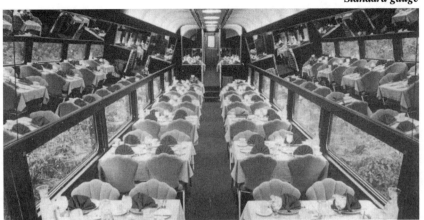

**Description:** One-hour and three-hour train rides through Michigan wetlands.

**Schedule:** Coe Rail: April through October, Sundays 1 and 2:30 p.m. Dinner Train: year round, except Mondays and certain holidays. Departs Tuesdays, Wednesdays, Thursdays, and Saturdays at 7 p.m., Fridays at 7:30 p.m., and Sundays at 5 p.m.

**Admission/Fare:** Standard fare: adults, $9; children (2-10) and seniors (65+), $8. Three-hour ride: $69.50 per person, includes five-course meal and entertainment.

**Locomotives/Rolling Stock:** GR-10 no. 52; EL/NJT nos. 4315 and 4317; Milw/PVTC/CRLE no. 165; C&EI no. 85258; caboose no. 60; ATSF/Amtrak no. 9604, PRR nos. 9604, 9605, and 9600; more.

**Special Events:** Coe Rail: Easter Bunny Special, Hobo Halloween, Santa Train. Dinner Train: Special Charters, seats 232.

**Nearby Attractions/Accommodations:** Henry Ford Museum, Greenfield Village, Detroit/Windsor Casinos.

**Location/Directions:** I-96 to exit 162, north on Novi Rd., west on Maple Rd., north on Pontiac Trail, 100 yards, cross tracks, turn right into parking lot.

**Site Address:** 840 N. Pontiac Trail, Walled Lake, MI
**Mailing Address:** 840 N. Pontiac Trail, Walled Lake, MI 48390
**Telephone:** (248) 960-9440
**Fax:** (248) 960-9444
**E-mail:** info@michiganstarclipper.com
**Internet:** www.michiganstarclipper.com

CHARLES WILLER

**Description:** The Little River Railroad offers a 25-mile round trip steam excursion departing from White Pigeon Depot to Sturgis and return. Lasting about 2 hours and 45 minutes, the run goes through forest, farm, and city scenery.

**Schedule:** Subject to change. Call for current status.

**Admission/Fare:** Adults, $15; children 3-11, $8; families, $50 (two adults, three or more children). Short runs, adults, $7; children, $4. Group rates for 20 or more.

**Locomotives/Rolling Stock:** No. 110, 1911 Baldwin 4-6-2, former Little River Railroad–the smallest standard gauge Pacific locomotive ever built; combination car no. 2594, former Chicago & Alton; *Hiawatha* coaches, former Milwaukee Road; open-air cars; World War II troop car; cabooses, former Baltimore & Ohio.

**Nearby Attractions/Accommodations:** Shipshewana Auction, Dutchman Essenhaus–Amish cooking, Kalamazoo Air Museum.

**Location/Directions:** Indiana Toll Road, exit 107, north on Indiana 13 to U.S. 12, east to traffic light in White Pigeon. Go south and follow signs. Call or write for brochure.

**Site Address:** 413 Elkhart St., White Pigeon, MI
**Mailing Address:** 13187 State Route 120, Middlebury, IN 46540
**Telephone:** (219) 825-9182
**Internet:** //2mm.com/info/rr/

# MINNESOTA & WESTERN RAILROAD
*Train ride, display*
*Standard and 12" gauge*

DONALD B. LIND

**Description:** Train ride, section car only at this date, ½ mile on standard gauge track. Twelve-inch gauge 4-4-0 is being rebuilt, will run on 1000 feet of track.

**Schedule:** Memorial Day through Labor Day: Mondays through Fridays, 10 a.m. to 5 p.m.; Sundays, 12 to 5 p.m.

**Admission/Fare:** Adults, $5; senior citizens, $4.

**Locomotives/Rolling Stock:** Ex-M&StL 2-8-0 no. 471, Baldwin 1910; ex-Coronet Phosphate Mine (Florida) 2-6-2T no. 5, H.K. Porter 1911. Four open-platform passenger cars: ex-DSS&A no. D977, 1888; ex-WC no. W331, 1885; ex-MSt.P&SSM no. 1925, 1887; ex-WC no. 965/no. 56, 1899. Many other freight and passenger cars.

**Special Events:** Eighth Annual Railroad Days, South Haven, last Saturday in July.

**Nearby Attractions/Accommodations:** Thayer Hotel 1895, golf courses, museum, restaurant, campground, heart of lake country, scenic drive.

**Location/Directions:** From junction of I-454 and Highway 55 go 35 miles west on 55. Or take I-94 to Monticello exit, then south on Highway 25 for 5 miles, then west on Highway 37 for 9 miles to Highway 55, then 3 miles west to milepost 47.8 on ex-Soo Line/Canadian Pacific main line.

*Coupon available, see coupon section.

**Site Address:** 8619 State Hwy. 55 NW, Annandale, MN
**Mailing Address:** 8619 State Hwy. 55 NW, Annandale, MN 55302-2445
**Telephone:** (320) 274-3733

**Description:** Ironworld Discovery Center, perched on the edge of the Glen open-pit iron mine, showcases the iron range's rich industrial, cultural and ethnic history. Included in the Ironworld experience is a 2.5-mile rail trip along the edge of Glen Mine.

**Schedule:** Daily, mid-June through early September, 9:30 a.m. to 5 p.m. Extended hours for special events.

**Admission/Fare:** Adults, $8; seniors, $7; students (7-17), $6; 6 and under, free. Add $1 for special events.

**Locomotives/Rolling Stock:** Two 16-ton electric trolleys; 45-ton diesel electric switching locomotive; caboose; boxcar, three observation cars; miscellaneous railroad repair equipment.

**Special Events:** Polkafest, June; European Holiday Festival Finlandia and Scandinavian Holiday, July; All Star Days, August. Call for more specific information.

**Nearby Attractions/Accommodations:** For more information, please contact the Iron Trail Convention and Visitor's Bureau at (800) 777-8497.

**Location/Directions:** Hwy. 169 west in Chisholm, Minnesota.

**Site Address:** Hwy. 169 West, Chisholm, MN
**Mailing Address:** PO Box 392, Chisholm, MN 55719
**Telephone:** (218) 254-7959 or (800) 372-6437
**Fax:** (218) 254-7972
**E-mail:** marketing@ironworld.com
**Internet:** www.ironworld.com

## END-O-LINE RAILROAD PARK
## AND MUSEUM
*Museum, display, layout*

**Description:** A working railroad yard including a rebuilt enginehouse on its original foundation, an original four-room depot, a water tower, an 1899 section-foreman's house, and an outhouse. The turntable, built in 1901 by the American Bridge Company and still operable, is the only one left in Minnesota on its original site. A general store and one-room schoolhouse can also be seen. A replica of the coal bunker is used as a picnic shelter and gift shop. The buildings contain various exhibits and displays of railroad artifacts, photographs, memorabilia, and equipment. The freight room in the depot has an HO scale model train layout of the railroad yards in Currie, complete with steam engine sound effects, authentic structures, and local countryside. A bicycle/pedestrian paved pathway connects the railroad park to Lake Shetek State Park (6 miles round trip).

**Schedule:** Memorial Day through Labor Day: Mondays through Fridays, 10 a.m. to 12 noon and 1 to 5 p.m.; weekends, 1 to 5 p.m. Last tour 4 p.m.

**Admission/Fare:** Adults, $3; students, $2; household, $10.

**Locomotives/Rolling Stock:** Georgia Northern steam engine no. 102; Grand Trunk Western caboose; Brookville diesel switcher, more.

**Nearby Attractions/Accommodations:** Lake Shetek State Park, Laura Ingalls Wilder Museum, Pipestone National Monument, campgrounds.

**Location/Directions:** Highway 30 to Currie, go ¾ mile north on County Road 38.

**Site Address:** 440 N. Main St., Currie, MN
**Mailing Address:** 440 N. Mill St., Currie, MN 56123
**Telephone:** (507) 763-3708
**E-mail:** louise@endoline.com
**Internet:** www.endoline.com

# THE OLD DEPOT RAILROAD MUSEUM
*Museum*

**Description:** A former Great Northern depot built in 1913 is filled with railroad memorabilia and pictures. This 33 x 100-foot country depot has two waiting rooms, an agent's office, and a large freight room, as well as a full basement. Authentic recorded sounds of steam locomotives and the clicking of the telegraph key create the realistic feel of an old small-town depot. Items displayed include lanterns, telegraph equipment, semaphores, and other signals; section crew cars, a hand pump car, and a velocipede; tools and oil cans; depot and crossing signs; buttons, badges, service pins, and caps; a large date-nail collection; and many baggage carts. Also included are children's toy trains, an HO scale model railroad, and many railroad advertising items. Interpretation of the items is provided. Static ½ scale train on display.

**Schedule:** Memorial Day through October 1: daily, 10 a.m. to 4:30 p.m.

**Admission/Fare:** Adults, $2.50; children under age 12, $1.

**Special Events:** Red Rooster Day, Labor Day.

**Nearby Attractions/Accommodations:** Six other museums along Highway 12.

**Locomotives/Rolling Stock:** Caboose; two boxcars.

**Location/Directions:** Fifty miles west of Minneapolis on U.S. Highway 12. Fourteen miles north of Hutchinson on State Highway 15.

**Site Address:** 651 W. Highway 12, Dassel, MN
**Mailing Address:** PO Box 99, Dassel, MN 55325
**Telephone:** (320) 275-3876
**Fax:** (320) 275-3933

# LAKE SUPERIOR & MISSISSIPPI RAILROAD
*Train ride*
*Standard gauge*

DAVE SCHAUER

**Description:** The train ride is 6 miles along the St. Louis River on a historical railroad right-of-way (1870).

**Schedule:** Weekends, 10:30 a.m. and 1:30 p.m.

**Admission/Fare:** Adults, $8; seniors, $7; children, $6.

**Locomotives/Rolling Stock:** GE center-cab 50-ton; ACF coach 1914; Pullman coach 1912; flatcar 1928.

**Nearby Attractions/Accommodations:** Duluth Zoo is across the street.

**Location/Directions:** Go west on Grand Ave. to Fremont St.

  TRAIN   Radio frequency: 160.380

**Site Address:** 6930 Fremont St., Duluth, MN
**Mailing Address:** PO Box 16211, Duluth, MN 55816-0211
**Telephone:** (218) 624-7549
**Fax:** (218) 728-6303
**Internet:** www.lsmrr.org

# LAKE SUPERIOR RAILROAD MUSEUM
*Train ride, dinner train, museum, display, layout*
*Standard gauge, narrow gauge, HO*

BRUCE OJARD PHOTOGRAPHY

**Description:** The Lake Superior Railroad Museum has one of the largest and most diverse collections of railroad artifacts, including the Great Northern's famous "William Crooks" locomotive and cars of 1861; Northern Pacific Railway no. 1, The "Minnetonka" built in 1870; the Soo line's first passenger diesel, FP7 no. 2500A; Duluth, Missabe & Iron Range 2-8-8-4 no. 227, displayed with revolving drive wheels and recorded sound; an 1887 steam rotary snowplow; other steam, diesel, and electric engines; a Railway Post Office car; a dining-car china exhibit; freight cars; work equipment; an operating electric single-truck streetcar; and much railroadiana.

**Schedule:** Museum–year round. Train/trolley–Memorial Day weekend through Labor Day weekend. Hours: Memorial Day to Mid-October, 9:30 a.m. to 6 p.m. Mid-October to Memorial Day, 10 a.m. to 5 p.m. Monday through Saturday and 1 p.m. to 5 p.m. Sunday.

**Admission/Fare:** Combination tickets (museum and train), $6 to $20.

**Special Events:** Steam train weekends.

**Nearby Attractions/Accommodations:** Downtown Duluth, Canal Park, Duluth waterfront; Bayfront Park.

**Location/Directions:** I-35 exit downtown Duluth/Michigan St.

**Site Address:** 506 W. Michigan St., Duluth, MN
**Mailing Address:** 506 W. Michigan St., Duluth, MN 55802
**Telephone:** (218) 733-7590
**Fax:** (218) 733-7596
**E-mail:** museum@lsrm.
**Internet:** www.lsrm.org

**Minnesota, Duluth**

## NORTH SHORE SCENIC RAILROAD
*Train ride, dinner train*
*Standard gauge*

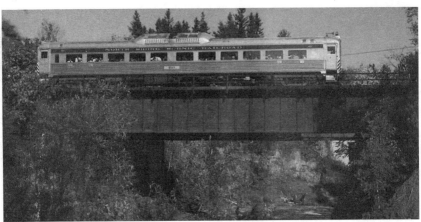

TIM SCHANDEL

**Description:** Formerly the Duluth Missabe & Iron Range Railway's Lake Front Line, this railroad's 26 miles of track run between the depot in downtown Duluth, along the Lake Superior waterfront, and through the residential areas and scenic woodlands of northeastern Minnesota to the Two Harbors Depot, adjacent to DM&IR's active taconite yard and ship-loading facility. The line offers 1½-, 2½-, and 6-hour round trips with departures from Duluth.

**Schedule:** To Lester River–Memorial Day to Labor Day, Sunday through Thursday, 12:30 and 3 p.m.; Friday and Saturday, 10 a.m., 12:30 and 3 p.m. Pizza train–Wednesday through Saturday, 6:30 p.m. Two Harbors–Friday and Saturday, 10:30 a.m. Reduced schedule, Labor Day to mid-October.

**Admission/Fare:** Lester River–adults, $9.50; children, $5. Pizza train–adults, $16.50; children, $11.50. Two Harbors–adults, $18; children, $8.

**Locomotives/Rolling Stock:** DM&IR SD18 no. 193; GN SD45 no. 400; GN NW5 no. 192; Soo Line FP7 no. 2500; DM&IR and GN coaches; more.

**Special Events:** Steam excursions, dinner trains, murder mystery train, beer tasting train.

**Location/Directions:** Duluth–Duluth Depot, Michigan St., downtown.

Radio frequency: 160.920

**Site Address:** 506 W. Michigan St., Duluth, MN
**Mailing Address:** 506 W. Michigan St., Duluth, MN 55802
**Telephone:** (218) 722-1273 and (800) 423-1273
**Fax:** (218) 733-7596
**E-mail:** museum@lsrm.org
**Internet:** www.lsrm.org

# MINNESOTA TRANSPORTATION MUSEUM
# EXCELSIOR STREETCAR LINE
*Museum, streetcar*
*Standard gauge*

LOUIS HOFFMAN

**Description:** Ride on a historic streetcar, approximately ½ mile, including a tour of a restoration facility.

**Schedule:** Memorial Day weekend through September: Thursdays, 3 to 6 p.m.; Saturdays, 10 a.m. to 4 p.m.; Sundays, 1 to 4 p.m.

**Admission/Fare:** $1; 4 and under, free.

**Locomotives/Rolling Stock:** Streetcar.

**Special Events:** Fourth of July, Apple Day.

**Nearby Attractions/Accommodations:** Steamboat Minnehaha

**Location/Directions:** West Highway 7, County Road 19 to Water St. Trolley stop at Lyman Park.

**Site Address:** 328 Lake St., Excelsior, MN
**Mailing Address:** 328 Lake St., Excelsior, MN 55331
**Telephone:** (952) 474-2115 and (800) 711-2591
**Fax:** 952-474-2192
**E-mail:** lmdminne78@9west.net
**Internet:** www.mtmuseum.org

**Minnesota, Minneapolis** MINNESOTA TRANSPORTATION MUSEUM
COMO-HARRIET STREETCAR LINE
*Train ride, museum*
*Standard gauge*

AARON ISAACS

**Description:** A 2-mile, 15-minute round trip on a restored portion of the former Twin City Rapid Transit Company's historic Como-Harriet route. Streetcars operate over a scenic line through a wooded area between Lakes Harriet and Calhoun. This is the last operating portion of the 523-mile Twin City Lines system, abandoned in 1954. The Linden Hills Station, a re-creation of the 1900 depot located at the site, houses changing historical displays about electric railways in Minnesota.

**Schedule:** May 18 through September 3: weekends, holidays, 12:30 p.m. to dusk. Mondays through Fridays, 6:30 p.m. to dusk. May before Memorial Day and September after Labor Day: weekends, 12:30 p.m. to dusk. October: weekends 12:30 to 5 p.m.

**Admission/Fare:** $1.50; children under age 4 are free. Chartered street-cars–$60 per half hour.

**Locomotives/Rolling Stock:** No. 265, 1915 Duluth St. Railway (TCRT Snelling Shops, St. Paul); no. 322, 1946 Twin City Lines PCC (St. Louis Car Co.); no. 1300, 1908 Twin City Lines (Snelling Shops).

**Nearby Attractions/Accommodations:** Lake Harriet Park.

**Location/Directions:** I-35W, 46th St. west to Lake Harriet Parkway, parkway to west shore at Linden Hills Station. Metro transit routes 6 and 28.

St. Paul      **Radio frequency: 161.355**

**Site Address:** 2330 W. 42nd St., Minneapolis, MN
**Mailing Address:** 193 E. Pennsylvania Ave., St. Paul, MN 55101-4319
**Telephone:** (651) 228-0263 and (800) 711-2591
**Internet:** www.mtmuseum.org

**MINNESOTA TRANSPORTATION MUSEUM**
**MINNEHAHA DEPOT**
*Museum, display*

ERIC MORTENSEN, MINNESOTA HISTORICAL SOCIETY

**Description:** Built in 1875, the Minnehaha Depot replaced an even smaller Milwaukee Road depot on the same site. Milwaukee Road agents quickly nicknamed the depot the "Princess" because of its intricate architectural details. Until Twin City Rapid Transit Company streetcars connected Minnehaha Falls Park to the city, as many as 13 passenger trains per day served the depot. It remained in service, primarily handling freight, for many years. Located at the south end of the Canadian Pacific South Minneapolis branch, operated by the Minnesota Commercial Railway, once a through route to the south, the depot sees occasional freight movements and often hosts visiting private cars. Visitors may tour the depot, which appears much as it did when in service as a typical suburban station. Exhibits include telegraphy demonstrations and historic photographs of the depot and its environs.

**Schedule:** Memorial Day weekend through Labor Day weekend: Sundays and holidays, 12:30 to 4:30 p.m.

**Admission/Fare:** Donations appreciated.

**Nearby Attractions/Accommodations:** Fort Snelling State Park, Historic Fort Snelling, Mall of America.

**Location/Directions:** In Minnehaha Falls Park just off State Highway 55 (Hiawatha Ave.). Metro transit routes 7 and 20.

St. Paul

**Site Address:** 4926 Minnehaha Ave., Minneapolis, MN
**Mailing Address:** 193 E. Pennsylvania Ave., St. Paul, MN 55101-4319
**Telephone:** (651) 228-0263 and (800) 711-2591
**E-mail:** corbin@plethora.net
**Internet:** www.mtmuseum.org

# NORTH STAR RAIL, INC.
## FRIENDS OF THE 261
*Train ride*
*Standard gauge*

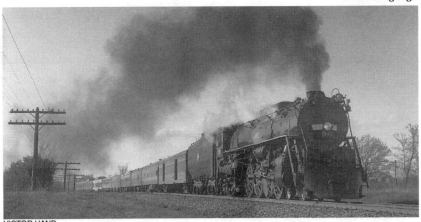

VICTOR HAND

**Description:** North Star Rail, Inc., operates a day-long steam-powered excursion over various Class 1 railroads.

**Schedule:** Varies with trip. Call or write for information.

**Admission/Fare:** Varies. Reservations recommended.

**Locomotives/Rolling Stock:** No. 261 1944 Alco 4-8-4, former Milwaukee Road class S3, leased to North Star Rail by the National Railroad Museum in Green Bay, Wisconsin.

**Site Address:** Minneapolis, MN
**Mailing Address:** 4322 Lakepoint Ct., Shoreview, MN 55126
**Telephone:** (651) 765-9812
**Fax:** (651) 490-1985 (call first)
**Internet:** www.261.com

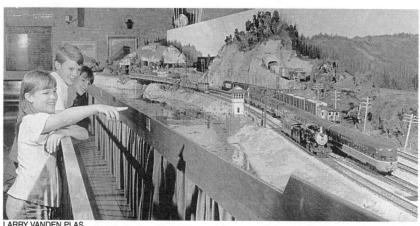

LARRY VANDEN PLAS

**Description:** Operating 3,000-square-foot O scale model of Minneapolis, St. Paul, and Mississippi River from the 1930s to the 1950s, plus one of the best displays of railroad art, maps, and photographs. Located in former Northern Pacific Como Shops, now Bandana Square.

**Schedule:** Year round, Sundays 12 noon to 5 p.m. Closed Mondays. Tuesdays, 11 a.m. to 3 p.m. and 6 to 8 p.m. Wednesdays and Thursdays, 11 a.m. to 3 p.m. Fridays, 11 a.m. to 7 p.m. Saturdays 10 a.m. to 6 p.m.

**Admission/Fare:** $2; under 5, free.

**Locomotives/Rolling Stock:** Full-size GTW 0-8-0 in front of building.

**Special Events:** Night Trains, Circus Train Day, Northern Pacific Day, Great Northern Day, Soo Line Day, etc. Check or request schedule.

**Nearby Attractions/Accommodations:** Restaurants, gift, hobby, book and art shops located in Bandana Square. Como Park (zoo, picnic, etc.) within a mile. The Mall of America, Gibbs Farm; more.

**Location/Directions:** In Bandana Square, on north side of Energy Park Dr., between Lexington and Sneling Avenues, one mile north of I-94.

**Site Address:** 1021 Bandana Blvd. East, St. Paul, MN
**Mailing Address:** 1021 Bandana Blvd. East, Suite 222, St. Paul, MN 55108
**Telephone:** (651) 647-9628
**E-mail:** tcmrm@tcmrm.org
**Internet:** www.tcmrm.org

**Description:** Museum with Great Northern steam locomotive and depot.

**Schedule:** Memorial Day through Labor Day: weekdays, 9 a.m. to 5 p.m.; weekends, 1 to 5 p.m.; September through May: weekdays, 9 a.m. to 5 p.m.

**Admission/Fare:** Free.

**Locomotives/Rolling Stock:** Great Northern 2523 P-2 class Baldwin.

**Nearby Attractions/Accommodations:** Schwanke Tractor and Car Museum.

**Location/Directions:** 610 N.E. Business 71, Willmar, Minnesota. Follow the signs at the north, south, and east edges of the city.

**Site Address:** 610 N.E. Highway 71, Willmar, MN
**Mailing Address:** 610 N.E. Highway 71, Willmar, MN 56201
**Telephone:** (320) 235-1881
**E-mail:** kandhist@wecnet.com

**Admission/Fare:** Adults and seniors, $1; under 12, $.50.

**Locomotives/Rolling Stock:** 1923 steam engine no. 841.

**Location/Directions:** Thirty-two miles north of Jackson, Mississippi. Exit 133 off I-55; Vaughan is one mile east off the exit.

**Site Address:** 10901 Vaughan Rd., #1, Vaughan, MS
**Mailing Address:** 10901 Vaughan Rd., #1, Vaughan, MS 39179
**Fax:** (662) 673-9864

**BELTON, GRANDVIEW & KANSAS CITY RAILROAD COMPANY**
*Train ride, museum*

GARY HANOLD

**Description:** Six-mile round trip aboard a NYC coach used in the movie *Biloxi Blues*. The train is pulled by a B&O GP9. Customized charter trips are available and encouraged. Static displays include two steam engines and numerous other rolling stock.

**Schedule:** May through October, weekends, 2 p.m.

**Admission/Fare:** $6.50 per person; 2 and under, free.

**Locomotives/Rolling Stock:** B&O GP9 no. 6142; Frisco 1918 Baldwin 2-10-0 no. 1632; Okmulgee no. 5 Alco 2-8-0; KCS observation lounge; ATSF instruction car; Wabash heavyweight and baggage car; NYC no. 4365 1920 coach; MoPac 1972 wide vision caboose; UP 1928 wood CA-1 caboose.

**Special Events:** Ice cream train, Fridays, 7 p.m. National Storyteller's Celebration, April. Pumpkin Patch Express, October. Children's Halloween trains on Halloween weekend. Specialty and discount days.

**Nearby Attractions/Accommodations:** Pres. Truman's farm home, Kansas City, Missouri, country club plaza shopping district, Westport entertainment area, KC Royals baseball, several switching yards, more.

**Location/Directions:** From 435 and Hwy. 71, take U.S. 71 south to Route Y. Follow Route Y through traffic light to Commercial St., turn right and go 4 blocks. Yards and depot are on your left.

        M

**Site Address:** 502 Walnut, Belton, MO
**Mailing Address:** 502 Walnut, Belton, MO 64012
**Telephone:** (816) 331-0630
**E-mail:** bgkcrr@aol.com
**Internet:** www.orgsites.com/mo/beltonrailroad

**BRANSON SCENIC RAILWAY**
*Train ride*
*Standard gauge*

**Description:** This railway operates a 40-mile, 1¾-hour round trip through the Ozark foothills over the former Missouri Pacific White River Route, now operated by the Missouri & North Arkansas Railroad. Most trips take passengers south into Arkansas, across Lake Taneycomo and two high trestles, and through two tunnels. The original 1906 Branson depot houses the railway's ticket office, waiting room, gift shop, and business offices.

**Schedule:** Excursions–Mid-March through mid-December: 9 and 11:30 a.m., 2 and 5 p.m. Dinner train–May through December: Saturdays 5 p.m.

**Admission/Fare:** Call 800-2TRAIN2 for fares.

**Locomotives/Rolling Stock:** No. 98 F9PH BSR no. 265; GP30M BSR, former B&O; "Silver Garden" dome car, former CBQ; "Silver Island" dome, former CBQ; "Silver Terrace" dome, former CBQ, "Silver Chef," former CBQ.

**Special Events:** Downtown see Plumb Nellie Days and Fiddler's Contest.

**Nearby Attractions/Accommodations:** Theme park, historic downtown, restaurants, flea market, crafts festivals, lake, campgrounds, lodging.

**Location/Directions:** Downtown Branson, ¾ mile east of U.S. 65.

**Site Address:** 206 E. Main St., Branson, MO
**Mailing Address:** PO Box 924, Branson, MO 65615
**Telephone:** (417) 334-6110 and (800) 2TRAIN2
**Fax:** (417) 336-3909
**Internet:** www.bransontrain.com

# SILVER DOLLAR CITY THEME PARK
*Train ride*
*Narrow gauge*

**Description:** The Silver Dollar Steam Train takes guests on a fun-filled 20-minute trip back to the 1880s on a tour through the splendid Ozark Mountains.

**Schedule:** April through December, departures every 30 minutes. Days of operation vary with operation of theme park.

**Admission/Fare:** Free with paid admission to theme park.

**Locomotives/Rolling Stock:** 1938 engine no. 13 Orenstein 2-4-0, Koppel, Germany; 1934 engine no. 43 Orenstein 2-4-0, Koppel, Germany; 1940 engine no. 76 2-4-0, Germany.

**Special Events:** Sing-Along Steam Train (caroling rides) during Old Time Christmas, November and December.

**Nearby Attractions/Accommodations:** Branson, Missouri.

**Location/Directions:** Highway 76, approximately 5 miles west of Branson.

**Site Address:** Silver Dollar City Theme Park, West Highway 76, Branson, MO
**Mailing Address:** 399 Indian Pt. Rd., Branson, MO 65616
**Telephone:** (800) 952-6626
**Internet:** www.silverdollarcity.com

# Guide to Tourist Railroads and Museums
## 2002 GUEST COUPONS
### Arranged alphabetically by state

**YUMA VALLEY RAILWAY**
With coupon: Adults $1 off; seniors $1 off;
children $1 off
Valid April 2002 through March 2003

**THE TRAIN PLACE**
With coupon: Buy any sandwich, get sandwich of
equal or lesser value free
Valid April 2002 through March 2003

**ROARING CAMP & BIG TREES
RAILROAD**
Regular price: Adults $15.50, children $10.50
With coupon: Adults $13.95, children $9.45
Valid April 2002 through March 2003
Maximum discount 6 persons per coupon

**SANTA CRUZ, BIG TREES & PACIFIC
RAILWAY**
Regular price: Adults, $17, seniors $17, children $12
With coupon: Adults, $16.30, seniors $16.30, children $10.80
Valid April 2002 through March 2003
Maximum discount 6 persons per coupon

**LOMITA RAILROAD MUSEUM**
Regular price: Adults $2, seniors $2
With coupon: Adults $1, seniors $1
Valid April 2002 through March 2003

**ELDORADO EXPRESS RAILROAD**
Regular price: Adults $2, seniors $2
With coupon: Adults $1, seniors $1
Valid April 2002 through March 2003
Maximum discount 1 person per coupon

**GOLDEN STATE MODEL RAILROAD
MUSEUM**
With coupon: Buy one admission get
equal price admission free
Valid April 2002 through March 2003

**SAN DIEGO MODEL RAILROAD
MUSEUM**
With coupon: Buy one admission get
equal price admission free
Valid April 2002 through March 2003
Maximum discount 1 person per coupon

**SAN DIEGO RAILROAD MUSEUM**
With coupon: Buy one admission get
equal price admission free
Valid April 2002 through March 2003
Maximum discount 1 person per coupon

**CRIPPLE CREEK AND VICTOR NARROW
GAUGE RAILROAD**
Regular price: Adults $9, seniors $8, children $5
With coupon: Adults $8, seniors $7, children $4
Valid April 2002 through March 2003
Maximum discount 4 persons per coupon

**OLD HUNDRED GOLD MINE TOUR**
Regular price: Adults $14.95, seniors $13.95, children $7.95
With coupon: Adults $13.95, seniors $12.95, children $6.95
Valid April 2002 through March 2003

**SHORE LINE TROLLEY MUSEUM**
Regular price: Adults $6, seniors $5, children $3
With coupon: Adults $5.50, seniors $4.50, children $2.50
Valid April 2002 through March 2003
Maximum discount $3 per coupon

| | |
|---|---|
| **THE TRAIN PLACE**<br>CAPITOLA, CA<br>GUIDE TO TOURIST RAILROADS AND MUSEUMS<br>2002 GUEST COUPON | **YUMA VALLEY RAILWAY**<br>YUMA, AZ<br>GUIDE TO TOURIST RAILROADS AND MUSEUMS<br>2002 GUEST COUPON |
| **SANTA CRUZ, BIG TREES & PACIFIC RAILWAY**<br>FELTON, CA<br>GUIDE TO TOURIST RAILROADS AND MUSEUMS<br>2002 GUEST COUPON | **ROARING CAMP & BIG TREES RAILROAD**<br>FELTON, CA<br>GUIDE TO TOURIST RAILROADS AND MUSEUMS<br>2002 GUEST COUPON |
| **ELDORADO EXPRESS RAILROAD**<br>LONG BEACH, CA<br>GUIDE TO TOURIST RAILROADS AND MUSEUMS<br>2002 GUEST COUPON | **LOMITA RAILROAD MUSEUM**<br>LOMITA, CA<br>GUIDE TO TOURIST RAILROADS AND MUSEUMS<br>2002 GUEST COUPON |
| **SAN DIEGO MODEL RAILROAD MUSEUM**<br>SAN DIEGO, CA<br>GUIDE TO TOURIST RAILROADS AND MUSEUMS<br>2002 GUEST COUPON | **GOLDEN STATE MODEL RAILROAD MUSEUM**<br>POINT RICHMOND, CA<br>GUIDE TO TOURIST RAILROADS AND MUSEUMS<br>2002 GUEST COUPON |
| **CRIPPLE CREEK AND VICTOR NARROW GAUGE RAILROAD**<br>CRIPPLE CREEK, CO<br>GUIDE TO TOURIST RAILROADS AND MUSEUMS<br>2002 GUEST COUPON | **SAN DIEGO RAILROAD MUSEUM**<br>SAN DIEGO, CA<br>GUIDE TO TOURIST RAILROADS AND MUSEUMS<br>2002 GUEST COUPON |
| **SHORE LINE TROLLEY MUSEUM**<br>EAST HAVEN, CT<br>GUIDE TO TOURIST RAILROADS AND MUSEUMS<br>2002 GUEST COUPON | **OLD HUNDRED GOLD MINE TOUR**<br>SILVERTON, CO<br>GUIDE TO TOURIST RAILROADS AND MUSEUMS<br>2002 GUEST COUPON |

# Guide to Tourist Railroads and Museums
## 2002 GUEST COUPONS
### Arranged alphabetically by state

**CONNECTICUT TROLLEY MUSEUM**
Regular price: Adults $6, seniors $5, children $3
**With coupon: Adults $5, seniors $4, children $2.50**
Valid April 2002 through March 2003
Maximum discount 2 adults and 4 children per coupon

**ESSEX STEAM TRAIN AND RIVERBOAT RIDE**
Regular price: Adults $18.50, children $9.50
**With coupon: Adults $16.50, children $8.50**
Valid April 2002 through March 2003

**FLORIDA GULF COAST RAILROAD MUSEUM, INC.**
Regular price: Adults $10, children $6
**With coupon: Adults $8, children $5**
Valid April 2002 through March 2003
Maximum discount 1 person per coupon

**KENNESAW CIVIL WAR MUSEUM**
**With coupon: Buy one admission get equal price admission free**
Valid April 2002 through March 2003

**ROUNDHOUSE RAILROAD MUSEUM**
**With coupon: Buy one admission get equal price admission free**
Valid April 2002 through March 2003

**NORTHERN PACIFIC DEPOT RAILROAD MUSEUM**
Regular price: Adults $2, seniors $1.50, children $1
**With coupon: Adults $1.50, seniors $1, children $.75**
Valid April 2002 through March 2003

**HISTORIC PULLMAN FOUNDATION**
**With coupon: Buy one admission get equal price admission free**
Valid April 2002 through March 2003
Maximum discount 2 persons per coupon

**ILLINOIS RAILWAY MUSEUM**
Regular price: Adults $8, seniors $6, children $6
**With coupon: Adults $7, seniors $5, children $5**
Valid April 2002 through March 2003

**VALLEY VIEW MODEL RAILROAD**
Regular price: Adults $5, seniors $4, children $2.50
**With coupon: Adults $4, seniors $3, children $2**
Valid April 2002 through March 2003

**HESSTON STEAM MUSEUM**
**With coupon: Buy one admission get equal price admission free**
Memorial Day through Labor Day, 2002
Maximum discount 4 persons per coupon

**TRAINLAND U.S.A.**
**With coupon: Buy one admission get equal price admission free**
Valid April 2002 through March 2003
Maximum discount 4 persons per coupon

**RAILSWEST RAILROAD MUSEUM**
Regular price: Adults $4, children $1.50
**With coupon: Adults $3.50, children $1**
Valid April 2002 through March 2003

**ESSEX STEAM TRAIN AND
RIVERBOAT RIDE**
ESSEX, CT
GUIDE TO TOURIST RAILROADS AND MUSEUMS
2002 GUEST COUPON

**CONNECTICUT TROLLEY MUSEUM**
EAST WINDSOR, CT
GUIDE TO TOURIST RAILROADS AND MUSEUMS
2002 GUEST COUPON

**KENNESAW CIVIL WAR MUSEUM**
KENNESAW, GA
GUIDE TO TOURIST RAILROADS AND MUSEUMS
2002 GUEST COUPON

**FLORIDA GULF COAST
RAILROAD MUSEUM, INC.**
PARRISH, FL
GUIDE TO TOURIST RAILROADS AND MUSEUMS
2002 GUEST COUPON

**NORTHERN PACIFIC
DEPOT RAILROAD MUSEUM**
WALLACE, ID
GUIDE TO TOURIST RAILROADS AND MUSEUMS
2002 GUEST COUPON

**ROUNDHOUSE RAILROAD MUSEUM**
SAVANNAH, GA
GUIDE TO TOURIST RAILROADS AND MUSEUMS
2002 GUEST COUPON

**ILLINOIS RAILWAY MUSEUM**
UNION, IL
GUIDE TO TOURIST RAILROADS AND MUSEUMS
2002 GUEST COUPON

**HISTORIC PULLMAN FOUNDATION**
CHICAGO, IL
GUIDE TO TOURIST RAILROADS AND MUSEUMS
2002 GUEST COUPON

**HESSTON STEAM MUSEUM**
HESSTON, IN
GUIDE TO TOURIST RAILROADS AND MUSEUMS
2002 GUEST COUPON

**VALLEY VIEW MODEL RAILROAD**
UNION, IL
GUIDE TO TOURIST RAILROADS AND MUSEUMS
2002 GUEST COUPON

**RAILSWEST RAILROAD MUSEUM**
COUNCIL BLUFFS, IA
GUIDE TO TOURIST RAILROADS AND MUSEUMS
2002 GUEST COUPON

**TRAINLAND U.S.A.**
COLFAX, IA
GUIDE TO TOURIST RAILROADS AND MUSEUMS
2002 GUEST COUPON

## Guide to Tourist Railroads and Museums
## 2002 GUEST COUPONS
## Arranged alphabetically by state

### GREAT PLAINS TRANSPORTATION MUSEUM, INC.
**With coupon: Buy one admission get equal price admission free**
Valid April 2002 through March 2003
Maximum discount 1 person per coupon

### KENTUCKY RAILWAY MUSEUM
Regular price: Adults $12.50/$15, children $8
**With coupon: Adults $11.50/$14, children $7**
Valid April 2002 through March 2003
Maximum discount 4 persons per coupon

### SOUTHERN FOREST HERITAGE MUSEUM
Regular price: Adults $5, seniors $5, children $2.50
**With coupon: Adults $4.25, seniors $4.25, children $2**
Valid April 2002 through March 2003

### SANDY RIVER & RANGELEY LAKES RAILROAD
Regular price: Adults $3, seniors $3
**With coupon: Adults and seniors are free**
Valid April 2002 through March 2003
Maximum discount 1 person per coupon

### B&O RAILROAD MUSEUM
Regular price: Adults $8, seniors $7
**With coupon: Adults $7, seniors $6**
Valid April 2002 through March 2003

### BALTIMORE STREETCAR MUSEUM
**With coupon: Buy one admission get equal price admission free**
Valid April 2002 through March 2003
Maximum discount 4 persons per coupon

### BRUNSWICK RAILROAD MUSEUM
**With coupon: Buy one admission get equal price admission free**
Valid April 2002 through March 2003

### NATIONAL CAPITAL TROLLEY MUSEUM
**With coupon: Buy one admission get equal price admission free**
Valid April 2002 through March 2003
Maximum discount 2 persons per coupon

### OLD COLONY AND FALL RIVER RAILROAD MUSEUM
Regular price: Adults $2, seniors $1.50, children $1
**With coupon: Adults $1, seniors $.75, children $.50**
Valid April 2002 through March 2003

### SHELBURNE FALLS TROLLEY MUSEUM
Regular price: Adults $2, seniors $2
**With coupon: Adults $1, seniors, free**
Valid April 2002 through March 2003

### WENHAM MUSEUM
Regular price: Adults $5, seniors $4, children $3
**With coupon: Adults $4, seniors $3, children $2**
Valid April 2002 through March 2003

### JUNCTION VALLEY RAILRAOD
Regular price: Adults $5, seniors $4.75, children $4.25
**With coupon: Adults $4.50, seniors $4.25, children $3.80**
Valid April 2002 through March 2003

| | |
|---|---|
| **KENTUCKY RAILWAY MUSEUM**<br>NEW HAVEN, KY<br>GUIDE TO TOURIST RAILROADS AND MUSEUMS<br>2002 GUEST COUPON | **GREAT PLAINS TRANSPORTATION**<br>**MUSEUM, INC.**<br>WICHITA, KS<br>GUIDE TO TOURIST RAILROADS AND MUSEUMS<br>2002 GUEST COUPON |
| **SANDY RIVER &**<br>**RANGELEY LAKES RAILROAD**<br>PHILLIPS, ME<br>GUIDE TO TOURIST RAILROADS AND MUSEUMS<br>2002 GUEST COUPON | **SOUTHERN FOREST HERITAGE**<br>**MUSEUM**<br>LONG LEAF, LA<br>GUIDE TO TOURIST RAILROADS AND MUSEUMS<br>2002 GUEST COUPON |
| **BALTIMORE STREETCAR MUSEUM**<br>BALTIMORE, MD<br>GUIDE TO TOURIST RAILROADS AND MUSEUMS<br>2002 GUEST COUPON | **B&O RAILROAD MUSEUM**<br>BALTIMORE, MD<br>GUIDE TO TOURIST RAILROADS AND MUSEUMS<br>2002 GUEST COUPON |
| **NATIONAL CAPITAL TROLLEY**<br>**MUSEUM**<br>COLESVILLE, MD<br>GUIDE TO TOURIST RAILROADS AND MUSEUMS<br>2002 GUEST COUPON | **BRUNSWICK RAILROAD MUSEUM**<br>BRUNSWICK, MD<br>GUIDE TO TOURIST RAILROADS AND MUSEUMS<br>2002 GUEST COUPON |
| **SHELBURNE FALLS TROLLEY MUSEUM**<br>SHELBURNE FALLS, MA<br>GUIDE TO TOURIST RAILROADS AND MUSEUMS<br>2002 GUEST COUPON | **OLD COLONY AND FALL RIVER**<br>**RAILROAD MUSEUM**<br>FALL RIVER, MA<br>GUIDE TO TOURIST RAILROADS AND MUSEUMS<br>2002 GUEST COUPON |
| **JUNCTION VALLEY RAILROAD**<br>BRIDGEPORT, MI<br>GUIDE TO TOURIST RAILROADS AND MUSEUMS<br>2002 GUEST COUPON | **WENHAM MUSEUM**<br>WENHAM, MA<br>GUIDE TO TOURIST RAILROADS AND MUSEUMS<br>2002 GUEST COUPON |

# Guide to Tourist Railroads and Museums
## 2002 GUEST COUPONS
### Arranged alphabetically by state

## MICHIGAN AUSABLE VALLEY RAILROAD

Regular price: Adults $3, seniors $3, children $3
**With coupon: Adults $2, seniors $2, children $2**
Valid April 2002 through March 2003

## HUCKLEBERRY RAILROAD

**With coupon: Buy one admission get equal price admission free**
Valid April 2002 through March 2003
Maximum discount 1 person per coupon

## IRON MOUNTAIN IRON MINE

Regular price: Adults $7, seniors, $6, children $6
**With coupon: Adults $6, seniors $5, children $5**
Valid April 2002 through March 2003

## TOONERVILLE TROLLEY TRAIN AND BOAT TOURS

**With coupon: 10% off any tour**
Valid April 2002 through March 2003
Maximum discount 6 persons per coupon
(Not valid in connection with other discounts)

## MINNESOTA & WESTERN RAILROAD

Regular price: Adults $5, seniors $4, children $2
**With coupon: Adults $4, seniors $3, children $1**
Valid April 2002 through March 2003
Maximum discount 5 persons per coupon

## WABASH FRISCO & PACIFIC STEAM RAILWAY

Regular price: Adults $2
**With coupon: Adults $1.50**
Valid April 2002 through March 2003
Maximum discount 6 persons per coupon

## PATEE HOUSE MUSEUM

**With coupon: Buy one admission get equal price admission free**
Valid April 2002 through March 2003

## FREMONT & ELKHORN VALLEY RAILROAD

Regular price: Adults $12, seniors $12, children $7
**With coupon: Adults $10.80, seniors $10.80, children $6**
Valid April 2002 through March 2003

## HARTMANN MODEL RAILROAD, LTD.

Regular price: Adults $6, seniors $5, children $4
**With coupon: Adults $5, seniors $4, children $3**
Valid April 2002 through March 2003

## BLACK RIVER & WESTERN RAILROAD

**With coupon: Buy one admission get equal price admission free**
Valid April 2002 through March 2003

## CUMBRES & TOLTEC SCENIC RAILROAD

**With coupon: 10% discount**
Valid April 2002 through March 2003

## SANTA FE SOUTHERN RAILWAY

Regular price: Adults $32/$45, seniors $27/$40, children $18/$32
**With coupon: Adults $28.80/$40.50, seniors $24.30/$36, children $16.20/$28.80**
Valid April 2002 through March 2003
Maximum discount 8 persons per coupon

**HUCKLEBERRY RAILROAD**
FLINT, MI
GUIDE TO TOURIST RAILROADS AND MUSEUMS
2002 GUEST COUPON

**MICHIGAN AUSABLE VALLEY RAILROAD**
FAIRVIEW, MI
GUIDE TO TOURIST RAILROADS AND MUSEUMS
2002 GUEST COUPON

**TOONERVILLE TROLLEY TRAIN AND BOAT TOURS**
SOO JUNCTION, MI
GUIDE TO TOURIST RAILROADS AND MUSEUMS
2002 GUEST COUPON

**IRON MOUNTAIN IRON MINE**
IRON MOUNTAIN, MI
GUIDE TO TOURIST RAILROADS AND MUSEUMS
2002 GUEST COUPON

**WABASH FRISCO & PACIFIC STEAM RAILWAY**
GLENCOE , MO
GUIDE TO TOURIST RAILROADS AND MUSEUMS
2002 GUEST COUPON

**MINNESOTA & WESTERN RAILROAD**
ANNANDALE, MN
GUIDE TO TOURIST RAILROADS AND MUSEUMS
2002 GUEST COUPON

**FREMONT & ELKHORN VALLEY RAILROAD**
FREMONT, NE
GUIDE TO TOURIST RAILROADS AND MUSEUMS
2002 GUEST COUPON

**PATEE HOUSE MUSEUM**
ST. JOSEPH, MO
GUIDE TO TOURIST RAILROADS AND MUSEUMS
2002 GUEST COUPON

**BLACK RIVER & WESTERN RAILROAD**
FLEMINGTON, NJ
GUIDE TO TOURIST RAILROADS AND MUSEUMS
2002 GUEST COUPON

**HARTMANN MODEL RAILROAD, LTD.**
INTERVALE, NH
GUIDE TO TOURIST RAILROADS AND MUSEUMS
2002 GUEST COUPON

**SANTA FE SOUTHERN RAILWAY**
SANTA FE, NM
GUIDE TO TOURIST RAILROADS AND MUSEUMS
2002 GUEST COUPON

**CUMBRES & TOLTEC SCENIC RAILROAD**
CHAMA, NM
GUIDE TO TOURIST RAILROADS AND MUSEUMS
2002 GUEST COUPON

# Guide to Tourist Railroads and Museums
## 2002 GUEST COUPONS
### Arranged alphabetically by state

**TROLLEY MUSEUM OF NEW YORK**
Regular price: Adults $3, seniors $2, children $2
**With coupon: Adults $1.50, seniors $1, children $1**
Valid April 2002 through March 2003

**MEDINA RAILROAD MUSEUM**
Regular price: Adults $5, seniors $4, children $3
**With coupon: Adults $4, seniors $3, children $2**
Valid April 2002 through March 2003

**ADIRONDACK SCENIC RAILROAD**
**With coupon: Buy one admission get
equal price admission free**
Valid April 2002 through March 2003

**CHARLOTTE TROLLEY, INC.**
**With coupon: Buy one admission get
equal price admission free**
Valid April 2002 through March 2003

**NORTH CAROLINA
TRANSPORTATION MUSEUM**
Regular price: Adults $5, seniors $4, children $4
**With coupon: Adults $4, seniors $3, children $3**
Valid April 2002 through March 2003
Maximum discount 4 persons per coupon

**FORT LINCOLN TROLLEY**
Regular price: Adults $5, seniors $5
**With coupon: Adults $4, seniors $4**
Valid April 2002 through March 2003

**BUCKEYE CENTRAL SCENIC
RAILROAD**
Regular price: Adults $7, seniors $7, children $5
**With coupon: Adults $6, seniors $6, children $4**
Valid April 2002 through March 2003
Maximum discount $6 per coupon

**TRAIN-O-RAMA**
Regular price: Adults $5, seniors $4, children $3
**With coupon: Adults $4, seniors $3, children $2**
Valid April 2002 through March 2003
Maximum discount 6 persons per coupon

**HARMAR STATION**
Regular price: Adults $5, seniors $4
**With coupon: Adults $4, children $3**
Valid April 2002 through March 2003

**HOCKING VALLEY SCENIC RAILWAY**
**With coupon: $1 off admission**
Valid April 2002 through March 2003
Maximum discount 2 coupons per family

**WASHINGTON PARK & ZOO RAILWAY**
Regular price: Adults $2.75, seniors $2, children $2
**With coupon: Adults $2.20, seniors $1.60, children $1.60**
Valid April 2002 through March 2003

**CROOKED RIVER DINNER TRAIN**
Regular price: Adults $71
**With coupon: Adults $66**
Valid April 2002 through March 2003

**MEDINA RAILROAD MUSEUM**
MEDINA, NY
GUIDE TO TOURIST RAILROADS AND MUSEUMS
2002 GUEST COUPON

**TROLLEY MUSEUM OF NEW YORK**
KINGSTON, NY
GUIDE TO TOURIST RAILROADS AND MUSEUMS
2002 GUEST COUPON

**CHARLOTTE TROLLEY, INC.**
CHARLOTTE, NC
GUIDE TO TOURIST RAILROADS AND MUSEUMS
2002 GUEST COUPON

**ADIRONDACK SCENIC RAILROAD**
OLD FORGE, NY
GUIDE TO TOURIST RAILROADS AND MUSEUMS
2002 GUEST COUPON

**FORT LINCOLN TROLLEY**
MANDAN, ND
GUIDE TO TOURIST RAILROADS AND MUSEUMS
2002 GUEST COUPON

**NORTH CAROLINA
TRANSPORTATION MUSEUM**
SPENCER, NC
GUIDE TO TOURIST RAILROADS AND MUSEUMS
2002 GUEST COUPON

**TRAIN-O-RAMA**
MARBLEHEAD, OH
GUIDE TO TOURIST RAILROADS AND MUSEUMS
2002 GUEST COUPON

**BUCKEYE CENTRAL SCENIC RAILROAD**
HEBRON, OH
GUIDE TO TOURIST RAILROADS AND MUSEUMS
2002 GUEST COUPON

**HOCKING VALLEY SCENIC RAILWAY**
NELSONVILLE, OH
GUIDE TO TOURIST RAILROADS AND MUSEUMS
2002 GUEST COUPON

**HARMAR STATION**
MARIETTA, OH
GUIDE TO TOURIST RAILROADS AND MUSEUMS
2002 GUEST COUPON

**CROOKED RIVER DINNER TRAIN**
REDMOND, OR
GUIDE TO TOURIST RAILROADS AND MUSEUMS
2002 GUEST COUPON

**WASHINGTON PARK & ZOO RAILWAY**
PORTLAND, OR
GUIDE TO TOURIST RAILROADS AND MUSEUMS
2002 GUEST COUPON

# Guide to Tourist Railroads and Museums
## 2002 GUEST COUPONS
### Arranged alphabetically by state

### STOURBRIDGE LINE RAIL EXCURSIONS
**With coupon: Buy one admission get equal price admission free**
Valid April 2002 through March 2003
Excludes tickets over $20
Maximum discount 2 persons per coupon

### WANAMAKER, KEMPTON & SOUTHERN, INC.
Regular price: Adults $6, seniors $6, children $3
**With coupon: Adults $5, seniors $5, children $2**
Valid April 2002 through March 2003

### NEW HOPE & IVYLAND RAILROAD
Regular price: Adults $9.95, seniors $8.95, children $6.95
**With coupon: Adults $8.95, seniors $7.95, children $5.95**
Valid April 2002 through March 2003

### ROCKHILL TROLLEY MUSEUM
Regular price: Adults $4.95, children $1.95
**With coupon: Adults $4.50, children $1.50**
Valid April 2002 through March 2003
Maximum discount 1 person per coupon

### ROADSIDE AMERICA
**With coupon: Buy one admission get equal price admission free**
Valid April 2002 through March 2003
Group rates excluded

### CHOO CHOO BARN
Regular price: Adults $5, seniors $5, children $3
**With coupon: Adults $3.75, seniors $3.75, children $2.25**
Valid April 2002 through March 2003

### PENNSYLVANIA TROLLEY MUSEUM
**With coupon: Buy one admission get equal price admission free**
Valid April 2002 through March 2003
Maximum discount 2 persons per coupon

### TIOGA CENTRAL RAILROAD
Regular price: Adults $10, seniors $9, children $5
**With coupon: Adults $9, seniors $8, children $4**
Valid April 2002 through March 2003

### THOMAS T. TABER MUSEUM OF THE WYCOMING COUNTY HISTORICAL SOCIETY
**With coupon: Buy one admission get equal price admission free**
Valid April 2002 through March 2003

### CHATTANOOGA CHOO-CHOO
**With coupon: Buy one admission get equal price admission free.**
Valid April 2002 through March 2003
Maximum discount $2 per coupon

### TENNESSEE VALLEY RAILROAD MUSEUM
**With coupon: $1 off regular adult price, $.50 off regular children's price**
Valid April 2002 through March 2003
Maximum discount 2 persons per coupon

### CASEY JONES MUSEUM AND TRAIN STORE
Regular price: Adults $4, seniors $3.50
**With coupon: Adults $3, seniors $2.50**
Valid April 2002 through March 2003

**WANAMAKER, KEMPTON & SOUTHERN, INC.**
KEMPTON, PA
GUIDE TO TOURIST RAILROADS AND MUSEUMS
2002 GUEST COUPON

**STOURBRIDGE LINE RAIL EXCURSIONS**
HONESDALE, PA
GUIDE TO TOURIST RAILROADS AND MUSEUMS
2002 GUEST COUPON

**ROCKHILL TROLLEY MUSEUM**
ROCKHILL FURNACE, PA
GUIDE TO TOURIST RAILROADS AND MUSEUMS
2002 GUEST COUPON

**NEW HOPE & IVYLAND RAILROAD**
NEW HOPE, PA
GUIDE TO TOURIST RAILROADS AND MUSEUMS
2002 GUEST COUPON

**CHOO CHOO BARN**
STRASBURG, PA
GUIDE TO TOURIST RAILROADS AND MUSEUMS
2002 GUEST COUPON

**ROADSIDE AMERICA**
SHARTLESVILLE, PA
GUIDE TO TOURIST RAILROADS AND MUSEUMS
2002 GUEST COUPON

**TIOGA CENTRAL RAILROAD**
WELLSBORO, PA
GUIDE TO TOURIST RAILROADS AND MUSEUMS
2002 GUEST COUPON

**PENNSYLVANIA TROLLEY MUSEUM**
WASHINGTON, PA
GUIDE TO TOURIST RAILROADS AND MUSEUMS
2002 GUEST COUPON

**CHATTANOOGA CHOO-CHOO**
CHATTANOOGA, TN
GUIDE TO TOURIST RAILROADS AND MUSEUMS
2002 GUEST COUPON

**THOMAS T. TABER MUSEUM OF THE WYCOMING COUNTY HISTORICAL SOCIETY**
WILLIAMSPORT, PA
GUIDE TO TOURIST RAILROADS AND MUSEUMS
2002 GUEST COUPON

**CASEY JONES MUSEUM AND TRAIN STORE**
JACKSON, TN
GUIDE TO TOURIST RAILROADS AND MUSEUMS
2002 GUEST COUPON

**TENNESSEE VALLEY RAILROAD MUSEUM**
CHATTANOOGA, TN
GUIDE TO TOURIST RAILROADS AND MUSEUMS
2002 GUEST COUPON

# Guide to Tourist Railroads and Museums
## 2002 GUEST COUPONS
### Arranged alphabetically by state

**AGE OF STEAM RAILROAD MUSEUM**
**With coupon: Buy one admission get**
**equal price admission free**
Valid April 2002 through March 2003
Maximum discount 2 persons per coupon

**CENTER FOR TRANSPORTATION**
Regular price: Adults $5, seniors $4.50, children $2.50
**With coupon: Adults $4, seniors $3.50, children $1.50**
Valid April 2002 through March 2003

**RAILROAD AND HERITAGE MUSEUM**
**With coupon: Buy one admission get**
**equal price admission free**
Valid April 2002 through March 2003
Maximum discount 2 persons per coupon

**HEBER VALLEY RAILROAD**
Regular price: Adults $14/$21, senior$11/$18, children $8/$12
**With coupon: Adults $11/$18, seniors $8/$15, children $5/$9**
Valid April 2002 through March 2003

**OGDEN UNION STATION**
**With coupon: Buy one admission get**
**equal price admission free**
Valid April 2002 through March 2003

**MT. RAINIER SCENIC RAILROAD**
Regular price: Adults $11.50, seniors $10.50, children $8.50
**With coupon: Adults $10.50, seniors $9.50, children $7.50**
Valid April 2002 through March 2003

**NORTHWEST RAILWAY MUSEUM**
**With coupon: Buy one admission get**
**equal price admission free**
Valid April 2002 through March 2003
Maximum discount 2 persons per coupon

**NORTHERN PACIFIC RAILWAY MUSEUM**
Regular price: Adults $2, seniors $1, children $1
**With coupon: Adults $1, seniors $.50, children $.50**
Valid April 2002 through March 2003

**HARPERS FERRY TOY TRAIN MUSEUM & JOY LINE RAILROAD**
Regular price: Adults $1.50, seniors $1.50, children $1.50
**With coupon: Adults $1, seniors $1, children $1**
Valid April 2002 through March 2003

**COLLIS P. HUNTINGTON RAILROAD HISTORICAL SOCIETY, INC.**
**With coupon: 10% off per person, no limit**
Valid April 2002 through March 2003

**COLFAX RAILROAD MUSEUM, INC.**
Regular price: Adults $2, seniors $2, children $1
**With coupon: Adults $1.50, seniors $1.50, children $.50**
Valid April 2002 through March 2003

**EAST TROY ELECTRIC RAILROAD MUSEUM**
**With coupon: Buy one admission get**
**equal price admission free**
Valid April 2002 through March 2003
Maximum discount 2 persons per coupon

**CENTER FOR TRANSPORTATION**
GALVESTON ISLAND, TX
GUIDE TO TOURIST RAILROADS AND MUSEUMS
2002 GUEST COUPON

**AGE OF STEAM RAILROAD MUSEUM**
DALLAS, TX
GUIDE TO TOURIST RAILROADS AND MUSEUMS
2002 GUEST COUPON

**HEBER VALLEY RAILROAD**
HEBER CITY, UT
GUIDE TO TOURIST RAILROADS AND MUSEUMS
2002 GUEST COUPON

**RAILROAD AND HERITAGE MUSEUM**
TEMPLE, TX
GUIDE TO TOURIST RAILROADS AND MUSEUMS
2002 GUEST COUPON

**MT. RAINIER SCENIC RAILROAD**
ELBE, WA
GUIDE TO TOURIST RAILROADS AND MUSEUMS
2002 GUEST COUPON

**OGDEN UNION STATION**
OGDEN, UT
GUIDE TO TOURIST RAILROADS AND MUSEUMS
2002 GUEST COUPON

**NORTHERN PACIFIC RAILWAY MUSEUM**
TOPPENISH, WA
GUIDE TO TOURIST RAILROADS AND MUSEUMS
2002 GUEST COUPON

**NORTHWEST RAILWAY MUSEUM**
SNOQUALMIE, WA
GUIDE TO TOURIST RAILROADS AND MUSEUMS
2002 GUEST COUPON

**COLLIS P. HUNTINGTON RAILROAD HISTORICAL SOCIETY, INC.**
KENOVA, WV
GUIDE TO TOURIST RAILROADS AND MUSEUMS
2002 GUEST COUPON

**HARPERS FERRY TOY TRAIN MUSEUM & JOE LINE RAILROAD**
HARPERS FERRY, WV
GUIDE TO TOURIST RAILROADS AND MUSEUMS
2002 GUEST COUPON

**EAST TROY ELECTRIC RAILROAD MUSEUM**
EAST TROY, WI
GUIDE TO TOURIST RAILROADS AND MUSEUMS
2002 GUEST COUPON

**COLFAX RAILROAD MUSEUM, INC.**
COLFAX, WI
GUIDE TO TOURIST RAILROADS AND MUSEUMS
2002 GUEST COUPON

# Guide to Tourist Railroads and Museums
## 2002 GUEST COUPONS
### Arranged alphabetically by state

### NATIONAL RAILROAD MUSEUM
**With coupon: Buy one admission get**
**equal price admission free**
Valid April 2002 through March 2003
Maximum discount 1 person per coupon

### CAMP FIVE
Regular price: Adults $15
**With coupon: Adults $13.50**
Valid April 2002 through March 2003
Maximum discount 2 persons per coupon

### WHISKEY RIVER RAILWAY
**With coupon: Buy one admission get**
**equal price admission free**
Valid April 2002 through March 2003
Unlimited persons per coupon

### CANADIAN MUSEUM OF RAIL TRAVEL
**With coupon: 10% off full tours only**
Valid April 2002 through March 2003

### PRINCE GEORGE RAILWAY AND FORESTRY MUSEUM
**With coupon: 20% off regular gate fee**
Valid April 2002 through March 2003

### REVELSTOKE RAILWAY MUSEUM
Regular price: Adults $6, seniors $5, children $3
**With coupon: Adults $4, seniors $3.75, children $2.25**
Valid April 2002 through March 2003
Maximum discount 5 persons per coupon

### WEST COAST RAILWAY HERITAGE PARK
Regular price: Adults $6, seniors $5, children $5
**With coupon: Adults $3, seniors $2.50, children $2.50**
Valid April 2002 through March 2003

### KETTLE VALLEY STEAM RAILWAY SOCIETY
**With coupon: Buy one admission get**
**equal price admission free**
Valid April 2002 through March 2003
Maximum discount 1 person per coupon

### VANCOUVER'S DOWNTOWN HISTORIC RAILWAY
**With coupon: Buy one admission get**
**equal price admission free**
Valid April 2002 through March 2003
Maximum discount 4 persons per coupon

### FORT ERIE RAILROAD MUSEUM
**With coupon: Buy one admission get**
**equal price admission free**
Valid April 2002 through March 2003
Maximum discount 4 persons per coupon

### HULL-CHELSEA-WAKEFIELD STEAM TRAIN
Regular price: Adults $29, seniors $26
**With coupon: Adults $26, seniors $23**
Valid April 2002 through March 2003

### CHAUDIERE-APPALACIAN TOURIST TRAIN
Regular price: Adults $24.95
**With coupon: Adults $22.95**
Valid April 2002 through March 2003

| | |
|---|---|
| **CAMP FIVE**<br>LAONA, WI<br>GUIDE TO TOURIST RAILROADS AND MUSEUMS<br>2002 GUEST COUPON | **NATIONAL RAILROAD MUSEUM**<br>GREEN BAY, WI<br>GUIDE TO TOURIST RAILROADS AND MUSEUMS<br>2002 GUEST COUPON |
| **CANADIAN MUSEUM OF RAIL TRAVEL**<br>CRANBROOK, BC<br>GUIDE TO TOURIST RAILROADS AND MUSEUMS<br>2002 GUEST COUPON | **WHISKEY RIVER RAILWAY**<br>MARSHALL, WI<br>GUIDE TO TOURIST RAILROADS AND MUSEUMS<br>2002 GUEST COUPON |
| **REVELSTOKE RAILWAY MUSEUM**<br>REVELSTOKE, BC<br>GUIDE TO TOURIST RAILROADS AND MUSEUMS<br>2002 GUEST COUPON | **PRINCE GEORGE RAILWAY<br>AND FORESTRY MUSEUM**<br>PRINCE GEORGE, BC<br>GUIDE TO TOURIST RAILROADS AND MUSEUMS<br>2002 GUEST COUPON |
| **KETTLE VALLEY STEAM<br>RAILWAY SOCIETY**<br>SUMMERLAND, BC<br>GUIDE TO TOURIST RAILROADS AND MUSEUMS<br>2002 GUEST COUPON | **WEST COAST RAILWAY HERITAGE<br>PARK**<br>SQUAMISH, BC<br>GUIDE TO TOURIST RAILROADS AND MUSEUMS<br>2002 GUEST COUPON |
| **FORT ERIE RAILROAD MUSEUM**<br>FORT ERIE, ON<br>GUIDE TO TOURIST RAILROADS AND MUSEUMS<br>2002 GUEST COUPON | **VANCOUVER'S DOWNTOWN<br>HISTORIC RAILWAY**<br>VANCOUVER, BC<br>GUIDE TO TOURIST RAILROADS AND MUSEUMS<br>2002 GUEST COUPON |
| **CHAUDIERE-APPALACIAN TOURIST<br>TRAIN**<br>VALLEE-JONCTION, PQ<br>GUIDE TO TOURIST RAILROADS AND MUSEUMS<br>2002 GUEST COUPON | **HULL-CHELSEA-WAKEFIELD<br>STEAM TRAIN**<br>HULL, PQ<br>GUIDE TO TOURIST RAILROADS AND MUSEUMS<br>2002 GUEST COUPON |

# WABASH FRISCO & PACIFIC RAILWAY
## "THE UNCOMMON CARRIER"

*Train ride*
*12" gauge*

DAVID J. NEUBAUER

**Description:** A 2-mile, 30-minute round trip over a former Missouri Pacific right-of-way along the scenic Meramec River through wooded areas and over three bridges. Two and, sometimes, three trains are operated consecutively with meets out on the line. The 150th anniversary of the original Pacific RR going through Glencoe in 1852 will be in 2002.

**Schedule:** May through October: Sundays, 11:15 a.m. to 4:15 p.m.

**Admission/Fare:** $2; children under age 3 ride free. No reservations.

**Locomotives/Rolling Stock:** Eight steam locomotives; 1907 no. 171 4-4-0 and coal burner; no. 180 4-4-0 coal; no. 102 2-6-2 coal; no. 300 4-4-2 oil; no. 400 4-6-2 oil; no. 434 4-6-4 oil; no. 350 4-4-4 coal being rebuilt as 4-6-4; no. 401 4-6-2 coal; 37 cars; roundhouse; turntables; and a wye.

**Special Events:** Member's Day, June.

**Nearby Attractions/Accommodations:** Museum of Transportation; Union Pacific and Burlington Northern Santa Fe main lines, Eureka, Missouri.

**Location/Directions:** Twenty-five miles west of St. Louis. I-44 (Eureka), exit 264, north on Route 109 for 3.5 miles to Old State Rd., make two right turns to depot on Washington St. and Grand Ave.

*Coupon available, see coupon section.

       **Radio frequency: 151.955**

**Site Address:** Foot of Washington St. and Grand Ave., Wildwood, MO
**Mailing Address:** 1569 Ville Angela Ln., Hazelwood, MO 63042-1630
**Telephone:** (636) 587-3538
**E-mail:** jmjrr@apci.net
**Internet:** www.wfprr.org

# ST. LOUIS, IRON MOUNTAIN & SOUTHERN RAILWAY
*Train ride, dinner train*
*Standard gauge*

**Description:** A 2-hour, 10-mile train ride on antique coaches, plus a New York Central A/C coach pulled by diesel Y-8 engine or occasional steam engine.

**Schedule:** September, October, April, and May, weekends, 11 a.m., 1, 2, and 5 p.m. June through August, weekends, 11 a.m., 1, 2, and 5 p.m., Wednesdays and Fridays, 1 p.m. November and December, Saturdays, 11 a.m. and 2 p.m.

**Admission/Fare:** Adults, $15; children, $8. Dinner runs, $24.50; Murder Mystery Dinner, $39.

**Locomotives/Rolling Stock:** 1946 H.K. Porter, steam 2-4-2 65T; 1947 Cummins diesel-electric 900 h.p.; 1929 MoPac caboose; two ex-Illinois Central commuter cars; two B&O cabooses 1971; diesel locomotive, PRR no. 5898; BN caboose; Southern Railroad caboose.

**Special Events:** Civil War Reenactment, October; Murder Mystery, New Years Eve; James Gang Train Robbery, some weekends.

**Nearby Attractions/Accommodations:** Trail of Tears State Park; Mississippi River; Burtordsville Mill and covered bridge; motels and restaurants.

**Location/Directions:** Highway I-55, exit 99, two hours south of St. Louis. From exit 99, four miles south on Highway 61 to Jackson, intersection of Highway 61/25/72.

**Site Address:** 505 E. Jackson Blvd., Jackson, MO
**Mailing Address:** PO Box 244, Jackson, MO 63755
**Telephone:** (573) 243-1688 and (800) 455-RAIL
**Fax:** (573) 243-1688
**Internet:** www.rosecity.net/trains

RICHARD A. EICHHORST

**Description:** F.O.L.K.S. supports the Kirkwood Amtrak station by providing passenger amenities. The station, built in 1893, is listed in the national register of historic places. Exhibits provided by the Museum of Transportation and the American Association of Railroaders, Inc.

**Schedule:** Daily, 8 a.m. to 8 p.m.

**Admission/Fare:** Station, free. Fares for excursions vary according to destination and activity.

**Special Events:** Kirkwood Jct. Festival, May; Kirkwood Station Celebration, first Sunday in November; train watchers gather every Saturday and Sunday afternoon. Sightseeing and dinner excursions on Amtrak trains are offered each month.

**Nearby Attractions/Accommodations:** Museum of Transportation; Route 66 State Park; Wabash, Frisco & Pacific Railway.

**Location/Directions:** In downtown Kirkwood at Kirkwood (Lindbergh) Blvd.

**Site Address:** 110 W. Argonne Road, Kirkwood, MO
**Mailing Address:** PO Box 221122, Kirkwood, MO 63122
**Telephone:** (314) 752-3148

GARY CHILCOTE

**Description:** Patee House Museum was headquarters for the Pony Express in 1860. The former hotel is now a museum of communications and transportation featuring a steam locomotive, mail car, antique cars, trucks, fire trucks, buggies, and wagons. On the grounds is the Jesse James Home, where the outlaw was killed.

**Schedule:** April through October, daily 10 a.m. to 5 p.m. during summer months; otherwise, 10 a.m. to 4 p.m. November through March, weekends only.

**Admission/Fare:** Adults, $3.50; seniors, $3; students ages 6-17, $2; under age 6 are free with family.

**Locomotives/Rolling Stock:** 1892 Baldwin 4-4-0 no. 35, backdated by Burlington in 1933 to resemble Hannibal & St. Joseph locomotive no. 35.

**Special Events:** Vintage carousel opens in 2002.

**Nearby Attractions/Accommodations:** Home of Jesse James, Pony Express Museum, Doll Museum, Firefighters Museum, Old Smokehouse Restaurant.

**Location/Directions:** From Highway 36 take the 10th St. exit, follow 10th St. north to right on Mitchell to 12th St.

*Coupon available, see coupon section.

**Site Address:** 1202 Penn, St. Joseph, MO
**Mailing Address:** PO Box 1022, St. Joseph, MO 64502
**Telephone:** (816) 232-8206
**Fax:** (816) 232-3717
**Internet:** www.stjoseph.net/ponyexpress/

## AMERICAN ASSOCIATION OF RAILROADERS
### *Train ride, dinner train*
### *Standard*

RICHARD A. EICHHORST

**Description:** Sponsors more than 50 rail activities each year. These events include industry tours, one-day sightseeing excursions, dinner excursions, mystery destination adventures, and mainline Amtrak tours. The organization also charters private sleepers, coaches, and observation cars for operation on Amtrak trains and regional railroads. Several train tours in Canada and at least one extended European tour are scheduled each year. The highlight of 2001 was the operation of a special Union Pacific train behind "Challenger 3985."

**Schedule:** Year round. At least three activities every month.

**Admission/Fare:** Varies. Determined by distance, activities, and amenities.

**Locomotives/Rolling Stock:** The organization prides itself on often being the "first" or "last" rail organization to ride certain lines and/or equipment. Frequently charters trains and/or private cars.

**Special Events:** An annual slide show the first weekend in March to preview the previous year. The "Nostalgia Program" brings back historic subjects from the last 35 years. Several excursions (free for members) aboard the organization's 1958 GM PD4104 Trailways bus.

**Nearby Attractions/Accommodations:** Museum of Transportation and "The Cabooseum" (see A.R.C.H.E.S.), St. Louis.

**Location/Directions:** Sent with tickets.

**Site Address:** St. Louis and Kirkwood, MO; Alton, IL
**Mailing Address:** 4351 Holly Hills Blvd., St. Louis, MO 63116
**Telephone:** (314) 752-3148

**AMERICAN RAILWAY CABOOSE HISTORICAL
EDUCATIONAL SOCIETY, INC. (A.R.C.H.E.S.)**
*Caboose museum*
*Standard gauge*

RICHARD A. EICHHORST

**Description:** The Caboose Museum has at least one of their 30 "cabeese" on
display at any given time. While a permanent location is being
planned, the equipment is stored at ten different locations in Missouri
and Illinois. Some of these cabooses are on loan to other rail museums.
In addition to the interpretive center that is open to the public,
ARCHES is an international association with members in 33 states and
Canada. The members have printed a 220-page book, "Cabeese in
America," which lists over 5,000 cabooses that have been preserved and
are used for other purposes. List price is $24.95, discounted to members.

**Schedule:** April 6, May 4, June 1, July 6, August 3, September 7, and
October 5: write or call for schedule and date of Annual Meeting.

**Admission/Fare:** Donations appreciated.

**Cabooses:** A&S, ATSF, B&O, C&O, C&NW, CC, CGW, Essex Terminal, Frisco,
IC, Manufacturers, Milwaukee, Missouri Pacific, N&W, RI, Soo,
Southern, TRRA, and Union Pacific.

**Special Events:** Caboose Chili Cook-off, Caboose Chase excursions, Santa
on Amtrak, Rail Caboose tours, one Western Caboose tour and one
Eastern tour each year. Charters and special trains.

**Location/Directions:** Varies. Write for specific date information.

       M

 St. Louis & Kirkwood, MO / Alton, IL

**Site Address:** St. Louis, MO
**Mailing Address:** PO Box 2772, St. Louis, MO 63116
**Telephone:** (314) 752-3148
**E-mail:** arches.org

**RAILROAD HISTORICAL MUSEUM, INC.**
*Museum*
*Standard*

**Description:** This stationary historical train is a museum within a museum, as it contains Frisco steam locomotive no. 4524 with tender, BN Express car, double-deck passenger car and BN caboose, all enclosed within a 40 x 400 x 8-foot chain-link fence, with railroad antiques, artifacts, and memorabilia, both within the fence and within the cars and locomotive.

**Schedule:** Saturdays, 2 to 4 p.m., mostly from April through November, weather permitting. (The weather must be sunny and dry and at least 60 degrees.) Also open by special group request.

**Admission/Fare:** Free. Donations accepted.

**Locomotives/Rolling Stock:** Frisco steam locomotive, no. 4524 with stoker tender and power boosters; BN express car, no. 976100, double-deck passenger car seating 100 on lower deck and 60 on the upper level; more.

**Special Events:** Frisco Days, two days in June.

**Nearby Attractions/Accommodations:** Bass Pro Shop; Dickerson Park Zoo; Grant Beach Park; Wild Animal Paradise, 12 miles east; Branson and Silver Dollar City, 40 miles south.

**Location/Directions:** From I-44 exit 77, go south on Kansas Expressway, turn east on Division St. Go ¾ mile and turn south on Grant Ave., two blocks to 1400 N. Grant, then turn west on Lynn St. to the museum entrance at Grant Beach Park.

**Site Address:** Grant Beach Park, 1400 N. Grant Ave., Springfield, MO
**Mailing Address:** 2033 S. Eureka Ave., Springfield, MO 65804
**Telephone:** (417) 881-3327

FOEREST TRENT

**Description:** Located in a 1910 passenger depot, the Springfield & Ozark Railway is a ¼ inch, O scale railroad that is modeled after an old branch line that became part of the St. Louis & San Francisco Railway in 1885. This 20 x 66-foot layout is a point-to-point, with reversing loops and a yard at each end. Up to four mainline and four yard trains can be operated simultaneously.

**Schedule:** The trains operate on the first Tuesday of every month, 7:30 p.m. until around 9 p.m., except on holidays, then operation is moved to the following Tuesday.

**Admission/Fare:** Free. Tax deductible donations accepted.

**Special Events:** Extra holiday operations Tuesday, December 10, 17, and 24.

**Nearby Attractions/Accommodations:** BN-SF mainline, Amtrak station in Kirkwood, The Magic House, Museum of Transport, St. Louis Live Steamers, Six Flags Over St. Louis, the Wabash Frisco & Pacific Railroad, Gateway Arch.

**Location/Directions:** Three miles west of St. Louis, Missouri, on the north side of I-44. Use exit 280 (Elm Ave.). Travel north ⅛ mile to stoplight at Big Bend Blvd. Turn left and travel about two blocks, cross the railroad tracks, and you are there.

**Site Address:** 8833 Big Bend Blvd., Webster Groves, MO
**Mailing Address:** 855 Windemere Ave., Des Peres, MO 63131-4531
**Telephone:** (314) 966-5227
**E-mail:** kc0esl@juno.com
**Internet:** www.geocities.com/bbrrclub/

KYLE BREHM

**Description:** Historic Great Northern Railroad Inn with caboose cottages.

**Schedule:** Year round: 7 a.m. to 10 p.m.

**Special Events:** Essex Express Railfan Weekend, May 3-5, 2002.

**Nearby Attractions/Accommodations:** Glacier National Park, Middle Fork of the Flathead River.

**Location/Directions:** On southern tip of Glacier National Park off Highway 2 between East and West Glacier in Essex, Montana.

**Site Address:** 290 Izaak Walton Inn Rd., Essex, MT
**Mailing Address:** 290 Izaak Walton Inn Rd., Essex, MT 59916
**Telephone:** (406) 888-5700
**Fax:** (406) 888-5200
**E-mail:** stay@izaakwaltoninn.com
**Internet:** www.izaakwaltoninn.com

# CHARLIE RUSSELL CHEW-CHOO
## DINNER TRAIN
### *Dinner train*

CHERIE NEUDICK

**Description:** Three and one-half hour narrated dinner train ride through the heart of Montana.

**Schedule:** Year round: June through September, Saturdays. Special trains occasionally.

**Fare/Admission:** Adults, $85; children 12 and under, $50.

**Locomotives/Rolling Stock:** Five stainless-steel Budd RDC cars

**Special Events:** Polar Express children's ride. Date to be announced.

**Nearby Attractions/Accommodations:** Many within a two-hour drive.

**Location/Directions:** 2.7 miles north of Lewistown, Montana on Highway 191, then west approximately 8 miles on Montana Highway 426, near mile marker 19.

**Site Address:** 408 NE Main St., Lewistown, MT
**Mailing Address:** Chamber of Commerce, PO Box 818, Lewiston, MT 59457
**Telephone:** (406) 538-2527
**Fax:** (406) 538-5437
**E-mail:** lewchamb@lewistown.net
**Internet:** www.lewistownchamber.com

**Description:** Daylight excursion train travels on original NPRR between Sandpoint, Idaho, and Livingston, Montana. We offer two-day trips on board with available motorcoach trips into Glacier and Yellowstone.

**Schedule:** June 7 through September 2, Fridays and Saturdays: eastbound from Sandpoint, Idaho. Sundays and Mondays: westbound from Livingston, Montana.

**Admission/Fare:** Contact sales office at 800-519-7245 for fares and availability.

**Locomotives/Rolling Stock:** Largest operators of ripple-sided Budd cars in the U.S. Cars are from Great Northern, NP Railway, CBQ, *Twin Cities Zephyr*, etc.

**Nearby Attractions/Accommodations:** Off-the-train tours include Yellowstone, Tetons, and Glacier National Parks. There are eight trips eastbound and eight trips westbound.

**Site Address:** 1055 Baldy Park Ave., Sandpoint, ID
**Mailing Address:** 1055 Baldy Park Ave., Sandpoint, ID 83864
**Telephone:** (800) 519-7245 and (208) 265-8618
**Fax:** (208) 265-8619
**E-mail:** information@montanarailtours.com
**Internet:** www.montanarailtours.com

227

# HISTORICAL MUSEUM AT FORT MISSOULA
*Museum, display, layout*
*Standard gauge*

RAILWAY MUSEUM

**Description:** County Historical Museum, on 32-acre site, with 13 historic structures depicting the history of western Montana.

**Schedule:** Memorial Day weekend through Labor Day weekend, Monday through Saturday, 10 a.m. to 5 p.m. and Sunday, 12 noon to 5 p.m. Labor Day weekend to Memorial Day weekend, Tuesday through Saturday, 12 noon to 5 p.m.

**Admission/Fare:** Adults, $3; seniors, $2, sudents, $1; children under 6 and members of the Friends of the Historical Museum, free.

**Locomotives/Rolling Stock:** Anaconda Copper Mining Co. Lumber Dept. 1923, Willamette Iron & Steel Works (3 Tr. Shay type) Const. no. 7; flatcars with log loads; Slide Jammer log loader; ACM "shuttle" car to transport lumberjacks; section motor car.

**Special Events:** Railroad Day, June 15; Forestry Day, April 27; Frontier Day, August 24; 4th of July Celebration; occasional operation of steam powered sawmill; motor cars on track; model railroad; Willamette cab tours.

**Nearby Attractions/Accommodations:** A Carousel for Missoula, Rocky Mountain Elk Foundation, Smokejumpers Visitor's Center, more.

**Location/Directions:** From I-90 take Reserve St. exit south to South Ave. (traffic signal). Turn right (west) on South Ave. to left at sign for museum.

**Site Address:** Bldg. #322 Fort Missoula, Missoula, MT
**Mailing Address:** Bldg. #322 Fort Missoula, Missoula, MT 59804
**Telephone:** (406) 728-3476
**Fax:** (406) 543-6277
**E-mail:** ftmslamuseum@montana.com
**Internet:** www.montana.com/ftmslamuseum

**MONTANA HERITAGE COMMISSION**
*Train ride, museum, display*
*30" gauge*

ANDY LIEDBERG

**Description:** Operating steam locomotive, rebuilt 30" gauge Mexican 2-8-0, former Ferrocaril Mexicano no. 12, built by Baldwin in 1910. It had been displayed at Edaville for many years. Also, Alder Gulch Short Line, tourist train with open-air cars that operates along Alder Gulch between Nevada City and Virginia City, Montana.

**Schedule:** Memorial Day through Labor Day, weather permitting, beginning at 11 a.m. Last run at 6:15 p.m.

**Admission/Fare:** C.A. Bovey train–$5. Steam train–$10 round trip.

**Locomotives/Rolling Stock:** Ferrocaril Mexicano no. 12 steam locomotive, built by Baldwin; C.A. Bovey gas-powered train.

**Nearby Attractions/Accommodations:** Historic mining towns Virginia and Nevada City.

**Location/Directions:** State Highway 287 between Ennis and Sheridan, Montana.

**Site Address:** Nevada City, MT
**Mailing Address:** PO Box 338, Virginia City, MT 59755
**Telephone:** (406) 843-5247
**Fax:** (406) 841-4004
**E-mail:** juljohnson@state.mt.us

# ROCK ISLAND DEPOT
## RAILROAD MUSEUM
### *Museum, display*

JEFFERSON COUNTY HISTORICAL SOCIETY

**Description:** Established in 1996 in the historic Rock Island Depot, which also housed the Western Division Headquarters for the Rock Island Railroad, built in 1914. The collection consists of Rock Island artifacts, from conductors' uniforms and train order hoops to baggage carts and caboose stoves, as well as local history involving the railroad. Includes a model railroad display, separate freight house and formal gardens. Restoration of the building is ongoing, as is development of rolling stock display.

**Schedule:** Year round: Wednesdays, Thursdays, and Sundays, 1 to 5 p.m.

**Admission/Fare:** Suggested donation.

**Special Events:** Annual Christmas at the Depot, second weekend in December; Annual Rock Island Rail Days, second weekend in June.

**Nearby Attractions/Accommodations:** Rock Creek Station State Historical Park, Homestead National Monument, golf, dining, Oregon Trail, camping.

**Location/Directions:** Seventy-five miles southwest of Lincoln, Nebraska, west on I-80, south on Nebraska Highway 15.

**Site Address:** 910 Second St., Fairbury, NE
**Mailing Address:** 910 Second St., Fairbury, NE 68352
**Telephone:** (402) 729-5131
**E-mail:** fairburyridepot@alltel.net
**Internet:** www.jeffersoncountyhistory.com

## FREMONT & ELKHORN VALLEY RAILROAD
## NRHS NEBRASKA CHAPTER
*Train ride, dinner train, museum*
*Standard gauge*

**Description:** Take a ride through history on a 30-mile round trip from Fremont to Hooper over rails laid in 1869. Ride on cars built in 1924 and 1925. Enjoy the scenic Elkhorn Valley.

**Schedule:** April 20, 2002 to October 27, 2002. Dinner train, year round.

**Admission/Fare:** Adults, $12; children 12 and under, $7; under age 3 ride free.

**Locomotives/Rolling Stock:** EMD SW1200, Davenport 44-ton no. 1481 under restoration; CB&Q RPO; "Lake Bluff" passenger car; 1927 "Fort Andrew" passenger car; BN wide-vision caboose.

**Special Events:** Open House, April 20-21; fireworks ride in Hooper on the 4th of July; John C. Fremont Days, second weekend in July; Santa Claus runs; others.

**Nearby Attractions/Accommodations:** Nebraska Railway Museum, May Museum, antique shopping, Motor Plex, Hooper, Nebraska, historical Main St.

**Location/Directions:** Approximately 35 miles northwest of Omaha. Highway 275 exit 23rd St., travel west through Fremont, turn south on Somers Ave.

*Coupon available, see coupon section.

**Site Address:** 1835 N. Somers Ave., Fremont, NE
**Mailing Address:** PO Box 191, Fremont, NE 68026
**Telephone:** (402) 727-0615
**Fax:** (402) 727-0615
**E-mail:** fevr@teknetwork.com
**Internet:** www.geocities.com/heartland/hills/4184/fevr.html

# FREMONT DINNER TRAIN
*Dinner train*
*Standard gauge*

RUDY DANIELS

**Description:** Thirty-mile round trip up the Elkhorn Valley to the historic town of Hooper, Nebraska.

**Schedule:** Year round. November through April, Saturdays, 6:30 p.m. May through October, Saturdays, 7:30 p.m. June through December, Fridays, 7:30 p.m. May through November, Sundays, 1:30 p.m. Occasionally January through April.

**Admission/Fare:** $39.95-$63.95 (Sunday afternoons; evenings with dinner theater.)

**Locomotives/Rolling Stock:** Power car no. 1315 (ex-Milw. baggage dorm); dining cars no. 101 (ex-IC); no. 102 (ex-CN); no. 104 (ex-CN); no. 765 lounge diner (ex-CN); no. 193 storage car (ex-Milw. parlor); no. 410 power car (ex-Nickel Plate).

**Special Events:** July 4th picnic dinner run, including fireworks display.

**Nearby Attractions/Accommodations:** Fremont Antique District; May Museum; Fremont State Lakes.

**Location/Directions:** Thirty-five miles northwest of Omaha; 50 miles north of Lincoln; 75 miles south of Sioux City, Iowa.

**Site Address:** 1835 N. Somers Ave., Fremont, NE
**Mailing Address:** 650 N. "H," St., Fremont, NE 68025
**Telephone:** 800) 942-7245
**Fax:** (402) 727-0915
**E-mail:** fdt@fremont-online.com
**Internet:** www.fremont-online.com/fdt

232

**Description:** Museum with 1890s Railroad Town and limited viewable railroad exhibit stock.

**Schedule:** October 16 through April 30: Mondays through Saturdays, 9 a.m. to 5 p.m., Sundays 1 to 5 p.m. May 1 through October 15: 9 a.m. to 5 p.m. daily.

**Admission/Fare:** Write, call, fax or internet for information.

**Special Events:** Call, write, fax or internet for 2002 calendar of events.

**Nearby Attractions/Accommodations:** Contact Grand Island/Hall County Convention and Visitor's Bureau for detailed information.

**Location/Directions:** Four short minutes north of I-80, exit 312, Grand Island, Nebraska.

**Site Address:** 3133 W. Highway 34, Grand Island, NE
**Mailing Address:** 3133 W. Highway 34, Grand Island, NE 68801
**Telephone:** (308) 385-5316
**Fax:** (308) 385-5028
**E-mail:** marketing@stuhrmuseum.org
**Internet:** www.stuhrmuseum.org

**Description:** Housed in the former Union Pacific train station, Durham WHM explores the history of Omaha through interactive exhibits and displays, as well as bringing regional, national, and world-renowned touring exhibitions to Omaha. In cooperation with the former UP Museum, the DWHM displays the Union Pacific collection, including six railroad cars.

**Schedule:** Tuesdays through Saturdays, 10 a.m. to 5 p.m. and Sundays 1 to 5 p.m. Closed Mondays and most major holidays.

**Admission/Fare:** Adults, $5; seniors, $4; children ages 3-12, $3.50; under age 3 are free.

**Locomotives/Rolling Stock:** Baldwin 4-6-0 1243; Pullman 6-4-6 National Command; Pullman 1914 business car; Pullman 1949 barber shop lounge SP2906.

**Special Events:** Christmas, weekends in December. Ethnic Holiday Festival, December.

**Nearby Attractions/Accommodations:** Joslyn Art Museum, Henry Doorley Zoo, Omaha Golden Spikes baseball, Strategic Air Command Museum.

**Location/Directions:** I-80, exit 13th St., north to Pacific St., east to Tenth St., go one block north.

**Site Address:** 801 S. Tenth St., Omaha, NE
**Mailing Address:** 801 S. Tenth St., Omaha, NE 68108
**Telephone:** (402) 444-5071
Fax: (402) 444-5391

# OMAHA ZOO RAILROAD
*Train ride*
*30" gauge*

AARON ZOEKO

**Description:** Passengers take a guided 1¾-mile, 20- to 30-minute trip through the zoo grounds, seeing hundreds of animals, including many rare and endangered species. Steam is scheduled 11 a.m. to 4 p.m.

**Schedule:** Seven days a week, Memorial Day through Labor Day. Weekends only April through Memorial Day and Labor Day through October.

**Admission/Fare:** Adults, $2.50; children under 12, $1.50; under 3 free round trip. (subject to change on Jan. 1)

**Locomotives/Rolling Stock:** Locomotives no. 395-104, 1890 Krauss 0-6-2T; no. 119 1968 Crown 4-4-0 narrow gauge replica of Union Pacific no. 119; passenger cars; 11 open-air coaches; caboose; ballast diner; Fairmont MT14 motor car.

**Special Events:** Member's Day, with free train ride to zoo members; Halloween Terror Train during zoo-sponsored Halloween party, children in costume ride free.

**Nearby Attractions/Accommodations:** Omaha Spikes baseball, Children's Museum, Western Heritage Museum; plenty of hotels/motels and restaurants.

**Location/Directions:** I-80 and Tenth St.

**Site Address:** 3701 S. Tenth St., Omaha, NE
**Mailing Address:** 3701 S. Tenth St., Omaha, NE 68107
**Telephone:** (402) 733-8401
**Fax:** (402) 733-7868
**Internet:** www.omahazoo.com

# NEVADA STATE RAILROAD MUSEUM
*Museum*
*Standard and narrow gauge*

**Description:** The Nevada State Railroad Museum houses over 50 pieces of railroad equipment from Nevada's past and is considered one of the finest regional railroad museums in the country. Included in the collection are seven steam locomotives and several restored coaches and freight cars. The bulk of the equipment is from the Virginia & Truckee Railroad, America's richest and most famous short line. Museum activities include operation of historic railroad equipment, handcar races, lectures, an annual railroad history symposium, changing exhibits, and a variety of special events. We offer steam train or motorcar rides on weekends, spring through fall, on the museum's one-mile loop track.

**Schedule:** Call or write for information.

**Admission/Fare:** Adults, $2; children under 18, free. Fares vary.

**Locomotives/Rolling Stock:** No. 25, 1905 Baldwin 4-6-0; no. 18, "Dayton," 1873 Central Pacific 4-4-0; and no. 22, "Inyo," 1875 Baldwin 4-4-0; all former V&T. No. 1, "Glenbrook," 1875 Baldwin narrow-gauge 2-6-0, former Carson & Tahoe Lumber & Fluming Co.; no. 8, 1888 Cooke 4-4-0, former Dardanelle & Russellville; no. 1, "Joe Douglass," 1882 Porter narrow gauge 0-4-2T, former Dayton, Sutro & Carson Valley. Coaches nos. 3, 4, 8, 11, 12, 17, and 18, express/mail nos. 14 and 21, caboose-coaches nos. 9, 10, and 15, and 11 freight cars, all former V&T; more.

**Location/Directions:** Highways 50 and 395, at the south end of town.

     M arm TRAIN

**Site Address:** 2180 S. Carson St., Carson City, NV
**Mailing Address:** 2180 S. Carson St., Carson City, NV 89701
**Telephone:** (775) 687-6953
**Internet:** www.nsrm-friends.org

# NEVADA NORTHERN RAILWAY MUSEUM
*Train ride, dinner train, museum, display*
*Standard gauge*

**Description:** This museum features steam train operation. Call or write for schedule.

**Schedule:** May through September.

**Special Events:** Raildays, Labor Day weekend.

**Nearby Attractions/Accommodations:** Great Basin National Park, Pony Express Trail, KOA, Ruth Mining Pits.

**Location/Directions:** East Central Nevada on U.S. 93/50/6.

**Site Address:** 1100 Ave. "A," East Ely, NV
**Mailing Address:** PO Box 150040, East Ely, NV 89315
**Telephone:** (775) 289-2085
**Fax:** (775) 289-6284
**E-mail:** nnry@mwpower.net
**Internet:** www.nevadanorthernrailway.net

**EUREKA & PALISADE RAILROAD**
*Train ride*
*36" gauge*

DANIEL MARKOFF

**Description:** Occasional historic display and operation on various host railroads.

**Schedule:** Call or write for details.

**Admission/Fare:** Call or write for details.

**Locomotives/Rolling Stock:** Eureka & Palisade locomotive no. 4 "Eureka," Baldwin Locomotive Works 1875, American standard 4-4-0, narrow gauge.

**Special Events:** Varies, depending on host railroad. When not in service, locomotive is not on public display. Call or write for details.

**Nearby Attractions/Accommodations:** Nevada State Railroad Museum, Boulder City. Las Vegas, with hotels, gaming, shows. The best of the Old West in the rest of Nevada.

**Location/Directions:** Not open to the public.

  TRAIN

**Site Address:** Private
**Mailing Address:** 820 S. Seventh St., Suite A, Las Vegas, NV 89101
**Telephone:** (702) 383-3327

# VIRGINIA & TRUCKEE RAILROAD CO.

*Train ride*
*Standard gauge*

**Description:** A 5-mile round trip from Virginia City to the town of Gold Hill through the heart of the historic Comstock mining region. A knowledgeable conductor gives a running commentary on the area and on the 126-year-old railroad.

**Schedule:** May 25 through October 21.

**Admission/Fare:** Adults, $5.50; children 5-12, $2.75; children under age 5 ride free.

**Locomotives/Rolling Stock:** 1916 Baldwin 2-8-0 no. 29, former Longview Portland & Northern; 1907 Baldwin 2-6-2 no. 8, former Hobart Southern; 1888 Northwestern Pacific combine and coach; former Tonopah & Tidewater coach; former Northern Pacific caboose; 1919 0-6-0 no. 30, former Southern Pacific.

**Special Events:** Party and Night train, once a month during the season.

**Nearby Attractions/Accommodations:** Historic Virginia City, mines, mansions, shops.

**Location/Directions:** Twenty-one miles from Reno, 17 miles from Carson City.

**Site Address:** Washington and "F" Streets, Virginia City, NV
**Mailing Address:** PO Box 467, Virginia City, NV 89440
**Telephone:** (775) 847-0380

# THE MOUNT WASHINGTON COG RAILWAY
*Train ride*
*4'8"gauge*

**Description:** Climb aboard the world's first mountain-climbing cog railway to the summit of Mount Washington, the highest peak in the Northeast. Rain or shine, this three-hour round-trip journey on one of seven enclosed and heated coaches is a unique vacation experience for all ages. Visit our new base station with museum, restaurant, and gift shop. This is a National Historic Engineering Landmark, built in 1869.

**Schedule:** Early May through early November: call for schedule. Reservations recommended.

**Admission/Fare:** Adults, $44; seniors, $40; children ages 6-12, $30; under age 6 are free unless occupying a seat.

**Locomotives/Rolling Stock:** Seven coal-fired steam engines; seven enclosed heated coaches; one speeder.

**Location/Directions:** Located in the heart of New Hampshire's White Mountains at the base of the Presidential Mountain Range. I-93, exit 35, Route 3 north, Route 302 east to Cog Railway Base Rd. Site is located 165 miles from Boston, Massachusetts, and 105 miles from Manchester, New Hampshire.

†See ad on page A-2.

**Site Address:** Base Rd., Mt. Washington, NH
**Mailing Address:** Base Rd., Mt. Washington, NH 03589
**Telephone:** (800) 922-8825 and (603) 278-5404
**Fax:** (603) 278-5830
**Internet:** www.thecog.com

**HARTMANN MODEL RAILROAD, LTD.**
*Train ride, museum, display, layout*

**Description:** Housed in two buildings, each 8,000 square feet, is a railroad display for all ages. This site features many operating layouts, from G to Z scales, including a replica of Crawford Notch, New Hampshire, in the mid-1950s to early 1960s. Visitors can see several other detailed operating layouts with trains winding through tunnels, over bridges, and past miniature stations and buildings, and Thomas the Tank Engine operates by a light-sensor system. Also on display are about 5,000 model locomotives and coaches, American and European. Come and see our operating outdoor railroad and take a ride with us. Six to eight-minute train ride on 12" narrow gauge trains, if dry weather.

**Schedule:** Year round: daily, 10 a.m. to 5 p.m.

**Admission/Fare:** Adults, $6; seniors, $5; children ages 5-12, $4; group rates available.

**Nearby Attractions/Accommodations:** Storyland, 1 mile north; Conway Scenic Railroad, 4 miles south.

**Location/Directions:** Four miles north of North Conway in the White Mountains.

*Coupon available, see coupon section.

**Site Address:** Town Hall Rd. and Route 302/16, Intervale, NH
**Mailing Address:** PO Box 165, Intervale, NH 03845
**Telephone:** (603) 356-9922
**Fax:** (603) 356-9958
**E-mail:** info@hartmannrr.com
**Internet:** www.hartmannrr.com

New Hampshire, North Woodstock

CAFE LAFAYETTE
DINNER TRAIN
*Dinner train*
*Standard gauge*

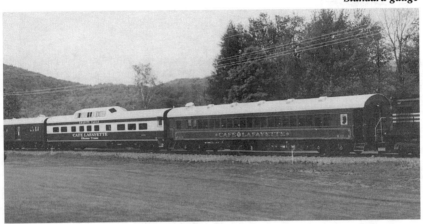

CHET BURAK

**Description:** Experience a leisurely two-hour evening train ride spent criss-crossing the picturesque Pemigewasset River. As dinner is served, period music keeps time with the rail's rhythmic rumbling. See magnificent mountain vistas and lush New England forests during this 20-mile round trip. After dinner, with the compartment lights down low, watch a dramatic New England sunset outside your window.

**Schedule:** Mother's Day through last Saturday in October. Call for details.

**Admission/Fare:** Adults, $46.95; children, 3-11 $29.95; age 2 and under, $7.50 minimum.

**Locomotives/Rolling Stock:** 1923 Pennsylvania Railroad caboose; 1924 Pullman dining car no. 221, former NYC; 1953 Army kitchen car; 1954 CN cafe coach no. 3207; 1952 Pullman dome car, former MoPac/Illinois Central no. 2211

**Nearby Attractions/Accommodations:** Heart of the White Mountain National Forest, Old Man of the Mountain, Franconia Notch State Park. White Mountain Central Railway, Cog Railroad, Mount Washington, Hobo Railroad, Winnepesaukee Scenic Railroad.

**Location/Directions:** I-93, exit 32 on Route 112 midway between Lincoln and North Woodstock, New Hampshire.

**Site Address:** Route 112, North Woodstock, NH
**Mailing Address:** RR1 Box 85, Lincoln, NH 03251
**Telephone:** (603) 745-3500 and (800) 699-3501 (outside NH)
**Fax:** (603) 745-3535
**Internet:** www.cafelafayette.com or www.nhdinnertrain.com

**KLICKETY KLACK
MODEL RAILROAD**
*Layout*

**Description:** Operate a turntable, a quarry train, carnival rides, trolley, Thomas the Tank and Percy; visit a circus, castle, lighthouse, villages and city; see a smoking factory and steam ships in the harbor. All of this is possible at Klickety-Klack, where over two dozen HO, N, and On30 scale trains run over 1,500 feet of track. This miniature collection includes 150 locomotives, 400 freight and passenger cars, 2,000 "people" and much more. This railroad represents over 75,000 hours of work by many dedicated people.

**Schedule:** July 1 through Labor Day: Mondays through Saturdays, 10 a.m. to 5:30 p.m. September through June: Thursdays through Saturdays, 10 a.m. to 5 p.m.

**Admission/Fare:** Adults, $4; children 3-12, $3.

**Nearby Attractions/Accommodations:** Mount Washington, New Hampshire lake region.

**Location/Directions:** At the junction of Routes 28 and 109A.

**Site Address:** 8 Elm St., Wolfeboro Falls, NH
**Mailing Address:** PO Box 205, Wolfeboro Falls, NH 03896
**Telephone:** (603) 569-5384

**New Jersey, Farmingdale**

NEW JERSEY MUSEUM OF
TRANSPORTATION, INC.
*Train ride, display*
*36" gauge*

GARY S. CRAWFORD

**Description:** Pine Creek Railroad is the operating exhibit of the New Jersey Museum of Transportation, Inc., founded in 1952.

**Schedule:** Weekends, April through October, 12 to 4:30 p.m. Daily, July through August, 12 to 4:30 p.m.

**Admission/Fare:** $2 per person; higher fare for special events.

**Locomotives/Rolling Stock:** Ely-Thomas Lumber Co. Shay no. 6; Surrey, Sussex & Southampton no. 2-6-2 no. 26.

**Special Events:** Easter Express, Palm Sunday and Easter weekends; Machinery Day, June Flag Day weekend; Railroader's Day, Sunday after Labor Day; Christmas Express, four weekends starting Thanksgiving weekend.

**Nearby Attractions/Accommodations:** Minutes from Jersey Shore attractions.

**Location/Directions:** Garden State Parkway exit 98, I-195 exit 31, follow signs to Allaire State Park.

**Site Address:** Allaire State Park, Route 524, Wall Township, Monmouth County, NJ
**Mailing Address:** PO Box 622, Farmingdale, NJ 07727-0622
**Telephone:** (732) 938-5524
**E-mail:** crawsat@juno.com
**Internet:** www.njmt.org

244

# BLACK RIVER & WESTERN RAILROAD
*Train ride*
*Standard*

ELIZABETH GRISWOLD

**Description:** The Black River & Western offers a steam/diesel excursion through the rolling hills of Hunterdon County. The 1-hour, 10-minute ride travels between Flemington and Ringoes.

**Schedule:** April through December: weekends departing Flemington Station 11:30 a.m., 1, 2:30, and 4 p.m. July through August: add Thursdays and Fridays (no 4:00 p.m. train on weekdays).

**Admission/Fare:** Adults, $8; children 3-12, $4; under 3 free. Groups/private charters available.

**Locomotives/Rolling Stock:** 1937 Alco 2-8-0 no. 60; 1956 EMD GP9 no. 752; 1950 EMD GP7 no. 780; nos. 752 and 780 GP7 diesels; nos. 1848 and 1849 GP9s; no. 820 NW 1200; nos. 8142 and 8159 SW1200s; nos. 320-323 commuter cars, former Central of New Jersey; more.

**Special Events:** Children ride free, March 16; Easter Bunny Express, March 23-24, 29-30. Great Train Robbery, May 18-19 and Sept. 21-22; Mixed Freight, July 19; Columbus Day, October 7; Halloween Express, October 26-27; Santa Express, November 29-30, December 1, 7-8, 14-15.

**Location/Directions:** Route 202 to Flemington Circle, 12W through second circle, after railroad tracks turn right on Stangl Rd., station is on right.

*Coupon available, see coupon section.

         Radio frequency: 161.085

**Site Address:** Route 12 and Stangl Rd., Flemington, NJ
**Mailing Address:** PO Box 200, Ringoes, NJ 08551
**Telephone:** (908) 782-6622
**Fax:** (908) 782-8251
**E-mail:** psgrinfo@brwrr.com
**Internet:** www.brwrr.com

**PHILLIPSBURG RAILROAD
HISTORIANS**
*Train ride, museum, display
9.5" gauge*

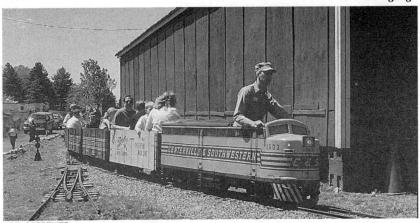

PAUL CARPENITO

**Description:** Miniature train ride on the Centerville & Southwestern Railroad. Speeder car rides on selected open house days.

**Schedule:** May 1 through October 1: Sundays, 10 a.m. to 4 p.m. Open houses with train rides in May, July, and September.

**Admission/Fare:** Donations accepted. Train ride, $1.

**Locomotives/Rolling Stock:** Ingersoll-Rand GE 45-tonner; L&HR caboose; CNJ caboose no. 91197; lowside gondola; L&HR flanger; Centerville & Southwestern, two locomotives and 31 cars.

**Special Events:** Call for 2002 schedule.

**Nearby Attractions/Accommodations:** Crayola Factory, Two Rivers Landing Canal and Museum.

**Location/Directions:** U.S. Route 22, exit at South Main St., follow over black bridge. Museum entrance is across from Joe's Steak Shop and behind Noto/Wyncoop Funeral Home.

     M

**Site Address:** Cross St. and Pine Alley, Phillipsburg, NJ
**Mailing Address:** 292 Chambers St., Phillipsburg, NJ 08805
**Telephone:** (908) 213-1722 and (908) 859-1277
**E-mail:** prrh@angelfire.com
**Internet:** www.angelfire.com/nj/prrh

# MODEL RAILROAD CLUB, INC.
## *Layout*

ROBERT SALFI

**Description:** Large model railroad club featuring fully-scenicked 40 x 40-foot HO scale and 20 x 27-foot N scale operating layouts. Major expansion of HO layout under construction.

**Schedule:** Saturdays, 1 to 4 p.m.

**Admission/Fare:** Adults, $2; children under age 12, $1.

**Special Events:** Annual Light and Sound Show and Open House, three weekends beginning Thanksgiving weekend. Call or visit our website for details.

**Nearby Attractions/Accommodations:** Less than one hour from New York City. Many family-oriented activities in our general area, including museums, major and minor league baseball, and other attractions.

**Location/Directions:** Route 22 east, off Jefferson Ave. (in back of Home Depot), approximately three miles from the Garden State Parkway.

**Site Address:** 295 Jefferson Avenue, Union, NJ
**Mailing Address:** PO Box 1146, Union, NJ 07083-1146
**Telephone:** (908) 964-8808 (recorded message)
**Internet:** www.tmrci.com

# WHIPPANY RAILWAY MUSEUM
## *Museum*
### *Standard gauge*

STEVEN HEPLER

**Description:** Visit the Whippany Railway Museum, headquartered in the restored 1904 freight house of the Morristown & Erie, with its outstanding collection of railroad artifacts and memorabilia. Take a leisurely stroll through a railroad yard lost in time, complete with fieldstone depot, coal yard, wooden water tank, and historic rail equipment. The museum also features an extensive outdoor G scale model train layout, an indoor O gauge train layout, and a display of ocean liner memorabilia. Educational and fun for all ages.

**Schedule:** April through October: Sundays, 12 to 4 p.m.

**Admission/Fare:** Museum–adults, $1; children under age 12, $.50. Special event train fare–adults, $8; children under age 12, $5.

**Locomotives/Rolling Stock:** Morris County Central no. 4039, an 0-6-0 built in 1942 by the American Locomotive Company; railbus no. 10 built in 1918 by the White Motor Company for the Morristown & Erie; more.

**Special Events:** Easter Bunny Express, G Scale Trains and Father's Day, Pumpkin Festival, Halloween Express, Santa Claus Special, more.

**Nearby Attractions/Accommodations:** Morris Museum, General Washington's headquarters, Jockey Hollow National Historic Site.

**Location/Directions:** At the intersection of Route 10 west and Whippany Rd. in Morris County.

       arm  Newark & Metropark Sta.

**Radio frequency:** 160.230

**Site Address:** 1 Railroad Plaza, Whippany, NJ
**Mailing Address:** PO Box 16, Whippany, NJ 07981-0016
**Telephone:** (973) 887-8177
**E-mail:** paultup@optonline.net
**Internet:** www.WhippanyRailwayMuseum.org

# TOY TRAIN DEPOT
*Train ride, museum, display, and layout*
*16" gauge*

HASKELL

**Description:** Two MTC F-7 16" diesels, Baltimore & Ohio, Union Pacific, transport three-car loads south to Live Tree, Dead Grass, Rosebud, Southhoop, and New Bridge. The round trip is 20 minutes.

**Schedule:** Year round: Wednesdays through Sundays, 12 to 4:30 p.m.

**Admission/Fare:** $2.

**Locomotives/Rolling Stock:** MTC 16" F-7 Baltimore & Ohio; MTC 16" F-7 Union Pacific; MTC 16" 4-4-0 1865 steam replica.

**Special Events:** Cottonwood Festival, Alamogordo, New Mexico Labor Day weekend, park/ride.

**Nearby Attractions/Accommodations:** Dog Canyon Museum, Oliver Lee State Park, Lincoln National Forest, Alamogordo Sacramento Mountain Roadbed tours.

**Location/Directions:** North end of Alameda Park is located on N. White Sands Blvd. in Alamogordo.

**Site Address:** 1991 N. White Sands Blvd., Alamogordo, NM
**Mailing Address:** 1991 N. White Sands Blvd., Alamogordo, NM 88310
**Telephone:** (505) 437-2855
**E-mail:** railfanexxmexico@hotmail.com
**Internet:** www.toytraindepot.homestead.com

**New Mexico, Chama**
**Colorado, Antonito**

**CUMBRES & TOLTEC**
**SCENIC RAILROAD**
*Train ride*
*36" gauge*

**Description:** The Cumbres & Toltec Scenic Railroad is the finest remaining example of the original Denver & Rio Grande narrow gauge railroad, built in the 1880s to reach the mines at Silverton. Unspoiled scenery awaits you as you travel through the spectacular San Juan Mountains. You'll pass over high bridges and through tunnels, alongside ghostly rock formations and restored company towns.

**Schedule:** Memorial Day weekend through mid-October: daily departures from both Antonito, 10 a.m., and Chama, 10:30 a.m.

**Admission/Fare:** Adults, $38-$58; children, $19-$29; senior, handicapped and group discounts.

**Locomotives/Rolling Stock:** Locomotives: ex-D&RGW K27 463 (BLW 1903, 21788); ex-D&RGW K36 483, 484, 487, 488, and 489 (BLW 1925); and ex-D&RGW K37 497 (BLW 1980), converted to narrow gauge 1930). Rolling stock: passenger cars constructed in the 1970s and 1980s, over 140 pieces of ex-D&RGW equipment from 1880 to 1968.

**Special Events:** Opening Day, May 26; others to be announced later.

**Nearby Attractions/Accommodations:** Antonito: Great Sand Dunes National Monument, Taos, Santa Fe, Royal Gorge. Chama: Santa Fe, Durango (D&SNGRR), Mesa Verde.

*Coupon available, see coupon section. †See ad on the inside back cover.

Radio frequency: 160.305, 161.505

**Site Address:** U.S. 285, Antonito, CO / 500 Terrace Ave., Chama, NM
**Mailing Address:** PO Box 789, Chama, NM 87520
**Telephone:** (505) 756-2151
**Fax:** (505) 756-2694
**E-mail:** rrinfo@cumbrestoltec.com
**Internet:** www.cumbrestoltec.com

# CLOVIS DEPOT
# MODEL TRAIN MUSEUM
*Museum, display, layout*

PHIL WILLIAMS

**Description:** The Clovis Depot has been restored to its condition in the 1950-60 era and has displays of historic documents and memorabilia covering its use and the history of the AT&SF in New Mexico along the Belen Cutoff since the turn of the century. Also featured are nine model railroad layouts depicting the history of toy trains, the development of the railroad in both Australia and Great Britain, and the Clovis Yard and adjacent city in 1950-60. Live BNSF train operations can be viewed from the dispatcher's position and platform with some 75-100 trains passing each day. We provide a one-hour guided tour of the museum and model railroad layouts, including running the model trains and other displays.

**Schedule:** Wednesdays through Sundays, 12 to 5 p.m. Closed September and February, as well as Easter, Thanksgiving, Christmas, and New Year's Day.

**Admission/Fare:** Call or write for information.

**Locomotives/Rolling Stock:** Fairmont Railway motor car.

**Nearby Attractions/Accommodations:** Blackwater Draw Museum, Blackwater Draw Archaeological site, Norman Petty Studios.

**Location/Directions:** In a restored ATSF passenger depot adjacent to BNSF main line, two blocks west of Main St. on U.S. 60/84.

**Site Address:** 221 W. First St., Clovis, NM
**Mailing Address:** 221 W. First St., Clovis, NM 88101
**Telephone:** (505) 762-0066 and (888) 762-0064
**E-mail:** philipw@3lefties.com
**Internet:** www.clovisdepot.com

# SANTA FE SOUTHERN RAILWAY
*Train ride, dinner train*
*Standard gauge*

MARK ROUNDS

**Description:** The Santa Fe Southern offers 2½-hour, 3½-hour, and 4½-hour excursions with freight movement. Scenic trains year round; April through October, Friday highball and Saturday barbecue dinner trains.

**Schedule:** Gift shop/ticket office, 9 a.m. to 5 p.m. Monday through Saturday; 11 a.m. to 5 p.m., Sunday.

**Admission/Fare:** Adult fares $32 to $55; senior (60+) discount.

**Locomotives/Rolling Stock:** GP 7 no. 92; GP 7 no. 93; New Jersey no. 1158; Great Northern no. 144; Super Chief Club "Acoma"; Santa Fe Pleasure Dome "Plaza Lamy."

**Special Events:** Valentine's Dinner, February 14; Easter, April 14-15; 4th of July barbecue and fireworks; Fiesta barbecue, September 8; Halloween Mystery Theater, October 27; post-Thanksgiving barbecue, November 23; Santa Claus and caroling trains, December 15-24; New Year's Eve dinner, December 31.

**Nearby Attractions/Accommodations:** Santa Fe downtown, art galleries, museums, fine clothing, restaurants, within walking distance of depot.

**Location/Directions:** I-25 at St. Francis to Cerrillos, turn right to Guadalupe, turn left, depot on left at Tomasita's Restaurant.

*Coupon available, see coupon section.

**Site Address:** 410 S. Guadalupe St., Santa Fe, NM
**Mailing Address:** 410 S. Guadalupe St., Santa Fe, NM 87501
**Telephone:** (505) 989-8600 or (888) 989-8600
**Fax:** (505) 983-7620
**E-mail:** depot@sfsr.com
**Internet:** www.sfsr.com

# ARCADE & ATTICA RAILROAD
*Train ride, dinner train, museum*
*Standard gauge*

PETER SWANSON

**Description:** A 90-minute excursion ride in coaches built in 1915, pulled by the last American-made steam locomotive in New York State.

**Schedule:** Memorial weekend through October: weekends, 12:30 and 3 p.m. July through August: Wednesdays, 12:30 and 3 p.m.; Fridays 1 p.m.

**Admission/Fare:** Adults, $10; seniors, $9; children, $7.

**Locomotives/Rolling Stock:** 1920 American steam locomotive; 1915 DL&W coaches.

**Special Events:** Civil War, children's trains, Easter Bunny ride, Santa runs, and Murder Mystery runs.

**Nearby Attractions/Accommodations:** Letchworth State Park.

**Location/Directions:** Forty miles south of Buffalo, 75 miles east of Rochester. On Route 39 near Route 98.

**Site Address:** 278 Main St., Arcade, NY
**Mailing Address:** 278 Main St., Arcade, NY 14009
**Telephone:** (716) 492-3100
**Fax:** (716) 492-0100
**E-mail:** 11k@anarr.com
**Internet:** anarr.com

# DELAWARE & ULSTER RAILRIDE
*Train ride, museum, display*
*Standard gauge*

AARON KELLER

**Description:** Nineteen miles of rail offering a 1-hour or 1¾-hour trip through the scenic Catskill Mountains. Operates on the route of the historic Ulster & Delaware Railroad.

**Schedule:** End of May through end of October: weekends and holidays. July and August: Wednesdays through Sundays. Departs at 10 a.m., 1 and 2:30 p.m.

**Admission/Fare:** Short trip–adults, $7; seniors, $6; children, $5; under age 3 ride free. Long trip–adults, $10; seniors, $8; children, $6; under age 3 ride free.

**Locomotives/Rolling Stock:** D&H no. 5017 RS36 Alco; no. 5106 1953 Alco S-4, former Chesapeake & Ohio; no. 1012 1954 Alco S-4, former Ford Motor Co.; M-405 1928 J.G. Brill Co. diesel-electric rail car, former New York Central; two slat cars with benches, former PRR; two boxcars, former NYC; 44-ton locomotive, former Western Maryland.

**Special Events:** Train Robberies, Tractor Pulls, Twilight Runs, Fall Foliage, Halloween Train, A Day Out with Thomas™, Santa Train.

**Location/Directions:** Route 28, in Arkville, 45 miles west of New York State Thruway.

Radio frequency: 161.385

**Site Address:** Route 28, Arkville, NY
**Mailing Address:** PO Box 310, Stamford, NY 12167
**Telephone:** (800) 225-4132 and (845) 586-DURR
**Fax:** (607) 652-2822
**Internet:** www.durr.org

**MARTISCO STATION MUSEUM**
**CENTRAL NEW YORK CHAPTER NRHS**
*Museum, display, layout*

**Description:** The Martisco Station Museum is a brick Victorian structure erected in 1870 for the New York Central and Hudson River Railroad. Located in a picturesque setting, the restored two-story passenger station houses a collection of railroad mementos of the local area. The adjacent former Pennsylvania Railroad diner houses additional displays. Presently the track passing the station is used five days per week by the Finger Lakes Railway.

**Schedule:** May through October: Sundays 1 to 5 p.m.

**Admission/Fare:** Donations appreciated.

**Locomotives/Rolling Stock:** Pennsylvania Railroad diner.

**Special Events:** Christmas at the Station, December.

**Location/Directions:** New York Route 174, halfway between the villages of Camillus and Marcellus, at the end of Martisco Rd.

**Site Address:** Martisco Rd., Camillus, NY
**Mailing Address:** PO Box 229, Marcellus, NY 13108-0229
**Telephone:** (315) 488-8208
**Fax:** (315) 487-2849
**E-mail:** CNYNRHS@aol.com
**Internet:** www.rrhistorical2.com/cnynrhs

**CENTRAL SQUARE STATION MUSEUM**
**CENTRAL NEW YORK CHAPTER NRHS**
*Museum, display*

**Description:** The Central New York Chapter NRHS is a former joint station of the New York Ontario & Western Railway and the New York Central Railroad, built in 1909. The restored one-story wood passenger station houses a collection of railroad artifacts from the local area.

**Schedule:** May through October: Sundays 12 to 5 p.m.

**Admission/Fare:** Free.

**Locomotives/Rolling Stock:** 0-4-0 steam locomotive no. 53 American Locomotive Co.; 0-4-0 narrow gauge steam no. 22; Brill car no. M-39; 25-ton G.E. diesel no. 7; Fairmont Rail motor car, 0-4-0T steam engine from Solvay Process.

**Nearby Attractions/Accommodations:** St. Lawrence Seaway, Thousand Islands, Adirondack Park.

**Location/Directions:** Railroad St. in Central Square, off Route 11 south of town, close to Route 81.

       M

**Site Address:** Railroad St., Central Square, NY
**Mailing Address:** PO Box 229, Marcellus, NY 13108-0229
**Telephone:** (315) 488-8208
**Fax:** (315) 487-2849
**E-mail:** CNYNRHS@aol.com
**Internet:** www.rrhistorical2.com/cnynrhs

**Description:** The Chester Historical Society's charter is for the promotion and preservation of the local history of the town and village of Chester, New York. The town was settled in the early 1700s. The first shipment of fresh milk to New York City by rail was made in 1842 via the Erie Railroad. The museum is housed in a 1915 Erie Railroad station on the former Erie main line in Chester, New York. This Arts-and-Crafts-influenced passenger station replaced the original 1841 station in 1915. After sitting in disuse for several decades, it opened on June 12, 1999, as Chester's Local History Museum.

**Schedule:** May through October: Saturdays 9 a.m. to 1 p.m. Groups by appointment anytime.

**Nearby Attractions/Accommodations:** The station is located in Historic Downtown, along the Orange Pathways Heritage Trail and within walking distance to refreshments, restaurants, antique shops, etc. Twenty miles west of West Point.

**Location/Directions:** New York State Thruway exit 16. Take Route 17 west 10 miles, exit 126 "Chester," straight at light onto Academy Ave. Left Main St., right at firehouse and continue on Main St. through downtown Chester. Station on left.

**Site Address:** 1915 Erie Railroad Station, 19 Winkler Pl., Chester, NY
**Mailing Address:** 47 Main St., Chester, NY 10918
**Telephone:** (845) 469-2591
**E-mail:** chester_historical@mac.com

# COOPERSTOWN & CHARLOTTE VALLEY RAILROAD

*Train ride, museum*
*Standard gauge*

ARIC PEERY

**Description:** A 16-mile, two-hour round trip from Cooperstown to Milford and back. Milford is the site of the Milford Park Railway, a home-built narrow gauge railroad, and a small museum in the 1869 depot. The entire operation is run by the Leatherstocking Railway Museum.

**Schedule:** May through October, daytime excursions. Call, write, or see website for days of operation and departure times.

**Admission/Fare:** Adults, $8; seniors (62+), $7; children 4-12, $5; under 4 free.

**Locomotives/Rolling Stock:** NYSW NW2 no. 116 (in its original NYO&W scheme); three DL&W passenger cars; D&H caboose no. 35723; EL caboose no. C316; D&H big-hook crane no. 30021; more.

**Special Events:** April through December; call, write, or see website for listing of specific events, dates, times, and fares.

**Nearby Attractions/Accommodations:** National Baseball Hall of Fame, the Farmers Museum, Glimmerglass State Park, National Soccer Hall of Fame, The Elm Inn of Milford.

**Location/Directions:** I-88, exit 17, north on Route 28 for 8 miles to Milford. East on Route 166 about one block, turn right before railroad crossing.

 **Radio Frequency: 151.670**

**Site Address:** E. Main St. (New York Route 166), Milford, NY
**Mailing Address:** PO Box 681, Oneonta, NY 13820-0681
**Telephone:** (607) 432-2429
**Fax:** (607) 433-0747
**E-mail:** lrhs@lrhs.com
**Internet:** www.lrhs.com

# ALCO BROOKS RAILROAD DISPLAY
*Display*
*Standard gauge*

**Description:** Located at the Chautauqua County Fairgrounds since 1987, the display features an original Alco-Brooks steam locomotive, a wood-sided boxcar housing displays of Chautauqua County commerce and railroads along with a gift shop, and a restored wooden caboose. Other items of interest at the site are a Nickel Plate work car, an Erie Railroad concrete telephone booth, a New York Central harp switch stand, a Pennsylvania Railroad cast-iron crossing sign, a DAV&P land line marker, and an operating crossing flasher.

**Schedule:** June 1 through August 31: Saturdays, 1 to 3 p.m., weather permitting. Open daily during special events or by appointment.

**Admission/Fare:** Donations appreciated.

**Locomotives/Rolling Stock:** 1916 Alco-Brooks 0-6-0 no. 444, former Boston & Maine; 1907 Delaware & Hudson 22020 wood-sided boxcar; 1905 New York Central 19224 wooden caboose.

**Special Events:** Chautauqua County Antique Auto Show and Flea Market, May 17-19. Chautauqua County Fair, July 22-28.

**Nearby Attractions/Accommodations:** Dunkirk Historical Museum, Dunkirk Lighthouse, Chautauqua Institution, Four Points Hotel Sheraton, Brookside Manor bed and breakfast.

**Location/Directions:** I-90, exit 59, to Chautauqua County Fairgrounds.

**Site Address:** 1089 Central Ave., Chautauqua County Fairgrounds, Dunkirk, NY
**Mailing Address:** Historical Society of Dunkirk, 513 Washington Ave., Dunkirk, NY 14048
**Telephone:** (716) 366-3797
**E-mail:** davrr@netsync.net

# NEW YORK & LAKE ERIE RAILROAD
*Train ride*
*Standard*

**Description:** Twenty or 30-mile scenic rail excursions through western New York's beautiful rural countryside. Trains travel over historic Erie Railroad trackage. All trains have station stops in a quaint rural village.

**Admission/Fare:** Adults, $17; children, $4.

**Locomotives/Rolling Stock:** NYLE Alco Century 425 no. 1013; NYLE Alco Century 425 no. 6101.

**Special Events:** Railroad Days and Taste of Amish excursions, June and September; fall foliage excursions; Ghost and Goblin Train, last weekend in October; Christmas at the Depots, November.

**Nearby Attractions/Accommodations:** Within 1½ hours from Niagara Falls and casino; Darien Lake Amusement Park, Chautauqua Lake.

**Location/Directions:** Gowanda is 30 miles south of Buffalo, New York. Station is ½ mile east of Route 62, center of Gowanda. Take Water St. to Commercial St.

**Site Address:** 50 Commercial St., Gowanda, NY
**Mailing Address:** PO Box 309, Gowanda, NY 14070
**Telephone:** (716) 532-5716
**Fax:** (716) 532-9128
**E-mail:** nyletour@aol.com

# RAILROAD MUSEUM OF LONG ISLAND
*Museum, display*

**Description:** Greenport consists of an 1890s Long Island Railroad freight station with exhibits depicting the development of railroad industry on Long Island. Riverhead houses a large collection of vintage LIRR equipment.

**Schedule:** Call or write for information.

**Admission/Fare:** Call or write for information.

**Locomotives/Rolling Stock:** LIRR G5s 4-6-0 no. 39; LIRR RS-3 no. 1556; BEDT 0-6-0T no. 16; LIRR double-decker no. 200; LIRR "Jaws" snowplow no. W-83; LIRR caboose no. C-68; LIRR RPO no. 4209; more.

**Nearby Attractions/Accommodations:** Riverhead–Splish Splash Waterpark, Tanger Outlet Mall. Greenport–historic Greenport waterfront district.

**Location/Directions:** Call or write for directions or check website.

**Site Address:** Fourth St. at the tracks, Greenport, NY, and 416 Griffing Ave., Riverhead, NY
**Mailing Address:** PO Box 726, Greenport, NY 11944
**Telephone:** (631) 477-0439 or (631) 727-7920
**E-mail:** twinforks@mail.peconic.net
**Internet:** www.bitnik.com/RMLI

## HUDSON VALLEY RAILROAD SOCIETY/RAILROAD STATION
*Museum, display, layout*

LARRY LALIBERTE

**Description:** This museum is a restoration of a 1914 railroad station by a railroad club. It relates the history of the station and the Roosevelt and Vanderbilt connection. Operating display layouts.

**Schedule:** Year round: Mondays 7 to 10 p.m. Mid-June through mid-September: weekends 11 a.m. to 5 p.m. Memorial Day and July 4.

**Admission/Fare:** Free. Donations appreciated.

**Nearby Attractions/Accommodations:** Franklin Delano Roosevelt home and library, Vanderbilt mansion, Old Rhinebeck Aerodome, bicycle tours, hiking trails, golf course, river tours, Mills Norrie State Park, hotels, motels, bed and breakfast, restaurants.

**Location/Directions:** East on E. Market St. from U.S. 9 (historic signs posted on U.S. 9) to bottom of hill. Station in Town Park on right.

**Site Address:** Riverfront Park, 34 River Road, Hyde Park, NY
**Mailing Address:** PO Box 135, Hyde Park, NY 12538
**Telephone:** (845) 229-2338
**E-mail:** revaul@aol.com
**Internet:** www.hydeparkstation.com

# TROLLEY MUSEUM OF NEW YORK
*Train ride*
*Standard gauge*

MARILYN JENNINGS

**Description:** This museum was established in 1955 and moved to its present location in 1983, becoming part of the Kingston Urban Cultural Park. A 2.5-mile, 40-minute round trip takes passengers from the foot of Broadway to Kingston Point, with stops at the museum in both directions. A gas-powered railcar operates on private right-of-way and in-street trackage along Rondout Creek to the Hudson River over part of the former Ulster & Delaware Railroad main line. An exhibit hall features trolley exhibits and a theater.

**Schedule:** Memorial weekend to Columbus Day: 12 to 5 p.m. Last ride departs at 4:30 p.m. Charters available.

**Admission/Fare:** Adults, $3; seniors and children, $2.

**Locomotives/Rolling Stock:** Eleven trolleys; eight rapid transit cars; Whitcomb diesel-electric; Brill model 55 interurban.

**Special Events:** Shad Festival, May 4-5; Mother's Day (moms ride free); Father's Day (dads ride free); Santa Days, December 7-8.

**Nearby Attractions/Accommodations:** Hudson River Maritime Museum, Senate House, Catskill Mountains, Urban Cultural Park.

**Location/Directions:** In the historic Rondout Waterfront area of Kingston. Call or write for directions or see map on web page.

*Coupon available, see coupon section.

Rhinecliffe

Radio Frequency: 462.175

**Site Address:** 89 E. Strand, Kingston, NY
**Mailing Address:** PO Box 2291, Kingston, NY 12402
**Telephone:** (845) 331-3399
**E-mail:** info@tmny.org
**Internet:** www.tmny.org

# MAYBROOK RAILROAD
## HISTORICAL SOCIETY
### *Museum*

**Description:** The museum offers photographs and memorabilia.

**Schedule:** April through October: weekends, 1 to 4 p.m.

**Admission/Fare:** Free.

**Locomotives/Rolling Stock:** Caboose no. 512

**Nearby Attractions/Accommodations:** Museum Village in Monroe, New York, includes model railroad of Orange County; Erie Depot Museum in Port Jervis; O&W Railroad Historical Society archives in Middletown.

**Location/Directions:** I-84 to exit 5; 2 miles south on Route 208. Located in rear of Maybrook Library.

**Site Address:** 101 Main St., Maybrook, NY (rear of library)
**Mailing Address:** PO Box 105, Maybrook, NY 12543
**Telephone:** (914) 427-2591

# CATSKILL MOUNTAIN RAILROAD
*Train ride*
*Standard gauge*

HARRY G. JAMESON III

**Description:** This railroad, which operates over trackage of the former Ulster & Delaware Railroad, offers a 6-mile, one-hour round trip to Phoenicia along the scenic Esopus Creek, through the heart of the beautiful Catskill Mountains. Tourists, inner-tubers, and visitors interested in fishing or canoeing may ride one way or round trip.

**Schedule:** Weekends and holidays. May 25 through September 2, 11 a.m. to 5 p.m.; September 7 through October 27, 12 to 4 p.m.

**Admission/Fare:** Adults, $6; children 4-11, $4; under age 4 are free.

**Locomotives/Rolling Stock:** No. 1, "The Duck," 1942 Davenport 38-ton diesel-mechanical, former U.S. Air Force; no. 2, "The Goat," H.K. Porter 50-ton diesel-electric, former U.S. Navy; no. 2361, 1952 Alco RS-1, former Wisconsin Central (Soo Line).

**Special Events:** Twilight Limited excursions with music and refreshments at the Empire State Railway Museum; Teddy Bear Train; Leaf Peeper Specials; Halloween Train. Call for schedule.

**Nearby Attractions:** World's largest kaleidoscope. Tubing the Esopus Creek. Museums, sports activities, restaurants, lodging, campgrounds, state parks, scenic sites.

**Location/Directions:** New York State Thruway, exit 19 (Kingston), and travel west 22 miles on Route 28 to the railroad depot in Mt. Pleasant.

          TRAIN

**Site Address:** Route 28, Mt. Pleasant, NY
**Mailing Address:** PO Box 46, Shokan, NY 12481
**Telephone:** (845) 688-7400
**Fax:** (845) 657-7257
**E-mail:** spiegler@netstep.com

**Description:** Located in a 1905 New York Central freight depot. Displays include rail maintenance tools, models, equipment, and memorabilia. We have a portable HO scale layout on loan and a 200 x 14-foot HO scale layout is under construction.

**Schedule:** Year round: Mondays through Saturdays 12 to 7 p.m. and Sundays 12 to 5 p.m.

**Admission/Fare:** Adults, $5; seniors, $4; children, $3.

**Locomotives/Rolling Stock:** Five 1948 Budd coaches, former NYC Empire State Express coaches from WNY Railway Historical Society; Nickel Plate Road RS11 Alco Diesel 1952 owned by Genesee Valley Transportation.

**Special Events:** Two-hour, 34-mile rail excursions are on select dates in summer and fall. Call for schedule.

**Nearby Attractions/Accommodations:** Niagara Falls, Buffalo, Rochester, Six Flags Darien Lake Amusement Park, Lockport Locks & Canal Cruises, Ridge Road Station gift shop.

**Location/Directions:** North of I-90, exit 48A, village of Medina at intersection of New York 63 and New York 31. One block west of Main St., next to railroad tracks.

*Coupon available, see coupon section.

        M

**Site Address:** 530 West Ave., Medina, NY
**Mailing Address:** 530 West Ave., Medina, NY 14103
**Telephone:** (716) 798-6106
**Fax:** (716) 798-1829
**E-mail:** rrmuseum@tigdata.net
**Internet:** www.railroadmuseum.net

# NORTH CREEK RAILWAY
## DEPOT MUSEUM
### *Museum*

TOM RYAN

**Description:** A restored 1872 train depot that houses a museum with exhibits on regional socioeconomic history, including the history of skiing at Gore Mountain, Ted Roosevelt's ride to the presidency, mining, logging, and the railroad.

**Schedule:** Tuesday through Sunday, 11 a.m. to 4 p.m.

**Admission/Fare:** Adults, $2; children, $1.

**Special Events:** Theodore Roosevelt Weekend, October 12-14.

**Nearby Attractions/Accommodations:** Upper Hudson River Railroad Scenic Train. Gore Mountain Ski Center. Garnet Hill Mine.

**Location/Directions:** Exit 23 Northway to Route 28 to North Creek.

   M arm

**Site Address:** 5 Railroad Pl., North Creek, NY
**Mailing Address:** PO Box 156, North Creek, NY 12853
**Telephone:** (518) 251-5842
**Fax:** (518) 251-5599
**E-mail:** georgereed@juno.com
**Internet:** www.northcreekraildepot.org

# UPPER HUDSON RIVER RAILROAD
*Train ride, museum*
*Standard gauge*

**Description:** A 2-hour scenic trip along the Hudson River in the Adirondack Mountains. Depart from the restored station where Teddy Roosevelt learned he was President, the oldest station in Adirondacks.

**Schedule:** May, June, September, and October: weekends. Summer: daily. Fall: Wednesdays through Sundays. Departures at 10 a.m. and 1 p.m.

**Admission/Fare:** Adults, $12; seniors, $11; children, $8.

**Locomotives/Rolling Stock:** Alco RS-36 no. 5019; Alco S-1 no. 5; L&N custom coach, 1920s CN coaches; CNJ coach; open air flatcar; LV caboose.

**Special Events:** Restoration of 90-foot turntable will be complete in 2002.

**Nearby Attractions/Accommodations:** Adjacent to North Creek Rail Depot Museum; Adirondack Museum; Cooperfield Inn; numerous restaurants, lodging; close to all Warren County/Lake George attractions.

**Location/Directions: Interstate** Exit 87 Exit 23, Route 9 north, Route 28 west to North Creek.

**Site Address:** 3 Railroad Pl., North Creek, NY
**Mailing Address:** 3 Railroad Pl., North Creek, NY 12853
**Telephone:** (518) 251-5334
**Fax:** (518) 251-5332
**E-mail:** uhrr@netheaven.com
**Internet:** www.UpperHudsonRiverRR.com

## BULLTHISTLE MODEL RAILROAD
## SOCIETY AND MUSEUM
*Museum, display, layout*

ERIC ROBB

**Description:** Featured are an operating HO layout of the O&W yards in Norwich, New York, circa 1950; O and S gauge antique train layouts; a modern N gauge layout; displays feature historically significant memorabilia.

**Schedule:** Year round. Thursdays, Fridays and Saturdays, 2 to 4 p.m. or by appointment.

**Admission/Fare:** Donations appreciated.

**Special Events:** Railroad Days, June.

**Nearby Attractions/Accommodations:** Adirondack Scenic Railroad; Cooperstown & Charlotte Valley Railroad; Chenango County Museum; Northeast Classic Car Museum.

**Location/Directions:** New York Route 12 to New York Route 23, turn east and go approximately two blocks. Museum is on the left 100 yards past railroad crossing. From east, New York Route 23 to Norwich. Museum is on the right before railroad crossing.

**Site Address:** 33 Rexford St. (New York Route 23), Norwich, NY
**Mailing Address:** 33 Rexford St., Norwich, NY 13815
**Telephone:** (607) 334-4522
**E-mail:** eled@ascent.net

## ADIRONDACK SCENIC RAILROAD
*Train ride, museum*
*Standard gauge*

**Description:** Rides from one hour to five hours round trip out of Utica, Thendara, and Saranac Lake–Lake Placid. Outstanding depots.

**Schedule:** Varies. Phone (315) 369-6290 (Thendara), (315) 724-0700 (Utica) and (518) 891-3238 (Saranac Lake)

**Admission/Fare:** Adults, $8 to $28; children $4 to $14.

**Locomotives/Rolling Stock:** Locomotives: 705 EMD SW1; 8223 Alco RS3; 105 GE 44-ton; 2064 Alco C420; 1508 EMD F7; 4243 Alco C424; 1500 EMD F7; also many passenger cars and work cars.

**Special Events:** Rail Fan Days, train robberies, Model Railroad Shows, cocktail runs, Halloween and Santa runs, steam trains, milk trains, meet the Adirondack authors, artwork sale on train.

**Nearby Attractions/Accommodations:** Old Forge Lake Cruises; McCauley Mountain Chairlift Rides; Arts Center/Old Forge; Old Forge Hardware; Enchanted Forest/Water Safari; Great Camp Sagamore; The Adirondack Museum; the W.W. Durant, Raquette Lake Navigation Co.; Adirondack Scenic Railroad, Return Trip; restaurants, lodging. For Lake Placid/Saranac Lake attractions, visit our website.

**Location/Directions:** Three locations–too complex–send for information.

*Coupon available, see coupon section.

**Site Address:** Thendara Station, Old Forge, NY; Falvo Station on Lee St., Utica, NY; Lake Placid and Saranac Lake train stations
**Mailing Address:** PO Box 84, Thendara, NY 13472. **Phone:** See above.
**Fax:** (315) 369-2479
**E-mail:** train@telenet.net
**Internet:** www.adirondackrr.com

# TIOGA SCENIC RAILROAD
*Train ride, dinner train*
*Standard gauge*

**Description:** A 22-mile round trip aboard early 1900s vintage train. The trip lasts about two hours.

**Schedule:** July through October.

**Admission/Fare:** From $6 to $30.

**Locomotives/Rolling Stock:** Tioga Scenic Railroad SW1 no. 40; OH Railway SW12 no. 1216; OH Railway RS18u no. 1811; two DL&W coaches built 1922; open-air car from the 1890s; two dining cars from the 1940s.

**Nearby Attractions/Accommodations:** Wineries, Finger Lakes, Hickory Park camping, Tioga Park flea market, Historic Owego shopping.

**Location/Directions:** Twenty miles west of Binghamton, Route 17, exit 64. Follow Route 96 north; after the railroad underpass turn left.

**Site Address:** 25 Delphine St., Owego, NY
**Mailing Address:** 25 Delphine St., Owego, NY 13827
**Telephone:** (607) 687-6786
**Fax:** (607) 687-6817
**E-mail:** TSRR40@clarityconnect.com
**Internet:** www.tiogascenicrailroad.com

**EMPIRE STATE RAILWAY MUSEUM**
*Museum, display, layout*

**Description:** This is an all-volunteer membership organization dedicated to bringing alive the history of Catskill Mountain railroads, their people, and the towns they served. The museum is located in a former Ulster & Delaware railroad station, which celebrated its 100th anniversary in 1999.

**Schedule:** Memorial Day through Columbus Day: weekends and holidays 11 a.m. to 4 p.m.

**Admission/Fare:** Suggested donation–adults, $3; seniors and students, $2; children under age 12, $1; families, $5.

**Locomotives/Rolling Stock:** No. 23, 1910 Alco 2-8-0, former Lake Superior & Ishpeming under restoration; 1920 D&H dining car "Lion Gardner"; 1926 CV autocarrier; 1920 B&M railway post office car.

**Special Events:** Photo exhibit, lectures, slide shows, Santa Claus Special

**Nearby Attractions/Accommodations:** Catskill Mountain Railroad, Delaware Ulster rail ride, New York state campgrounds at Woodland Valley and Wilson State Park, hiking, fishing in Catskill Forest Preserve, tube rides on Esopus Creek.

**Location/Directions:** New York State Thruway to exit 19, then Route 28 west to Phoenicia.

       M

**Site Address:** Off High St., Phoenicia, NY
**Mailing Address:** PO Box 455, Phoenicia, NY 12464
**Telephone:** (845) 688-7501
**Internet:** www.esrm.com

New York, Rochester

## NEW YORK MUSEUM
## OF TRANSPORTATION
*Train ride, museum, layout*
*Standard gauge*

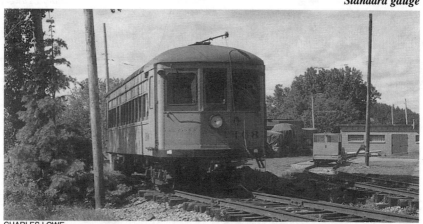

CHARLES LOWE

**Description:** The site includes trolleys, rail and road vehicles, related artifacts and exhibits, an 11 x 21 operating HO model railroad, and a video/photo gallery. A 2-mile track car ride connects with the Rochester & Genesee Valley Railroad Museum, departing every half-hour.

**Schedule:** Museum–year round, Sundays, 11 a.m. to 5 p.m. Groups by appointment. Ride–May through October, weather permitting.

**Admission/Fare:** Adults, $5; seniors, $4; students ages 5-15, $3. Includes entry to NYMT, Rochester & Genesee Valley Railroad Museum, and ride. Lower rates November through April.

**Locomotives/Rolling Stock:** Rochester & Eastern interurban car no. 157; North Texas Trac. interurban car no. 409; P&W cars nos. 161 and 168; Elmira, Corning & Waverly no. 107; Philadelphia snow sweeper no. C-130; Rochester Railway no. 437; Batavia Street Railway no. 33; more.

**Special Events:** Transportation Day, mid-May; Model Steam and Gas Engines, July; Diesel Days, August.

**Nearby Attractions/Accommodations:** Finger Lakes Region, Niagara Falls, Arcade & Attica Railroad, Genesee Country Museum, George Eastman House Museum of Photography.

**Location/Directions:** I-90, exit 46, south 3 miles on I-390, exit 11. Route 251 west 1.5 miles, right on E. River Rd., 1 mile to museum entrance.

Radio Frequency: 160.440

**Site Address:** 6393 E. River Rd., W. Henrietta, NY
**Mailing Address:** PO Box 136, W. Henrietta, NY 14586
**Telephone:** (716) 533-1113
**Internet:** www.nymt.mus.ny.us

273

# ROCHESTER & GENESEE VALLEY RAILROAD MUSEUM

*Train ride, museum*
*Standard gauge*

CHRIS HAUF

**Description:** The museum, housed in a restored 1908 Erie Railroad station, displays railroad artifacts from western New York railroads. On outdoor tracks are a number of railroad cars and diesel locomotives open for display. Museum has tours and track car rides.

**Schedule:** May through October: Sundays, 11 am. to 5 p.m. Visits at other times by appointment.

**Admission/Fare:** Adults, $5; seniors, $4; children 5-15, $3.

**Locomotives/Rolling Stock:** 1946 GE 80-ton diesel, former Eastman Kodak; 1953 Alco RS-3, former Lehigh Valley; 1953 Alco S-4, former Nickel Plate; 1941 GE 45-ton, former Rochester Gas & Electric; Fairbanks-Morse H12-44, former U.S. Army.

**Special Events:** Diesel Days, mid-July.

**Nearby Attractions/Accommodations:** Strong Museum, Eastman House, Genesee Country Museum, Frontier Stadium, New York Museum of Transportation.

**Location/Directions:** All regularly scheduled Sunday tours start at the New York Museum of Transportation (previous page). The depot itself is located on Route 251, just west of East River Rd.

**Site Address:** 6393 E. River Rd., Henrietta, NY
**Mailing Address:** PO Box 23326, Rochester, NY 14692-3326
**Telephone:** (716) 533-1431
**E-mail:** mikeb123@rochester.rr.com
**Internet:** www.transportation.mus.ny.us

        **SALAMANCA RAIL MUSEUM**
*Museum*

**Description:** Fully restored BR&P depot and freight house. Artifacts and photographs tell the history of railroads in western New York and Pennsylvania. For children, the museum grounds offer the permanent display of a boxcar, a crew camp car, and the chance to explore two cabooses.

**Schedule:** April through December: Mondays through Saturdays, 10 a.m. to 5 p.m. and Sundays, 12 to 5 p.m. Closed Mondays in April, October, November, and December.

**Admission/Fare:** Donations appreciated.

**Locomotives/Rolling Stock:** B&O caboose; P&WV caboose; Erie crane crew car; Conrail boxcar; Jordan spreader; DL&W electric commuter coach.

**Nearby Attractions/Accommodations:** Allegany State Park, Seneca Iroquois National Museum, Holiday Valley Summer-Winter Resort, Chautauqua Institution.

**Location/Directions:** Downtown Salamanca on New York Route 17/U.S. I-86, Route 219.

**Site Address:** 170 Main St., Salamanca, NY
**Mailing Address:** 170 Main St., Salamanca, NY 14779
**Telephone:** (716) 945-3133

**Description:** Five-hundred-foot display of some 40 historical scenes (Troy, Saratoga, Lake George, New York, and Rutland, Vermont) from the Hudson-Champlain Valley, all set in 1950.

**Schedule:** One Saturday per month, 12 to 4 p.m. Call or check website for dates.

**Admission/Fare:** $5 per person. The exhibit is not for children under 53 inches tall.

**Location/Directions:** Located opposite Troy High School, just south of Route 7.

**Site Address:** Burdett Ave., Troy, NY
**Mailing Address:** RMRRS, RPI Student Union, 110 8th St., Troy, NY 12180
**Telephone:** (518) 276-2971
**Fax:** (518) 276-6920
**E-mail:** mrrs@rpi.edu
**Internet:** www.union.rpi.edu/railroad

**Description:** A children's museum with hands-on interactive displays concerning science, natural science, history, and culture. Frequent craft activities and events.

**Schedule:** Tuesdays through Fridays, 10 a.m. to 5 p.m.; Saturdays, 10 a.m. to 4:30 p.m.; Sundays, 12 to 4:30 p.m.

**Admission/Fare:** $3.50 per person; 9 months and younger, free.

**Locomotives/Rolling Stock:** We have a stationary locomotive and cars for viewing: New York Central 0-6-0; Adirondack Alco; Santa Fe passenger car; Pennsylvania Railroad caboose.

**Nearby Attractions/Accommodations:** Utica Zoo.

**Location/Directions:** 311 Main St., next door to Union Station train station.

**Site Address:** 311 Main St., Utica, NY
**Mailing Address:** 311 Main St., Utica, NY 13501
**Telephone:** (315) 724-6129
**Fax:** (315) 724-6120 (call first)
**E-mail:** caryi@aol.com

VIRGIL HURLEY

**Description:** Our museum is located in a former Piedmont & Northern Railway depot. The outside display consists of railroad cars and a GE 25-ton diesel-electric switcher. The inside displays consist of various articles from the Piedmont & Northern Railway and the Southern Railway, as well as O scale model trains, an HO scale layout, and a gift area.

**Schedule:** Wednesdays through Saturdays, 10:30 a.m. to 4:30 p.m.; Sundays, 1:30 to 4:40 p.m.

**Admission/Fare:** Donations are accepted.

**Locomotives/Rolling Stock:** GE 25-ton diesel-electric switcher, formerly used by Duke Power at their River Bend steam station; Southern Railway caboose no. X662, built in 1951; sleeper-lounge car the "Keystone State," built by Pullman in 1955 for the New York, New Haven & Hartford; more.

**Special Events:** Third Saturday in May, Belmont's "Garibaldi Days" spring festival across the street in Stowe Park.

**Nearby Attractions/Accommodations:** Daniel Stowe Botanical Gardens in Belmont; Schiele Museum in Gastonia; Museum of the New South and Discovery Place in Charlotte; Carowinds amusement park in Charlotte on the North Carolina–South Carolina state line.

**Location/Directions:** Belmont is 10 miles west of Charlotte; the museum is a mile off I-85 in the downtown area.

**Site Address:** 4 N. Main St., Belmont, NC 28012
**Mailing Address:** Piedmont Carolinas Chapter NRHS, PO Box 11753, Charlotte, NC 28220
**Telephone:** (704) 825-4403
**Internet:** www.webserve.net/piedmont-nrhs

# NEW HOPE VALLEY RAILWAY
*Train ride*
*Standard gauge*

GRAY LACKEY

**Description:** Eight-mile round trip over 4 miles of the original Norfolk Southern Railway's Durham Branch on a diesel-powered train with open cars and cabooses. Other equipment and displays at this site.

**Schedule:** May through December: first Sunday of month, departures at 12, 1, 2, 3, and 4 p.m.

**Admission/Fare:** Adults, $6; children, $4.

**Locomotives/Rolling Stock:** 80-ton GE and Whtcomb; 45-ton GE; 50-ton Whitcomb; 0-4-0T steam engine; cabooses, freight cars.

**Special Events:** Halloween Train, Santa Claus Train.

**Nearby Attractions/Accommodations:** Jordan Lake, camping, fishing, boating, Shearon Harris Nuclear Power Plant tours, Ramada Inn in Apex, North Carolina.

**Location/Directions:** Eight miles south of Apex on State Route 1011. In Bonsal turn right on Daisey St., 300 feet on left.

**Radio frequency: 160.425**

**Site Address:** 5121 Daisey St., Bonsal, NC
**Mailing Address:** PO Box 40, New Hill, NC 27562
**Telephone:** (919) 362-5416
**E-mail:** nhvry@mindspring.com
**Internet:** www.mindspring.com/~nhvry

279

**CHARLOTTE TROLLEY, INC.**
*Trolley ride*

**Description:** 1.2-mile ride through historic South End in vintage streetcar.

**Schedule:** Year round: Friday and Saturday, 10 a.m. to 9 p.m.; Sunday 10 a.m. to 6 p.m.; leaving the barn on the hour and the half hour.

**Admission/Fare:** Round trip, $2; children under 13, free; groups, $1 each; handicap accessible.

**Locomotives/Rolling Stock:** No. 1 Charlotte Electric Railway by United Electric Car Co. 1914 for Piraeus, Greece; no. 13 Philadelphia Suburban Transp. by St. Louis Car Co. 1949 modified double-end PCC; no. 85 Southern Public Utilities homebuilt 1927 no. 407 South Carolina Power Co. JG Brill 1922 for Virginia Railway & Power Co. (Richmond), four-wheel Birney, was Virginia Railway & Power no. 1520 then Ft. Collins Municipal Railway no. 25-II; Ashville Power & Light no. 117 4-wheel Birney Brill 1927.

**Special Events:** Monthly pub crawl; annual gala; Volunteer Day, May 20 ; Labor Day barbecue; New Year's.

**Nearby Attractions/Accommodations:** Restaurants, shops, galleries, tea house, antiques, and convention center.

**Location/Directions:** South 1 mile from town on South Blvd. at Atherton Mill.

*Coupon available, see coupon section.

**Site Address:** 2104 South Blvd., Charlotte, NC
**Mailing Address:** 2104 South Blvd., Charlotte, NC 28203
**Telephone:** (704) 375-0850
**Fax:** (704) 375-0553
**E-mail:** clttrolley@aol.com
**Internet:** www.charlottetrolley.org

**GREAT SMOKY MOUNTAINS RAILROAD**
*Train ride, dinner train, museum*
*Standard gauge*

LAVIDGE AND ASSOCIATES

**Description:** Departures from Dillsboro and Bryson City's historic depot, traveling through scenic mountains of North Carolina. White water rafting packages, gourmet dinner and mystery theater trains.

**Schedule:** January through December: schedule varies with season. Call or write for schedule and reservations.

**Admission/Fare:** Adults, $28 and up; children under age 13, $14 and up. Varies seasonally. Steam excursions, add $5 per adult. Ages 21+, $7 upgrade to club car. Some lunch options.

**Locomotives/Rolling Stock:** No. 1702, 1942 Baldwin 2-8-0, former U.S. Army; nos. 711 and 777, EMD GP7s; nos. 210 and 223, EMD GP35s.

**Special Events:** Santa Express, featuring the story of "Polar Express," December; Day Out with Thomas event, July/August; spring and fall wine trains.

**Nearby Attractions/Accommodations:** Smoky Mountains National Park, Cherokee Indian Reservation, Biltmore estate, whitewater rafting.

**Location/Directions:** From Asheville, I-40 west to exit 27 to U.S. 74 west. Exit 81 for Dillsboro, or exit 67 for Bryson City. From Atlanta, 85 to 441 North.

**Site Address:** 119 Front St., Dillsboro, NC or Depot St., Bryson City, NC
**Mailing Address:** PO Box 397, Dillsboro, NC 28725
**Telephone:** (800) 872-4681 or (828) 586-8811
**Fax:** (828) 586-8806
**E-mail:** traininfo@gsmr.com
**Internet:** www.gsmr.com

# NATIONAL RAILROAD MUSEUM
# AND HALL OF FAME
*Museum, display, layout*

**Description:** The museum exhibits include photographs, maps, displays, a gift shop, a model railroad layout, four pieces of rolling stock, and a recreated telegraph office. The SAL locomotive 1114 SDP 35 and caboose SAL 5241 are on display at the museum.

**Schedule:** Year round: Saturdays 10 a.m. to 5 p.m.; Sundays 1 to 5 p.m.; during the week by appointment.

**Admission/Fare:** Free, donations appreciated.

**Locomotives/Rolling Stock:** SAL locomotive 1114 SDP 35; SAL caboose 5241; replica of the "Tornado" built in 1892 at Raleigh, North Carolina.

**Nearby Attractions/Accommodations:** North Carolina Motor Speedway, Morrow Mountain State Park, Town Creek Indian Mound, North Carolina Zoo, Pee Dee National Wildlife Refuge, Pinehurst, over 40 golf courses.

**Location/Directions:** In Hamlet, at the stop light on Highway 74 and Raleigh, go across Raleigh St. The museum is on the right in the middle of that block.

**Site Address:** 23 Hamlet Ave., Hamlet, NC
**Mailing Address:** PO Box 1583, Hamlet, NC 28345
**Telephone:** (910) 582-3317 (residence) or (910) 582-3337

**NORTH CAROLINA TRANSPORTATION MUSEUM AT HISTORIC SPENCER SHOPS**
*Museum*
*Standard gauge*

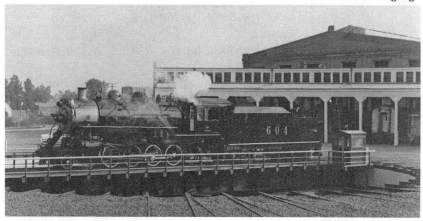

**Description:** Thirty-minute narrated train ride around property. Steam powered on weekends, April through Labor Day. Exhibits on inland transportation automobiles.

**Schedule:** April through October, museum open Monday through Saturday, 9 a.m. to 5 p.m. and Sundays, 1 to 5 p.m.; November through March, Tuesday through Saturday, 10 a.m. to 4 p.m. and Sundays, 1 to 4 p.m.

**Admission/Fare:** Train ride–adults, $5; seniors (60+) and children 3-12, $4. Turntable ride–$.50 per person.

**Locomotives/Rolling Stock:** SR E8 6900; SR FP76133; N&W GP9 620; SRGP302601–all operating. Several more locomotives and cars on display in roundhouse. Operating steam includes Graham County Shay 1925 and BC&G 2-8-0 no. 604.

**Special Events:** Rail Days, last weekend in April; Steamfest, September 29; A Day Out with Thomas (times vary from year to year).

**Nearby Attractions/Accommodations:** Dan Nicolas Park, Rowan Museum, several restaurants and hotels.

**Location/Directions:** I-85 exit 79 (Spencer). Follow signs to museum.

*Coupon available, see coupon section.

**Site Address:** 411 S. Salisbury Ave., Spencer, NC
**Mailing Address:** PO Box 165, Spencer, NC 28159
**Telephone:** (704) 636-2889 or (800) NCTMFUN
**Fax:** (704) 639-1881
**E-mail:** nctm<nctrans@vnet.net>
**Internet:** www.nctrans.org

CHARLES KERNAN

**Description:** Museum housed in the 1900 ACL freight office building. Interact with our extensive artifact collection, model train layouts (HO and Lionel), and children's hands-on learning area. Climb aboard the 1910 Baldwin steam locomotive and red caboose.

**Schedule:** March 15 through October 14: Monday through Saturday, 10 a.m. to 5 p.m.; Sunday, 1 to 5 p.m. October 15 through March 14: Monday through Saturday, 10 a.m. to 4 p.m.; Closed Thanksgiving, Christmas Eve, Christmas Day, New Year's Day, and Easter Sunday.

**Admission/Fare:** Adults, $3; seniors (60+)/military, $2; children 3-12, $1.50; 2 and under and members are free; group rates available.

**Locomotives/Rolling Stock:** 1910 Baldwin steam locomotive 4-6-0 no. 250; SCL no. 01036; ACL caboose no. 01983; 1963 RF&P boxcar no. 2379.

**Special Events:** Model Railroad Show, January; Azalea Festival, April; Riverfest, October.

**Nearby Attractions/Accommodations:** Battleship U.S.S. *North Carolina*, Fort Fisher State Historical Site, beaches, Best Western Coast Line Inn.

**Location/Directions:** Highway 17 into downtown Wilmington (turns into Market St.), turn right on Water St., four blocks ahead, three-story brick building.

        M arm

**Site Address:** 501 Nutt St., Wilmington, NC
**Mailing Address:** 501 Nutt St., Wilmington, NC 28401
**Telephone:** (910) 763-2634
**Fax:** (910) 763-2634 (call first)
**Internet:** www.wilmington.org/railroad

**Description:** One-and-a-half-mile train ride; operating turntable; scale steam train ride; steam threshing and plowing; steam sawmills; operating steam shovel; large steam engines.

**Schedule:** Labor Day weekend, Friday through Monday, 8 a.m. to 8 p.m.

**Admission/Fare:** Daily ticket, $8; season ticket, $12; 14 years and under, free.

**Locomotives/Rolling Stock:** Ex Soo Line 0-6-0 switcher no. 353, a Porter 0-4-0, three wooden cabooses, 10 other cars.

**Nearby Attractions/Accommodations:** Fargo Moorhead, 35 miles; lodging, restaurants, museums, Maplewood State Park, lakes and campgrounds.

**Location/Directions:** Rollag, Minnesota. Ten miles south of Hawley, Minnesota on Highway 32.

        M

**Mailing Address:** 2610 1st Ave., Fargo, ND 58102
**Telephone:** (701) 232-4484
**Internet:** www.rollag.com

**Description:** A 9-mile round trip from Mandan to Ft. Abraham Lincoln State Park along the Heart River. We have a restored American Car Co. streetcar and an eight-bench open car.

**Schedule:** Memorial Day through Labor Day: daily departures 1, 2, 3, 4, 5 p.m.

**Admission/Fare:** Adults, $5; children 5-10, $3; under 5 are free.

**Locomotives/Rolling Stock:** American Car Co. streetcar no. 102; eight-bench open car.

**Nearby Attractions/Accommodations:** Fort Lincoln State Park, Lewis and Clark Riverboats, Mandan Railroad Museum.

**Location/Directions:** I-94 to Highway 1806 to Third St. SE; east on Third St. SE about five blocks.

*Coupon available, see coupon section.

**Site Address:** Third St. SE, Mandan, ND
**Mailing Address:** 29 Captain Leach Dr., Mandan, ND 58554
**Telephone:** (701) 663-9018

## OLD SOO DEPOT TRANSPORTATION MUSEUM & WESTERN HISTORY RESEARCH CENTER
### *Museum*

DENNIS LUTZ, M.D.

**Description:** Museum and Research Center in completely restored 1912 Soo Line Depot. Museum focuses on transportation history of the American West, including GN, NP, Soo, Milwaukee Road, and Amtrak.

**Schedule:** Call or write for information.

**Admission/Fare:** Donations accepted.

**Locomotives/Rolling Stock:** Burlington Northern Santa Fe, Canadian Pacific, and Amtrak trains frequently operating beside or across from building.

**Nearby Attractions/Accommodations:** Taube Art Museum, Railroad Museum of Minot, Charlie's Main Street Cafe, Dragon Delight.

**Location/Directions:** North end of Main St. in downtown Minot, along the main line of the Canadian Pacific and Burlington Northern Sante Fe Railroads.

**Site Address:** 15 N. Main St., Minot, ND
**Mailing Address:** PO Box 2148, Minot, ND 58702
**Telephone:** (701) 852-2234

# RAILROAD MUSEUM OF MINOT
*Museum*

**Description:** A mile-long train ride through Roosevelt Park on the Magic City Express train. A ⅜ scale model of a Great Northern F-8 locomotive no. 1177 and four cars.

**Schedule:** Train–May through August, weekdays 1 to 5 p.m.; weekends 1 to 8 p.m. Museum–Mondays, Wednesdays, Fridays, 10 a.m. to 12:00 noon; Saturdays 1 to 4 p.m.

**Admission/Fare:** $2, which includes one free train ride, one free admission to museum, under 5 free.

**Locomotives/Rolling Stock:** Burlington caboose no. 12183; Soo Line caboose no. 32; speeder cars; baggage cart.

**Special Events:** Railroad Days, second weekend (Friday-Saturday) of June; Family Day, third Saturday of July.

**Nearby Attractions/Accommodations:** Roosevelt park, zoo and pool.

**Location/Directions:** Going east on E. Central takes you to the north end of the park, where we are. The zoo is at the south end of the park. Museum is one block east of Main St.

      M

**Site Address:** 19 First St. NE, Minot, ND
**Mailing Address:** PO Box 74, Minot, ND 58703
**Telephone:** (701) 852-7091

# BONANZAVILLE U.S.A.
*Museum, display, layout*
*Standard gauge*

R.A. YOUNG

**Description:** A 12-acre historical village with static displays of the Embden, North Dakota, Depot and train shed and the Kathryn, North Dakota, Depot with Spud Valley Model Railroad layout. See 40 other buildings serving as small museums representing life in the Red River Valley between 1880 and 1920.

**Schedule:** May and October, Mondays through Fridays, 9 a.m. to 5 p.m. June through September, daily, 9 a.m. to 6 p.m.

**Admission/Fare:** Adults, $6; juniors, $3; age 5 and under, free.

**Locomotives/Rolling Stock:** Rome locomotive 4-4-0; Northern Pacific wood caboose no. 1628; wood russell plow, former NP; NP steel 80-ton passenger coach, no. 1360.

**Special Events:** Pioneer Days, third weekend in August.

**Nearby Attractions/Accommodations:** Red River Zoo, Children's Museum, Plains Art Museum, F-M Redhawks baseball, Cass County Campground, Days Inn.

**Location/Directions:** I-94, exit 343 to West Fargo.

**Site Address:** 1351 W. Main Ave., West Fargo, ND
**Mailing Address:** PO Box 719, West Fargo, ND 58078
**Telephone:** (701) 282-2822
**Fax:** (701) 282-7606
**E-mail:** info@bonanzaville.com
**Internet:** www.bonanzaville.com

**MAD RIVER & NKP RAILROAD SOCIETY, INC.**
*Museum, display, layout*

GEORGE LEADER

**Description:** Steps and open doors welcome all who come to the hands-on museum.

**Schedule:** Memorial Day through Labor Day: daily, 1 to 5 p.m.; May, September, and October: weekends only.

**Admission/Fare:** Adults, $3; children, $1; subject to change.

**Locomotives/Rolling Stock:** Alco RSD 12 NKP no. 329; EMD GP30 NKP no. 900; FM H1244 Milw. no. 740; Wabash F7 diesel no. 671; PRR RPO car; NKP dynamometer car; three NKP cabooses; N&W caboose; troop sleeper car; refrigerator cars; four passenger cars, including the first dome car built; and various other cars and equipment.

**Special Events:** Limited number of bus/rail tours throughout the year. Call for information. Guided tours, if scheduled in advance.

**Nearby Attractions/Accommodations:** Cedar Point Amusement Park, Sorrowful Mother Shrine, Seneca Caverns, Historic Lyme Village.

**Location/Directions:** Two blocks south of downtown. Follow our green signs.

**Site Address:** 353 Southwest St., Bellevue, OH
**Mailing Address:** 233 York St., Bellevue, OH 44811-1377
**Telephone:** (419) 483-2222
**E-mail:** madriver@onebellevue.com
**Internet:** www.onebellevue.com/madriver/

**CARROLLTON-ONEIDA-MINERVA RAILROAD**
**ELDERBERRY LINE**
*Train ride*
*Standard gauge*

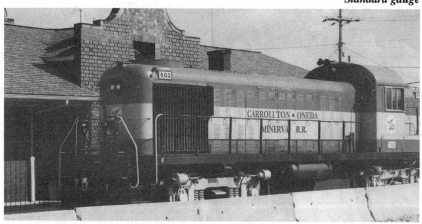

**Description:** Travel 14 miles between Carrollton and Minerva through areas of light industry, farmland, marshland, and forest, with one-hour layover in Minerva. The train ride is 28 miles round trip.

**Schedule:** Mid-June through October: weekends. December: Christmas runs. Call for information and schedules.

**Admission/Fare:** Adults, $12; children 2-12, $9. Group rates available.

**Locomotives/Rolling Stock:** 1952 Alco RS-3 locomotive; 1926 ES New Jersey coach; three 1937 coaches, former Canadian.

**Special Events:** Fall Foliage, October. Christmas trains start Thanksgiving weekend.

**Nearby Attractions/Accommodations:** Atwood Lodge, sailing, fishing, Pro Football Hall of Fame, McKinley's monument.

**Location/Directions:** Site is 100 miles south of Cleveland, 25 miles south of Canton, and 60 miles west of Pittsburgh, Pennsylvania.

**Site Address:** 203 2nd St. NW, Carrollton, OH
**Mailing Address:** 220 Wayne Ave., Carrollton, OH 44615
**Telephone:** (330) 627-2282
**Fax:** (330) 627-3624
**E-mail:** elderbrr@raex.com
**Internet:** www.advantagepages.com/elderberry

DALE W. BROWN

**Description:** Founded in 1938, this club has an exhibit area in the former Cincinnati Union Terminal's control Tower A, which was the operating and dispatching center for the passenger terminal's operations from 1933 to 1973. The Tower overlooks the busy Norfolk Southern and CSX yard, main lines, and the former Southern Railway bridge to Kentucky. It was restored in 1991 by the CRRC as their meeting location, library and display area. The CRRC has displays and an extensive library, and photo collection in Tower A, and occasionally operates special charter train excursions on both mainline and local shortline railroads in the area.

**Schedule:** Memorial Day through Labor Day, Saturdays, 10 a.m. to 5 p.m. and Sundays, 12 to 5 p.m. September through May, one hour less.

**Admission/Fare:** Free. Parking, $3.50 all day.

**Locomotives/Rolling Stock:** No. 2435 Cincinnati street railways curved sider streetcar on display in the Cincinnati History Museum inside the museum center.

**Special Events:** Summerail show and sale, Saturday, August 3, 2002; slide shows, railroad show and sale pre-summerail show, August 2, 2002.

**Nearby Attractions/Accommodations:** Bengals football, Cincinnati Reds baseball, zoo, aquarium, Kings Island amusement park.

**Location/Directions:** Exits 2A, 1H, or 1F on I-75 and Ezzard Charles Dr.

**Site Address:** 1301 Western Ave., Cincinnati, OH
**Mailing Address:** PO Box 14157, Cincinnati, OH 45242-7142
**Telephone:** (513) 561-RAIL (7245)
**Internet:** www.cincinnatirrclub.org

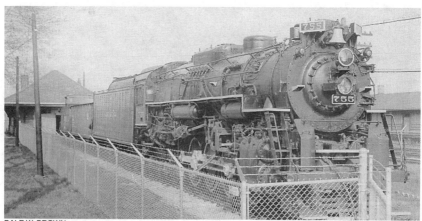

DALE W. BROWN

**Description:** Displays of railroad memorabilia and an HO scale model railroad.

**Schedule:** Memorial Day through Labor Day; daily, 12 to 5 p.m.

**Admission/Fare:** Donations appreciated.

**Locomotives/Rolling Stock:** No. 755, 1944 Lima 2-8-4, former Nickel Plate. A 90-ton hopper car and a wooden caboose, both former Bessemer & Lake Erie.

**Nearby Attractions/Accommodations:** Within a mile of Lake Erie.

**Location/Directions:** In the old New York Central station at Depot and Mill streets, north of U.S. 20 and I-90. Blue-and-white locomotive signs point the way to the museum.

**Site Address:** Conneaut, OH
**Mailing Address:** PO Box 643, Conneaut, OH 44030
**Telephone:** (440) 599-7878

293

# CARILLON HISTORICAL PARK
*Train ride, museum*
*Standard and 7½" gauge*

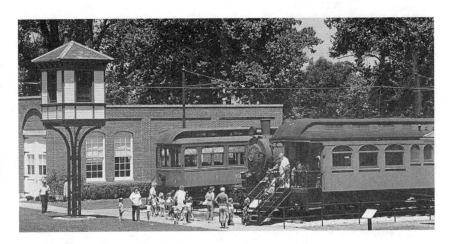

**Description:** Indoor and outdoor history museum. Carillon features a new transportation center with rolling stock, 1894 railroad station, 1907 watch tower, canal lock, two bridges, and scheduled rides on a small scale live-steam railroad.

**Schedule:** April through October, Mondays through Saturday, 9:30 a.m. to 5 p.m., Sundays, 12 to 5 p.m.

**Admission/Fare:** Annual ride-on family membership, $12. Park entry will be the same until April 1, 2002, when new admission prices will be: Adults, $5; seniors, $4; children 3-17, $3.

**Locomotives/Rolling Stock:** Featuring the James F. Dicke Family Transportation Center collection: The 1835 "John Quincy Adams," 1903 summer trolley, 1904 Kuhlman interurban, 1923 B&O caboose; more.

**Special Events:** Rail and Steam Festival, Saturday and Sunday Memorial Day weekend.

**Nearby Attractions/Accommodations:** U.S. Air Force Museum, Sunwatch Indian Village, Wright Brothers Memorial, Dayton Aviation Heritage National Historical Park, Marriott, Holiday Inn.

**Location/Directions:** I-75 exit 51, east on Edwin C. Moses Blvd., right over bridge, right on Patterson Blvd., right on Carillon Blvd. to entrance.

          M

**Site Address:** 1000 Carillon Blvd., Dayton, OH
**Mailing Address:** 1000 Carillon Blvd., Dayton, OH 45409
**Telephone:** (937) 293-2841
**Fax:** (937) 293-5798

# AUGLAIZE VILLAGE
*Museum, display, layout*

DENNIS GRIME

**Schedule:** June through Labor Day, weekends; first Sunday in October.

**Admission/Fare:** Adults, $3; children, $1.

**Locomotives/Rolling Stock:** C&O wood caboose, 9000 series, motor cars, hand car.

**Special Events:** Johnny Appleseed Day, first Sunday in October; Steam Show, second weekend in June; Blacksmith Show and Cowboy Shoot, weekend after the 4th.

**Nearby Attractions/Accommodations:** Independence Dam; a mall, and many motels and restaurants

**Location/Directions:** On Krouse Rd., three miles west of Defiance, Ohio and one mile south of U.S. 24 West.

         M

**Site Address:** Krouse Rd., Defiance, OH
**Mailing Address:** PO Box 801, Defiance, OH 43512
**Telephone:** (419) 784-0107 and (419) 782-7255
**E-mail:** dennisgrime@hotmail.com
**Internet:** www.defiance-online.com/auglaize

# THE DENNISON RAILROAD DEPOT MUSEUM
*Train ride, museum, layout*
*N scale*

**Description:** The museum, restaurant, and gift shop are housed in a restored 1873 Pennsylvania Railroad depot. Train rides from May through December: all-day excursions, murder mysteries, fall foliage trips, and holiday trips.

**Schedule:** Year round: Tuesdays through Saturdays, 11 a.m. to 5 p.m. Sundays, 11 a.m. to 3 p.m. Tours by appointment.

**Admission/Fare:** Range from $7 to $100.

**Locomotives/Rolling Stock:** See website: www.ohiocentralrr.com for train ride rolling stock. On display: 1940s Thermos Bottle Vulcan engine; caboose; freight cars; C&O engine no. 2700.

**Special Events:** Railroad festival, third week of May.

**Nearby Attractions/Accommodations:** Amish Country, Roscoe Village, Zoar and Schoennbrunn (Ohio Historical Society sites).

**Location/Directions:** Located halfway between Columbus, Ohio, and Pittsburgh, Pennsylvania, 18 miles east of I-77 and 36 miles north of I-70. At the junction of Routes 250, 36, and 800.

**Site Address:** 400 Center St., Dennison, OH
**Mailing Address:** PO Box 11, Dennison, OH 44621
**Telephone:** (740) 922-6776
**Fax:** (740) 922-0105
**E-mail:** depot@tusco.net
**Internet:** www.dennisondepot.org

**Description:** Carvings of the evolution of the steam engine, carved of ivory, ebony, and walnut.

**Schedule:** Daily, 9 a.m. to 5 p.m. Closed major holidays.

**Admission/Fare:** Adults, $8; students (6-17), $4.

**Nearby Attractions/Accommodations:** Gateway to Ohio's Amish Country.

**Location/Directions:** I-77 exit no. 83, east on Route 211 ¼ mile.

**Site Address:** 331 Karl Ave., Dover, OH
**Mailing Address:** 331 Karl Ave., Dover, OH 44622
**Telephone:** (330) 343-7513
**Fax:** (330) 343-1443
**E-mail:** info@warthers.com
**Internet:** www.warthers.com

# NORTHWEST OHIO RAILROAD PRESERVATION, INC.
*Train ride, display*
*15" gauge*

**Description:** Live steam 2-6-2 Prairie-type locomotive with open-seat coaches.

**Schedule:** Call, fax, or write for information; we are under construction.

**Locomotives/Rolling Stock:** B&O 200-ton steam wrecking derrick no. X-45; several motorcars (speeders), 1890s boxcar.

**Nearby Attractions/Accommodations:** Amusement parks, museums, restaurants, lodging, campgrounds, state park, scenic sites.

**Location/Directions:** Northeast corner of I-75 and County Road 99, exit 161.

     M

**Site Address:** 11732 County Rd. 99, Findlay, OH
**Mailing Address:** 11732 County Rd. 99, Findlay, OH 45840-9602
**Telephone:** (419) 423-2995
**Fax:** (419) 423-4258

# BUCKEYE CENTRAL SCENIC RAILROAD

*Train ride*
*Standard gauge*

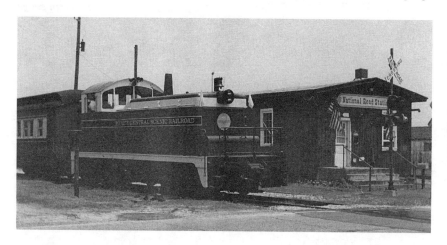

**Description:** We offer a scenic 1.5-hour round trip excursion through the rolling hills of central Ohio on historic Shawnee branch of the old B&O. Travel in vintage passenger coaches or in the open-air gondola. On your journey pass over a steel bridge and two trestles.

**Schedule:** Memorial Day weekend through mid-October: weekend departures at 1 and 3 p.m.

**Admission/Fare:** Adults, $7; children (2-12), $5.

**Locomotives/Rolling Stock:** SW-1 no. 8599; open gondola; four Canadian National coaches.

**Special Events:** Haunted Halloween Trains, Santa Claus Specials, Wild West/Train Robbery. Call for dates.

**Nearby Attractions/Accommodations:** Flint Ridge State Park, Buckeye Lake, Dawes Arboretum, Heissy Museum, the Olde Mill, village of Granville.

**Location/Directions:** I-70, exit Route 13N to Route 40, turn left; or I-70, exit Route 79N to Route 40, turn right. Located on Route 40.

*Coupon available, see coupon section.

**Site Address:** 5501 National Rd. SE, Hebron, OH
**Mailing Address:** PO Box 242, Newark, OH 43058-0242
**Telephone:** (740) 366-2029
**Fax:** (614) 891-5847

# CUYAHOGA VALLEY
# SCENIC RAILROAD
*Train ride*
*Standard gauge*

**Description:** The CVSR in Northeastern Ohio runs through the heart of Cuyahoga Valley National Park. Each 26-mile trip is a different adventure filled with fun, excitement, natural beauty, and historic sites. Ride comfortably in vintage climate-controlled coaches built between 1939 and 1940. The coaches originally saw passenger service on the NYC and Santa Fe Railroads.

**Schedule:** February through May, November and December: weekends. June through August: Wednesdays through Sundays. October: daily.

**Admission/Fare:** $11 to $20.

**Locomotives/Rolling Stock:** Alco FPA 4s nos. 15 and 14; Alco FPA 4s nos. 1822, 800, and 4099; 2014 General Motors.

**Special Events:** Maple Sugar Express. Wine Tasting Train. Easter Bunny Express, Easter Day. Fall Color Train, daily in October. Christmas Tree Adventure, weekends in December. Polar Express, weeknights in December.

**Nearby Attractions/Accommodations:** Hale Farm Village, Holiday Inn Richfield, Sea World, Cleveland Indians/Browns, Stan Hywet Hall and Gardens.

**Location/Directions:** I-77 to Rockside Rd.

**Site Address:** Old Riverside Rd., Independence, OH
**Mailing Address:** PO Box 158, Peninsula, OH 44264-0158
**Telephone:** (800) 468-4070 and (330) 657-2000
**Fax:** (330) 657-2080
**E-mail:** webmaster@cvsr.com
**Internet:** www.cvsr.com

# AC&J SCENIC LINE RAILWAY
*Train ride*
*Standard gauge*

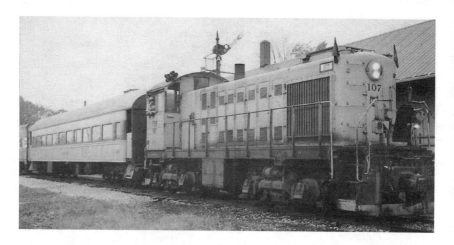

**Description:** Enjoy a one-hour 12-mile round trip over the last remaining portion of the New York Central's Ashtabula-to-Pittsburgh "High Grade" passenger main line. Ride in vintage passenger cars pulled by a first-generation diesel. A family educational adventure.

**Schedule:** June 15 through October 27: departures at 12:30, 2, and 3:30 p.m.

**Admission/Fare:** Adults, $7; seniors, $6; children, $5; under age 3 are free when not occupying a seat.

**Locomotives/Rolling Stock:** No. 107, 1950 Alco S-2 diesel, former Nickel Plate and Fairport, Painesville & Eastern; no. 518, 1948 Alco S-2 diesel, former Erie and Centerior Energy plant switcher; no. 1022 former Erie passenger coach; no. 425 former Nickel Plate caboose; nos. 7133 and 7155 former Long Island Railroad commuter cars.

**Special Events:** Murder Mystery trains, spring and fall.

**Nearby Attractions/Accommodations:** Adjacent Jefferson Depot, Victorian Perambulator Museum, Geneva-on-the Lake, Pymatuning Resort area.

**Location/Directions:** I-90 from east/west exit Ohio 11 south, to Ohio 46 and south to Jefferson, left at second light on E. Jefferson St. to tracks. Or north on Route 11, exit 307 west to Jefferson, right at second light to tracks.

**Site Address:** E. Jefferson St., Jefferson, OH
**Mailing Address:** PO Box 517, Jefferson, OH 44047-0517
**Telephone:** (440) 576-6346
**Fax:** (440) 576-8848

# JEFFERSON DEPOT, INC.
*Museum*

**Description:** Jefferson Depot is a restored 1872 Lake Shore & Michigan Southern Railroad station/museum. It features a 1918 PRR caboose, a quaint 1848 church, circuit-rider barn, an 1838 one-room schoolhouse, and a general store; train rides next door.

**Schedule:** June through September: Sundays 1 to 4 p.m. Group tours by appointment. Buses welcome.

**Admission/Fare:** Adults, $2; children, free.

**Special Events:** Strawberry Festival and Craft Bazaar, June 15-16. Fall Foliage Train/Bus Trip, October 5.

**Nearby Attractions/Accommodations:** On site: Jefferson Depot Historic Village; campgrounds, Pymatuning State Park, many restaurants and lodging nearby.

**Location/Directions:** From I-90, south on I-11 to State Route 46 south to E. Jefferson St. From I-11, north to State Route 307 west to State Route 46 north, to E. Jefferson St.

            M

**Site Address:** 147 E. Jefferson St., Jefferson, OH
**Mailing Address:** PO Box 22, Jefferson, OH 44047
**Telephone:** (440) 293-5532 and (352) 343-8256
**E-mail:** duttonjg@hotmail.com
**Internet:** http://members.tripod.com/jeffersonhome

**Description:** Train-O-Rama is Ohio's largest operating multi-gauge train layout. It is also a gift/hobby store.

**Schedule:** Year round; Mondays through Saturdays, 11 a.m. to 5 p.m.; Sundays, 1 to 5 p.m. Extended summer hours: Mondays through Saturdays, 10 a.m. to 6 p.m.; Sundays 1 to 6 p.m.

**Fare/Admission:** Adults, $5; seniors, $4; children (4-11), $3.

**Nearby Attractions/Accommodations:** Near East Harbor State Park and Lake Erie Islands; also near Cedar Point.

**Location/Directions:** State Route 2 to State Route 269 north to Route 163 east. E. Harbor Rd. is Route 163 east.

*Coupon available, see coupon section.

**Site Address:** 6732 E. Harbor Rd., Route 163 E., Marblehead, OH
**Mailing Address:** 6732 E. Harbor Rd., Marblehead, OH 43440
**Telephone:** (419) 734-5856
**Fax:** (419) 660-0133
**E-mail:** trainorama@aol.com
**Internet:** www.trainorama.net

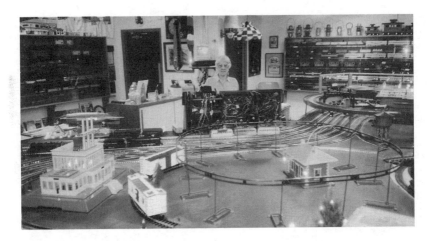

**Description:** A model railroad museum and operating layout featuring over 18 trains running simultaneously in standard, O, and G gauge. Over 275 locomotives are on display: Lionel, American Flyer, Ives, Williams, and others. Features a single-track with four trains crossing automatically in a double loop.

**Schedule:** Year round: daily, 11 a.m. to 5 p.m.

**Admission:** Adults, $5; seniors, $4; children under 10 are free with paying adult; families, $15.

**Special Events:** Sternwheel Festival, weekend after Labor Day.

**Nearby Attractions/Accommodations:** Butch's Cola Museum, Children's Toy and Doll Museum, Valley Gem Sternwheel, Showboat Becky Thatcher, Rossi Pasta Factory, Fenton Art Glass Company and Outlet, historic Lafayette Hotel, Ohio River Museum.

**Location/Directions:** I-77 and Ohio Route 7.

*Coupon available, see coupon section.

     M

**Site Address:** 220 Gilman St., Harmar Village, Marietta, OH
**Mailing Address:** 220 Gilman St., Marietta, OH 45750
**Telephone:** (740) 374-9995
**Fax:** (740) 373-7808
**E-mail:** jmoberg@charter.net
**Internet:** www.harmarstation.com

## MARION UNION STATION ASSOCIATION
*Museum, layout*

**Description:** This museum and model railroad club is a train viewer's paradise. Sixty to 70 CSX-NS freight trains pass by daily on average, to the north, south, east, and west.

**Schedule:** Year round: Tuesdays through Fridays, 10 a.m. to 2 p.m. May through September, most weekends, 2 to 5 p.m. Model Railroad–Sundays, 2 to 4 p.m.

**Admission/Fare:** Donations appreciated ($2 per person suggested).

**Locomotives/Rolling Stock:** Erie/EL caboose no. C-306; 3-ton Plymouth model TLC; AC interlocking tower.

**Special Events:** Chicken barbecue, first Sunday in October. Model train show, first Saturday in December.

**Nearby Attractions/Accommodations:** Call Visitor's Bureau at (800) 371-6688.

**Location/Directions:** Route 309 on west side of Marion (between railroad tracks).

**Site Address:** 532 W. Center St., Marion, OH
**Mailing Address:** 532 W. Center St., Marion, OH 43302
**Telephone:** (740) 383-3768
**Fax:** (740) 383-3768
**E-mail:** unionstation@marion.net

## LUCAS COUNTY/MAUMEE VALLEY HISTORICAL SOCIETY
*Museum, display*

**Description:** The depot is part of a five-building museum complex. Guided tours cover the entire complex. The depot and caboose are authentically furnished. Railroad memorabilia are on display.

**Schedule:** Wednesdays through Sundays, 1 to 4 p.m.

**Fare/Admission:** Adults $3.50; children $1.50.

**Locomotive/Rolling Stock:** Caboose and baggage car.

**Special Events:** Model train exhibit in depot for Harvest Days, October 29; Christmas by the River, November 8 through December 31.

**Nearby Attractions/Accommodations:** Toledo Zoo, Toledo Museum of Art, Toledo Mud Hens baseball, Tony Pacos Restaurant, Ft. Meigs.

**Location/Directions:** The museum is on River Rd. in downtown Maumee and can be reached easily from U.S. routes 20 and 24.

**Site Address:** 1031 River Rd., Maumee, OH
**Mailing Address:** 1031 River Rd., Maumee, OH 43537
**Telephone:** (419) 893-9602
**Fax:** (419) 893-3108
**Internet:** www.maumee.org/wolcott/wolcott.htm

# HOCKING VALLEY SCENIC RAILWAY

*Train ride, museum*
*Standard gauge*

**Description:** Hocking Valley Scenic Railway offers a 14-mile round trip at 12 noon and a 22-mile round trip at 2:30 p.m. All regular scheduled trains stop at an 1850s village for 30 minutes.

**Schedule:** Memorial weekend through first weekend in November: weekends, 12 and 2:30 p.m.; Santa Trains: last weekend in November and first three weekends in December; Santa Trains depart at 11 a.m. and 2:30 p.m.

**Admission/Fare:** 12 p.m.–adults, $8, children 3-12, $5; 2:30 p.m.–adults, $11, children 3-12, $7. Santa trains–adults, $11, children 3-12, $7.50.

**Locomotives/Rolling Stock:** GP7 C&O 5833; BLH switcher 4005; GE 45-ton Industrial 7315; B&O combine "City of Athens"; three RI commuter cars, "City of Logan," "City of Nelsonville," and "Village of Haydenville"; 1941 60-ton center cab Whitcombe.

**Special Events:** Check web site: www.hvsr.com

**Nearby Attractions/Accommodations:** Hocking Hills area; Old Man's Cave, campgrounds, Lakes hiking trails Nelsonville; Victorian Square, restored 1800s opera house, famous Dew Hotel, Robbins Crossing 1850s village.

**Location/Directions:** From Columbus take U.S. 33 east to Nelsonville second traffic signal on right.

*Coupon available, see coupon section.

**Site Address:** 33 Canal St., Nelsonville, OH
**Mailing Address:** PO Box 427, Nelsonville, OH 45764
**Telephone:** (800) 967-7834 and (614) 470-1300
**Fax:** (740) 753-1152
**Internet:** www.hvsr.com

# TROLLEYVILLE, U.S.A.

*Train ride, museum,*
*Standard gauge*

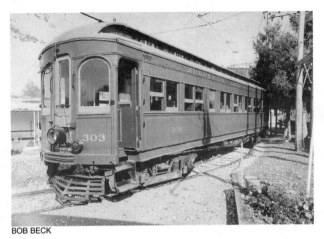

BOB BECK

**Description:** Streetcars and miscellaneous railroad equipment are on display. The museum is located in the 1875 restored B&O Berea Depot. Ride on over 2.5 miles of track.

**Schedule:** May through November: weekends. June through September: Wednesdays, Fridays, and weekends.

**Admission/Fare:** Adults, $5.50; seniors, $4.50; children 3-11, $3.50; 2 and under, free.

**Locomotives/Rolling Stock:** Thirteen streetcars; 13 interurban; four work cars and locomotives; two boxcars; two cabooses; miscellaneous motorcars.

**Special Events:** Easter Egg Hunt, 4th of July, Train Shows, Halloween.

**Nearby Attractions/Accommodations:** Cedar Point, Geauga Lake Amusement Park, Six Flags, Rock and Roll Hall of Fame, Museum of Science and Industry.

**Location/Directions:** I-480, exit 6A, 2 miles south, west side of road in shopping center.

 **Radio frequency: 43.7**

**Site Address:** 7100 Columbia Rd., Olmsted Township, OH
**Mailing Address:** 7100 Columbia Rd., Olmsted Township, OH 44138
**Telephone:** (440) 235-4725
**Fax:** (440) 427-1431
**E-mail:** cliff@trolleyvilleusa.org
**Internet:** www.trolleyvilleusa.org

## ORRVILLE RAILROAD
## HERITAGE SOCIETY
*Train ride, museum, display*
*Standard gauge*

ROBERT CUTTING

**Description:** Mainline trips, all-day rides, 50 to 120 miles in length.

**Schedule:** Depot open Saturdays, May through October, 10 a.m. to 4 p.m. Trips vary year to year. Send for information.

**Admission/Fare:** Depot tours, no charge. Mainline trips, fares vary per trip.

**Locomotives/Rolling Stock:** Ex-New Haven GP-9 PRR; N5C caboose; five Budd passenger coaches; ex-Amtrak baggage car; privately owned caboose and passenger cars; switch block tower.

**Special Events:** Depot Days, second weekend of June; Open House, Friday and Saturday after Thanksgiving.

**Nearby Attractions/Accommodations:** Amish Country; Rubbermaid store; Smucker Jam and Jelly store; new motel at junction of Routes 57 and 30 (3 miles south).

**Location/Directions:** Twelve miles south of I-76; 3 miles north of Route 30, on Route 57.

**Site Address:** 145 Depot St., Orrville, OH
**Mailing Address:** PO Box 11, Orrville, OH 44667
**Telephone:** (330) 683-2426
**Fax:** (330) 682-2426
**Internet:** www.orrvillerailroad.com

DAN FEICHT

**Description:** The Cedar Point and Lake Erie (CP&LE) railroad is a 15-minute train ride that covers a two-mile trip around the Frontiertown section of Cedar Point Amusement Park/resort.

**Schedule:** To be determined.

**Admission/Fare:** To be determined.

**Locomotives/Rolling Stock:** "Myron H."1922 Vulcan 0-4-0 rebuilt as 2-4-0; "Albert" 1910 Davenport 2-6-0; "George R." 1942 H.K. Porter Co. 0-4-0 rebuilt as 2-4-0; "Jennie K." 1909 H.K. Porter Co. 1-4-0 rebuilt as 2-4-0; "Judy K." Vulcan 0-4-0 rebuilt as 2-4-0.

**Site Address:** 1 Cedar Point Dr., Sandusky, OH
**Mailing Address:** 1 Cedar Point Dr., Sandusky, OH 44870-5259
**Telephone:** (419) 627-2350
**Fax:** (419) 627-2200
**E-mail:** BEdwards@cedarpoint.com
**Internet:** www.cedarpoint.com

# OHIO RAILWAY MUSEUM
*Train ride, museum*
*Standard gauge*

DAVE BUNGE

**Description:** Museum offers a 3-mile round trip on historic trolley-interurban cars.

**Schedule:** May through October: Sundays, 1 to 5 p.m.

**Admission/Fare:** Adults, $3.50; seniors, $2.50; children, $1.50.

**Locomotives/Rolling Stock:** N&W no. 578 Pacific Steam; OPS no. 21 interurban; passenger cars, street cars, and interurbans.

**Special Events:** Ghost Trolley, Santa Trolley, State Fair, Twilight Trolley Excursions.

**Nearby Attractions/Accommodations:** Ohio Historical Museum, Polaris Amphitheatre, Columbus Zoo, many hotels and restaurants.

**Location/Directions:** I-71 to State Route 161 exit, west to Worthington.

    M arm

**Site Address:** 990 Proprietors Rd., Worthington, OH
**Mailing Address:** Box 777, Worthington, OH 43085
**Telephone:** (614) 885-7345
**Internet:** www.ohiorailwaymuseum.org

**Description:** Trains, trains, and more trains running everywhere! Exhibits include an outdoor G scale garden railroad, a 28 x 48-foot Lionel layout, HO and N scale layouts, and a wagon-train ride through the park.

**Schedule:** March 15 through September 15: Tuesdays through Saturdays, 10 a.m. to 5 p.m.; Sundays, by appointment. September 15 through March 15: by appointment only.

**Admission/Fare:** Donations appreciated.

**Special Events:** Main Line Train Show, first Saturday after 4th of July.

**Nearby Attractions/Accommodations:** Osage Hills State Park, candle factory, restaurants, motels, Bartlesville, Oklahoma (12 miles).

**Location/Directions:** U.S. 75 to County Road 2700, east 2 miles to stop sign, north 1.5 blocks to entrance.

**Site Address:** 26811 N. 3990 Rd., Ramona, OK
**Mailing Address:** 26811 N. 3990 Rd., Ramona, OK 74061
**Telephone:** (918) 336-5821 and (800) 345-5821

# CHOCTAW CABOOSE MUSEUM
*Museum, display*

**Description:** Walk-through museum, static displays.

**Schedule:** Memorial Day through Labor Day, Saturdays, 10 a.m. to 4 p.m. and Sundays, 2 to 5 p.m.

**Admission/Fare:** Free.

**Location/Directions:** Corner of N.E. 23rd St. and Henney Rd.

**Site Address:** Corner of N.E. 23rd St. and Henney Rd., Choctaw, OK
**Mailing Address:** PO Box 364, Choctaw, OK 73020
**Telephone:** (405) 390-2771

**Description:** Our museum of working trains includes a 30 x 40-foot layout with a circus, mountains, and lakes.

**Schedule:** Year round: daily, 9 a.m. to 5 p.m.

**Admission/Fare:** Free; donations appreciated.

**Special Events:** Cherokee Strips Days, September 18. Cherokee Strip Museum, restaurants, motels; Perry, Oklahoma, is 10 miles away.

**Location/Directions:** On I-35 exit 185. Go 10 miles west on Highway 164 and ¼ mile south.

**Site Address:** Route 1, Box 113, Covington, OK
**Mailing Address:** Route 1, Box 113, Covington, OK 73730
**Telephone:** (580) 336-2823

# RAILROAD MUSEUM OF OKLAHOMA
*Museum, display, layout*
*Standard gauge*

ROBERT CHESTER

**Description:** This museum, housed in a 1926-27 former Santa Fe freighthouse, has one of the largest collections of railroad memorabilia in the midwest. It is focused on preserving historically significant railroad equipment. Recapture the essence of railroad days as you climb aboard a 1925 steam locomotive, wander through cabooses from eight different railroads, and view eleven different types of freight cars.

**Schedule:** Year round: Tuesday through Friday, 1 to 4 p.m. Saturdays, 9 a.m. to 1 p.m. Sundays, 2 to 5 p.m. Other times by appointment.

**Admission/Fare:** By donation.

**Locomotives/Rolling Stock:** 1925 Frisco Baldwin 4-8-2 no. 1519; Vulcan Chemicals 1965 GE 50-ton class BB switcher; renovated BN, NP, RI, MoP, SL&SF, MK&T, and UP cabooses; 1928 automobile boxcar; 1937 three-dome tank car; 1953 single-dome tank car; 1930 boxcar; 1920 gondola.

**Special Events:** Two model railroad swap meets; Christmas party; Railroad Appreciation Day, April; two caboose excursions each year.

**Nearby Attractions/Accommodations:** Water park, winery, Science and Discovery Center, Cherokee Strip, Midgley and Veterans museums.

**Location/Directions:** Enid is 30 miles west of I-35 in north central Oklahoma on Routes 60, 81, 64, 412. Museum is six blocks northwest of downtown square.

         M

**Site Address:** 702 N. Washington, Enid, OK
**Mailing Address:** 702 N. Washington, Enid, OK 73701
**Telephone:** (580) 233-3051

**KIRKPATRICK AIR SPACE MUSEUM AT OMNIPLEX**
*Museum, display*

**Description:** The Toy Train Collection features the M.G. Martin Model Train Exhibit, a complete 1,000-square-foot layout that features several toy trains running through a miniature town, including an industrial area, an agricultural area, and an amusement area. The layout is maintained and operated by the Toy Train Operating Society, Sooner Division. The Parlor Car is a 1929 Missouri Pacific Railroad Car built by the Pullman Company and used for executive business. The car has four staterooms, three bathrooms, a dining salon, an observation parlor, a kitchen, and an open observation platform.

**Schedule:** Museum exhibits open Labor Day through Memorial Day, Monday through Friday 9 a.m. to 5 p.m., Saturday 9 a.m. to 6 p.m., Sunday, 11 a.m. to 6 p.m.; Memorial Day through Labor Day, Monday through Saturday 9 a.m. to 6 p.m., Sunday 11 a.m. to 6 p.m.

**Admission/Fare:** Museum: adults, $7.50; seniors, $6.75; children 6-12, $6; children 3-5, $5.

**Nearby Attractions/Accommodations:** National Cowboy and Western Heritage Center, Oklahoma City Zoo, Remington Rack horse racing facility, Softball Hall of Fame, Oklahoma Firefighters Museum; more.

**Location/Directions:** I-35 to N.E. 50th St. Next door to the Oklahoma City Zoo and directly across from Remington Park.

**Site Address:** 2100 N.E. 52nd St., Oklahoma City, OK
**Mailing Address:** 2100 N.E. 52nd St., Oklahoma City, OK 73111
**Telephone:** (405) 602-6664
**Fax:** (405) 602-3766
**E-mail:** kholding@omniplex.org; omnipr@omniplex.org
**Internet:** www.omniplex.org

**WAYNOKA AIR-RAIL MUSEUM**
*Museum*

SANDIE OLSON

**Description:** An air-rail museum featuring the Santa Fe Railroad, Harvey House, Transcontinental Air Transport, German prisoner-of-war paintings, vintage video, museum store, and more in the beautifully restored Harvey House, an ISTEA project.

**Schedule:** Museum and restaurant open Thursday, Friday, and Saturday evenings and by appointment.

**Admission/Fare:** $2 to museum.

**Locomotives/Rolling Stock:** Hudson Bay 2511 locomotive GP7.

**Nearby Attractions/Accommodations:** Little Sahara State Park with great dune riding, Curtis Hill for train watching, Sod House Museum, Alabaster Caverns, Great Salt Plains for bird watching and crystal digging. Museum is located on Oklahoma's fastest and busiest rail line, 50 to 100 trains daily.

**Location/Directions:** From Oklahoma City, west on I-40 to U.S. 281, northwest on U.S. 281 to Waynoka. The museum is at the west end of Waynoka St. on BNSF main line.

         M

**Site Address:** 202 S. Cleveland, Waynoka, OK
**Mailing Address:** PO Box 193, Waynoka, OK 73860
**Telephone:** (580) 824-4211
**Fax:** (580) 824-0921
**E-mail:** sandieo@pldi.net
**Internet:** www.pldi.net/~harpo

JOHN SHANNON

**Description:** The museum contains an extensive display of railroad antiques and artifacts of the Rock Island Line and other railroads.

**Schedule:** Year round by chance or appointment. Call or write for information.

**Admission/Fare:** Free.

**Locomotives/Rolling Stock:** Rock Island boxcar no. 5542; UP caboose no. 25865.

**Location/Directions:** On historic Route 66. Main St., across from "Yukon's Best Flour" wheat elevator.

**Site Address:** Third and Main Streets, Yukon, OK
**Mailing Address:** 410 Oak Ave., Yukon, OK 73099-2640
**Telephone:** (405) 354-5079

**CANBY DEPOT MUSEUM**
*Museum*

BERGMAN PHOTOGRAPHY

**Schedule:** Thursday through Sunday, 1 to 4 p.m. Closed January and February.

**Admission/Fare:** Free. Donations accepted.

**Locomotives/Rolling Stock:** Caboose no. HMS7810M.

**Special Events:** Pancake Breakfast, July 4th. Victorian Garden Party, July 22. Open House, September. Antique Appraisals, October through April.

**Nearby Attractions/Accommodations:** Clackamas County Fairgrounds (fair in August). Molalla River State Park Canby Ferry Crossing. Willamette River, Flower Farmer Miniature Train Rides.

**Location/Directions:** Highway 99 East and Pine St. Seven miles south of Oregon City.

       M

**Site Address:** 888 N.E. Fourth Ave., Canby, OR
**Mailing Address:** PO Box 160, Canby, OR 97013
**Telephone:** (503) 266-6712
**Fax:** (503) 266-9775
**E-mail:** depotmuseum@canby.com
**Internet:** www.canby.com/chamber/depot/depot.htm

**PHOENIX & HOLLY RAILROAD**
*Train ride*
*24" gauge*

FLOWER FARMER

**Description:** Visitors can ride through acres of flowers at the Flower Farmer and enjoy a 1¾-mile ride with a stopover at "Box Curve" station and pet the farm animals (July through September).

**Schedule:** May through October: weekends and holidays 11 a.m. to 6 p.m. Weekdays, groups only. October: open daily, Pumpkin Patch Trips; Haunted Train Rides, last three weeks of October, dusk to 9 p.m.

**Admission/Fare:** Adults, $3.50; children age 12 and under and seniors (65+), $3. Groups, weekdays by appointment. October Haunted Trains: adults, $3.50; children $3.

**Locomotives/Rolling Stock:** "Sparky" the diesel locomotive purpose-built; diesel locomotive 5.5" scale; DRG&W side-rod diesel; gondolas; flatcar; caboose.

**Special Events:** Pumpkin Run to pumpkin patch, month of October. Haunted Train Rides, Christmas lights.

**Nearby Attractions/Accommodations:** Swan Island, Dahlia Farm, Canby Ferry, state parks, city parks, golf. Swan Island Dahlia Festival, last two weeks in August.

**Location/Directions:** I-5 to Canby exit, to Holly St., turn left one mile to site.

**Site Address:** 2512 N. Holly St., Canby, OR
**Mailing Address:** 2512 N. Holly St., Canby, OR 97013-9118
**Telephone:** (503) 266-3581
**Fax:** (503) 263-4027
**E-mail:** lgarre@falconpc.com
**Internet:** www.narrowgaugerr.com

# MOUNT HOOD RAILROAD AND
# DINNER TRAIN
*Train ride, dinner train*
*Standard gauge*

**Description:** Built in 1906, this historic railroad takes passengers on four-hour tours from the Columbia Gorge to the foothills of Mt. Hood. The trip aboard the Excursion Train comprised of 1910-20 Pullman coaches, concession car, and caboose is narrated one way. The 1940s Dinner & Brunch Train offers excellent four-course dining. Special events occur throughout the year.

**Schedule:** April through December. Excursion Train: 10 a.m. and 3 p.m. Brunch Train: 11:50 a.m. Dinner Train: Friday, 6:30 p.m., Saturday, 5:30 p.m. (4:30 p.m. October through December).

**Admission/Fare:** Excursion Train: adults, $22.95; seniors, $20.95; children, $14.95. Brunch Train: $56. Dinner Train: $69.50. Murder Mystery Dinner Trains: $79.50.

**Locomotives/Rolling Stock:** Two GP 9s; 1910 and 1920 Pullmans; 1940s dining cars.

**Special Events:** Festivals, Train Robberies, Circus Train, Christmas Tree Trains, Murder Mystery Trains

**Nearby Attractions/Accommodations:** Mt. Hood; Columbia River National Scenic Area; biking, hiking, wind surfing, golf; historic hotels.

**Location/Directions:** Sixty miles east of Portland on I-84, exit 63 right to Cascade St., left to parking lot.

**Site Address:** 110 Railroad Ave., Hood River, OR
**Mailing Address:** 110 Railroad Ave., Hood River, OR 97031
**Telephone:** (800) TRAIN-61 (872-4661) and (541) 386-3556
**Fax:** (541) 386-2140
**E-mail:** www.mthoodrr@gorge.net
**Internet:** www.mthoodrr.com

# OREGON ELECTRIC RAILWAY
# HISTORICAL SOCIETY
*Train ride*
*Standard*

BOB SPARKES

**Description:** Scenic 7-mile trip on a trolley along the Willamette River from Lake Oswego to Portland.

**Schedule:** June through August: Wednesdays through Sundays and holidays, 10 a.m. to 6 p.m. September through May: weekends and holidays, weather permitting.

**Admission/Fare:** Round trip: Adults, $8; seniors, $7; children, $4.

**Locomotives/Rolling Stock:** Blackpool no. 48; Broadway no. 813.

**Nearby Attractions/Accommodations:** Tillamook Ice Creamery Restaurant, Willamette Park, Riverplace Marina.

**Location/Directions:** Highway 43 to Lake Oswego. Trolley depot located at 311 N. State St. (Highway 43) at Foothills Rd.

       M arm

**Site Address:** Lake Oswego, OR
**Mailing Address:** PO Box 308, Lake Oswego, OR 97034
**Telephone:** (503) 222-2226
**Internet:** www.trainweb.org

# WASHINGTON PARK & ZOO RAILWAY
### Train ride
### 30" gauge

GEORGE BAETJER

**Description:** Four-mile round trip from the zoo through Washington Park, to the Portland rose gardens ad Japanese garden.

**Schedule:** Memorial Day weekend through September 30: round trip, daily. Spring: short loop ride around edge of zoo grounds. First train normally at 10:30 a.m. Trains depart at frequent intervals.

**Admission/Fare:** Round trip–adults, $2.75; seniors (65+)/youth (3-11), $2. Zoo admission required to ride the zoo railway.

**Locomotives/Rolling Stock:** Steam locomotive no. 1; Virginia & Truckee replica; diesel locomotive no. 2, GM Aerotrain replica; diesel locomotive no. 5, "Oregon Express."

**Nearby Attractions/Accommodations:** Portland Rose Gardens, Japanese Gardens, International Forestry Center, Portland Children's Museum.

**Location/Directions:** Two miles west of Portland City Center, on U.S. Highway 26. Zoo is on MAX light rail line; get off at Washington Park Station.

*Coupon available, see coupon section.

 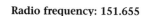 **Radio frequency: 151.655**

**Site Address:** Oregon Zoo, 4001 SW Canyon Rd., Portland, OR
**Mailing Address:** 4001 SW Canyon Rd., Portland, OR 97221
**Telephone:** (503) 226-1561
**Fax:** (503) 226-6836
**Internet:** www.oregonzoo.org

# CROOKED RIVER DINNER TRAIN
*Dinner train*
*Standard gauge*

**Description:** Three-hour, 38-mile round trip through the scenic Crooked River Valley. A four-course meal is served by characters from the Wild West and a murder mystery or train robbery is performed.

**Schedule:** Year round on weekends.

**Admission/Fare:** Adults: $59 to $71, per person; children 4-12, $38; children 3 and under, $20.

**Locomotives/Rolling Stock:** 1940s Milwaukee Road railcars.

**Special Events:** New Year's Eve party train; holiday brunch trains, Easter; holiday mystery trains, December. Railroad Days (with Shay steam engine), September. Mother's Day, Father's Day, Thanksgiving.

**Nearby Attractions/Accommodations:** Smith Rock State Park, High Desert Museum, Newberry Crater, Lava Cast Forest, Crater Lake.

**Location/Directions:** Located near intersection of Highway 97 and O'Neil Junction. Follow the signs.

*Coupon available, see coupon section.

**Site Address:** 4075 N.E. O'Neil Rd., Redmond, OR
**Mailing Address:** PO Box 387, Redmond, OR 97756
**Telephone:** (541) 548-8630
**Fax:** (541) 548-8702
**E-mail:** crookedriverrailroad.com
**Internet:** www.dintrain@coinet.com

# SUMPTER VALLEY RAILROAD
*Train ride, museum*
*36" gauge*

**Description:** A 5-mile one-way or 10-mile round trip.

**Schedule:** Memorial Day through September: McEwen, 10 a.m., 12:30, and 3 p.m. Sumpter, 11:30 a.m. and 2 p.m. One way only at 4:30 p.m.

**Admission/Fare:** Adults, round trip, $9, and one way, $6; children 6-16, $6.50/$4.50; families, $20/$15.

**Locomotives/Rolling Stock:** No. 19 Mikado (oil/steam); no. 3 Heisler (wood/steam); no. 101 diesel switcher; nos. 1101 and 1102 open-air car; no. 20 coach; no. 5 caboose; nos. 1101 and 1102 Sumpter Valley Ry.; no. 19 American (Sumpter Valley Ry.); no. 3 Heisler (W.H. Eccles Lumber Co.); no. 20 E.M. Eccles; no. 5 Sumpter Valley Ry.; work cars, gondola cars, cabooses, and more.

**Special Events:** Night trains, round trip with dinner and entertainment: July through September, first Saturdays of each month. Flea market in Sumpter, major holidays in summer.

**Nearby Attractions/Accommodations:** Oregon Interpretive Center/Museum, Oregon Trail Museum, Sunridge Hotel and restaurant, Sumpter Park RV, Phillips Lake with camping.

**Location/Directions:** Hwy. 7, 22 miles southwest of Baker City off I-84.

**Site Address:** Dredge Loop Rd., McEwen, OR
**Mailing Address:** PO Box 389, Baker City, OR 97814
**Telephone:** (541) 894-2268 and (541) 523-3453
**E-mail:** lmcx@eoni.com
**Internet:** www.svry.com

## ALTOONA RAILROADERS MEMORIAL MUSEUM
*Train ride, museum, display, layout*
*Standard gauge*

PETER D. BARTON

**Description:** America's newest interactive railroad museum reflecting life and labor of railroad workers..

**Schedule:** April through October: daily, 9 a.m. to 5 p.m.; November through March: Tuesdays through Sundays, 9 a.m. to 5 p.m. Closed Mondays.

**Admission/Fare:** Adults, $8.50; seniors, $7.75; children, $5. Combo with Horseshoe Curve NHL: Adults, $10; seniors, $9; children, $5.50.

**Locomotives/Rolling Stock:** PRR K4s no. 1361 locomotive; PRR/General Electric GG1 no. 4913; Vulcan Iron Works saddle tank locomotive no. 2826; Baldwin Locomotive Works diesel electric VO-660 no. 6712; Pullman; the "Loretto," private car of Charles Schwaab.

**Special Events:** Railfest, first weekend in October. Heritage Holidays and Model Trains, November 23 through December. Thomas Play Day, November 3.

**Nearby Attractions/Accommodations:** Horseshoe Curve National Historic Landmark; Allegheny Portage Railroad National Historic Site; East Broad Top Railroad; DelGrosso's Family Park.

**Location/Directions:** I-99, exit 33.

    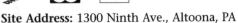

**Site Address:** 1300 Ninth Ave., Altoona, PA
**Mailing Address:** 1300 Ninth Ave., Altoona, PA 16602
**Telephone:** (814) 946-0834
**Fax:** (814) 946-9457
**E-mail:** admin@railroadcity.com
**Internet:** www.railroadcity.com

# HORSESHOE CURVE NATIONAL HISTORIC LANDMARK
*Museum, display*

**Description:** Contemporary mainline mountain railroading, exhibit hall, food service, incline plane, gift shop.

**Schedule:** April through October: daily, 10 a.m. to 7 p.m.; November through December: Tuesdays through Sundays, 10 a.m. to 4 p.m. Closed January through March.

**Admission/Fare:** Adults, $3.50, seniors, $3, children, $1.75. Horseshoe Curve and Railroaders Memorial Museum: adults, $10; seniors, $9; children, $5.50

**Locomotives/Rolling Stock:** PRR GP9 diesel electric no. 7048.

**Special Events:** Railfest, first weekend in October; Moonlight at the Curve, December 7-8, 6 to 9 p.m.; Heritage Holidays, December 17-21; Horn & Whistle Fair, May 18-19.

**Nearby Attractions/Accommodations:** Altoona Railroaders Memorial Museum, Allegheny Portage Railroad National Historic site, East Broad Top Railroad.

**Location/Directions:** I-99, exit 31.

**Mailing Address:** 1300 Ninth Ave., Altoona, PA 16602
**Telephone:** (814) 946-0834
**Fax:** (814) 946-9457
**E-mail:** admin@railroadcity.com
**Internet:** www.railroadcity.com

# PIONEER TUNNEL COAL MINE AND STEAM TRAIN
### *Train ride*
### *Narrow gauge*

**Description:** Scenic ride along the Mahanoy Mountain behind a steam loco-motive of the 0-4-0 type built in 1927 by the Vulcan Iron Works of Wilkes-Barre, Pennsylvania. Guides tell the story of strip mining, boot-legging and the Centralia Mine Fire. Also available is a tour of a real anthracite coal mine in open mine cars pulled by a battery-operated mine motor. Mine guides tell the story of anthracite coal mining.

**Schedule:** April: weekday mine tours: 11 a.m., 12:30 and 2 p.m. Memorial Day through Labor Day: daily mine tours 10 a.m. to 6 p.m. Mine tours and steam train–May, September, October: weekday mine tours 11 a.m., 12:30 and 2 p.m. train tours for reserved groups only; weekend mine and train run continuously.

**Admission/Fare:** Steam train–adults, $5; children under age 12, $3.50. Mine–adults, $7; children under age 12, $4.50. Group discounts.

**Locomotives/Rolling Stock:** A spare "lokie" of the 0-4-0 type built by Vulcan Iron Work; two battery-powered mine motors.

**Special Events:** Tenth Annual Pioneer Day, August 17; coal mine tours, steam train rides, large craft fair, ethnic foods, live music, more.

**Nearby Attractions/Accommodations:** Pennsylvania Museum of Anthracite Mining.

**Location/Directions:** I-81, exit 36W (Frackville). Rt. 61 north to Ashland.

**Site Address:** 19th and Oak Streets, Ashland, PA
**Mailing Address:** 19th and Oak Streets, Ashland, PA 17921
**Telephone:** (570) 875-3850
**Fax:** (570) 875-3301
**Internet:** www.pioneertunnel.com

# BELLEFONTE HISTORICAL RAILROAD
### Train ride
### Standard gauge

W.M. RUMBERGER

**Description:** Scheduled and special trips over the 60-mile Nittany & Bald Eagle Railroad to Lemont, Vail (Tyrone), and Mill Hall. Fall foliage and Christmas runs offered. The Bellefonte Station, a restored former Pennsylvania Railroad structure built in 1888, houses an operating N gauge layout of the Bellefonte-Curtin Village route, as well as historical photos and memorabilia of area railroading. A snowplow and caboose under restoration are displayed beside the station.

**Schedule:** May 30 through September 30: weekends and holidays. October and December: special runs only. Call for information.

**Admission/Fare:** Adults, $8 and up; children 3-11, $5 and up.

**Locomotives/Rolling Stock:** No. 9167, 1952 RDC-1; and 1962 No. 1953; air-conditioned passenger cars. Can be configured for meal service.

**Special Events:** Spring, Fall, Christmas trains.

**Nearby Attractions/Accommodations:** Curtin Village, Bald Eagle State Park, Penn State University, Victorian Bellefonte, Historic Boalsburg, Penns Cave.

**Location/Directions:** Central Pennsylvania, less than 5 miles from exit 23 and 24, I-80.

**Site Address:** The Train Station, Bellefonte, PA
**Mailing Address:** 320 W. High St., Train Station, Bellefonte, PA 16823
**Telephone:** (814) 355-0311
**Fax:** (814) 353-0511
**E-mail:** countyseat@aol.com

Pennsylvania, Gallitzin

# ALLEGHENY PORTAGE RAILROAD NATIONAL HISTORIC SITE
*Museum*
*Standard gauge*

**Description:** This site preserves the remains of the incline railway used to portage canal boats over the Allegheny Mountains. It includes the original railroad trace, inclines and levels, visitor center, Lemon House Tavern, and Engine House Exhibit Shelter no. 6. Visitor Center includes films, exhibits, models.

**Schedule:** Year round: daily 9 a.m. to 5 p.m. Extended hours in summer. Closed Veteran's Day, President's Day, Thanksgiving, Christmas, and New Year's Day.

**Admission/Fare:** Adults 17 and older, $2; national park passes honored.

**Locomotives/Rolling Stock:** 1893 Pangborn model of the "Lafayette."

**Special Events:** Summer: National Park Service ranger costumed demonstrations of stone cutting, log hewing, lifestyles of the past. Summer Saturdays: Evening on the Summit concert lecture series. Summer Sundays: Heritage Hike series, hikes and bus tours of portage route.

**Nearby Attractions/Accommodations:** Gallitzin Tunnels, Johnstown Flood National Memorial, state parks.

**Location/Directions:** U.S. 22, Gallitzin exit.

**Site Address:** 110 Federal Park Rd., Gallitzin, PA
**Mailing Address:** 110 Federal Park Rd., Gallitzin, PA 16641
**Telephone:** (814) 886-6150
**Fax:** (814) 886-6117
**Internet:** www.nps.gov/alpo/

# GETTYSBURG SCENIC RAILWAY
*Train ride, display*
*Standard gauge*

**Description:** Depart from the historic 1884 depot that welcomed thousands of Civil War veterans back to Gettysburg, and enjoy a nostalgic 1¾-hour excursion to Aspers, passing through the renowned Adams County apple orchards. Visit website for information on special event trains.

**Schedule:** Summer, departures every afternoon and two round trips on weekends; off-peak season, weekends. Visit web site for more details.

**Admission/Fare:** Adults, $16; children 4-15, $9; 3 and under, free.

**Locomotives/Rolling Stock:** Locomotive PREX 401 EMD F-7A, formerly B&LE 726A; locomotive PREX 402 EMD F-7A, formerly C&NW 406; double-decker open car; combine/snack car; six celestial-roofed heavy-weight passenger cars.

**Special Events:** Civil War Train Raids; Easter Bunny Train; Ghost Train.

**Nearby Attractions/Accommodations:** Renowned Civil War sites and breathtaking scenery. Many fine campgrounds, hotels, unique shops, and restaurants.

**Location/Directions:** One block from the downtown Square on North Washington St.

**Site Address:** 106 N. Washington St., Gettysburg, PA
**Mailing Address:** 106 N. Washington St., Gettysburg, PA 17325
**Telephone:** (717) 334-6932
**Fax:** (717) 334-0291
**E-mail:** scenic@gettysburgrail.com
**Internet:** www.gettysburgrail.com

**Description:** This museum features an extensive collection of model trains and a collection of items dealing with military railroads; it also offers a simulated train ride following President Lincoln to Gettysburg.

**Schedule:** Summer hours 9 to 9.

**Admission/Fare:** Adults, $5.95; children 6-11, $3.50.

**Nearby Attractions/Accommodations:** In the center of Gettysburg attractions: Gettysburg National Military Park, Visitor Center, Cyclorama.

**Location/Directions:** Steinwehr Ave. (Business 15 south).

**Site Address:** 425 Steinwehr Ave., Gettysburg, PA
**Mailing Address:** 425 Steinwehr Ave., Gettysburg, PA 17325
**Telephone:** (717) 334-5678
**Internet:** www.gettysburgbattlefieldtours.com

## GREENVILLE RAILROAD
## PARK AND MUSEUM
*Museum*

**Admission/Fare: Free.** Donations accepted.

**Locomotive/Rolling Stock:** Static equipment. World's largest steam switch locomotive built in 1936 by Baldwin 0-10-2 S/N 61910; antique Erie flatcar; B&LE iron ore car; UP caboose; Wheeling & Lake Erie caboose and B&LE caboose.

**Nearby Attractions/Accommodations:** Deer and Animal Park; Pymatuning State Park and Dam; Canal Museum Tara Inn and Restaurants; Thiel Collage; Coneaut Lake Park.

**Location/Directions:** Fourteen miles east of I-79; 22 miles north of I-80.

      M arm

**Site Address:** 314 Main St., Greenville, PA
**Mailing Address:** 314 Main St., Greenville, PA 16125
**Telephone:** (724) 588-9501 (Patty Marantis)

# STOURBRIDGE LINE
# RAIL EXCURSIONS
*Train ride*
*Standard gauge*

**Description:** Scenic round-trip rides from Honesdale to Hawley (24 miles) and Honesdale to Lackawaxen-on-the-Delaware (50 miles). The ride parallels the shimmering Lackawaxen River and closely follows the route of the Delaware & Hudson Canal.

**Schedule:** Easter through early December, on scheduled weekends.

**Admission/Fare:** Varies by ride.

**Locomotive/Rolling Stock:** 1949 EMD BL2 no. 54, former Bangor & Aroostook.

**Nearby Attractions/Accommodations:** Claws 'n Paws Wild Animal Park, Wayne County Historical Society and Museum Shop, Dorflinger Glass Museum, Lake Wallenpaupack, historic downtown Honesdale.

**Location/Directions:** Northeastern Pennsylvania, 24 miles from Scranton.

*Coupon available, see coupon section.

**Site Address:** 303 Commercial St., Honesdale, PA
**Mailing Address:** 303 Commercial St., Honesdale, PA 18431
**Telephone:** (570) 253-1960 and (800) 433-9008
**Fax:** (570) 253-1322
**E-mail:** waynecoc@sunlink.net
**Internet:** www.waynecountycc.com and www.stourbridgerail.com

# RAIL TOURS, INC.
*Train ride*
*Standard*

**Description:** A 40-minute, eight-mile round trip; a 1¾-hour, 19-mile round trip; or a 2¾-hour, 33-mile round trip over the former Jersey Central's Nesquehoning branch line. Rides go to Nesquehoning, Lake Hauto, or Hometown Trestle (161 feet high).

**Schedule:** Mid-May through October, weekends and holidays.

**Admission/Fare:** Varies. Call or write for information.

Locomotives/Rolling Stock: Nos. 7545, 7579, and 7580 former Conrail EMD GP-10 diesels; no. 581, former Santa Fe EMD CF-7 diesel; former Jersey Central and Reading coaches; various cabooses.

**Special Events:** Easter Bunny trains; Santa Claus trains; Flaming Foliage Rambles.

**Location/Directions:** In Northeastern Pennsylvania off I-476, exit 75. Take Route 209 south to downtown Jim Thorpe.

**Site Address:** 2 Lehigh Ave., Jim Thorpe, PA
**Mailing Address:** PO Box 285, Jim Thorpe, PA 18229
**Telephone:** (570) 325-4606
**Fax:** (610) 250-0968
**E-mail:** bigjohn@epix.net
**Internet:** www.railtours-inc.com

# WANAMAKER, KEMPTON & SOUTHERN, INC.
*Train ride*
*Standard gauge*

**Description:** A 6-mile, 40-minute round trip through scenic Pennsylvania Dutch country over part of the former Reading Company's Schuylkill & Lehigh branch. Restored stations relocated from Joanna and Catasauqua, Pennsylvania; original circa 1874 Wanamaker station; operating HO gauge model layout.

**Schedule:** May through October: weekends. Call or write for detailed schedule.

**Admission/Fare:** Adults, $56; children 3-11, $3; age 2 and under ride free.

**Locomotives/Rolling Stock:** No. 2, 1920 Porter 0-4-0T, former Colorado Fuel & Iron; no. 65, 1930 Porter 0-6-0T, former Safe Harbor Water Power; no. 7258 1942 GE diesel electric 45-ton, former Birdsboro Corp.; coaches nos. 1494 and 1474 and combine no. 408, all former Reading Company; coach no. 582, former Lackawanna; assorted freight cars and caboose, former Lehigh & New England; steel and wood cabooses, former Reading.

**Special Events:** Mother's Day Special, Kids' Fun Weekend, Harvest Moon Special, Halloween Train, Santa Claus Special. Write for schedule.

**Nearby Attractions/Accommodations:** Hawk Mountain, Crystal Cave.

**Location/Directions:** Depot is located at Kempton on Routes 143 or 737, a short distance north of I-78. The site is 20 miles west of Allentown.

*Coupon available, see coupon section.

**Site Address:** 42 Community Center Rd., Kempton, PA
**Mailing Address:** PO Box 24, Kempton, PA 19529
**Telephone:** (610) 756-6469
**E-mail:** info@wknsrr.com
**Internet:** www.wknsrr.com

# DUTCH WONDERLAND FAMILY AMUSEMENT PARK
*Train ride*
*24" gauge*

**Description:** A 48-acre amusement park geared to families with a variety of rides and attractions. Live shows include the Great American High Diving Show. The Wonderland Special has seating for 56 guests and is a scenic 7-minute ride through the park. We also offer a monorail ride.

**Schedule:** Weekends, spring and fall. Daily, Memorial Day through Labor Day.

**Nearby Attractions/Accommodations:** Discover Lancaster County History Museum, Old Mill Stream Camping Manor, Amish Farm and House, Outlets (Tanger and Rockvale). Hotels: Host, Ramada, McIntosh, Continental Inn.

**Location/Directions:** Four miles east of Lancaster on Route 30.

**Site Address:** 2249 Route 30E, Lancaster, PA
**Mailing Address:** 2249 Route 30E, Lancaster, PA 17602
**Telephone:** (717) 291-1888
**Fax:** (717) 291-1595
**E-mail:** info@dutchwonderland.com
**Internet:** www.dutchwonderland.com

# KNOX & KANE RAILROAD
*Train ride*
*Standard gauge*

**Description:** This line offers one round trip each operating day to Kane and the Kinzua Bridge over a former Baltimore & Ohio branch line. Passengers may board at Marienville for a 96-mile, 8-hour trip or at Kane for a 32-mile, 3½-hour trip. The 2,053-foot-long, 301-foot-high Kinzua Bridge, built in 1882 to span the Kinzua Creek Valley, was at the time the highest bridge in the world. It is on the National Register of Historic Places and is a National Historic Civil Engineering Landmark.

**Schedule:** June and September: Friday through Sunday. July and August: Tuesday through Sunday. Early October: Wednesday through Sunday. Depart Marienville 8:30 a.m.; depart Kane 10:30 a.m.

**Admission/Fare:** From Marienville: adults, $22; children, $14. From Kane: adults, $16; children, $9. Advance reservations suggested. Box lunches available by advance order, $5.50.

**Locomotives/Rolling Stock:** No. 38, 1927 Baldwin 2-8-0, former Huntington & Broad Top Mountain; no. 44, Alco diesel; no. 58, Chinese 2-8-2 built in 1989; Porter Switcher no. 1; steel coaches; open cars; two snack and souvenir cars.

**Location/Directions:** In northwestern Pennsylvania, about 20 miles north of I-80.

**Site Address:** S. Forest St., Marienville, PA
**Mailing Address:** PO Box 422, Marienville, PA 16239
**Telephone:** (814) 927-6621
**Fax:** (814) 927-8750

# MIDDLETOWN & HUMMELSTOWN RAILROAD
*Train ride, dinner train, museum*
*Standard gauge*

WENDELL DILLINGER

**Description:** An 11-mile, 1¼-hour round trip through Swatara Creek Valley with narration and singalongs.

**Schedule:** Memorial Day through Labor Day, weekends; Thursdays and Fridays in May; Tuesdays, Thursdays, Saturdays, and Sundays in July and August; Sundays only in September; weekends in October.

**Admission/Fare:** Adults, $9; children 3-11, $4.50. Add $1 on steam weekends. Special events train pricing varies.

**Locomotives/Rolling Stock:** Regular train consist: GE 65-ton nos. 1 and 2 with DL&W coaches; freight locomotives NSS Alco T6 no. 1016; WM Alco S6 no. 151; CN 2-6-0 no. 91; three SEPTA PCCs; more.

**Special Events:** Sweetheart Special; Easter Express; Mother's Special; Colonial Craft Fair; Moonlight Specials; Barbecue Express; Train Robberies; "Civil War Remembered" re-enactment; Fall Foliage Specials and Haunted Trains; Santa Express, Christmastime Dinner Train, and New Year's Eve Celebration Train.

**Nearby Attractions/Accommodations:** Hershey Park, Chocolate World, Pennsylvania Dutch Country, Gettysburg Battlefield, more.

**Location/Directions:** Pennsylvania Turnpike, exit 19 to Route 283 to Middletown and Hummelstown exit; go south, turn right on Main St., left on Race St.

**Site Address:** Race St., Middletown, PA, at railroad track
**Mailing Address:** 136 Brown St., Middletown, PA 17057
**Telephone:** (717) 944-4435, ext. 0
**Fax:** (717) 944-7758
**E-mail:** riderail@ptdprolog.net
**Internet:** www.800padutch.com/mhrr.html and www.mhrailroad.com

# NEW HOPE & IVYLAND RAILROAD
*Train ride, dinner train*
*Standard gauge*

**Description:** Enjoy a 50-minute, 9-mile round trip to Lahaska, Pennsylvania, and return. Passengers can ride in coach, open-air car, or air-conditioned parlor car.

**Schedule:** Year round. Call or visit website for schedule.

**Admission/Fare:** Adults, $9.95; seniors, $8.95; children, $6.95; under age 2, $1.50.

**Locomotives/Rolling Stock:** Lancaster & Chester Baldwin Consolidation no. 40; Conrail Penn Central Pennsylvania EMD GP30 no. 2198; CSX family lines GE C30-8 no. 7087.

**Special Events:** Easter Trains, Father's Day cab ride giveaways; Train Robbery; Halloween trains, Santa Claus trains.

**Nearby Attractions/Accommodations:** Downtown New Hope, Lambertville, Peddlers Village.

**Location/Directions:** New Hope exit 51 off of I-95. North 10 miles into downton New Hope, left on Bridge Street, one block driveway on right.

*Coupon available, see coupon section.

**Site Address:** 32 W. Bridge St., New Hope, PA
**Mailing Address:** 32 W. Bridge St., New Hope, PA 18938
**Telephone:** (215) 862-2332
**Fax:** (215) 862-2150
**Internet:** www.newhoperailroad.com

RODNEY BLYSTONE

**Description:** A restored New York Central passenger station built in 1899 by the Lake Shore & Michigan Southern houses an extensive collection of displays. The museum is adjacent to CSX and NS main lines. A passenger/freight station built in 1869 by LS&MS is also on the grounds.

**Schedule:** Memorial Day through Labor Day: Wednesdays through Sundays and holidays, 1 to 5 p.m. May, September, and October: weekends, 1 to 5 p.m.

**Admission/Fare:** Donations appreciated.

**Locomotives/Rolling Stock:** NYC U25B no. 25001 CSS&SB "Little Joe" electric locomotive; no. 8202 Heisler fireless 0-6-0; heavyweight Pullman sleeping cars; CB&Q heavyweight baggage no. 1530; GN lightweight diner no. 1251; passenger and freight cars, cabooses.

**Special Events:** Wine Country Harvest Festival, September 28-29. Christmas-at-the-Station, December 7-8, 14-15. Call or write for additional special events.

**Nearby Attractions/Accommodations:** Peek'nPeak Resort, Presque Isle State Park, Lake Erie nature walks, beaches and marinas.

**Location/Directions:** At Wall and Robinson Streets. Fifteen miles east of Erie, 2 miles north of I-90, exit 41, three blocks south of U.S. 20.

**Site Address:** 31 Wall St., North East, PA
**Mailing Address:** PO Box 571, North East, PA 16428-0571
**Telephone:** (814) 825-2724

Pennsylvania, Philadelphia

## THE FRANKLIN INSTITUTE
## SCIENCE MUSEUM
*Museum, display, layout*
*Standard gauge*

**Description:** The nostalgic Baldwin 60000 steam locomotive has become part of an exciting new attraction. "The Train Factory" transports visitors to an active turn-of-the-century train works where they feel the steam, hear the noise of the machines, and meet some of the people who worked to create America's locomotives. Visitors explore original and modern train technology as they journey through the sections of this exhibit including, The Machine Shop, The Track Shop, Research and Development, Accident Investigation, and the Baldwin 60000 test run. The Franklin Institute is located at 20th Street and the Benjamin Franklin Parkway in downtown Philadelphia, within walking distance of Suburban Station.

**Schedule:** Year round: daily, 9:30 a.m. to 5 p.m.

**Admission/Fare:** Call or check website for information.

**Locomotives/Rolling Stock:** Baldwin 60000.

**Location/Directions:** Center city Philadelphia.

30th Street, ¼ mile away

**Site Address:** 20th St. and the Ben Franklin Parkway, Philadelphia, PA
**Mailing Address:** 222 N. 20th St., Philadelphia, PA 19103
**Telephone:** (215) 448-1200
**Fax:** (215) 448-1235
**Internet:** www.fi.edu

**Description:** The museum is located in two historic buildings at the southern operating terminus of the East Broad Top Railroad during the era of common-carrier operation. On display are exhibits related to the history of the East Broad Top Railroad.

**Schedule:** June through mid-October: Saturdays 10 a.m. to 5 p.m.; Sundays 1 to 5 p.m.

**Admission/Fare: Free.** Donations appreciated.

**Locomotives/Rolling Stock:** EBT maintenance-of-way wood handcar; EBT combination passenger-baggage car no. 16 (stored off-site).

**Special Events:** Summer Open House, June 1-2. EBT Rebirthday Celebration, August 10. Fall Open House and Reunion, October 12-13.

**Nearby Attractions/Accommodations:** East Broad Top Railroad, Broad Top Area Coal Miners Museum, Raystown Lake.

**Location/Directions:** Approximately 17 miles southwest of Orbisonia/Rockhill Furnace (EBT and U.S. 522), 30 miles southeast of Huntingdon (U.S. 22), and 20 miles north of Breezewood (I-70, I-76, and U.S. 30).

**Site Address:** Main St., Robertsdale, PA
**Mailing Address:** PO Box 68, Robertsdale, PA 16674
**Telephone:** (814) 625-2388
**E-mail:** febt@aol.com
**Internet:** www.febt.org

**EAST BROAD TOP RAILROAD**
*Train ride*
*36" gauge*

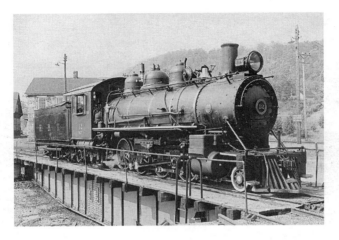

**Description:** The East Broad Top Railroad, chartered in 1856, is the last operating narrow-gauge railroad east of the Mississippi. The road hauled coal, freight, mail, express, and passengers for more than 80 years. Today the East Broad Top offers passengers a 10-mile, 50-minute ride through the beautiful Aughwick Valley with its own preserved locomotives; the ride takes passengers from the historic depot at Rockhill Furnace to the picnic grove, where the train is turned. On display are the railroad yard with shops, operating roundhouse, and turntable. Dates, times, and fares are subject to change. Call or write for latest information.

**Schedule:** June through October: weekends, 11 a.m., 1 and 3 p.m.

**Admission/Fare:** Adults, $9; children, $6.

**Locomotives/Rolling Stock:** 1911 Baldwin locomotive 2-8-2 no. 12; 1912 Baldwin locomotive 2-8-2 no. 14; 1914 Baldwin locomotive 2-8-2 no. 15; 1918 Baldwin locomotive 2-8-2 no. 17; all original East Broad Top Railroad.

**Special Events:** Fall Spectacular, Columbus Day Weekend.

**Nearby Attractions/Accommodations:** Raystown Lake, Rockhill Trolley Museum.

**Location/Directions:** Pennsylvania Turnpike exit Willow Hill or Fort Littleton.

**Site Address:** Rockhill Furnace, PA
**Mailing Address:** PO Box 158, Rockhill Furnace, PA 17249
**Telephone:** (814) 447-3011
**Fax:** (814) 447-3256

**ROCKHILL TROLLEY MUSEUM**
*Train ride*
*Standard*

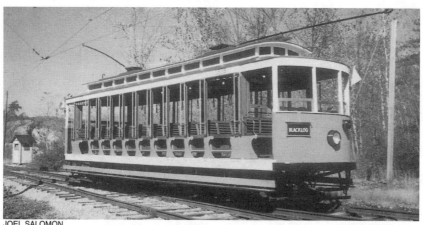

JOEL SALOMON

**Description:** A 10-mile, 50-minute ride through the beautiful Aughwick Valley, taking passengers from the historic depot at Rockhill Furnace to the picnic grove, where the train is turned. On display are the railroad yard with shops, operating roundhouse, and turntable. A new 3,000-foot track into the Blacklog Narrows offers a 3-mile trolley ride. Dates, times, and fares are subject to change. Call or write for latest information.

**Schedule:** Memorial Day weekend through October: weekends and holidays. Weekday tours by arrangement.

**Admission/Fare:** Adults, $4.95; children, $1.95.

**Locomotives/Rolling Stock:** No. 163, 1924 Brill curveside car, former York Railways (Pennsylvania); Philadelphia & Western bullet car no. 205; no. 1875 1912 open car; Johnston Traction Co. double-truck car no. 311.

**Special Events:** Fall Spectacular, Columbus Day weekend. Santa's Trolley, first Saturday in December.

**Nearby Attractions/Accommodations:** Raystown Lake, Altoona Railroader Museum, East Broad Top Railroad, Swigart Antique Car Museum.

**Location/Directions:** Twenty miles north of exit 13 of Pennsylvania Turnpike, adjacent to East Broad Top Railroad.

*Coupon available, see coupon section.

**Site Address:** Meadow St., Rockhill Furnace, PA
**Mailing Address:** 1003 N. Chester Rd., West Chester, PA 19380
**Telephone:** (610) 692-4107 and (814) 447-9576 (weekends)
**E-mail:** sgurley@prodigy.net
**Internet:** www.rockhilltrolley.org

# KISKI JUNCTION RAILROAD
*Train ride*
*Standard gauge*

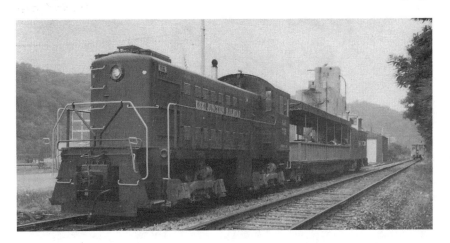

**Description:** Take a one-hour scenic ride along the Kiski River on a real working freight shortline railroad. Bring your own picnic lunch, and eat right on the cars with tables as we go. Reservations are required.

**Schedule:** Memorial Day weekend through Halloween: Tuesdays 2 p.m. (mixed freight run–discount tickets and half-hour longer ride); Wednesdays 7 p.m.; weekends 2 p.m. Group rates and rides available weekdays.

**Admission/Fare:** Adults, $8; seniors, $7; children 12-17, $6; children 4-11, $4; age 3 and under, free.

**Locomotives/Rolling Stock:** Alco S1 no. 7135; P&LE cabin car no. 500; KJR transfer cabin no. 200; KJR flatcar no. 44; KJR coach no. 1154.

**Nearby Attractions/Accommodations:** Crooked Creek State Park.

**Location/Directions:** Thirty miles northeast of Pittsburgh on the Allegheny and Kiski Rivers. Route 66 north out of Leechburg, two miles to Schenley Rd., turn west, travel 4 miles.

**Site Address:** 48 Railroad St., Schenley, PA
**Mailing Address:** PO Box 48, Schenley, PA 15682-0048
**Telephone:** (724-) 295-5577
**E-mail:** info@kiskijunction.com
**Internet:** www.kiskijunction.com

## STEAMTOWN NATIONAL HISTORIC SITE
*Train ride, museum, display, layout*
*Standard gauge*

**Description:** A 27-mile round trip steam excursion operates between Scranton and Moscow, Pennsylvania. The site's visitor facilities include two museums, a theater, a visitor center, restored portions of the roundhouse, and a museum store. Roundhouse tours, locomotive shop tours, preservation shop tours, and various additional programs will be offered. Many locomotives and cars are on display in the buildings and in the historic Delaware, Lackawanna & Western Railroad yards.

**Schedule:** 9 a.m. to 5 p.m.

**Admission/Fare:** Museum: adults, $8; seniors, $7; children, $3. Excursion: adults, $12; seniors, $10; children, $6.

**Special Events:** Rail Expo and The Polar Express..

**Nearby Attractions/Accommodations:** Lackawanna County Trolley Museum, Lackawanna County Coal Mine Tour, Everhart Museum, more.

**Location/Directions:** Downtown Scranton. Entrance is at intersection of Lackawanna and Cliff Avenues.

**Site Address:** Lackawanna and Cliff Avenues, Scranton, PA
**Mailing Address:** 150 S. Washington Ave., Scranton, PA 18503
**Telephone:** (570) 340-5200 and (888) 693-9391
**E-mail:** stea_visitor_information@nps.gov
**Internet:** www.nps.gov/stea

**Description:** Roadside America, an idea born in June 1903, is a childhood dream realized. More than 60 years in the making by Laurence Gieringer, it is housed in a new, modern, comfortable, air-conditioned building and covers more than 8,000 square feet of space. The display includes 2,570 feet of track for trains and trolleys and 250 railroad cars. O gauge trains and trolleys run among the villages.

**Schedule:** July 1 through Labor Day: weekdays, 9 a.m. to 6:30 p.m.; weekends, 9 a.m. to 7 p.m. September 6 through June 30: weekdays, 10 a.m. to 5 p.m.; weekends, 10 a.m. to 6 p.m.

**Admission/Fare:** Adults, $4.50; senior citizens, $4; children 6-11 years old, $2; children 5 and under free.

**Location/Directions:** I-78, exit 8, between Allentown and Harrisburg.

*Coupon available, see coupon section.

**Site Address:** Shartlesville, PA
**Mailing Address:** P.O. Box 2, Shartlesville, PA 19554
**Telephone:** (610) 488-6241
**Internet:** www.roadsideamericainc.com

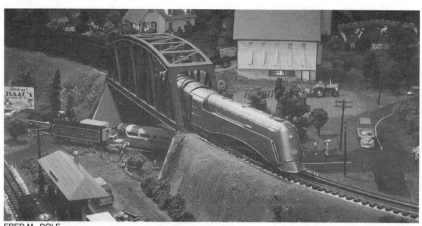

FRED M. DOLE

**Description:** A 1,700-square-foot display of Lancaster County in miniature, built by hand, mostly by one family. Twenty operating O, HO, and N trains and over 150 animated engines and vehicles.

**Schedule:** March 23 through January 5: daily 10 a.m. to 5 p.m. Last tour starts at 4:30 p.m. Closed major holidays.

**Admission/Fare:** Adults, $5; children 5-12, $3; under age 5 are free.

**Special Events:** Canned Food Fridays, free admission with non-perishable food item for local food bank, December 6, 13, and 20.

**Location/Directions:** Located along Route 741 east of Strasburg.

*Coupon available, see coupon section.

**Site Address:** Route 741 East, Strasburg, PA
**Mailing Address:** PO Box 130, Strasburg, PA 17579
**Telephone:** (717) 687-7911 and (800) 450-2920
**Fax:** (717) 687-6529 and (800) 886-3819
**E-mail:** info@choochoobarn.com
**Internet:** www.choochoobarn.com

# THE NATIONAL TOY TRAIN MUSEUM
*Museum*

**Description:** Five operating layouts, toy trains from the mid-1800s to the present day. Continuous toy train videos.

**Schedule:** Daily, May 1 through October 31; weekends, April, November and December, 10 a.m. to 5 p.m.

**Admission/Fare:** Adults (13-64), $3; seniors (65+), $2.75; children 6-12, $1.50; under 5, free; family rate, $9.

**Nearby Attractions/Accommodations:** Choo Choo Barn, Railroad Museum of Pennsylvania, Strasburg Railroad, Hershey Park, Longwood Gardens.

**Location/Directions:** From U.S. 30: south on Pennsylvania 896, east on Pennsylvania 741, north on Paradise Ln. One block from railroad tracks.

**Site Address:** 300 Paradise Ln., Strasburg, PA
**Mailing Address:** PO Box 248, Strasburg, PA 17579-0248
**Telephone:** (717) 687-8976
**Fax:** (717) 687-0742
**E-mail:** toytrain@traincollectors.org
**Internet:** www.traincollectors.org

## RAILROAD MUSEUM
## OF PENNSYLVANIA
### *Museum*

**Description:** The museum displays a fine collections of over 100 steam, electric, and diesel-electric locomotives, passenger and freight cars, and related memorabilia. The 100,000-square-foot Rolling Stock Hall exhibits equipment dating from 1825 to 1992. Also interactive education center and Whistle Stop Shop museum store.

**Schedule:** Mondays through Saturdays 9 a.m. to 5 p.m.; Sundays 12 to 5 p.m. Closed Mondays, November through March and some holidays.

**Admission/Fare:** Adults 13-59, $6; seniors, $5.50; students 6-12, $4; under age 6 are free; families, $16. Group rates available.

**Locomotives/Rolling Stock:** See above.

**Special Events:** Charter Day, March 10. Pennsy Days, June 1-2. Reading Railroad Days, July 5-7. Railroad Circus Days, August 15-18. Home for the Holidays, December 26. (Events subject to change without notice. Additional events may be scheduled.)

**Nearby Attractions/Accommodations:** Strasburg Railroad, National Toy Train Museum, Choo Choo Barn, Pennsylvania Dutch attractions.

**Location/Directions:** Ten miles east of Lancaster on Route 741.

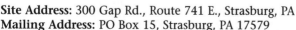

**Site Address:** 300 Gap Rd., Route 741 E., Strasburg, PA
**Mailing Address:** PO Box 15, Strasburg, PA 17579
**Telephone:** (717) 687-8628
**Fax:** (717) 687-0876
**E-mail:** info@rrmuseumpa.org
**Internet:** www.rrmuseumpa.org

## STRASBURG RAIL ROAD
*Train ride, dinner train*
*Standard gauge*

**Description:** A 45-minute trip into the past. The train travels through beautiful Lancaster County farmland as it journeys from Strasburg to Amtrak's Leaman Place interchange at Paradise. The East Strasburg Station mall features four gift shops, one restaurant, fudge shop, old time portrait studio, and the exquisite "Paradise" business car. Just across the street is the Railroad Museum of Pennsylvania.

**Schedule:** February 17 through April 7, weekends. April 8 through October 27, daily. October 28 through December 15, weekends and Friday after Thanksgiving. December 26 through 31, daily. Times vary.

**Admission/Fare:** Adults, $9 and up; children 3-11, $4.50 and up. Group rates available.

**Locomotives/Rolling Stock:** No. 90, 2-10-0 ex-GW; no. 475 4-8-0 ex-N&W; no. 89 2-6-0 ex-GT; no. 31 0-6-0 ex-CN; no. 972 4-6-0 ex-CPR; no. 4 0-4-0 ex-RDG; GE 44-ton ex-PRR 9331; Plymouths nos. 1 and 2; very early 20th century wooden passenger cars; over a dozen early freight cars; reserved dining car, parlor car, and lounge car seating and service available; open-sided observation cars.

**Special Events:** A Day Out with Thomas events, Easter Bunny Trains, Pumpkin Trains, Santa Trains. Call for dates.

**Location/Directions:** On Route 741 one mile east of Strasburg.

**Site Address:** Route 741, 301 Gap Rd., Strasburg, PA
**Mailing Address:** PO Box 96, Strasburg, PA 17579
**Telephone:** (717) 687-7522
**Fax:** (717) 687-6194
**E-mail:** srrtrain@strasburgrailroad.com
**Internet:** www.strasburgrailroad.com

**OIL CREEK & TITUSVILLE RAILROAD**
*Train ride*

BETTY M SQUIRE

**Description:** Twenty-seven-mile, 2½-hour train ride through "The Valley That Changed the World."

**Schedule:** Mid-June through October. June and September: weekends, 11 a.m. July, August, and October: Wednesdays through Sundays, 11 a.m. October weekends, 11 a.m. and 3:30 p.m. School excursions: May 14-16, 21-23, and October 2-3, 9-10.

**Admission/Fare:** Adults, $10; seniors (60+), $9; students 3-17, $6. Under 3, no charge.

**Locomotives/Rolling Stock:** 1947 Alco S-2 no 75; caboose no. 10 built by Elgin, Joliet & Eastern Railroad approximately 1923; railway post office car.

**Special Events:** Murder Mysteries and more. Call, write, or e-mail for more information.

**Nearby Attractions/Accommodations:** Drake Well Museum, Oil Creek State Park, Tyred Wheels Auto Museum.

**Location/Directions:** Route 8 north or south to Titusville, watch for signs.

**Site Address:** 409 S. Perry St., Titusville, PA
**Mailing Address:** 7 Elm St., Oil City, PA 16301
**Telephone:** (814) 676-1733
**Fax:** (814) 677-2192
**E-mail:** ocandt@usachoice.net
**Internet:** //octrr.clarion.edu

# PENNSYLVANIA TROLLEY MUSEUM
*Train ride, museum, display*
*5'2½" gauge, standard gauge*

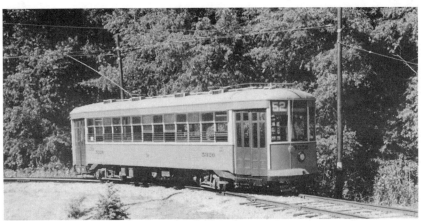

SCOTT R. BECKER

**Description:** A scenic 3.5-mile round-trip trolley ride, just extended for 2002! Also guided tour of carbarn and restoration shop, the film "Pennsylvania's Trolleys in a Changing Landscape," gift shop, and picnic area.

**Schedule:** Weekends, April through December; daily, Memorial Day through Labor Day, 11 a.m. to 5 p.m.

**Admission/Fare:** Adults, $6; seniors (65+), $5; children 2-15, $3.50. Admission includes trolley rides and tours.

**Special Events:** Easter Bunny Trolley, March 23, 30. Anything on Wheels weekend, June 29-30. Pumpkin Patch Trolley, October 12-13, 19-20. Santa Trolley, November 29-30, December 1, 7-8 and 14-15. Trolleys & Toy Trains, December 21-22, 26-30.

**Nearby Attractions/Accommodations:** Washington County Fairgrounds, The Meadows Racetrack, LeMoyne House, David Bradford House, Meadowcroft Museum of Rural Life. Pittsburgh is 30 miles away.

**Location/Directions:** Thirty miles southwest of Pittsburgh. Take I-79 south to exit 41 Racetrack Rd. or I-79 north to exit 40 Meadowlands. Follow museum signs 3 miles.

*Coupon available, see coupon section.

**Site Address:** One Museum Rd., Washington, PA
**Mailing Address:** One Museum Rd., Washington, PA 15301-6133
**Telephone:** (724) 228-9256 and (877) PA-TROLLEY
**Fax:** (724) 228-9675
**E-mail:** ptm@pa-trolley.org
**Internet:** www.pa-trolley.org

**TIOGA CENTRAL RAILROAD**
*Train ride, dinner train*
*Standard gauge*

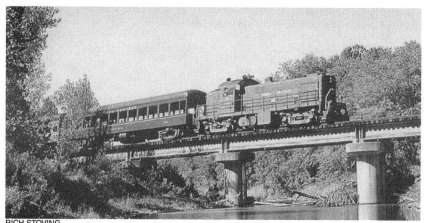
RICH STOVING

**Description:** A 1½-hour excursion through beautiful north central Pennsylvania countryside; 24 miles round trip.

**Schedule:** Saturdays and Sundays, May 11 through October 20; departures at 11 a.m., 1 and 3 p.m.

**Admission/Fare:** Adults, $10; seniors (60+), $9; children 6-12, $5. Children under 6 free with paying adult.

**Locomotives/Rolling Stock:** Alco S2 no. 14; Alco R1 no. 62; Alco RS3 no. 506.

**Special Events:** Wellsboro Rail Days, October 26-27, special trains, longer runs, for rail fans.

**Nearby Attractions/Accommodations:** Grand Canyon of Pennsylvania, Ives Run Recreation Area, many fine restaurants and Main Street shopping in beautiful Wellsboro.

**Location/Directions:** Three miles north of Wellsboro on State Route 287. Wellsboro is on U.S. Route 6 east-west, and Pennsylvania Route 287 north-south; 35 miles south of Corning, New York.

*Coupon available, see coupon section.

**Radio frequency: 160.725**

**Site Address:** Muck Rd., Wellsboro Junction, PA
**Mailing Address:** PO Box 269, Wellsboro, PA 16901
**Telephone:** (570) 724-0990
**E-mail:** info@tiogacentral.com
**Internet:** www.tiogacentral.com

# WEST CHESTER RAILROAD
*Train ride, dinner train*
*Standard gauge*

**Description:** A 16-mile round trip from West Chester to Glen Mills. This line is the unused portion of SEPTA's R-3 Elwyn line, which is very scenic as it follows Chester Creek in western Delaware County through eastern Chester County.

**Schedule:** April, May, September through December: weekends. Charters available year round. Call for information on specials.

**Admission/Fare:** Adults, $10; children 2-12, $8.

**Locomotives/Rolling Stock:** No. 99 EMD GP-9 ex-B&O no. 6499; no. 1803 is DRS-18U Alco former CP 1803; Reading Blue Liners coaches nos. 9114, 9124, 9117, 9107; baggage car former Pennsy B-60 7551; more.

**Special Events:** Monthly dinner trains. Easter Bunny Express. West Chester Restaurant Festival, third weekend in September. Pratt & Co. Fall Festival, fourth weekend in September. Fall Foliage, October. Holiday Express, November. Santa Express, November and December.

**Nearby Attractions/Accommodations:** Valley Forge National Park, West Chester Restaurants, Chadds Ford, Brandywine Museum, Winterthur Longwood Gardens.

**Location/Directions:** Highway 202, exit Gay St./West Chester. Follow Gay to Matlack turning left, one block to Market, left at railroad station, one block on right.

**Radio frequency:** 160.6050

**Site Address:** 230 E. Market St., West Chester, PA
**Mailing Address:** PO Box 385, Yorklyn, DE 19736
**Telephone:** (610) 430-2233
**Fax:** (302) 995-5286

## THOMAS T. TABER MUSEUM OF THE
## LYCOMING COUNTY HISTORICAL SOCIETY
*Museum, layout*

TERRY WILD STUDIO

**Description:** History museum with model train exhibit.

**Schedule:** Open year round. May 1 through October 31: Tuesdays through Fridays, 9:30 a.m. to 4 p.m.; Saturdays, 11 a.m. to 4 p.m.; Sundays, 1 to 4 p.m. November 1 through April 30: Tuesdays through Fridays, 9:30 a.m. to 4 p.m.; Saturdays, 11 a.m. to 4 p.m. Closed major holidays.

**Admission/Fare:** Adult, $3.50; seniors, AARP/AAA, $3; children, $1.50.

**Special Events:** Toy Train Expo, December 9-10, 12 to 4 p.m. Area collectors have displays and layouts throughout the museum.

**Nearby Attractions/Accommodations:** Little League Museum, Genetti Hotel, amusement park, Reptile Land.

*Coupon available, see coupon section.

      M

**Site Address:** 858 W. Fourth St., Williamsport, PA
**Mailing Address:** 858 W. Fourth St., Williamsport, PA 17701-5824
**Telephone:** (570) 326-3326
Fax: (570) 326-3689
**E-mail:** lchsmuse@csrlink.net
**Internet:** www.lycoming.org/lchsmuseum

# WESTMORELAND HERITAGE RAILROAD
### *Train ride, museum*
### *Standard gauge*

**Description:** Train rides: north, 12 miles round trip; south, 16 miles round trip.

**Schedule:** April through early November, with some specials.

**Admission/Fare:** Adults, $10; children, $5.

**Locomotives/Rolling Stock:** Alco S-2; three Pennsy coaches; three cabooses, various roads.

**Special Events:** Easter Bunny; Train Robberies; Santa Train; other events.

**Nearby Attractions/Accommodations:** Museum, restaurants, lodging, campground.

**Location/Directions:** Pennsylvania Turnpike, exit 8 New Scranton. Follow U.S. 119 north, at fourth traffic light turn right, Depot St. one block. Park on the left.

**Site Address:** 1 Depot St., Youngwood, PA
**Mailing Address:** PO Box 444, Youngwood, PA 15697
**Telephone:** (724) 925-6543
**Internet:** www.whrr.org

358

**YOUNGWOOD RAILROAD MUSEUM**
*Train ride, museum, layout*
*Standard gauge*

**Description:** Ninety-minute ride with a 1949 Alco S2 and PRR coaches and cabooses from various lines. Operated by the Westmoreland Heritage Railroad.

**Schedule:** Train: Weekends, 11 a.m., 1 and 3 p.m. Memorial Day, July 4 and Labor Day, 12 noon, 2 and 4 p.m.

**Admission/Fare:** Adults, $9; children, $5. Includes admission to museum.

**Locomotives/Rolling Stock:** No. 2049 caboose, Penn Central; circa PRR caboose.

**Special Events:** Firecracker Special, July 4; Train Robbery, July 8; Scout's weekend, August 4-5; Rail Fan weekend, August 18-19; Bob's Day, August 30.

**Nearby Attractions/Accommodations:** Laurel Highlands, Idlewild Park.

**Location/Directions:** From the Pennsylvania Turnpike New Stanton exit 8 follow U.S. Route 119 north to Youngwood. Turn right on Depot St., go one block to the tracks. From U.S. Route 30 at Greensburg take U.S. Route 119 south to Youngwood. Turn left on Depot St., go two blocks to the tracks.

**Site Address:** 1 Depot St., Youngwood, PA
**Mailing Address:** PO Box 444, Youngwood, PA 15697
**Telephone:** (724) 925-7355 and (724) 925-6543
**Fax:** (724) 925-1158
**E-mail:** prrconductor@surfbest.net
**Internet:** www.ywdrailroadmuseum.com

# SOUTH CAROLINA RAILROAD MUSEUM
*Train ride, museum, display, layout*
*Standard gauge*

**Description:** A 6.6-mile round trip to Greenbrier and return over a portion of the former Rockton & Rion Railway. The route was built in the late 1800s as a quarry line to haul world-famous Winnsboro blue granite from the quarry to the Southern Railway at Rockton.

**Schedule:** June through October, first and third Saturdays. Museum gallery and yard tours, Sundays 1 to 4 p.m. (No train rides on Sundays.)

**Admission/Fare:** Adults, $5; children 2-12, $3; first-class, $9.

**Locomotives/Rolling Stock:** No. 2015 and 2028, 1950 SW-8; no. 33, 1946 GE 44-ton, former PRR; no. 76, 1951 Porter 50-ton, former U.S. Navy; no. 82, 1945 GE 45-ton, former U.S. Navy; and no. 44, 1927 Baldwin 4-6-0, former Hampton & Branchville (static display).

**Special Events:** Easter Bunny Train, Caboose Day, Santa Train. Call, write, or visit our website for exact dates.

**Nearby Attractions/Accommodations:** Downtown Winnsboro, South Carolina State Museum, Riverbanks Zoo.

**Location/Directions:** Take State Route 34 from I-26 or I-77 and follow the signs to Winnsboro. Then follow brown signs. The museum is located between State Route 34 and U.S. Highway 321, 3 miles south of Winnsboro.

**Radio frequency:** 151.865

**Site Address:** 110 Industrial Park Rd., Winnsboro, SC
**Mailing Address:** PO Box 643, Winnsboro, SC 29180
**Telephone:** (803) 635-9893
**E-mail:** info@scrm.org
**Internet:** www.scrm.org

**BLACK HILLS
CENTRAL RAILROAD**
*Train ride*
*Standard gauge*

RICH W. MILLS

**Description:** Passengers can take a two-hour round-trip journey between Hill City and Keystone. Experience a ride from the past as you travel through the Black Hills, seeing the old mine sights and Harney Peak.

**Schedule:** Mid-May through early October: daily. Departures added during summer season. Call, write, or e-mail for information.

**Admission/Fare:** Adults, $18; children 4-12, $10; age 3 and under are free. Group rates available for parties of 20 and up.

**Locomotives/Rolling Stock:** 1926 Baldwin 2-6-2 no. 104 saddle tank; 1919 Baldwin 2-6-2 no. 7; 1928 Baldwin 2-6-6-2 no. 110; 1880s-1910 passenger cars.

**Special Events:** Railroad Days, last weekend of June.

**Nearby Attractions/Accommodations:** Mt. Rushmore and Crazy Horse Memorials.

**Location/Directions:** Highway 16/385, 24 miles south of Rapid City or Keystone, Highway 16A.

**Site Address:** 222 Railroad Ave., Hill City, SD
**Mailing Address:** PO Box 1880, Hill City, SD 57745
**Telephone:** (605) 574-2222
**Fax:** (605) 574-4915
**E-mail:** office@1880train.com
**Internet:** www.1880train.com

# PRAIRIE VILLAGE
*Train ride, dinner train, museum, display*
*Standard and 24" gauge*

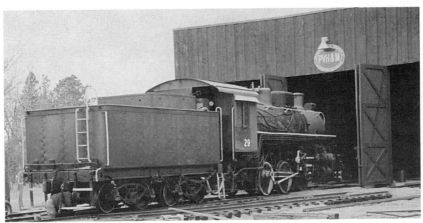

BILL NOLAN

**Description:** Prairie Village is an assembly of turn-of-the-century buildings. There are steam traction engines, gas tractors, and displays of farm equipment. A 2-mile loop of track is used for train rides. Buildings include the Wentworth Depot, Junius Depot, and roundhouse/turntable.

**Schedule:** Museum–May through September: daily, 9 a.m. to 6 p.m. Train–June through August and during Railroad Days and Jamboree: Sundays, 2, 3, and 4 p.m.

**Admission/Fare:** Museum–$5. Train–$3.

**Locomotives/Rolling Stock:** No. 29 Lima 0-6-0, former D&NE; no. 11 Alco 0-4-0T, ex-Deadwood Central; Orrenstein & Koppel 0-4-0T "Wilhelmine"; Baldwin 60T diesel; GE 80T diesel; rolling stock with snowplow, cabooses and passenger cars.

**Special Events:** Railroad Days, June. Car Show, August. Fall Jamboree, August.

**Nearby Attractions/Accommodations:** Camping available on grounds, Lake Herman State Park, Smith-Zimmermann State Museum, Madison.

**Location/Directions:** Prairie Village is 2 miles west of Madison on Highway 34. From Sioux Falls, take I-29 north to the Madison/Colman exit, then travel west on Highway 34 to Madison.

**Site Address:** W. Highway 34, Madison, SD
**Mailing Address:** PO Box 256, Madison, SD 57042-0256
**Telephone:** (800) 693-3644 and (605) 256-3644
**Fax:** (605) 256-4588
**E-mail:** prairiev@rapidnet.com
**Internet:** www.prairievillage.org

# CHATTANOOGA CHOO CHOO
*Museum, layout*

**Description:** Opened in 1909 as the Southern Railway's Terminal Station, this depot welcomed thousands of travelers during the golden age of railroads. Today, the restored station is the heart of the Chattanooga Choo Choo Holiday Inn, a 24-acre complex with a full range of entertainment. Forty-eight passenger cars are part of the 360-room hotel; two passenger cars serve as a formal restaurant and meeting/banquet room.

**Schedule:** Year round: Sundays through Saturdays, 10 a.m. to 8 p.m.

**Admission/Fare:** Adults, $2; children, $1; under age 6 are free.

**Locomotives/Rolling Stock:** Five to eight trains running in museum.

**Special Events:** Victorian Holidays Open House, December. Free outdoor entertainment, May through September.

**Nearby Attractions/Accommodations:** Tennessee Aquarium, IMAX Theater, Southern Belle Riverboat, Creative Discovery Museum, Coolidge Park, Rock City, Ruby Falls.

**Location/Directions:** I-24 exit 178, take S. Broad St. split and follow signs to Choo Choo.

*Coupon available, see coupon section.

**Site Address:** 1400 Market St., Chattanooga, TN
**Mailing Address:** 1400 Market St., Chattanooga, TN 37402
**Telephone:** (423) 266-5000 and (800) 872-2529
**Fax:** (423) 265-4635
**E-mail:** frontdesk@choochoo.com
**Internet:** www.choochoo.com

# LOOKOUT MOUNTAIN INCLINE RAILWAY
### *Train ride*

**Description:** The thrill of riding the Incline Railway has delighted guests for a century. As the incline climbs Lookout Mountain, Chattanooga's surrounding mountains and valleys come alive as the trolley-style railcars carry you cloud high. The breathtaking 72.7 percent grade of the track near the top give the Incline the distinction of being the steepest passenger railway in the world. See centennial exhibits depicting the history of one of Chattanooga's most unusual landmarks. Displays include rare photographs and points of interest on the mountain from late 1800s to present.

**Schedule:** Year round: Memorial Day through Labor Day, 8:30 a.m. to 9:30 p.m.; spring and fall, 9 a.m. to 6 p.m.; winter, 10 a.m. to 6 p.m. Hours are subject to change.

**Admission/Fare:** One way and round trip rates. Group rates.

**Location/Directions:** The lower station and free parking are located at the foot of Lookout Mountain, near I-24; three blocks south of Highways 11, 41, 64, and 72 on Highway 58.

**Site Address:** 827 E. Brow Rd., Lookout Mountain, TN
**Mailing Address:** 1827 E. Brow Rd., Lookout Mountain, TN 37350
**Telephone:** (423) 821-4224
**Fax:** (423) 821-9444
**Internet:** www.lookoutmtnattractions.com

# TENNESSEE VALLEY RAILROAD
*Train ride, display*
*Standard gauge*

STEVE FREER

**Description:** Daily, 45-minute round trip through pre-Civil War Missionary Ridge Tunnel. Dixie Land Excursions run on select weekends and most include a dining car luncheon. Special events throughout the year.

**Schedule:** April through November: Saturdays 10 a.m. to 5 p.m.; Sundays 11 a.m. to 5 p.m. Spring/fall weekdays 10 a.m. to 1 p.m. Summer weekdays 10 a.m. to 5 p.m.

**Admission/Fare:** Adults, $10.50; children 3-12, $5. Group rates/charters.

**Locomotives/Rolling Stock:** S160 2-8-0 no. 610; SR KSI 2-8-0 no. 630; SR MSI 2-8-2 no. 4501; K&T 2-8-2 no. 10; CN J7b no. 5288; Alco RSDI nos. 8669 and 8677; EMD GP7 no. 1824 and 1829; Budd RDC nos. 20 and 22.

**Special Events:** Spring Steam Up, March. Autumn Leaf Specials, October. Polar Express and Christmas Specials, November and December.

**Nearby Attractions/Accommodations:** Hamilton Place Mall retail center, Chattanooga Regional Airport, Tennessee Aquarium, Rock City, Ruby Falls, Incline Railway, Chattanooga Choo Choo complex, NMRA headquarters, and Kalmbach Memorial Library.

**Location/Directions:** I-75 exit 4 onto Highway 153 to Jersey Pike (fourth exit), follow brown directional signs ⅓ mile to TVRM.

*Coupon available, see coupon section.

Radio frequency: 160.425

**Site Address:** 4119 Cromwell Rd., Chattanooga, TN
**Mailing Address:** 4119 Cromwell Rd., Chattanooga, TN 37421-2119
**Telephone:** (423) 894-8028
**Fax:** (423) 894-8029
**E-mail:** info@tvrail.com
**Internet:** www.tvrail.com

# CASEY JONES MUSEUM
## AND TRAIN STORE
### Museum

**Description:** Visit the home and railroad museum of Casey Jones. Casey was living in this home at the time of his death in 1900. There are three layouts on display in the 1800s baggage car and a replica of no. 382, Casey's engine, along with souvenirs and a hobby shop. There is also a miniature train ride on a ¼-mile track.

**Schedule:** Year round: June, July, August, 8 a.m. to 8 p.m. September through May, 9 a.m. to 5 p.m.

**Admission/Fare:** Adults, $4; seniors, $3.50; children 6-12, $3; children age 5 and under are free. Lifetime passes available.

**Locomotives/Rolling Stock:** Rogers 4-6-0 locomotive; 1800s M&O baggage car; IC caboose you can sleep in; 1890s sleeper car; HO and O27 model train display.

**Nearby Attractions/Accommodations:** State Park, Shiloh National Military Park, Home of Buford Pusser, Adamsville.

**Location/Directions:** I-40 exit 80A onto 45, 45 seconds off Highway 45, look for caboose in the sky.

*Coupon available, see coupon section.

**Site Address:** 30 Casey Jones Ln., Jackson, TN
**Mailing Address:** 56 Casey Jones Ln., Jackson, TN 38305
**Telephone:** (901) 668-1222
**Fax:** (901) 664-7782
**E-mail:** ntaylor@caseyjonesvillage.com
**Internet:** www.caseyjones.com

# NASHVILLE, CHATTANOOGA & ST. LOUIS DEPOT AND RAILROAD MUSEUM

*Museum, display, layout*

MOORE STUDIOS

**Description:** The restored NC&StL Depot features a museum that reflects Jackson's history as West Tennessee's railroad hub. A working scale model depicts local railroad heritage. An Amtrak dining car, which seats up to 48 diners, can be rented for catered parties.

**Schedule:** Year round: Mondays through Saturdays, 10 a.m. to 3 p.m.

**Admission/Fare:** Free.

**Locomotives/Rolling Stock:** Former FEC (Bunn 1947) dining car, "Ft. Matanzas"; Southern caboose X421; C&O caboose 3255.

**Nearby Attractions/Accommodations:** Brooks Shaw's Old Country Store, Historic Casey Jones Home and Railroad Museum, Pinson Mounds State Archaeological Area, Cypress Grove Nature Park, Chickasaw Rustic State Park, Pringles Park, Home of West Tennessee Diamond Jaxx baseball.

**Location/Directions:** Turn off Highway 45 bypass onto Martin Luther King Dr. at the Jackson Main Post Office and go one block to S. Royal St. Turn right, proceed one block, depot is on the left.

**Site Address:** 582 S. Royal St., Jackson, TN
**Mailing Address:** 582 S. Royal St., Jackson, TN 38301
**Telephone:** (731) 425-8223
**Fax:** (731) 425-8682

## THREE RIVERS RAMBLER
*Train ride*
*Standard gauge*

**Description:** An hour-and-20-minute round trip excursion aboard our vintage train, which includes our newly restored 1925 steam engine "Lindy." The Three Rivers Rambler travels through east Tennessee farmland to the Three Rivers trestle, where the Franch Bread & Molsen Rivers meet to form the Tennessee River.

**Schedule:** March 30 through November 17, Saturdays, Sundays and most holidays, 1, 3:30, and 6 p.m.

**Admission/Fare:** Ages 13-54, $16.95; seniors 55+, $14.95; children 6-12, $9.95; under 5, free.

**Locomotives/Rolling Stock:** 1925 Baldwin 2-8-0 no. 203; 1925 Pullman office car "Resplendent"; three 1932 coach cars, 1942 open-air car, caboose.

**Nearby Attractions/Accommodations:** The Star of Knoxville Riverboat, restaurants, The Hyatt motel.

**Location/Directions:** Take I-40 to Knoxville, exit at Janer White Parkway (388A) to Neyland Dr. (158). Go one mile to stoplight at the Tennessee Grill. Park in Tennessee Grill lot C-18, cross Neylard and walk to train.

**Site Address:** L&N Station, 401 Henley St., Suite 5, Knoxville, TN
**Mailing Address:** 401 Henley St., Suite 5, Knoxville, TN 37902
**Telephone:** (865) 524-9411
**Fax:** (865) 546-3717
**Internet:** www.threeriversrambler.com

# LYNNVILLE RAILROAD PRESERVATION SOCIETY
*Museum, display*

**Description:** Rebuilt L&N depot, memorabilia, static display of rail cars and locomotive, HO scale model railroad in depot. There is a video theater in the restored coach, and a telegraph from the depot to the caboose.

**Schedule:** May through October: Thursdays and Fridays 11 a.m. to 4 p.m.; Saturdays 10 a.m. to 4 p.m.; Sundays through Wednesdays by appointment.

**Admission/Fare:** Adults, $2; children under age 12 are free.

**Locomotives/Rolling Stock:** 1927 Baldwin 2-6-2 locomotive; 1925 passenger coach NC&St.L; flatcar; Illinois Central caboose with L&N markings.

**Special Events:** Railroad Days, first weekend in May; music entertainment, street dance, and activities.

**Nearby Attractions/Accommodations:** Iron Horse Restaurant (seats 80 plus), trolley car emporium (mini-mall with full-sized horse-drawn trolley car and cafe). Local bed and breakfast.

**Location/Directions:** Seven miles west of exit 27 off I-65; 50 miles south of Nashville.

**Site Address:** Mill St., Lynnville, TN
**Mailing Address:** PO Box 158, Lynnville, TN 38472
**Telephone:** (931) 527-0564
**Fax:** (931) 527-0564
**E-mail:** oldtoot@pop.vsit.net
**Internet:** www.lynnvillerailroad.com

# TENNESSEE CENTRAL
# RAILWAY MUSEUM
*Train ride, museum, display, layout*
*Standard gauge*

STEVE JOHNSON

**Description:** Excursion train, hobby shop, railroad artifacts, modular HO and N scale model railroads.

**Schedule:** Saturdays 9 a.m. to 3 p.m. Fifteen to 20 excursion trains scheduled during the year.

**Admission/Fare:** Museum–free. Excursion train–varies.

**Locomotives/Rolling Stock:** EMD E8A TCRX 5764; EMD SW8 TC 52; former ATSF coaches; TCRX 4711, 4717, 4719, 4733, 4739; Budd buffet-diner TCRX 3113, 3119; Budd slumbercoach TCRX 2095; Pullman business car TC 102.

**Special Events:** Excursion trains for Valentine's Day, Easter, July 4th, Fall foliage, Christmas/Santa, more.

**Nearby Attractions/Accommodations:** Tennessee Titans NFL football, downtown Nashville, Grand Ole Opry House, Opryland Hotel, Nashville Toy Museum, Music Row, Nashville Arena, Opry Mills Shopping Mall.

**Location/Directions:** I-24/40 eastbound exit 212 Fesslers Ln. Left onto Fesslers Ln., 0.5 mile to left on Lebanon Rd., proceed 0.8 mile to right on Fairfield Ave. and follow sign to museum site.

**Radio frequency: 154.570**

**Site Address:** 220 Willow St., Nashville, TN
**Mailing Address:** 220 Willow St., Nashville, TN 37210-2159
**Telephone:** (615) 244-9001
**Fax:** (615) 244-2120
**E-mail:** hultman@nashville.com
**Internet:** http://home.hiwaay.net/~bgaddes/tcrm

Tennessee, Oak Ridge

# SOUTHERN APPALACHIA RAILWAY MUSEUM
*Train ride, dinner train, museum, display*
*Standard gauge*

CHRIS WILLIAMS

**Description:** A 14-mile, 90-minute train ride aboard air-conditioned coaches and dining car, plus caboose. Train travels former Southern Railway branch line through the former Manhattan Project K-25 facility. Limited number of evening dinner trains. Additional shortline railroad charters conducted across the United States.

**Schedule:** First and third Saturdays, April through September, plus additional weekends and Sundays in October, November, and December. 10 a.m., 12, 2 and 4 p.m. Reservations recommended.

**Admission/Fare:** Adults, $10; children age 12 and under, $7.50.

**Locomotives/Rolling Stock:** U.S. Atomic Energy Commission 1951 Alco RS-1 5310; Tennessee Valley Authority, formerly U.S. Army 1943 Alco S-2 7100 and 7125; Central of Georgia 1947; coaches nos. 663, 664, and 665.

**Special Events:** Fabulous Forties Festival, May 18; Heritage Open Car Show, June 1-2; Halloween Trains, October 26-27; Santa Claus Trains, December 14-15; 60th anniversary of Manhattan project.

**Nearby Attractions/Accommodations:** Museum of Appalachia, Great Smoky Mountains National Park, Big South Fork National River and Recreation Area, Oak Ridge Manhattan Project tours.

**Location/Directions:** Six miles north of I-40 exit 356 between Knoxville and Nashville at the East Tennessee Technology Park on Highway 58.

         M

**Radio frequency:** 160.425

**Site Address:** Highway 58 S., Oak Ridge, TN
**Mailing Address:** PO Box 5870, Knoxville, TN 37928
**Telephone:** (865) 241-2140
**Fax:** (865) 692-9505
**E-mail:** bjenninl@utk.edu
**Internet:** www.techscribes.com/sarm/sarm.htm

**DOLLYWOOD ENTERTAINMENT PARK**
*Train ride*
*36" gauge*

RICHARDS & SOUTHERN

**Description:** The *Dollywood Express,* located in the Village area of Dollywood, takes visitors on a 5-mile journey through this scenic park. As passengers ride on the authentic, coal-fired steam train, they can catch a glimpse of the different areas of Dollywood: Dreamland Forest, Rivertown Junction, The Village, Craftsman's Valley, Country Fair, Showstreet, Jukebox Junction, and Dollywood Boulevard. The *Dollywood Express* also takes visitors through replicas of a typical turn-of-the-century mountain village and logging community.

**Schedule:** Thirty-minute rides every hour during park operating hours.

**Admission/Fare:** Adults, $32; seniors, $27; children 4-11, $23.

**Locomotives/Rolling Stock:** "Klondike Katie," a 1943 Baldwin 2-8-2, former U.S. Army no. 192; "Cinderella," a 1939 Baldwin 2-8-2, former U.S. Army no. 70; open-air passenger cars.

**Special Events:** Festival of Nations, early April; Harvest Celebration, October; Smoky Mountain Christmas Festival, mid-November, December. School field trips. Special group rates.

**Nearby Attractions/Accommodations:** Numerous restaurants, lodging, shopping, and attractions in Pigeon Forge area.

**Location/Directions:** Call for directions.

**Site Address:** 1020 Dollywood Ln., Pigeon Forge, TN
**Mailing Address:** 1020 Dollywood Ln., Pigeon Forge, TN 37863-4101
**Telephone:** (865) 428-9488 and (800) DOLLYWOOD
**Internet:** www.dollywood.com

## LITTLE RIVER RAILROAD
## AND LUMBER COMPANY
### *Museum*

**Description:** Restored Shay locomotive, depot, steam sawmill, and collection of railroad and lumber company artifacts and photographs, and interpretive displays tell the story of the community.

**Schedule:** April, May, and September: weekends, Saturday 10 a.m. to 5 p.m. and Sunday 1 to 5 p.m. June through August, and October: daily, Monday through Friday, 10 a.m. to 2 p.m., Saturday, 10 a.m. to 5 p.m., and Sunday, 1 to 5 p.m.

**Admission/Fare:** Free. Donations appreciated.

**Locomotives/Rolling Stock:** Little River Shay no. 2147.

**Nearby Attractions/Accommodations:** Great Smoky Mountains National Park.

**Location/Directions:** U.S. Highway 321, Townsend, at western entrance to Great Smoky Mountains National Park. Eighteen miles east of Maryville and 15 miles southwest of Pigeon Forge.

**Site Address:** 7747 E. Lamar Alexander Pkwy., U.S. 321, Townsend, TN
**Mailing Address:** PO Box 211, Townsend, TN 37882
**Telephone:** (865) 448-2211
**Fax:** (865) 448-2312

# AGE OF STEAM RAILROAD MUSEUM
*Museum*
*Standard gauge*

**Description:** A fine collection of steam and early diesel era railway equipment, including a complete heavyweight passenger train featuring restored MKT dining car and "Glengyle," the oldest all-steel, all-room Pullman.

**Schedule:** Wednesdays through Sundays, 10 a.m. to 5 p.m.

**Admission/Fare:** Adults, $5; children age 12 and under, $2.50; 2 years and under, free.

**Locomotives/Rolling Stock:** Big Boy no. 4018, 1942 Alco 4-8-8-4 and "Centennial" no. 6913, EMD DDA40X, both former Union Pacific; no. 1625, 1918 Alco 2-10-0, former Eagle-Picher Mining Co.; more.

**Special Events:** Whistle Fair, June 16-17. Festival of Trains, August 11-12. Texas State Fair, September 28-October 21.

**Nearby Attractions/Accommodations:** The museum is located in Fair Park, a year-round collection of arts and cultural institutions housed in a restored art deco building originally constructed for the 1936 Texas centennial.

**Location/Directions:** Two miles east of downtown; I-30 westbound, exit 47A right onto Exposition Ave., left on Parry Ave.

*Coupon available, see coupon section.

        M arm

**Site Address:** 1105 Washington St., Fair Park, Dallas, TX
**Mailing Address:** PO Box 153259, Dallas, TX 75315-3259
**Telephone:** (214) 428-0101
**Fax:** (214) 426-1937
**E-mail:** info@dallasrailwaymuseum.com
**Internet:** www.dallasrailwaymuseum.com

# MCKINNEY AVENUE TRANSIT AUTHORITY
*Train ride*
*Standard gauge*

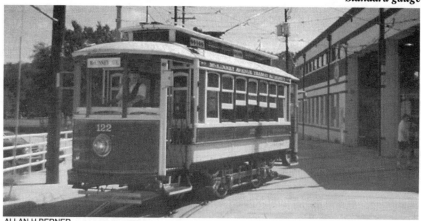

ALLAN H BERNER

**Description:** Four restored trolleys operate on 2.8 miles of track from downtown Dallas through the historic uptown area.

**Schedule:** Daily 10 a.m. to 10 p.m. Expansion to Citiplace subway station in January, 2002.

**Admission/Fare:** Adults, $1.50; seniors, $.50; children 2-12, $1.

**Locomotives/Rolling Stock:** 1906 Brill ex-Porto no. 122; 1913 Stone & Webster ex-DR&T no. 186; 1920 Birney ex-DR&T no. 636; and 1925 W-2 ex-Melbourne no. 369.

**Nearby Attractions/Accommodations:** Hard Rock Cafe, art galleries, antique shops, numerous restaurants with sidewalk cafe dining, historic hotels.

**Location/Directions:** Operates from downtown Dallas Arts District to the historic uptown area. From the DART St. Paul Light Rail Station walk four blocks north.

**Site Address:** Car barn at McKinney Ave. and Bowen St., Dallas, TX
**Mailing Address:** 3153 Oak Grove Ave., Dallas, TX 75204
**Telephone:** (214) 855-0006
**Fax:** (214) 855-5250
**Internet:** www.mata.org

**CENTER FOR TRANSPORTATION**
*Museum*

JIM CRUZ

**Description:** This major southwestern railroad museum has 42 cars, the Renfert collection of fine railroad dining china, Ghosts of Travelers Past, model railroad exhibits, and a mini train. The Union Pacific mini train holds 25 passengers and will operate from the museum through the Strand Historic District, Model Train Shop.

**Schedule:** Daily 10 a.m. to 4 p.m. Seasonal schedule, call or write for information.

**Admission/Fare:** Adults, $5; seniors, $4.50; children 4-12, $2.50; under age 4 are free.

**Locomotives/Rolling Stock:** Forty-two pieces of equipment, including steam locomotives; diesel-electric locomotives; passenger cars; cabooses; freight cars; maintenance-of-way cars.

**Location/Directions:** I-45 south, stay on Broadway, turn left on 24th St. Turn left on Santa Fe Pl., turn right into museum parking lot.

*Coupon available, see coupon section.

     M

**Site Address:** 123 Rosenberg, Galveston, TX
**Mailing Address:** 123 Rosenberg, Galveston, TX 77550
**Telephone:** (409) 765-5700
**Fax:** (409) 763-0936
**E-mail:** railroad@tamag.tamu.edu
**Internet:** www.tamug.tamu.edu/rrmuseum

# GULF COAST RAILROAD MUSEUM
*Museum*
*Standard gauge*

**Description:** Features a collection of locomotives, freight and passenger cars with a Texas emphasis. The museum is operated by Gulf Coast Chapter, National Railway Historical Society, Inc.

**Schedule:** March through November, Saturdays 11 a.m. to 5 p.m. and Sundays 1 to 4 p.m.

**Admission/Fare:** Adults $3; children 12 and under, $1.50.

**Locomotives/Rolling Stock:** ATSF "Verde Valley," Pullman; ATSF 3401 Budd RPO; ATSF 1890 Pullman end-door express car; ATSF 2350 Alco S2; MKT 6 cupola caboose; MKT "New Braunfels" coach; KCS "Good Cheer" observation-lounge; GM&O Alton parlor, SP 4696 caboose; HB&T 14 Alco S2; TM 510 Baldwin DS44-750; SP&S 50 baggage; CSOX 2198 tank car; MHAX 1237 helium car.

**Special Events:** Open House and Railroad Photography Contest in recognition of National Model Railroad month, first two weekends in November. Free admission.

**Nearby Attractions/Accommodations:** NASA/Space Center in Houston; Center for Transportation & Commerce at Galveston; Six Flags Houston.

**Location/Directions:** Exit Loop 610 north at McCarty Drive. Go west on McCarty Dr. to Mesa Dr., then left about 1.5 miles to the museum.

**Site Address:** 7390 Mesa Dr., Houston, TX
**Mailing Address:** PO Box 457, Houston, TX 77001-0457
**Telephone:** (713) 631-6612
**E-mail:** tom@kingswayrc.com
**Internet:** www.kingswayrc.com/gcst

## SIX FLAGS ASTROWORLD
*Train ride*
*36" gauge*

**Description:** Theme park attraction with ten featured roller coasters. Train ride is a complete 2-mile trip around AstroWorld and WaterWorld; takes about 20 minutes; shows all attractions and history.

**Schedule:** Open 11 a.m. to closing. Hours vary.

**Admission/Fare:** General use 48" and taller, $32.99 plus tax; children $19 plus tax; senior citizens, $26.99 plus tax; 2 and under free.

**Locomotives/Rolling Stock:** Two diesel locomotives; converted ore car.

**Special Events:** Fright Fest, Un Dia Padre, Gospel Celebration, Flag Day, concerts, Joy Fest, 4th of July Celebration.

**Nearby Attractions/Accommodations:** Radisson Astrodome Hotel, Residence Inn, Holiday Inn Astrodome, Astrodome, Astroarena, Rellant Stadium, WaterWorld.

**Location/Directions:** On I-610 exit Kirby; southwest of downtown, across from Astrodome complex.

**Site Address:** 9001 Kirby Dr., Houston, TX
**Mailing Address:** Attn: Public Relations, 9001 Kirby Dr., Houston, TX 77054
**Telephone:** (713) 799-8404 and Group Sales (713) 794-3291
**Fax:** (713) 799-8945
**Internet:** www.sixflags.com

**MARSHALL DEPOT INC.**
*Museum, display, layout*

BILL ROBINSON

**Description:** Amtrak Station, gift shop, museum displays, HO layout.

**Schedule:** Wednesdays through Saturdays, 10 a.m. to 4 p.m., Sundays 1 to 4 p.m. Group reservations with two days notice.

**Admission/Fare:** Adults, $3; seniors, $2; children $1.

**Locomotives/Rolling Stock:** UP caboose no. 25687.

**Special Events:** Stagecoach Days, third weekend in May. 4th of July Celebration. Fire Ant Festival, second weekend in October. Wonderland of Lights, Thanksgiving to December 31.

**Nearby Attractions/Accommodations:** Marshall Pottery, Starr Family Historic Park, Caddo Lake and State Park, Harrison County Historical Court House, Harrison County Historical Museum, Michelson Art Museum, T.C. Lindsey store in Jonesville.

**Location/Directions:** From I-20 exit 617 north on U.S. 59 3.8 miles (five traffic lights). West on U.S. 80 1 mile (three traffic lights). North three blocks on N. Washington, walk through tunnel.

**Site Address:** 800 N. Washington Ave., Marshall, TX
**Mailing Address:** 800 N. Washington Ave., Ste. 1, Marshall, TX  75670-2064
**Telephone:** (903) 938-9495
**Fax:** (903) 938-8248
**Internet:** www.rypn.org/mdi

# SQUARE HOUSE MUSEUM
*Museum, display*

**Description:** Eight buildings of displays and art galleries, including a 1912 church, two art galleries, local animal and bird display, a caboose, dugout, replica of early bank, dentist office, depot, blacksmith shop.

**Schedule:** Monday through Saturday, 9 a.m. to 5 p.m. and Sundays 1 to 5 p.m. Closed Christmas, New Year's, and Easter.

**Admission/Fare:** Free. Donations accepted.

**Locomotives/Rolling Stock:** ATSF caboose no. 1703R.

**Special Events:** Parade and Celebration, July 4. Museum Day, October 6, barbecue, country store, Pioneer Church.

**Nearby Attractions/Accommodations:** Palo Duro Park; musical outdoor drama; hotel, motel, restaurants.

**Location/Directions:** From Amarillo go 28 miles east on 60 to 207 north to intersection of Fifth St. From I-40 go 9 miles north at intersection with 207.

**Site Address:** Highway 207 (Elsie St.) and 5th St., Panhandle, TX
**Mailing Address:** PO Box 276, Panhandle, TX 79068
**Telephone:** (806) 537-3524
**Fax:** (806) 537-5628
**E-mail:** shm@squarehousemuseum.org
**Internet:** www.squarehousemuseum.org

# TEXAS STATE RAILROAD
*Train ride*
*Standard gauge*

BILL LANGFORD

**Description:** Established in 1893, the Texas State Railroad now carries visitors on a 4-hour, 50-mile round trip across 24 bridges as it travels through the heart of the east Texas rolling pine and hardwood forest. Victorian-style depots are located in Rusk and Palestine.

**Schedule:** March through November: weekends. June and July: Thursdays through Sundays.

**Admission/Fare:** Round trip–adults, $15; children, $9. One-way–adults, $10; children, $6.

**Locomotives/Rolling Stock:** No. 201, 1901 Cooke 4-6-0, former Texas & Pacific no. 316; no. 300, 1917 Baldwin 2-8-0, former Texas Southeastern no. 28; no. 400, 1917 Baldwin 2-8-2, former Magma Arizona no. 7; no. 500, 1911 Baldwin 4-6-2, former Santa Fe no. 1316; no. 610, 1927 Lima 2-10-4, former Texas & Pacific no. 610.

**Special Events:** Murder on the Dis-Oriented Express, Special Dogwood Excursion, Civil War and World War II re-enactments, Victoria Christmas train, starlight excursions.

**Nearby Attractions/Accommodations:** Rusk–nation's longest foot bridge. Palestine–National Scientific Balloon Base.

**Location/Directions:** Highway 84, 2 miles west of downtown Rusk, 3 miles east of downtown Palestine.

**Site Address:** 2503 W. 6th, Rusk, TX
**Mailing Address:** PO Box 39, Rusk, TX 78785
**Telephone:** (800) 442-8951 and (903) 683-2561
**Fax:** (903) 683-5634
**Internet:** www.tpwd.state.tx.us/park/railroad/

**Description:** One-third-mile ride behind Baldwin RS4 switcher with MP bay window caboose.

**Schedule:** Thursdays, Saturdays, and Sundays, 9 a.m. to 4 p.m.

**Admission/Fare:** Adults, $4; children 12 and under, $2.

**Locomotives/Rolling Stock:** Baldwin 2-6-0 Moscow Camden & St. Augustine Railroad; 0-4-0 saddle tank no. 1 Comal County Power Co.; three cabooses, UP, MP, MP transfer.

**Special Events:** Santa's Holiday Depot: Friday, Saturday, Sunday, December 8-10, 15-17, 22-23, 6:30 to 9 p.m.

**Nearby Attractions/Accommodations:** San Antonio

**Location/Directions:** North of airport on Wetmore Rd., 2½ miles north of I-410.

**Site Address:** 11731 Wetmore Rd., San Antonio, TX
**Mailing Address:** 11731 Wetmore Rd., San Antonio, TX 78247
**Telephone:** (210) 490-3554
**E-mail:** ttm@stic.net
**Internet:** www.txtransportationmuseum.org

MARV IRVING

**Description:** Housed in the 1910 Gulf, Colorado & Santa Fe depot in downtown Temple. Featuring early Santa Fe and Missouri-Kansas-Texas station equipment and furniture, including a working telegraph for train orders. Observation alcoves with dispatch radios allow visitors to watch and listen to current BNSF operations just outside the museum. Exhibits focus on the effect of railroading on Texas and westward expansion, including a collection of railroad timetables, passes, photographs, and Santa Fe's engineer's tracings for the Southern Division.

**Schedule:** Year round. Tuesdays through Saturdays, 10 a.m. to 4 p.m. and Sundays 12 to 4 p.m.

**Admission/Fare:** Adults, $4; seniors, $3; children 5+, $2.

**Locomotives/Rolling Stock:** No. 3423, 1921 Baldwin 4-6-2, former Santa Fe; no. 2301, 1937 Alco, the oldest surviving Santa Fe diesel; steel caboose no. 1556, former Gulf, Colorado & Santa Fe; more.

**Special Events:** Texas Train Festival, third weekend in September; specials.

**Nearby Attractions/Accommodations:** Lake Belton, camping, fishing.

**Location/Directions:** I-35 exit Adams/Central Ave. Go east on Central to 7th St. Turn right and enter parking lot. Enter on trackside.

*Coupon available, see coupon section.

**Site Address:** 315 W. Ave. B, Temple, TX
**Mailing Address:** 315 W. Ave. B, Temple, TX 76501
**Telephone:** (254) 298-5172
**Fax:** (254) 298-5171
**E-mail:** mirving@ci.temple.tx.us
**Internet:** www.rrdepot.org

# WICHITA FALLS RAILROAD MUSEUM
## *Museum*
### *Standard gauge*

DAVID H. GAINES

**Description:** The museum preserves the railroad history of Wichita Falls, Texas, and the surrounding area. Artifacts, displays, and the Wichita Falls Model Railroad Club HO gauge layout are housed in some of the museum's rail cars. The museum's yard is located on the site of the Wichita Falls Union Passenger Station and is adjacent to the Burlington Northern & Santa Fe's (former Fort Worth & Denver) Forth Worth to Texline main line.

**Schedule:** Year round: Saturdays, 12 to 4 p.m. and by appointment (unless temperature is below 32 degrees F or precipitation is falling).

**Admission/Fare:** Donations appreciated. Fee for special events.

**Locomotives/Rolling Stock:** FW&D 2-8-0 no. 304; MKT NW-2 no. 1029; FW&D RPO baggage no. 34; CB&Q power combine no. 7300; more.

**Special Events:** Zephyr Days Railroad Festival; check museum's website for specific dates and detailed information.

**Nearby Attractions/Accommodations:** Kell House Museum, Wichita Falls Police and Fire Museum, Texas Tourist Information Center, Econo Lodge, Holiday Inn Hotel & Suites, Radisson Inn at the Falls.

**Location/Directions:** From Holliday or Broad Streets, go toward downtown. At Ohio St. turn toward Ninth St.; at Ninth St. turn toward the BNSF tracks to museum's main gate. (Many downtown streets are one way.)

      M arm

**Site Address:** 500 Ninth St., Wichita Falls, TX
**Mailing Address:** PO Box 4242, Wichita Falls, TX 76308-0242
**Telephone:** (940) 723-2661 and (940) 692-6073
**E-mail:** wfrrm@wf.quik.com
**Internet:** www.wf.quik.com/wfrrm/wfrrm01.htm

# HEBER VALLEY RAILROAD
*Train ride, dinner train*
*Standard gauge*

MIKE LEWIS

**Description:** Historic train excursions from 90 minutes to 3½ hours. Travel across farmland, lake shore, and into a glacier-carved canyon.

**Schedule:** Year round. Daily in summer. Call for winter schedule or check website.

**Admission/Fare:** $14-$21. Discounts for children and senior citizens.

**Locomotives/Rolling Stock:** 1907 Baldwin steam 2-8-0s nos. 618 and 75; no. 1813 MRS1 (EMD); no. 1218 Davenport 44-ton; nos 270 and 250 Lackawanna coaches; no. 248 Clinchfield; nos. 365, 366, 501, 504 open-air cars; no. 3700 UP caboose; DRGW 7508 and 7510 coaches; more.

**Special Events:** BBQ train, Polar Express, Murder Mystery Train, "Haunted Canyon" Train, Sunset Special, Pioneer Day Old West Festival, Christmas Train.

**Nearby Attractions/Accommodations:** Homestead Resort, Heber Valley Railway Park, golf course, Cascade Springs.

**Location/Directions:** Forty-five minutes from Salt Lake City. Highway 40 to Heber City. Six blocks west of Main St. to train.

*Coupon available, see coupon section.

**Site Address:** 450 S. 600 W., Heber City, UT
**Mailing Address:** PO Box 609, Heber City, UT 84032
**Telephone:** (435) 654-5601 and (801) 581-9980
**Fax:** (435) 654-3709
**Internet:** www.hebervalleyrr.org

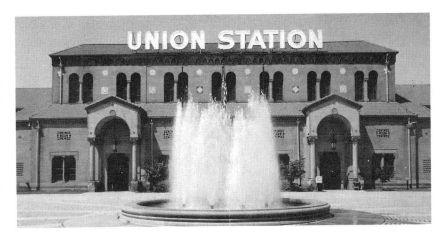

**Description:** Ogden Union Station is primarily a railroad museum. Other features include John M. Browning Museum, classic cars, natural history, and an art gallery.

**Schedule:** Mondays through Saturdays, 10 a.m. to 5 p.m.

**Admission/Fare:** Adults, $4; seniors 65+, $3; children under age 12, $2.

**Nearby Attractions/Accommodations:** Historic 25th Street shops and restaurants, Hill Aerospace Museum, Eccles Dinosaur Park.

**Location/Directions:** I-15 exit 344A, left at Wall Ave., north to Union Station.

*Coupon available, see coupon section.

**Site Address:** 2501 Wall Ave., Ogden, UT
**Mailing Address:** 2501 Wall Ave., Ogden, UT 84401
**Telephone:** (801) 629-8444 and (801) 629-8535
**Fax:** (801) 629-8555
**E-mail:** jeannieyoung@ci.ogden.ut.us
**Internet:** www.theunionstation.org

# TOOELE COUNTY RAILROAD MUSEUM
*Train ride, museum*
*7.5" gauge*

**Description:** Displays of mining, smelting, and railroading artifacts are located in the former Tooele Valley Railroad station and section house. An HO scale model railroad and a 7½" gauge mini-train operate on Saturdays.

**Schedule:** Memorial Day through Labor Day weekend: Museum–Tuesdays through Saturdays 1 to 4 p.m. Train–Saturdays 1 to 4 p.m.

**Admission/Fare:** Donations appreciated.

**Locomotives/Rolling Stock:** Static display standard gauge 2-8-0 Consolidation; cabooses.

**Nearby Attractions/Accommodations:** Benson Grist Mill, Donner Party Museum, Pony Express Station, Daughters of Utah Pioneers, restaurants.

**Location/Directions:** From Salt Lake City–I-80 west to exit 99, take Highway 36 to Tooele, Vine St. east to Broadway.

**Site Address:** 35 N. Broadway, Tooele, UT
**Mailing Address:** 90 N. Main St., Tooele, UT 84074
**Telephone:** (435) 882-2836 summer and (435) 843-2110 after September

**Description:** A museum specializing in Americana, folk art, and heritage.

**Schedule:** Late May through mid-October.

**Admission/Fare:** Two-day Pass: Adults, $17.50; children 6-14, $7.

**Locomotives/Rolling Stock:** 1890 railroad station; locomotive 220; private car.

**Nearby Attractions/Accommodations:** Burlington, Vermont.

**Location/Directions:** From I-89, exit 13. Seven miles south on Route 7 to Shelburne.

           M

**Site Address:** 6000 Shelburne Rd., Route 7, Shelburne, Vermont
**Mailing Address:** PO Box 10, Shelburne, VT 05482
**Telephone:** (802) 985-3346
**Fax:** (802) 985-2331
**E-mail:** info@shelburnemuseum.org
**Internet:** www.shelburnemuseum.org

**FAIRFAX STATION RAILROAD MUSEUM**
*Museum, layout*

**Description:** A restored Southern Railway depot rich in Civil War and local history. Clara Barton was a nurse here after the Second Battle of Manassas.

**Schedule:** Year round: Sundays, 1 to 4 p.m. Labor Day, 12 to 5 p.m.

**Admission/Fare:** Adults, $2; children 3-10, $1.

**Locomotives/Rolling Stock:** Caboose N&W 518606.

**Special Events:** Model train layouts, every third Sunday of the month. Annual Model Train Display, first weekend in December. Annual Civil War/Community Day, Quilt Show, Art Show.

**Nearby Attractions/Accommodations:** Washington, D.C., museums, Manassas Museum, Fairfax City Museum.

**Location/Directions:** Three miles south of Fairfax. Located ¼ mile from corner of Route 123 (Ox Rd.) and Fairfax Station Rd.

**Site Address:** 11200 Fairfax Station Rd., Fairfax Station, VA
**Mailing Address:** PO Box 7, Fairfax Station, VA 22039
**Telephone:** (703) 425-9225 and (703) 278-8833
**E-mail:** fxstn@fairfax-station.org
**Internet:** www.fairfax-station.org/

**Description:** This military-history museum displays items of transportation dating from 1776 to the present. Inside the 15,000-square-foot museum are dioramas and exhibits; on five acres outside are rail rolling stock, trucks, jeeps, amphibious marine craft, helicopters, aircraft, and an experimental hovercraft.

**Schedule:** Year round: Tuesdays through Sundays, 9:30 a.m. to 4:30 p.m. Closed Mondays and federal holidays.

**Admission/Fare:** Free.

**Locomotives/Rolling Stock:** Steam locomotive 2-8-0 no. 607; steam locomotive 0-6-0 no. V-1923; ambulance ward car no. 87568; steam wrecking crane; 40-T and 50T flatcars; cabooses; Berlin duty train cars.

**Nearby Attractions/Accommodations:** Camping, Colonial Williamsburg, Jamestown, Yorktown.

**Location/Directions:** I-64 exit 250A. Eleven miles south of Williamsburg.

**Site Address:** 300 Washington Blvd., Fort Eustis, VA
**Mailing Address:** 300 Washington Blvd., Fort Eustis, VA 23604
**Telephone:** (757) 878-1115
**Internet:** www.eustis.army.mil/DPTMSEC/museum.htm

MARK MILLIGAN

**Description:** Thirty-five-minute excursion ride on the Virginia Railway Express.

**Schedule:** June 1, 2002. 10 a.m. to 4 p.m.

**Admission/Fare:** Free. $5 per person for excursion train ride.

**Locomotives/Rolling Stock:** Locomotives and rolling stock provided by Norfolk Southern, Virginia Railway Express, and Amtrak.

**Special Events:** Railway Festival, June 1; memorabilia, modular exhibits, living history and folklore, rail excursions, children's amusements, and great food.

**Nearby Attractions/Accommodations:** Manassas Museum, Manassas Battlefield Park, Splashdown Water Park, locally owned restaurants, hotels, and campgrounds.

**Location/Directions:** From I-66 in Virginia take Route 234 business south. Follow for 7 miles. Turn left on Center St. Turn right on Main St. Cross over railroad tracks and festival is off to right.

**Site Address:** 9431 West St., Manassas, VA
**Mailing Address:** 9431 West St., Manassas, VA 20110
**Telephone:** (703) 361-6599 and (877) 848-3018
**Fax:** (703) 361-6942
**E-mail:** hmi@erols.com
**Internet:** www.visitmanassas.org

# EASTERN SHORE RAILWAY MUSEUM
*Museum*

JOHN E. BATES

**Description:** Restored 1920s Pennsylvania Railroad Station; original crossing shanty, toolshed, artifacts, gift shop. Home of Delmarva Chapter NRHS. Antique auto museum is also located on grounds.

**Schedule:** Year round: Mondays through Saturdays 10 a.m. to 4 p.m. and Sundays 1 to 4 p.m. November through March: closed Wednesdays.

**Admission/Fare:** $2; children under age 12 are free.

**Locomotives/Rolling Stock:** 1920s RF&P post office car; 1962 NKP caboose no. 473; 1949 Wabash caboose no. 2783; Seaboard Airline diner car no. 8011; 1950 RF&P Fairfax River; 1927 Pullman "Diplomat" parlor/observation car.

**Special Events:** Parksley Festival, first Saturday in June.

**Nearby Attractions/Accommodations:** Chincoteague Island, Kiptopeke State Park, Ocean City.

**Location/Directions:** Midway between Chesapeake Bay Bridge Tunnel and Salisbury, Maryland. Route 13, 2 miles west on State Route 176.

**Site Address:** 18468 Dunne Ave., Parksley, VA
**Mailing Address:** PO Box 135, Parksley, VA 23421
**Telephone:** (757) 665-RAIL

# OLD DOMINION RAILWAY MUSEUM
*Museum*

**Description:** The Old Dominion Railway Museum tells the story of Virginia's railroading heritage through artifacts, videos, and static displays. It is located within a few blocks of the 1831 birthplace of Virginia railroad operations. Through its affiliate, the Old Dominion Chapter, NRHS, seasonal rides are offered on the Buckingham Branch Railroad.

**Schedule:** Year round: Saturdays, 11 a.m. to 4 p.m. and Sundays, 1 to 4 p.m.

**Admission/Fare:** Donations appreciated.

**Locomotives/Rolling Stock:** RF&P express car 185; David M. Lea & Co. 0-4-0T no. 2; SCL caboose 21019; Seaboard System boxcar 111935; Fairmont motor car.

**Special Events:** Floodwall Guided Walking Tours, second Sunday of each month 2 p.m. Rides on Buckingham Branch Railroad, May, October, and December.

**Nearby Attractions/Accommodations:** Downtown Richmond tourist area, Richmond Floodwall Promenade, James River boating, fishing, nature walks, downtown canal.

**Location/Directions:** I-95 , exit 73 (Maury St.). Turn right onto Maury St., go two blocks. Turn left onto W. Second St., to right on Hull St., to museum on right.

       arm

**Site Address:** 102 Hull St., Richmond, VA
**Mailing Address:** PO Box 8583, Richmond, VA 23226
**Telephone:** (804) 233-6237
**Fax:** (804) 745-4735
**Internet:** www.odcnrhs.org

# VIRGINIA MUSEUM OF TRANSPORTATION, INC.
*Museum, display, layout*
*Standard gauge*

**Description:** Diesel, steam, and electric locomotives, railcars, trolleys, carriages, automobiles, trucks, aviation, and rocket. Interactive exhibits, large O gauge train layout, resource library and archives, and much more.

**Schedule:** Daily. Mondays through Saturdays, 10 a.m. to 5 p.m. and Sundays 12 to 5 p.m. Closed major holidays and Sundays and Mondays in January and February.

**Admission/Fare:** Adults, $6; seniors, $5; children 3-11, $4; under 3 free, plus Roanoke City admission tax.

**Locomotives/Rolling Stock:** No. 611, J class 4-8-4, former Norfolk & Western; no. 4, 1910 Baldwin class SA 0-8-0, former Virginian Railway; no. 6, 1897 Baldwin class G-1 2-8-0, former N&W; no. 763, 1994 Lima class S-2 2-8-4, former Nickel Plate; no. 1, Celanese 0400 fireless locomotive; many diesels, City of Roanoke trolley, and D.C. Transit trolley: more.

**Special Events:** Calendar of events available on website.

**Nearby Attractions/Accommodations:** Visitor Center, Blue Ridge Parkway, two national forests, two state parks on lakes, museums, zoo, hotels, restaurants, shopping, award-winning downtown Farmer's Market.

**Location/Directions:** I-81 to I-581, exit 5 to downtown Roanoke, follow signs.

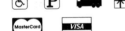

**Site Address:** 303 Norfolk Ave. SW, Roanoke, VA
**Mailing Address:** 303 Norfolk Ave. SW, Roanoke VA 24016
**Telephone:** (540) 342-5670
**Fax:** (540) 342-6898
**E-mail:** info@vmt.org
**Internet:** www.vmt.org

# REMLINGER FARMS RAILROAD
*Train ride*
*Narrow gauge*

**Description:** Child-based activities park with lunch service restaurant and farm market.

**Schedule:** Daily, June through September. Weekends and limited weekedays in October.

**Admission/Fare:** $5-$12 per person; unlimited activities.

**Locomotives/Rolling Stock:** Authentic miniature steam train, 24" narrow gauge.

**Special Events:** Octoberfest, weekends in October.

**Nearby Attractions/Accommodations:** Snoqualmie Falls, Salish Lodge.

**Location/Directions:** South of Carnation on State Hwy. 203.

**Site Address:** 32610 N.E. 32nd St., Carnation, WA
**Mailing Address:** PO Box 177, Carnation, WA 98014
**Telephone:** (425) 333-4135
**Fax:** (425) 333-4373
**E-mail:** www.remlingerfarms.com

## CHEHALIS-CENTRALIA
## RAILROAD ASSOCIATION
*Train ride, dinner train*
*Standard gauge*

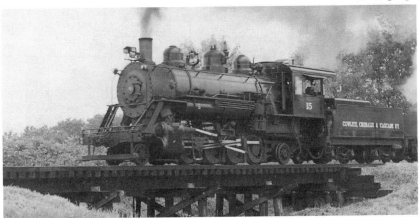

DON HARTMAN

**Description:** A 13-mile, 1¼-hour round trip or a 19-mile, 1¾-hour round trip over former Weyerhaeuser (Chehalis Western) trackage, former Milwaukee Road, from South Chehalis to Millburn or Ruth.

**Schedule:** May 26 through September: weekends. Depart Chehalis–1 and 3 p.m. Ruth trip–Saturdays, depart Chehalis 5 p.m. Ruth dinner train on select Saturdays requires advance reservations. Call for information.

**Admission/Fare:** Round trip–adults, $8; children 4-16, $5. Ruth trip–adults, $11; children, $8.

**Locomotives/Rolling Stock:** No. 15, 1916 Baldwin 90-ton 2-8-2, former Cowlitz, Chehalis & Cascade, former Puget Sound & Cascade no. 200. This engine had been displayed for 30 years in a local park; restoration was completed in 1989 by Mt. Rainier Scenic Railroad shop and volunteers from Lewis County; Milw. Z-frame 40-foot wood boxcar no. 711018 used as shop/supply car; also Milw. steel rib-side 40-foot boxcar.

**Nearby Attractions/Accommodations:** Motel, restaurants, campgrounds. One hour from Mt. Rainier Scenic Railroad's steam operation.

**Location/Directions:** Midway between Seattle, Washington, and Portland, Oregon. I-5 to exit 77. Turn west to first street south (Riverside Rd.). Proceed ¼ mile to Sylvenus St. Turn left one block to railroad tracks.

 **Radio frequency: 161.385 and 160.635**

**Site Address:** 1100 Sylvenus St., Chehalis, WA
**Mailing Address:** 1945 S. Market Blvd., Chehalis, WA 98532
**Telephone:** (360) 748-9593
**Fax:** (360) 748-9994
**E-mail:** ccrra@hotmail.com
**Internet:** www.ccrra.com

# DAYTON HISTORICAL DEPOT SOCIETY
*Museum*

**Description:** Oldest train depot in the state of Washington, fully restored and on the National Register of Historic Places. Used as a repository for train memorabilia and artifacts (mostly photos) from early Columbia County history.

**Schedule:** Tuesdays through Saturdays 10 a.m. to 5 p.m. Sundays and Mondays, by appointment.

**Admission/Fare:** $2 per person.

**Locomotives/Rolling Stock:** UP caboose 25219 built in 1952.

**Special Events:** Depot Days, third Saturday in September, celebrating railroad history in the northwest.

**Nearby Attractions/Accommodations:** Three historic districts, hotels and restaurants within walking distance.

**Location/Directions:** Coming through Dayton on Highway 12, turn north on Second St. one block.

       M arm

**Site Address:** 222 Commercial St., Dayton, WA
**Mailing Address:** PO Box 1881, Dayton, WA 99328
**Telephone:** (509) 382-2026

# MOUNT RAINIER SCENIC RAILROAD
*Train ride, display*
*Standard gauge*

MARTIN HANSEN

**Description:** Collection of five operating steam logging locomotives. 1½-hour excursion.

**Schedule:** June and September, weekends; July and August, daily; Santa Train, first three weekends of December.

**Admission/Fare:** Adults, $11.50, seniors, $10.50, children under 12, $8.50.

**Locomotives/Rolling Stock:** 2-8-2 71-ton Porter 1924; 70-ton 3-track Climax 1928; 90-ton 3-track Shay 1929; 70-ton 3-track Heisler 1912; Alco 2-8-2 85-ton 1929; all steam locomotives.

**Special Events:** Tacoma Railfan Days, first weekend in May. Elbe Railfan Days, end of June; Tacoma, Thanksgiving weekend.

**Nearby Attractions/Accommodations:** Thirteen miles from south entrance to Mount Rainier National Park.

**Location/Directions:** Take Highway 7 from Tacoma or Morton to Elbe.

*Coupon available, see coupon section.

**Site Address:** Elbe, WA
**Mailing Address:** PO Box 921, Elbe, WA 98330
**Telephone:** (888) s783-2611
**Fax:** (360) 569-2438
**Internet:** www.mrsr.com

# WASHINGTON STATE RAILROADS
# HISTORICAL SOCIETY MUSEUM
### *Museum*

**Description:** Museum with 1909 and 1910 Northern Pacific & Great Northern cabooses being restored in yard. Also 1900 Great Northern passenger car to be restored.

**Schedule:** April through December. Saturdays, 9 a.m. to 3 p.m.

**Admission/Fare:** Free. Donations appreciated.

**Locomotives/Rolling Stock:** Main rolling stock in Port of Pasco.

**Nearby Attractions/Accommodations:** BNSF hump yard and refueling facilities nearby; Franklin County History Society Museum

**Location/Directions:** Take 4th Ave. exit south from I-182 in Pasco. Turn east on Clark to Tacoma St. Turn south to 122 N. Tacoma Ave.

**Site Address:** 122 N. Tacoma Ave., Pasco, WA
**Mailing Address:** PO Box 552, Pasco, WA 99301
**Telephone:** (509) 543-4159
**E-mail:** wsrhs@hotmail.com
**Internet:** www.cbvcp.com/wsrhs

# SPIRIT OF WASHINGTON DINNER TRAIN
*Dinner train*
*Standard gauge*

**Description:** Experience the nostalgia of passenger rail as you ride and dine in our luxurious, vintage rail cars. The Spirit of Washington Dinner Train takes you on a 3½-hour excursion that showcases scenic views of the Puget Sound regions. The 45-mile round trip is enhanced by scenery of Lake Washington, the Olympic Mountains, the Seattle skyline, and Mount Rainier. You'll dine in comfort and elegance as your journey takes you to Woodinville's beautiful Columbia Winery. There, you'll sample fine Northwest wines and visit the cellar before returning to the depot.

**Schedule:** Call or write for information.

**Admission/Fare:** Regular Seating–$59.99 dinner; $49.99 lunch/brunch. Dome Seating–$69.99 dinner; $59.99 lunch/brunch. Also available for conventions, corporate parties, weddings, and special events up to 370.

**Locomotives/Rolling Stock:** Former Santa Fe coaches and dome lounge; former Reading "Crusade" observation car; fromer Milwaukee Road Super Dome.

**Nearby Attractions/Accommodations:** Seattle, Puget Sound.

**Location/Directions:** I-405 exit 2 (Route 162, Renton/Rainier Ave.), travel north to S. Third St., turn right, turn right again on Burnett Ave. S. for one block to depot.

**Site Address:** Renton, WA
**Mailing Address:** PO Box 835, Renton, WA 98057
**Telephone:** (206) 227-RAIL and (800) 876-RAIL
**Internet:** www.spiritofwashingtondinnertrain.com

# NORTHWEST RAILWAY MUSEUM
*Train ride, museum, display*
*Standard gauge*

**Description:** Operating railway museum with exhibits at the restored Queen Anne-style Snoqualmie Depot. Ten-mile round trip train excursions on restored heavyweight passenger coaches pulled with first-generation diesel locomotives.

**Schedule:** Train–April through October: Saturdays, Sundays, Memorial Day, and Labor Day. Museum and gift shop–year round. Memorial Day through Labor Day: 7 days/week 10 a.m. to 5 p.m. Labor Day through Memorial Day: Thursdays through Mondays 10 a.m. to 5 p.m.

**Admission/Fare:** Train–adults, $8; seniors (62+), $7; children 3-12, $6.

**Locomotives/Rolling Stock:** Kennecott Copper no. 201, Alco RSD-4; Weyerhaeuser Timber Co. no. 1 Fairbanks-Morse H-12-44; Spokane, Portland & Seattle nos. 272 and 276, Barney and Smith steel coaches; Spokane, Portland & Seattle no. 213, Barney and Smith wood coach; OWRR&NCO no. 1590, Pullman observation car; more.

**Special Events:** Mother's Ride Free, May 11-12. "Pops" on Us, June 15-16. Snoqualmie Railroad Days, August 3-4. Santa Train, November 30, December 1, December 7-8, and December 14-15.

**Nearby Attractions/Accommodations:** Snoqualmie Falls, hiking, Seattle.

**Location/Directions:** I-90, eastbound exit 27 or westbound exit 31.

*Coupon available, see coupon section.

**Site Address:** 38625 S.E. King St., Snoqualmie, WA
**Site Address:** 205 McClellan St., North Bend, WA
**Mailing Address:** PO Box 459, Snoqualmie, WA 98065-0459
**Telephone:** (425) 888-3030
**Fax:** (425) 888-9311
**E-mail:** visitorservices@trainmuseum.org
**Internet:** www.trainmuseum.org

**CAMP 6 LOGGING MUSEUM
AND PDQ&K RAILROAD**
*Train ride, museum*

TACOMA CHAPTER, NRHS COLLECTION

**Description:** Over 700 tons of steam-era logging and railroad equipment set up as a rail logging camp in the woods. Train makes a 20-minute run through the site every half hour.

**Schedule:** Museum–outside, year round; inside, March through October: Wednesdays through Sundays, 10 a.m. to 4 p.m. Logging Train–April through May: weekends 12 to 4 p.m.; June through September: weekends 12 to 6:30 p.m.

**Admission/Fare:** Museum–free. Train–ages 13-64, $3; 3-12 and 65-99, $1.75; under 3 and over 99, free.

**Locomotives/Rolling Stock:** KL&L Co. no. 7 Pacific Coast Shay no. 3346; 20T Whitcomb DM46 no. 40133; 8T Plymouth DLC no. 2689; 25T Ohio Steam Crane no. 3802; Rayonier Caboose no. 3; more.

**Special Events:** Santa Train, first three weekends of December, 10 a.m. to 4 p.m. $1.

**Nearby Attractions/Accommodations:** Within the Tacoma/Seattle area there are zoos, museums, national parks, pro sports, arts, and theaters, and a full range of tourist accommodations.

**Location/Directions:** I-5 north or south to Tacoma, then take State Route 16 west to Sixth Ave. and Pearl St. exit. Follow signs to Point Defiance Park and go two miles into park.

**Site Address:** 5400 N. Pearl St., Tacoma, WA
**Mailing Address:** PO Box 340, Tacoma, WA 98401-0340
**Telephone:** (253) 752-0047
**E-mail:** camp6museum@harbornet.com
**Internet:** www.camp-6-museum.org/c6.html

# NORTHERN PACIFIC RAILWAY MUSEUM
### *Dinner train, display*

HAROLD K. CHANDLER

**Description:** This museum operates a tourist train on the former Northern Pacific White Swan branch line. Passenger excursions are 20-mile round trips from Harrah to White Swan. The 1911 former NP railroad depot in Toppenish serves as the museum and gift shop. The freight house has been converted to an engine house and the former NP section foreman's house is also adjacent to the depot.

**Schedule:** Museum–May through November: weekends 10 a.m. to 5 p.m. Train–September through October: Saturdays 10:30 a.m.

**Fare/Admission:** Museum–adults, $2; seniors and children, $1; families, $5. Train–adults, $8; children, $5.

**Locomotives/Rolling Stock:** 1902 NP Baldwin 4-6-0 no. 1364; 1953 150-ton; two 1920s P70 heavyweights, former PRR; 1947 NP coach no. 588; NH combination coach; 1907 NP wooden caboose.

**Special Events:** Halloween Run. Christmas Run with Santa, first two Saturdays in December. Western Art & Rail Show, third weekend in August.

**Nearby Attractions/Accommodations:** Over 50 murals by noted artists.

**Location/Directions:** Twenty minutes south of Yakima, Washington.

*Coupon available, see coupon section.

      M arm

**Site Address:** 10 Asotin Ave., Toppenish, WA
**Mailing Address:** PO Box 889, Toppenish, WA 98948
**Telephone:** (509) 865-1911
**Internet:** nprymuseum.org/

403

## NEW TYGART FLYER, WEST VIRGINIA CENTRAL RAILROAD
*Train ride, dinner train*
*Standard gauge*

LARS O. BYRNE

**Description:** Choice of 24-, 58-, or 85-mile excursions over tracks of the West Virginia Central Railroad in the wild heart of West Virginia.

**Schedule:** May through October, Saturday and Sunday, with special runs during fall colors and in conjunction with local festivals. Call for details.

**Admission/Fare:** Rates start at $15 and vary according to choice of excursion. First-class service is also offered.

**Locomotives/Rolling Stock:** No. 82 ex-WM BL-2, 1948. The train is all-Pullman cars, including coach, dinette, and observation/lounge car.

**Special Events:** Battle of Laurel Hill Civil War re-enactment, July 8-9. Mountain State Forest Festival, October 3-7.

**Nearby Attractions/Accommodations:** Monongahela National Forest, Cheat Mountain Salamander Railbus Ride, Cass Scenic Railroad, Durbin & Greenbrier Valley Scenic Railroad, Revelle's Campground.

**Location/Directions:** Belington, West Virginia, is located on Route 250, 5 miles north of U.S. 33 in Barbour County. Elkins is located at the intersection of U.S. 33 and 250 in Randolph County in east central West Virginia.

**Site Address:** Watkins Ave., Belington, WV
**Mailing Address:** E. Main St., Durbin, WV 26264
**Telephone:** (304) 456-4935 and (877) 686-7245
**Fax:** (304) 456-5246
**E-mail:** jksmith@naumedia.net
**Internet:** www.mountainrail.com

# CASS SCENIC RAILROAD STATE PARK
*Train ride, dinner train, museum*
*Standard gauge*

**Description:** Cass Scenic Railroad is a state park that offers excursions powered by a steam-driven locomotive. We have overnight accommodations with camping nearby.

**Schedule:** May 26 through September 3 and October 1 through October 14, daily; September 7 through September 30, Fridays and weekends; October 18 through October 28, Thursdays, Fridays, and weekends. Cass to Whittaker, departs Cass 10:50 a.m., 1 and 3 p.m. Cass to Bald Knob, departs Cass 12 noon, except Mondays. (Cass to Bald Knob does operate on Memorial Day and Labor Day.)

**Admission/Fare:** Call or write for details. Prices vary with event. Group rates available. Reservations recommended.

**Locomotives/Rolling Stock:** No. 2 1928 Pacific Coast Shay; no. 4 1922 70-C Shay; no. 5 1905 80-C Shay; no. 6 1945 150-C Shay; no. 11 1923 formerly Pacific Coast Shay no. 3

**Nearby Attractions/Accommodations:** Green Bank National Radio Astronomy Observatory, Snowshoe Resort.

**Location/Directions:** State Route 28/92 between Dunmore and Green Bank in Pocahontas County, eastern West Virginia.

**Site Address:** Main St., Route 66, Cass, WV
**Mailing Address:** PO Box 107, Cass, WV 24927
**Telephone:** (304) 456-4300 and (800) 225-5982
**Fax:** (304) 456-4641
**E-mail:** cassrr@neumedia.net
**Internet:** www.neumedia.net/~cassrr/

## CHEAT MOUNTAIN SALAMANDER RAIL RIDE
*Train ride*
*Standard gauge*

**Description:** Thirty-six-, 88- or 118-mile mountain wilderness ride on top of Cheat Mountain through the spectacular Monongahela National Forest in east central West Virginia. Self-propelled railcoach crosses 4,066-foot mountain pass as it traverses one of the last great wilderness areas in the eastern United States. Elkins train climbs 3 percent grade to Inspirational High Falls of the Cheat River.

**Schedule:** Four-season operation. Limited to weekends only during winter. Call for details.

**Admission/Fare:** Fares range from $15 and up.

**Locomotives/Rolling Stock:** No. M-3, a self-propelled 50-passenger Edwards Railway Company motor coach; climate-controlled Pullman cars.

**Special Events:** Mountain State Forest Festival, October 1-9; Durbin Days, third week in July; special fall foliage runs.

**Nearby Attractions/Accommodations:** Monongahela National Forest, Durbin & Greenbrier Valley Scenic Railroad, Cass Scenic Railroad, New Tygart Flyer Scenic Railroad, National Radio Astronomy Observatory.

**Location/Directions:** Cheat Bridge is located on U.S. 250, 28 miles south of Elkins; Elkins is located at the intersection of U.S. 33 and 250 in east central West Virginia.

**Radio frequency: 161.175**

**Site Address:** Red Run Rd., Cheat Bridge, WV; and Davis Ave., Elkins, WV
**Mailing Address:** 3 E. Main St., Durbin, WV
**Telephone:** (304) 456-4935 and (877) 686-7245
**Fax:** (304) 456-5246
**E-mail:** jksmith@neumedia.net
**Internet:** mountainrail.com

# DURBIN & GREENBRIER VALLEY RAILROAD
*Train ride*
*Standard gauge*

KATHY SMITH

**Description:** A 10-mile, 1.5-hour round trip on ex-C&ORR Greenbrier Division along the upper Greenbrier River. Ride terminates at isolated Hevener station picnic area on the banks of the river.

**Schedule:** May 5 through October 28: Thursdays through Sundays, 11 a.m. and 2 p.m.

**Admission/Fare:** Adults, $8; seniors, $7; children 5-12, $5.50.

**Locomotives/Rolling Stock:** No. 1 "Little Leroi," 20-ton Whitcomb, 1936; open excursion car; 1926 ex-B&ORR wooden caboose.

**Special Events:** Durbin Days, third week in July; special fall colors trips in season; winter snowplow train, weather permitting.

**Nearby Attractions/Accommodations:** Monongahela National Forest, Cass Scenic Railroad, Cheat Mountain Salamander.

**Location/Directions:** 35 miles south of Elkins on U.S. 250.

**Site Address:** E. Main St., Route 250, Durbin, WV
**Mailing Address:** PO Box 44, Durbin, WV 26264
**Telephone:** (304) 456-4935 and (877) 686-7245
**Fax:** (304) 456-5246
**E-mail:** jksmith@neumedia.net
**Internet:** mountainrail.com

## HARPERS FERRY TOY TRAIN MUSEUM & JOY LINE RAILROAD
### Train ride, museum, display, layout

**Description:** One-half mile of 16-inch gauge track and a collection of antique toy trains in the museum

**Schedule:** April through October: weekends and holidays 9 a.m. to 5 p.m.

**Admission/Fare:** Adults, $1.50.

**Locomotives/Rolling Stock:** Two miniature train G-16; S-16; homebuilt 2-4-4T; four M.T. passenger cars; six freight cars; caboose; snowplow; work crane.

**Nearby Attractions/Accommodations:** Harpers Ferry National Park.

**Location/Directions:** Take 340 west one mile past Harpers Ferry and turn right onto Bakerton Rd. (Route 27), continue one mile and turn left.

*Coupon available, see coupon section.

**Site Address:** Bakerton Rd., Route 27, Harpers Ferry, WV
**Mailing Address:** Toy Train Museum, Rt. 3 Box 315, Harpers Ferry, WV 25425
**Telephone:** (304) 535-2521 and (304) 535-2291
**E-mail:** hfttm@aol.com
**Internet:** mountainrail.com

# COLLIS P. HUNTINGTON RAILROAD HISTORICAL SOCIETY, INC.

*Train ride, museum, display*
*Standard gauge*

JEAN CHAPMAN

**Description:** Museum and rail excursions.

**Schedule:** Museum: Memorial Day through late September, Sundays 2 to 5 p.m., also by appointment year round.

**Admission/Fare:** Museum–donations appreciated. Excursions–from $109.

**Locomotives/Rolling Stock:** C&O no. 1308 Mallet steam locomotive; two C&O coaches; C&O and VGN cabooses; operating hand car; boxcar; baggage car; concession car; RS-3 diesel locomotive former Reading engine; lounge car NYC no. 38.

**Special Events:** Annual New River Train Excursions, October. One-day 300-mile round trips. Tri-State Railroad Days, March, at Greenbo State Resort Park.

**Nearby Attractions/Accommodations:** Pilgrim Glass, Radio Museum, Highlands Museum and Discovery Center, Huntington Museum of Art, Blenko Glass, CSX, NS main lines, Greenbo Lake State Resort Park.

**Location/Directions:** Excursions: Seventh Ave. and Eighth St., Huntington. Museum: 14th St., West and Ritter Park.

*Coupon available, see coupon section.

**Site Address:** 1429 Chestnut St., Kenova, WV
**Mailing Address:** PO Box 451, Kenova, WV 25530
**Telephone:** (304) 453-1641
**Fax:** (304) 453-6120
**E-mail:** railtwo@aol.com
**Internet:** www.newrivertrain.com

**POTOMAC EAGLE
SCENIC RAIL EXCURSIONS**
*Train ride, dinner train
Standard gauge*

D. W. CORBITT

**Description:** A 35-mile, three-hour ride through the "trough" of the South Branch of the Potomac River on the South Branch Valley Railroad. All trips have first-class club and dining cars with meals included.

**Schedule:** May through August: Saturdays, 1 p.m. September: weekends 1 p.m. October: trains operate daily; call for schedule.

**Admission/Fare:** Three-hour trip: Coach–adults, $22; seniors, $20; children 3-14, $10. First-class club car, $49. Six-hour trip: Coach–adults, $40; seniors, $38; children 3-14, $20. First-class club car, $89.

**Locomotives/Rolling Stock:** GP9s, former Baltimore & Ohio; F units, former CSX; 1920s open-window coaches, former CN; 1950s-era lounge car, former C&O.

**Special Events:** All-day excursions, including Petersburg trip, home tours train to Moorefield, ride the whole railroad 100+ mile route, and Railfan Day with many photo run-bys.

**Location/Directions:** Train departs Wappocomo Station, 1.5 miles north of Romney on Route 28.

Cumberland, Maryland

**Site Address:** Route 28 North, Romney, WV
**Mailing Address:** Ticket Agent, 2306 35th St., Parkersburg, WV 26104
**Telephone:** (304) 424-0736
**Fax:** (304) 485-5901
**E-mail:** corbittdavid@hotmail.com
**Internet:** wvweb.com/www/potomac_eagle/

**Description:** O gauge 1400-square-foot model railroad display. Fourteen working tracks with detailed scenery, 1930s to mid-1950s.

**Schedule:** Daily 11 a.m. to 4 p.m.

**Admission/Fare:** Adults, $4.80; youth, $3.75.

**Locomotives/Rolling Stock:** Lionel, Williams, Weaver.

**Special Events:** Annual Model Railroad Show, January 19-20.

**Nearby Attractions/Accommodations:** Display is on the grounds of the Oglebay Family Resort and Conference Center.

**Location/Directions:** I-70 to Wheeling. Route 88 north. Follow signs.

**Site Address:** Oglebay Resort, Route 88, Wheeling, WV
**Mailing Address:** Oglebay Resort, Route 88, Wheeling, WV 26003
**Telephone:** (800) 624-6988 ext. 4010
**Fax:** (304) 243-4110
**E-mail:** smitch@oglebay-resort.com
**Internet:** www.oglebay-resort.com

# COLFAX RAILROAD MUSEUM, INC.
*Museum*
*Standard and narrow gauge*

HERBERT F. SAKALAUCKS JR.

**Description:** The museum houses a large collection of railroad memorabilia, an extensive reference library, and offers a ride on a railroad speeder.

**Schedule:** May and September: Saturday, 11 a.m. to 5 p.m.; Sunday, 1 to 5 p.m. June through August: Thursday and Friday, 11 a.m. to 4 p.m.; Saturday, 11 a.m. to 5 p.m.; Sunday, 1 to 5 p.m.

**Admission/Fare:** Adults, $2; children 7-14, $1; children 6 and under free.

**Locomotives/Rolling Stock:** Soo Line wooden caboose no. 273; Soo Line outside-braced boxcar no. 33400; Soo Line Barney & Smith coach no. 991; Milwaukee Road flanger no. 000931; two Canadian National speeders; velocipede; Algoma Century caboose no. 9517; two GE 3-foot gauge electric locomotives.

**Nearby Attractions/Accommodations:** Hoffman Hills State park, Red Cedar River, Altoona Roundhouse.

**Location/Directions:** Exit 52 off I-94 toward Chippewa Falls approximately ¾ mile, go north 8 miles on Highway 40 to Colfax. Take the first right after the railroad tracks; go one block and it's on the right.

*Coupon available, see coupon section.

**Site Address:** 500 Railroad, Colfax, WI
**Mailing Address:** PO Box 383, Colfax, WI 54730
**Telephone:** (715) 962-2076 and (715) 233-0434
**Fax:** (715) 235-3126
**E-mail:** colfaxrr@wwt.net

# EAST TROY ELECTRIC RAILROAD
## WISCONSIN TROLLEY MUSEUM
*Train ride, dinner train, museum*
*Standard gauge*

SCOTT PATRICK

**Description:** Ride restored trolleys or the museum's award-winning dinner train over Wisconsin's landmark railroad.

**Schedule:** Weekends, May 25 through October 27, 11:30 a.m. to 4 p.m.; Wednesdays through Fridays, June 19 through August 23, 10 a.m. to 1 p.m. Call for dinner train schedule.

**Admission/Fare:** Trolley ride–Adults, $8; children 3-11, $4; dinner train–$49.

**Locomotives/Rolling Stock:** CSS&SB 9, 11, 13, 21, 24, 25, 30, 111; CTA 35, 45, 4420, 4453; Duluth-Superior Streetcar 253; P&W 64; ETER 21; TMER&L 200, D23, L6, L8, and L9; CNS&MRR 228; SEPTA PCCs 2120 and 2185; TTC PCC 4617; WP&L 26 and TE-1.

**Special Events:** Call for complete schedule.

**Nearby Attractions/Accommodations:** Many nearby hotels, motels, B&Bs, historic attractions, and other family activities.

**Location/Directions:** One mile off I-43 on Highway 20, just 20 minutes north of Lake Geneva and 35 minutes southwest of Milwaukee.

*Coupon available, see coupon section.

**Site Address:** 2002 Church St., East Troy, WI
**Mailing Address:** PO Box 556, Waukesha, WI 53187-0556
**Telephone:** (262) 548-3837
**Fax:** (262) 548-0400
**Internet:** www.easttroyrr.org

**NATIONAL RAILROAD MUSEUM**
*Museum*
*Standard gauge*

**Description:** Home to over 70 pieces of railroad equipment. A new 26,000-square-foot exhibit hall houses Eisenhower's World War II command train, a Union Pacific Big Boy, and a Pennsylvania GG-1.

**Schedule:** Daily, 9 a.m. to 5 p.m. Train rides, May through September.

**Admission/Fare:** Adults, $7; seniors, $6; children 6-15, $5; 5 and under, free.

**Locomotives/Rolling Stock:** Union Pacific Big Boy no. 4017; Pennsylvania no. 4890 GG-1; General Motors Aerotrain; Eisenhower's World War II command train.

**Special Events:** Call for dates and details. Events throughout the year

**Location/Directions:** Highway 41 or 172, Ashland Ave. exit, travel north to Cormier Ave. and east three blocks.

*Coupon available, see coupon section.

**Site Address:** 2285 S. Broadway, Green Bay, WI
**Mailing Address:** 2285 S. Broadway, Green Bay, WI 54304
**Telephone:** (920) 437-7623
**Fax:** (920) 437-1291
**E-mail:** staff@nationalrrmuseum.org
**Internet:** www.nationalrrmuseum.org

JOHN BROEKER

**Description:** Steam locomotive Soo Line 1003 is operated on cooperating railroads for special longer duration trips. Trips are usually in conjunction with local historical or holiday celebrations in the Wisconsin, Illinois, Michigan, and Minnesota areas.

**Schedule:** Approximately two or three excursions are operated each year at varied locations and on various dates. Events will be noted by message at 847-438-6133 and through other advertising.

**Locomotives/Rolling Stock:** Soo Line 1003, 2-8-2, Class L1, built in 1913 and modernized by the Soo Line railroad in 1941. Its last regular operation was in 1955. The locomotive was restored and first operated again in November of 1996. Trains are assembled with vintage passenger cars as needed or requested.

**Special Events:** Call for dates and details. Events throughout the year

**Nearby Attractions/Accommodations:** Our trips are chosen to be in conjunction with a fair, festival, or other celebration that includes activities such as art fairs, unique food concessions, historic town tours, amusement rides, etc.

**Location/Directions:** Directions/map to special trip departure points are provided with ticket.

**Mailing Address:** Box 3466 RFD, Long Grove, IL 60047
**Telephone:** (847) 438-6133 and (651) 484-4843
**Internet:** www.sooline1003.com

415

**CAMP FIVE MUSEUM
FOUNDATION, INC.**
*Train ride, museum, display*

**Description:** Camp Five offers visitors a unique mix of history, steam railroading, and ecology. Visitors ride the *Lumberjack Special* steam train (2.5 miles one way) to the museum complex; once there, they take a guided surrey tour through beautiful forests managed on a perpetual-cycle basis. A hayrack/pontoon ride on the Rat River is also an optional offer. The logging museum features an early-transportation wing and an active blacksmith shop; half-hour steam engine video; nature center with northern Wisconsin wildlife diorama; petting corral; and a large outdoor display of logging artifacts.

**Schedule:** June 19 through August 31: Mondays through Saturdays: departures at 11 a.m., 12, 1, and 2 p.m.

**Admission/Fare:** Adults, $15; students 13-17, $10; children 4-12, $5; 3 and under, free; families, $40. Group discounts available.

**Locomotives/Rolling Stock:** 1916 Vulcan 2-6-2; cupola cabooses.

**Special Events:** Horse Pull, July 6; Heritage Festival, August 2-3; Fall Festival, September 21, 28, and October 5.

**Location/Directions:** West of Laona on Highway 8.

*Coupon available, see coupon section.

**Site Address:** 5480 Connor Farm Rd., Laona, WI
**Mailing Address:** 5480 Connor Farm Rd., Laona, WI 54541
**Telephone:** (800) 774-3414 and (715) 674-3414
**Fax:** (715) 674-7400
**E-mail:** mverich@camp5museum.org
**Internet:** www.camp5musuem.org

# PINECREST HISTORICAL VILLAGE
*Museum*

**Description:** Outdoor interpretive museum with 25 restored historic buildings and exhibit areas. Caboose 99006 recently restored and open for public viewing.

**Schedule:** Daily, May 1 through third Sunday in October; also, second weekend in December.

**Admission/Fare:** Adults, $6; children 6-17, $4; 5 and under, free

**Locomotives/Rolling Stock:** Soo Line 0-6-0 no. 321 steam locomotive, built in 1887; Wisconsin Central caboose no. 99006, built in 1886; Soo Line depot from Collins, Wisconsin, built in 1896.

**Special Events:** German Fest (July), Fall Harvest Festival (October), Christmas at Pinecrest (December).

**Nearby Attractions/Accommodations:** Food, lodging, and other attractions can be found in nearby Manitowoc and Two Rivers.

**Location/Directions:** Seven miles west of Manitowoc. From I-43 follow JJ 3 miles west to Pine Crest Ln.

     M

**Site Address:** 924 Pine Crest Ln., Town of Manitowoc Rapids, WI
**Mailing Address:** MCHS, PO Box 574, Manitowoc, WI 54221-0574
**Telephone:** (920) 684-5110 (seasonal), (920) 684-4445 (year round)
**Fax:** (920) 684-0573

# WHISKEY RIVER RAILWAY
*Train ride*
*16" gauge*

D. KLOMPMAKER COLLECTION

**Description:** A 2-mile scenic ride over the Wisconsin countryside, featuring many animals, including llamas, sheep, cattle, emu, longhorn steer, and zebra.

**Schedule:** Memorial Day through Labor Day: daily. October: weekends. December: daily.

**Admission/Fare:** $4.50; unlimited rides, $10.

**Locomotives/Rolling Stock:** Gene Autry's Daylight Melody Ranch Special; Oakland Acorn Pacific; Gracy's Atlantic 1919 8½-ton Pacific (built in house); McCallister collection, including Atlantic, Shay, and 2-8-8-4 Mallet.

**Nearby Attractions/Accommodations:** Amusement park, miniature golf.

**Location/Directions:** Located ¼ mile east of Highway 73 on Highway 19 in Marshall.

*Coupon available, see coupon section.

**Site Address:** 700 E. Main St., Marshall, WI
**Mailing Address:** 700 E. Main St., Marshall, WI 53559
**Telephone:** (888) 607-7735
Fax: (608) 655-4767
**E-mail:** gardyloo@jvlnet.com

## ZOOFARI EXPRESS
## MILWAUKEE COUNTY ZOO
*Train ride*
*15" gauge*

MIKE NEPPER

**Description:** This railroad has operated at the Milwaukee County Zoo since 1958, carrying over 13 million riders. The 1.25-mile trip across zoo property lasts about eight minutes.

**Schedule:** May through September: daily 10 a.m. to 4 p.m. March, April, October: weekends 10 a.m. to 4 p.m.

**Admission/Fare:** Zoo admission required–adults, $9; children 3-12, $6; parking, $6. Train–adults, $2; children, $1.

**Locomotives/Rolling Stock:** Sandley light locomotive and rolling stock–coal-fired steam locomotive 4-6-2 no. 1924; coal-fired steam locomotive 4-4-2 no. 1916; diesel hydraulic switcher no. 1958; F2 diesel hydraulic no. 1996; 12-passenger day coaches nos. 1080-1096.

**Nearby Attractions/Accommodations:** Wisconsin State Fair Park, Summerfest Grounds, Milwaukee County Stadium, Milwaukee Public Museum, Mitchell Park Domes, Wehr Nature Center, Whitnall Boerner Botanical Gardens, Cool Waters Water Park, Best Western Midway, Holiday Inn Express, Sheraton Inn Mayfair, Excel Inn, many restaurants and area attractions.

**Location/Directions:** Zoo is located 8 miles west of downtown Milwaukee at the intersection of I-94, I-894, and Highway 45.

**Site Address:** 10001 W. Bluemound Rd., Milwaukee, WI
**Mailing Address:** 10001 W. Bluemound Rd., Milwaukee, WI 53226
**Telephone:** (414) 771-3040
**Fax:** (414) 256-5410
**Internet:** www.milwaukeezoo.org

**Description:** Restored CNW depot complete with railroad artifacts.

**Schedule:** June through August: first and third Sundays, 1 to 4 p.m. or by appointment.

**Admission/Fare:** Donations appreciated.

**Locomotives/Rolling Stock:** U.S. Army no. 4555 renumbered U.S. Army no. 7436, built by Vulcan Iron Works 1941, sold to Laona & Northern Railway October 1948 to become engine 3101; Soo Line caboose no. 138; CNW caboose no. 11153; Laona & Northern engine 101.

**Special Events:** Rail Fest Days, second Sunday in August.

**Nearby Attractions/Accommodations:** Rainbow Motel, Marly's Restaurant, Mosquito Hill Nature Center, Memorial Park.

**Location/Directions:** Route 45 north to Business 45, High St. east to railroad tracks, north to the depot.

      M

**Site Address:** 900 Montgomery St., New London, WI
**Mailing Address:** 101 Beckert Rd., Apt. 204, New London, WI 54961-2500
**Telephone:** (920) 982-5186 and (920) 982-8557

**MID-CONTINENT RAILWAY
HISTORICAL SOCIETY**
*Train ride, museum*
*Standard gauge*

WILLIAM RAIA

**Description:** Seven-mile, 50-minute ride in rural setting. Trains depart from a restored 1894 C&NW depot. On display is an extensive collection of vintage freight, passenger, and company-service equipment. Caboose and cab rides are offered.

**Schedule:** Mid-May through Labor Day: daily 10:30 a.m., 12:30, 2, and 3:30 p.m. Weekends through late October.

**Admission/Fare:** Adults, $10; seniors, $9; children 3-12, $5.50; under 3, free. Cab ride, $26. Caboose: adult, $12; child, $6.50. Call or e-mail for first-class, dinner train, and group rates.

**Locomotives/Rolling Stock:** C&NW no. 1385, ALCO 4-6-0 (1907); Polson Logging Co. no. 2, Baldwin 2-8-2 (1912); WC&C no. 1; MLW 4-6-0 (1913); C&NW combine no. 7409; drovers caboose no. 10802; business car no. 440; Soo Line diner-lounge no. 2017; business car "Oak Park"; DM&IR caboose no. C-74; reefer no. 7122; GN coach no. 3261; more.

**Special Events:** Snow Train, February. Civil War, Weekend, July. WWI Weekend, August. Autumn Color Weekend, October. Santa Express, November. Call or e-mail for dates and times.

**Location/Directions:** Seven miles west of Baraboo. State Highway 136 to County Highway PF. Follow signs.

†See ad on page A-11.

**Site Address:** E8948 Museum Rd., North Freedom, WI
**Mailing Address:** PO Box 358, North Freedom, WI 53951-0358
**Telephone:** (608) 522-4261
**Fax:** (608) 522-4490
**E-mail:** midcon@baraboo.com
**Internet:** www.midcontinent.org

# OSCEOLA & ST. CROIX VALLEY RAILWAY
## MINNESOTA TRANSPORTATION MUSEUM
*Train ride, museum*
*Standard gauge*

JAKE LUECKEL

**Description:** Enjoy the scenic St. Croix River Valley on a 90-minute round trip between Osceola, Wisconsin, and Marine-on-St. Croix, Minnesota, or a 45-minute round trip through rural Wisconsin between Osceola and Dresser. See the restored Osceola Historical Depot, featuring exhibits about railroading and the Osceola area, and the U.S. Railway Post Office exhibits aboard Northern Pacific triple combine no. 1102.

**Schedule:** Memorial Day through October: weekends. Charters available during the week.

**Admission/Fare:** Marine trip–$7 to $13; Dresser trip–$5 to $10.

**Locomotives/Rolling Stock:** Northern Pacific no. 328 4-6-0 steam locomotive; NP no. 105 LST&T switcher engine; nos. 2604 and 2608 cars, former Rock Island; NP triple combine car no. 1102; DL&W no. 2232 commuter coach; Soo Line 559 1951 Electromotive 6P7; streamline coaches 1213 Great Northern *Empire Builder* and 1096 and 1097 Chicago & Northwestern *400.*

**Special Events:** Fireworks Express; fall leaves trip, September and October.

**Nearby Attractions/Accommodations:** Cascade Falls, St. Croix River, St. Croix Art Barn, Interstate Park, motels, and campgrounds.

**Location/Directions:** I-35W to Forest Lake, Highway 97 east to Highway 95, north to I-243 across the St. Croix River to Highway 35S, to Depot Rd.

Radio frequency: 161.355

**Site Address:** 114 Depot Rd., Osceola, WI
**Mailing Address:** PO Box 176, Osceola, WI 54020
**Telephone:** (715) 755-3570 and (800) 711-2591 and (651) 228-0263
**Fax:** (715) 294-3330
**E-mail:** oscvrlwy@centurytel.net
**Internet:** www.mtmuseum.org or www.trainride.org

# THE MINING MUSEUM AND
# ROLLO JAMISON MUSEUM
*Train ride, museum*
*24" gauge*

**Description:** Tour an 1845 lead mine, and ride a 1931 mine locomotive above ground. Tour home and farm exhibits in Rollo Jamison Museum. (The train ride is part of the mine tour and takes three to five minutes.)

**Schedule:** May through October: daily, 9 a.m. to 5 p.m. Self-guided exhibits, November through April, Monday through Friday, 9 a.m. to 4 p.m. Group tours available year round.

**Admission/Fare:** Adults, $6; seniors, $5; children 5-15, $2.50; under age 5 are free.

**Locomotives/Rolling Stock:** Whitcomb Co., Rochelle, Illinois, 1931 locomotive.

**Nearby Attractions/Accommodations:** First Capital Historic Site; University of Wisconsin-Platteville, Chicago Bears training camp; hotels and restaurants.

**Location/Directions:** Corner of Main St. and Virgin Ave. Three blocks north of Highway 151.

**Site Address:** 405 E. Main St., Platteville, WI
**Mailing Address:** PO Box 780, Platteville, WI 53818-0780
**Telephone:** (608) 348-3301
**Fax:** (608) 348-4640
**E-mail:** kleefiss@uwplatt.edu

**LITTLE FALLS RAILROAD & DOLL MUSEUM**
*Train ride, museum*
*24" gauge*

JIM BROWN

**Description:** Three-acre campus with doll museum building and train museum building. Picnic area, swings, 12" gauge train, 300 feet, being expanded to 2000 feet.

**Schedule:** April through November, daily except Wednesdays, 12 to 5 p.m.

**Admission/Fare:** Museum, $3; train ride, $1.50; both, $5.

**Locomotives/Rolling Stock:** Milwaukee bay window caboose 992175.

**Special Events:** Operating garden railroad daily, weather permitting.

**Nearby Attractions/Accommodations:** Wegner Grotto.

**Location/Directions:** 1.8 miles east of Cataract. Halfway between Sparta and Black River Falls on County Highway II.

         M

**Site Address:** 9208 County Highway II, Sparta, WI
**Mailing Address:** 9208 County Highway II, Sparta, WI 54656-6485
**Telephone:** (608) 272-3266
**Fax:** (608) 272-3266
**E-mail:** raildoll@centurytel.net
**Internet:** http://fp1.centurytel.net/raildoll

# RAILROAD MEMORIES MUSEUM
## Museum, layout

CARL SCHULT

**Description:** Historical, educational museum covering all aspects of railroading. Tools, equipment, track vehicles, memorabilia, and history from the 1800s. Many station signs, books, art, and rare uniforms. Guided tours, videos, models, eleven large rooms full and an 8 x 12-foot scale diorama of the Spooner yard and complex from the years when Spooner was a big, busy terminal.

**Schedule:** Memorial weekend through Labor Day weekend: daily, 10 a.m. to 5 p.m. Groups by appointment.

**Admission/Fare:** Adults, $3; children 6-12, $.50; under age 6 are free.

**Nearby Attractions/Accommodations:** Namekagon Scenic River System, Bulik's Amusement Park, Museum of Wood Carving, Heart O' North Rodeo, State Fish Hatchery, lodging, restaurants.

**Location/Directions:** Two blocks from Highways 70 and 63; in old CNW depot at Walnut and Front Streets.

       arm

**Site Address:** 424 Front St., Spooner, WI
**Mailing Address:** N8425 Island Lake Rd., Spooner, WI 54801
**Telephone:** (715) 635-3325; when closed, (715) 635-2752, 635-3833
**Internet:** www.spoonerwi.com/rail_museum.htm

# RIVERSIDE & GREAT NORTHERN RAILWAY

*Train ride, museum, display*
*15" gauge*

MARSHALL L. "PETE" DEETS

**Description:** A scenic 3-mile ride on railroad dating back to the 1850s, through rock cuts and thick forest just north of Wisconsin Dells. The R&GN is a living museum preserving miniature steam equipment and the facilities of the Sandley Light Railway Equipment Works, manufacturers of narrow gauge railroads for over 30 years.

**Schedule:** Memorial Day through Labor Day: daily 10 a.m. to 5:30 p.m., trains run every 45 minutes. Friday and Saturday, Sunset Specials run to dusk. May, October, November, and December: weekends 10 a.m. to 4 p.m., trains run on the hour. Weather permitting, call ahead to check operation schedule.

**Admission/Fare:** Adults, $6.50; seniors, $5; children 4-15, $4.50; under age four are free; family pass, $20.

**Locomotives/Rolling Stock:** No. 82 1957 4-4-0 steam engine former Milwaukee County Zoo engine; vertical boiler "Tom Thumb" steam engine; no. 95 SW-style diesel engine; more.

**Nearby Attractions/Accommodations:** Wisconsin Dells-Lake Delton area.

**Location/Directions:** West of Kilbourne Bridge in Wisconsin Dells. North on Stand Rock Rd. for about one mile to stop sign at railroad viaduct, turn right under viaduct and then left into driveway.

**Site Address:** N115 Highway N, Wisconsin Dells, WI
**Mailing Address:** N115 Highway N, Wisconsin Dells, WI 53965
**Telephone:** (608) 254-6367
**E-mail:** simstrains@compuserve.com
**Internet:** www.randgn.com

## ROUNDHOUSE RESTORATION, INC.
*Display*

RICHARD COLLIER

**Description:** Historic Depot Square includes restored 1900 depot, a replica of Evanston Chinese Joss House. Evanston Roundhouse and Railyards includes fully operational turntable.

**Schedule:** Winter–Mondays through Fridays, 8 a.m. to 5 p.m. Summer–Mondays through Fridays, 9 a.m. to 9 p.m.; Saturdays, 9 a.m. to 7 p.m.; and Sundays, 12 noon to 6 p.m.

**Admission/Fare:** Free.

**Special Events:** Roundhouse Festival, including model railroads, tours of roundhouse, arts and crafts, entertainment, food, usually second weekend in August.

**Nearby Attractions/Accommodations:** Wyoming Downs horseracing, summer months. Close to Park City and Salt Lake City, Utah, south of Yellowstone Park and Jackson, Wyoming. Restaurants, lodging, historic downtown. Uinta Mountains 20 miles south.

**Location/Directions:** On I-80, 85 miles east of Salt Lake City.

**Site Address:** 1500 Main St., Evanston, WY
**Mailing Address:** 1200 Main St., Evanston, WY 82930
**Telephone:** (307) 783-6320
**Fax:** (307) 783-6390
**E-mail:** urevan@allwest.net

**HERITAGE PARK HISTORICAL VILLAGE**
*Train ride*
*Standard gauge*

**Description:** Heritage Park is Canada's largest living historical village, where the past comes to life right in front of your eyes. We are a first-class summer tourist attraction and a year-round catering and convention facility.

**Schedule:** May long weekend through Labor Day weekend: daily, 9 a.m. to 5 p.m. October through Canadian Thanksgiving: weekends and holidays only.

**Admission/Fare:** Call or write for information.

**Locomotives/Rolling Stock:** Two port steam 0-4-0T 1909 compressed air; 1902 no. 3 Vul Steam 0-4-0T; 1905 no. 4 CP CPR steam 0-6-0; 1942 no. 2023 USA ALCO steam 0-6-0; 1944 no. 2024 Lima Steam 0-6-0; 1949 no. 5931 CPR MLW steam 2-10-4; 1944 no. 7019 CPR 1 MLW S2 1000.

**Special Events:** Opening weekend in May. Festival of Quilts, May. Railway Days and Father's Day, June. Canada Day, July. Hayshaker Days and Heritage Family Festival, August. Old Time Fall Fair and Fall Harvest Sale, September. October West, October. Call for information.

**Nearby Attractions/Accommodations:** Calgary Zoo, Olympic Park, Glenbow Museum, Fort Calgary, Alberta Science Centre.

**Location/Directions:** Follow Heritage Dr. west.

**Site Address:** 1900 Heritage Dr. SW, Calgary, AB
**Mailing Address:** 1900 Heritage Dr. SW, Calgary, AB Canada T2V 2X3
**Telephone:** (403) 259-1900
**Fax:** (403) 252-3528
**Internet:** www.heritagepark.ab.ca

# FORT EDMONTON PARK
*Train ride*
*Standard gauge*

**Description:** Nestled in Edmonton's river valley, Fort Edmonton Park is brought to life by costumed staff reenacting life as it was in Edmonton at the 1846 fur trading fort, and on the streets of 1885, 1905, and 1920. The train transports visitors through the park.

**Schedule:** May 19 through August 31: daily, Sundays in September.

**Admission/Fare:** Adults, $7.25; seniors and youth, 13-17 $5.50; children 2-12, $3.75; families, $22. Price includes train ride.

**Locomotives/Rolling Stock:** 1919 Baldwin 2-6-2 no. 107, former Oakdale & Gulf Railway (restored to its 1905 appearance).

**Special Events:** Call or write for information.

**Nearby Attractions/Accommodations:** Downtown Edmonton and West Edmonton Mall.

**Location/Directions:** Edmonton, Alberta.

          VIA

**Site Address:** Fox Dr. and Whitemud Dr., Edmonton, Alberta
**Mailing Address:** PO Box 2359, Edmonton, AB Canada T5J 2R7
**Telephone:** (780) 496-8787
**Fax:** (780) 496-8797
**Internet:** www.gov.edmonton.ab.ca/fort

**CANADIAN MUSEUM OF RAIL TRAVEL**
*Display, layout*
*Standard gauge*

WALTER LANZ

**Description:** Museum with static displays of restored vintage luxury train sets, plus a 3,000-square-foot oak-panelled Royal Alexandra Hall, carved oak fireplace (1906) and freight shed (1898). Tours vary from ½ hour to 1 hour in length. Open on occasion for light refreshments.

**Schedule:** Open all year, but seasonal hours vary. Call for information or check our website.

**Admission/Fare:** Prices vary for adults, seniors, students, and preschool; family discounts are given for prebooked tours. Check our website.

**Locomotives/Rolling Stock:** 1929 *Trans Canada Ltd.* complete set of 7 cars; 1907 Soo-Spokane train; other business cars, royal cars, and cars of state.

**Special Events:** Sam Steele Day, mid-June; Rockin in the Rockies Vintage Car Show, June; Gala Christmas dinner, annually in late November and early December.

**Nearby Attractions/Accommodations:** Fort Steele Heritage Town, Kimberley Bavarian Town, local campgrounds, restaurants, shops, golf courses, ski hills in winter.

**Location/Directions:** On Van Horne St. go north on Hwy. 3/95 in downtown Cranbrook. Parking at King St. intersection.

*Coupon available, see coupon section.

**Site Address:** One Van Horne St. (Highway 3/95), Cranbrook, BC
**Mailing Address:** Box 400, Cranbrook, BC Canada V1C 4H9
**Telephone:** (250) 489-3918
**Fax:** (250) 489-5744
**E-mail:** officeortours@trainsdeluxe.com
**Internet:** www.trainsdeluxe.com

## BRITISH COLUMBIA
## FOREST DISCOVERY CENTRE
*Train ride, museum*
*Narrow gauge*

**Description:** 1910 steam train ride (1½ miles long), forest discovery walks, historical collection, picnic and playground area, much more. One hundred acres to discover.

**Schedule:** Daily, Easter through Canadian Thanksgiving.

**Admission/Fare:** Adults, $8; seniors and students 13-18, $7; children 5-12, $4.50; under age 5 are free. Group rates available.

**Locomotives/Rolling Stock:** Bloedel Stewart & Welch no. 1; Hillcrest Lumber Co. no. 1; Shawnigan Lake Lumber Co. no. 2; Mayo Lumber Co. no. 3; Hillcrest Lumber Co. no. 9; locomotive no. 25; locomotive no. 24; no. 27 speeder; White Pass no. 1; Plymouth no. 26; Whitcomb no. 9; more.

**Special Events:** National Forestry Week, Mother's Day, Father's Day, Classic Tractors, Celebration of Steam, Labor Day Picnic, Terry Fox Run.

**Nearby Attractions/Accommodations:** Duncan Totem Tours, Native Heritage Centre, Chemainus Murals.

**Location/Directions:** Located five minutes north of Duncan off Trans Canada Highway.

         M VIA

**Site Address:** 2892 Drinkwater Rd., Duncan, BC
**Mailing Address:** 2892 Drinkwater Rd., Duncan, BC Canada V9L 6C2
**Telephone:** (250) 715-1113
**Fax:** (250) 715-1170
**E-mail:** bcfm@islandnet.com

## OKANAGAN VALLEY
## WINE TRAIN
*Dinner train*
*Standard gauge*

**Description:** A five-hour family attraction travelling from Kelowna to Vernon and return.

**Schedule:** Fridays and Saturdays, 5:30 p.m. to 10:30 p.m. Sundays, 11:00 a.m. to 5:00 p.m.

**Admission/Fare:** $91.95 per person plus GST.

**Locomotives/Rolling Stock:** 1954 CN Super Continental train cars.

**Location/Directions:** Downtown Kelowna at 600 Recreation Ave.

**Site Address:** 600 Recreation Ave., Kelowna, BC
**Mailing Address:** 11830 Kingsway Ave., Edmonton, AB Canada T5G 0X5
**Telephone:** (780) 488-8725 and (888) 674-8725
**Fax:** (780) 482-7666
**E-mail:** funtrain@telusplanet.net
**Internet:** www.okanaganvalleywinetrain.com

**BC RAIL**
*Train ride, dinner train*
*Standard gauge*

**Description:** *Whistler Northwind:* multi-day rail cruise. *Pacific Starlight* dinner train. Hudson day trip. *Cariboo Prospector* passenger train.

**Schedule:** *Cariboo Prospector* operates year round. All others, May to September.

**Admission/Fare:** Varies.

**Locomotives/Rolling Stock:** *Pacific Starlight:* five dining cars; three dome cars. Hudson daytrip ex-CPR 4069 F-unit and ex-CN coaches, CCF 1954. *Cariboo Prospector:* Budd RDCs. *Whistler Northwind:* three new dome cars, Colorado rail car, restored dining car.

**Location/Directions:** Located at the foot of Pemberton Ave., 20 minutes from downtown Vancouver.

        Vancouver VIA

**Site Address:** 1311 W. First St., North Vancouver, BC
**Mailing Address:** 1311 W. First St., North Vancouver, BC Canada V7P 1A7
**Telephone:** (800) 663-8238 and (604) 984-5246
**Fax:** (604) 984-5505
**E-mail:** passinfo@bcrail.com
**Internet:** www.bcrail.com/bcrpass

# ALBERNI PACIFIC RAILWAY
*Train ride, museum*
*Standard gauge*

BERT SIMPSON

**Description:** An 11-mile round trip from Port Alberni Station to McLean Mill National Historic Site.

**Schedule:** Late May through mid-October. Call or check website for schedule.

**Admission/Fare:** Adults, $20; seniors and youth, $15. Call or check website for other options.

**Locomotives/Rolling Stock:** 1929 Baldwin 90-ton 2-8-2 ST; 1954 Alco RS-3; 1942 GE 45-ton; more.

**Special Events:** Phone or see website for details.

**Nearby Attractions/Accommodations:** The station is located at Harbour Quay with shops, restaurants, and boat tours. The MacLean Mill National Historic Site celebrates the days of steam sawmilling and camp life.

**Location/Directions:** Port Alberni, on Vancouver Island, is a one-hour drive from Nanaimo, the B.C. Ferry terminal to the mainland.

**Site Address:** 3100 Kingsway Ave., Port Alberni, BC
**Mailing Address:** 3100 Kingsway Ave., Port Alberni, BC Canada V9Y 3B1
**Telephone:** (250) 723-1376
**Fax:** (250) 723-5910
**E-mail:** wviihs@uniserve.com
**Internet:** www.alberniheritage.com

# PRINCE GEORGE RAILWAY AND FORESTRY MUSEUM
*Museum*

**Description:** Portrays a history of the rail and forest industry of British Columbia. Speeder rides are offered.

**Schedule:** Daily, May through September, 10 a.m. to 6 p.m.

**Locomotives/Rolling Stock:** A variety of 50 pieces of rolling stock.

**Location/Directions:** At the east end of First Ave. beside Cottonwood Park.

*Coupon available, see coupon section.

      M VIA

**Site Address:** 850 River Rd., Prince George, BC
**Mailing Address:** 850 River Rd., Prince George, BC Canada V2L 5S8
**Telephone:** (250) 563-7351
**Fax:** (250) 7563-3697
**E-mail:** trains@pgrfm.bc.ca

# REVELSTOKE RAILWAY MUSEUM
*Museum*
*Standard gauge*

**Description:** History of the Canadian Pacific Railway from construction to present day, focusing on western Canada.

**Schedule:** Year round. July and August, 9 a.m. to 8 p.m. December through March, 1 to 5 p.m. April through June and September through November, 9 a.m. to 5 p.m.

**Admission/Fare:** Adults, $6; seniors, $5; youth, $3; children 6 and under, free; family, $13. Group rates available.

**Locomotives/Rolling Stock:** CP steam locomotive 5468; business car no. 4; caboose no. 437477; road repair car no. 404116; 40-foot flatcar no. 421237; service flanger no. 400573; Jordan spreader no. 402811; wedge plow no. 401027; baggage car no. 404944.

**Special Events:** Revelstoke Railway Days, third weekend in August.

**Nearby Attractions/Accommodations:** Revelstoke Hydroelectric Dam, Mt. Revelstoke and Glacier National Parks, British Columbia Interior Forestry Museum, City Museum, Canyon Hot Springs.

**Location/Directions:** Downtown Revelstoke, Victoria Rd. along the tracks.

*Coupon available, see coupon section.

**Site Address:** 719 Track St. W., Revelstoke, BC
**Mailing Address:** PO Box 3018, Revelstoke, BC Canada V0E 2S0
**Telephone:** (250) 837-6060 and (877) 837-6060 (toll free in North America)
**Fax:** (250) 837-3732
**E-mail:** railway@revelstoke.net
**Internet:** www.railwaymuseum.com

# WEST COAST RAILWAY
# HERITAGE PARK
*Museum*
*Standard gauge*

TREVOR MILLS

**Description:** One-kilometer miniature train ride.

**Schedule:** Year round: daily, 10 a.m. to 5 p.m. Closed Christmas and New Year's Day.

**Admission/Fare:** Adults, $6; seniors and students, $5; families, $18; children 5 and under, free.

**Locomotives/Rolling Stock:** PGE no. 2 Baldwin 2-6-2 1910; CPR business car "British Columbia" 1890; interurban sleeper "Clinton" 1923; BCE 960; BCE 941; CP 4069; locomotives; snowplows; cranes; cabooses.

**Special Events:** Hobgoblin Express, October 31. Christmas Lights in the Park, December. Scavenger Hunt, Easter Sunday. Canada Day, July 1. Mini Rail Days, August.

**Nearby Attractions/Accommodations:** Squamish Chief, Shannon Falls, Brennan Park Leisure Centre, Super 8 Motel.

**Location/Directions:** Highway 99, west on Industrial Way at Tim Horton's, follow signs to Government Rd. One hour north of Vancouver.

*Coupon available, see coupon section.

**Site Address:** 39645 Government Rd., Squamish, BC
**Mailing Address:** PO Box 2387, Squamish, BC Canada V0N 3G0
**Telephone:** (604) 898-9336
**Fax:** (604) 898-9349
**E-mail:** manager@wcra.org
**Internet:** www.wcra.org

## KETTLE VALLEY STEAM RAILWAY SOCIETY
### Train ride
### Standard gauge

DAVID WEST, WEST PHOTOGRAPHIC ARTS

**Description:** Enjoy a 90-minute journey traveling along cliffsides overlooking beautiful orchards and vineyards of the scenic Okanagan Valley, while enjoying a historical commentary.

**Schedule:** May, June, September, and October: weekends and Mondays 10:30 a.m. and 1:30 p.m. July and August: Thursdays through Mondays 10:30 a.m. and 1:30 p.m.

**Admission/Fare:** Adults, $14; seniors/students, $13; children 4-12, $10; age 3 and under are free. Group rates available with reservation for 20 or more.

**Locomotives/Rolling Stock:** 1924 Shay no. 3 locomotive; two vintage coaches, and two open-air cars.

**Special Events:** The Great Train Robberies and barbecues, Billy Miner Express, Teddy Bear Picnic, Hobo's Holiday, Wild West Express.

**Nearby Attractions/Accommodations:** Summerland is an old English theme town with many local festivals. Giants Head Park, Summerland Ornamental Gardens, Summerland Museum, many campgrounds, and beautiful beaches.

**Location/Directions:** Six kilometers off Highway 97, 45 kilometers south of Kelowna, 16 kilometers north of Penticton.

*Coupon available, see coupon section.

**Site Address:** 18404 Bathville Rd., Summerland, BC
**Mailing Address:** PO Box 1288, Summerland, BC Canada V0H 1Z0
**Telephone:** (250) 494-8422 and (877) 494-8424
**Fax:** (250) 494-8452
**E-mail:** kvr@telus.net
**Internet:** www.kettlevalleyrail.org

# BEAR CREEK PARK TRAIN
*Train ride*
*15" gauge*

**Description:** A ⅝-mile, eight-minute ride into Bear Creek Park's forest and gardens, through a tunnel with displays that change every two months, and over a trestle.

**Schedule:** January through November 29: daily, 10 a.m. to dark. November 29 through January 2: 10 a.m. to 10 p.m. for Christmas lights.

**Admission/Fare:** Adults, $2.50; seniors, $2; children, $1.75. Group discounts available.

**Locomotives/Rolling Stock:** 1967 Dutch-built steam engine based on Welsh mining design; 1988 Alan Keef diesel locomotive; covered British antique coaches, open touring coaches in summer.

**Special Events:** Easter Egg Treasure Hunt. Canada Day Exhibit. Halloween Haunted Forest, Christmas Enchanted Forest.

**Nearby Attractions/Accommodations:** Bear Creek Park is a 160-acre park with picnic facilities, art center, playground, water park, skate bowl, five-acre landscaped garden, walking trails, and sports fields.

**Location/Directions:** Twelve miles from U.S. border via King George Highway (99A); 20 miles from downtown Vancouver via Highway 1.

**Site Address:** 13750 88th Ave., Surrey, BC
**Mailing Address:** 13750 88th Ave., Surrey, BC Canada V3W 3L1
**Telephone:** (604) 501-1658
**Fax:** (604) 507-2620
**Internet:** www.bctrains.com

**ROCKY MOUNTAINEER RAILTOURS**
*Train ride*
*Standard gauge*

SCOTT ROWED

**Description:** Two-day all-daylight train service from Vancouver, British Columbia, to Jasper, Banff, and Calgary, Alberta, from mid-April to mid-October.

**Schedule:** Mid-April through mid-October: three departures per week. Four Christmas departures in December.

**Locomotives/Rolling Stock:** Nos. 800, 804, 805, 806, and General Motors GP40-2 locomotives. Passenger Cars–17 Dayniter 44-seat coaches, 1954 Canadian Car and Foundry, rebuilt 1972 and 1985-88; 20 cafe coaches; 48-seat no. 5749; 1949 Pullman, ten 72-seat bi-level dome coaches; Rader Railcar, more.

       VIA

**Site Address:** 1150 Station St., First Floor, Vancouver, BC
**Mailing Address:** 1150 Station St., First Floor, Vancouver, BC Canada V6A 2X7
**Telephone:** (800) 665-7245
**Fax:** (604) 606-7250
**E-mail:** brochure@rockymountaineer.com
**Internet:** www.rockymountaineer.com

**British Columbia, Vancouver**

**VANCOUVER'S DOWNTOWN
HISTORIC RAILWAY**
*Train ride*
*Standard gauge*

PAUL PHIBBS

**Description:** A 3-kilometer ride along the south side of False Creek.

**Schedule:** Mid-May through mid-October: weekends and holidays 12 to 5 p.m.

**Admission/Fare:** Adults, $2; seniors and children, $1. Charters, $150 per hour.

**Locomotives/Rolling Stock:** BCER interurban no. 1207 1905 all-wood passenger car; BCER interurban no. 1213 1913 steelside passenger car.

**Nearby Attractions/Accommodations:** Granville Island Public Market at west end of line. Science World (Omnimax theatre) at east end of line. VIA Rail/Amtrak station at east end of line, walking distance to Chinatown.

**Location/Directions:** First Ave. and Ontario St. Two blocks southwest of Skytrain's Main St. Station.

*Coupon available, see coupon section.

**Site Address:** 1601 Ontario St., Vancouver, BC
**Mailing Address:** TRAMS, 949 W. 41st Ave., Vancouver, BC Canada V52 2N5
**Telephone:** (604) 665-3903
**E-mail:** buses@telus.net
**Internet:** www.trams.bc.ca

**WINNIPEG RAILWAY MUSEUM**
*Museum*
*Standard gauge*

RON EINARSON

**Description:** Walk the passenger platforms of Winnipeg's Union Station trainshed and view numerous displays and artifacts dedicated to railroading in this region and where it began. View the first steam locomotive on the Canadian Prairies that started the development of the railways in the Canadian West. Displays and equipment will return you to yesteryear. You can also view the remaining tracks inside the trainshed that service VIA Rail Canada's premier train, the *Canadian*, and the northern Manitoba service, the *Hudson Bay* and CN main line.

**Schedule:** Winter hours: September 2 through June 3, Saturdays and Sundays, 12 to 4 p.m. Summer hours: June 6 through September 1, Thursdays through Sundays, 11 a.m. to 5 p.m.

**Admission/Fare:** Adults 16 and over, $2; children 15 and under, free. Donations also accepted. Tours arranged by appointment.

**Locomotives/Rolling Stock:** Canadian Pacific Railway (Joseph Whitehead contract no. 5) no. 1, known as the "Countess of Dufferin" 1872 Baldwin; CNR GMD1 no. 1900 City Hydro Mack Railbus B-1; more.

**Special Events:** Railway Days, mid-September.

**Nearby Attractions/Accommodations:** The Forks Historic Site, The Fort Garry.

**Location/Directions:** Main and Broadway. VIA Rail Canada Union Station. Entrance to the building from the Forks parking lot or Main St.

       M VIA

**Site Address:** VIA Rail Canada's Union Station, 123 Main St., Winnipeg, MB
**Mailing Address:** Box 48, 123 Main St., Winnipeg, MB Canada R3C 1A3
**Telephone:** (204) 942-4632
**Fax:** (204) 942-4632

# SALEM & HILLSBOROUGH RAILROAD

*Train ride, dinner train, museum, display*
*Standard gauge*

J.A. CLOWES

**Description:** One-hour, 5-mile one-way excursions. Three-hour, 10-mile diner train. Group charters. Museum and display of rolling stock and artifacts.

**Schedule:** Site and Museum: June 22 through September 2. Excursions: weekends, June 22 through September 2 and Wednesdays, July 3 through August 28. See web site for additional details.

**Admission/Fare:** Excursions: adults, $8.50; museum, $2; dining train, $27; senior, child, and family rates for certain events.

**Locomotives/Rolling Stock:** CN RSC 14, no. 1754; CN S12, no. 8245; GTR 1st Class, no. 2335; CN Colonist, no. 2737; Sunset dining train, 4 cars; displayed CN caboose 78727; plus CN F-1 no. 1009; double-end snow plow and various freight cars.

**Special Events:** Father's Day, June 16. Canada Day fireworks special, July 1. Homecoming Day, July 20. Fall Foliage, September 29.

**Nearby Attractions/Accommodations:** Waterfowl Park; Henry Steeves House; Hopewell Rocks; Fundy National Park; assortment of B&B and craft shops.

**Location/Directions:** New Brunswick Route 114 (route to Fundy Park) 15 miles south of Monston (Fundy Coastal Route).

 **Radio frequency: 166.050**

**Site Address:** 2847 Main St., Hillsborough, NB
**Mailing Address:** 2847 Main St., Hillsborough, NB Canada E4H 2X7
**Telephone:** (506) 734-3195 (summer) and (506) 734-3733 (winter)
**Fax:** (506) 734-3711
**E-mail:** jaclowes@istar.ca
**Internet:** http://shrailroad.go.to

**RAILWAY SOCIETY OF
NEWFOUNDLAND**
*Museum*
*Narrow gauge*

**Description:** One-hundred-year-old freight shed converted to a museum, containing historic artifacts and a display of locomotives and rail cars.

**Schedule:** June through August, 9 a.m. to 9 p.m.

**Admission/Fare:** $2 membership fee. Children under 17, free. Group rate, $20.

**Locomotives/Rolling Stock:** Baldwin steam locomotive no. 593 built in 1920; NF box baggage car no. 1598 built in 1954; steel baggage car no. 1900 built in 1943; steel passenger coach no. 758 built in 1949; steel diner coach no. 10 built in 1943; diesel locomotive no. 931 built in 1956; caboose no. 6072 built in 1956.

**Nearby Attractions/Accommodations:** Marbe Mountain Ski Lodge, Corner Brook Museum, Captain Cook site.

**Location/Directions:** Intersection of Riverside Dr. and Station Rd.

     M

**Site Address:** Station Rd., Corner Brook, NF
**Mailing Address:** PO Box 673, Corner Brook, NF Canada A2H 6G1
**Telephone:** (709) 634-5658
**Fax:** (709) 686-2081

**SYDNEY & LOUISBURG
RAILWAY MUSEUM**
*Museum, display*

**Description:** Original 1895 railway station housing railway and local history artifacts, rolling stock, and a gift shop.

**Schedule:** Mid-May, June, and September through mid-October: Mondays through Fridays 9 a.m. to 5 p.m. July and August: daily 8 a.m. to 7 p.m.

**Admission/Fare:** Donations appreciated.

**Special Events:** Canada Day Celebration, July 1. Annual Reunion, second Sunday in September.

**Nearby Attractions/Accommodations:** Restaurants, campgrounds, shops, theatre, and the Fortress of Louisbourg National Historic Park along with various types of accommodations.

**Location/Directions:** From Canso Causeway joining Cape Breton to Nova Scotia, take highway to Sydney, near Sydney on Route 125, take Route 22 to Louisbourg.

**Site Address:** 7330 Main St., Louisbourg, NS
**Mailing Address:** 7330 Main St., Louisbourg, NS Canada B1C 1P5
**Telephone:** (902) 733-2720
**Fax:** (902) 733-2157

# CHATHAM RAILROAD MUSEUM
*Museum*

GARY SHURGOLD

**Description:** The Chatham Railroad Museum is a retired Canadian National baggage car built in 1955 in Hamilton, Ontario.

**Schedule:** Mondays through Fridays, 9 a.m. to 4 p.m. and Saturdays 11 a.m. to 4 p.m.

**Admission/Fare:** Free. Donations accepted.

**Special Events:** Annual Railway Fun Day with special presentations.

**Nearby Attractions/Accommodations:** Chathem-Kent Museum.

**Location/Directions:** Located across from the Chatham Train Station.

      M

**Site Address:** 2 McLean St., Chatham, ON
**Mailing Address:** PO Box 434, Chatham, ON Canada N7M 5K5
**Telephone:** (519) 352-3097

**Description:** Allowing modern children and nostalgic seniors to visit one of the seven schools on wheels that taught children along the northern Ontario railways.

**Schedule:** May Victoria Day through Labor Day: Thursdays and Fridays 2 to 5 p.m.; weekends and holidays 1 to 5 p.m.

**Admission/Fare:** Free. Donations.

**Locomotives/Rolling Stock:** Canadian National 15089.

**Nearby Attractions/Accommodations:** Restaurants, lodging, campgrounds, state parks, 10 minutes from Lake Huron.

**Location/Directions:** Off Highway 4 near London, Ontario.

     VIA

**Site Address:** Victoria Terrace, Clinton, ON
**Mailing Address:** Box 488, Clinton, ON Canada N0M 1L0
**Telephone:** (519) 482-9583 (7 to 9 p.m.)

447

# COCHRANE RAILWAY AND PIONEER MUSEUM
### *Museum*

**Description:** This museum preserves a three-dimensional picture of the pioneer railway and homesteading days as a tribute to men and women who opened northern Ontario, an empire bigger than the territories of many United Nations members. A model train display aboard a former Canadian National coach introduces the main railway exhibits, which include a telegraph operator's corner, a ticket office, a document display, an insulator collection and uniforms. There is also a large varied display of photographs. Many of the pictures are from the large collection assembled by the Rev. W. L. Lawrence around 1912, for which the museum is now trustee. Also, in Train "Tim" Horton Memorial Museum is a display of hockey artifacts.

**Schedule:** June 23 through September 3: daily 8:30 a.m. to 8 p.m.

**Admission/Fare:** Adults, $2; seniors, $1; students/children, $1.50; families, $5. Group rates available.

**Locomotives/Rolling Stock:** No. 137 2-8-0, former Temiskaming & Northern Ontario.

**Special Events:** Museum Days, August.

          M

**Site Address:** 210 Railway St., Cochrane, ON
**Mailing Address:** PO Box 490, Cochrane, ON Canada P0L 1C0
**Telephone:** (705) 272-4361
**Fax:** (705) 272-6068
**E-mail:** towncoch@puc.net
**Internet:** www.town.cochrane.on.ca

# POLAR BEAR EXPRESS
*Train ride*
*Standard gauge*

ONTARIO NORTHLAND

**Description:** Summer excursion train to the edge of the Arctic, 186-mile train ride operating between Cochrane and Moosonee, Ontario.

**Schedule:** Late-June through Labor Day: daily except Fridays. Depart Cochrane 8:30 a.m., arrive Moosonee 12:50 p.m. Depart Moosonee 6:00 p.m., arrive Cochrane 10:05 p.m.

**Admission/Fare:** Adults, $56; seniors, $51; students, $48; children 5-11, $28; under age 5 are free. Family plan available. All fares include GST.

**Nearby Attractions/Accommodations:** Gold Mine Tour, Hunta Museum, The Station Inn.

**Location/Directions:** Highway 11 north through North Bay past New Liskeard to Cochrane.

**Site Address:** 200 Railway St., Cochrane, ON
**Mailing Address:** 555 Oak St. E., North Bay, ON Canada P1B 8L3
**Telephone:** (800) 268-9281
**Fax:** (705) 495-4745
**E-mail:** busrail@ontc.on.ca
**Internet:** www.polarbearexpress.ca

**Description:** This museum displays railroad-related exhibits in two train stations, one built in 1910 and another built in 1873; also on display are maintenance-of-way equipment, a steam engine, a caboose, and a fireless engine.

**Schedule:** Victoria Day through Labor Day: daily 9 a.m. to 5 p.m. Labor Day through Thanksgiving (October 8): weekends 9 a.m. to 5 p.m.

**Admission/Fare:** Adults, $2; children under age 13, $.50.

**Locomotives/Rolling Stock:** No. 6218, former Canadian National 4-8-4; Porter fireless locomotive.

**Nearby Attractions/Accommodations:** Niagara Falls, Fort Erie Historical Museum, Battlefield Museum, Historic Fort Erie, Mahoney Dolls House, Willoughby Museum.

**Location/Directions:** On Central Ave. between Gilmore Rd. and Wintemute, northwest of the west end of the Peace Bridge.

*Coupon available, see coupon section.

**Site Address:** Central Ave. and Oakes Park, Fort Erie, ON
**Mailing Address:** PO Box 339, Ridgeway, ON Canada L0S 1N0
**Telephone:** (905) 894-5322
**Fax:** (905) 894-6851

PIERRE OZORAK

**Description:** Relive railroad history at this restored railroad station, letting your imagination run down the tracks as you examine early railway equipment. Take a few minutes to relax in air-conditioned comfort while watching multi-media presentations like "Workin on the Railroad."

**Schedule:** June through September: Saturdays 9 a.m. to 12 p.m., Fridays and Sundays, 1 to 5 p.m.

**Admission/Fare:** Adults, $3; seniors/teens, $2; elementary students, $1. Group tours booked in advance, $2 each.

**Locomotives/Rolling Stock:** 1913 Shay logging locomotive; 1939 CN baggage car no. 8731; 1972 GTW caboose no. 79198; collection of CN maintenance jiggers (speeders).

**Special Events:** Pancake Breakfast and Train Show, June 18.

**Nearby Attractions/Accommodations:** Oriole Park Campground, Delaware Speedway, Little Beaver Restaurant, Komoka Provincial Park, Belamere Farm Market and Winery.

**Location/Directions:** Eight miles west of London on Glendon/ Commissioners Rd. Follow signs on Highway 401 and 402.

      M arm VIA

**Site Address:** 133 Queen St., Komoka, ON
**Mailing Address:** PO Box 22, Komoka, ON Canada N0L 1R0
**Telephone:** (519) 657-1912
**Fax:** (519) 657-6791
**E-mail:** railmus@komokarail.ca
**Internet:** www.komokarail.ca

# HALTON COUNTY RADIAL RAILWAY
*Museum*
*4'10⅞" gauge*

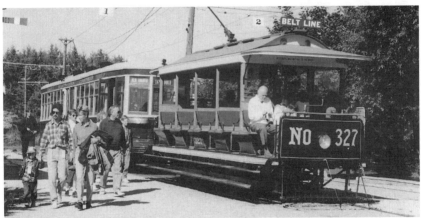

J.D. KNOWLES

**Description:** Ride 2 miles through scenic forest on a variety of restored streetcars, radials, subway and work cars. A special feature is that the line terminates in loops at both ends.

**Schedule:** May through October, weekends and holidays. July and August, daily. Special December events.

**Admission/Fare:** Adults, $7.50; seniors, $6.50; youth, $5.50; 3 and under and over 90, free. Grounds admission includes rides.

**Locomotives/Rolling Stock:** Open car no. 327 1893; Peter-Witt no. 2424, London & Port Stanley interurban no. 8, Jewitt 1915; Montreal & Southern counties interurban no. 107, Ottawa 1912, C.T.A. "L" car no. 48, track plow, sweeper, maintenance equipment.

**Special Events:** Wild flower weekend, streetcar and heritage day, car show, ice cream and starlight, Halloween fall trolley festival, Santa special, Christmas night shows.

**Nearby Attractions/Accommodations:** Conservation areas, Mohawk Race Track, antique shops, ostrich farm, Halton Region Museum, golf course, Canadian Warplane Heritage Museum, steam and technology museum.

**Location/Directions:** Highway 401 to exit 312 (Guelph Line), north for 9 miles or Highway 7 to Wellington Road 44, south for 3 miles.

**Site Address:** 13629 Guelph Line, Milton, ON
**Mailing Address:** PO Box 578, Milton, ON Canada L9T 5A2
**Telephone:** (519) 856-9802
**Fax:** (519) 856-1399
**E-mail:** streetcar@hcry.org
**Internet:** www.hcry.org

# CANADA SCIENCE AND TECHNOLOGY MUSEUM
### *Museum, display*

**Description:** This museum features all types of transportation, from Canada's earliest days to the present time. On display in the Steam Locomotives Hall are four huge steam locomotives, a CNR narrow gauge passenger car from Newfoundland, and a caboose. The visitors have access to two of the cabs, where sound effects give the feeling of live locomotives. The engines are meticulously restored, with polished rods and lighted number boards and class lights.

**Schedule:** Museum–May 1 to Labor Day: daily, 9 a.m. to 5 p.m. Labor Day through April: Tuesdays through Sundays, 9 a.m. to 5 p.m. Closed Mondays and Christmas Day. Free train ride with admission–July through August: Wednesdays and Sundays.

**Admission/Fare:** Adults, $6; seniors and students, $5; children 6-14, $2; children under age 6 are free; family of 2 adults/2 children, $12. Group rates available.

**Locomotives/Rolling Stock:** 1923 Shay steam locomotive; CN6400 4-8-4 Montreal 1936; CP926 4-6-0 1912; CP2858 4-6-4 Royal Hudson, Montreal 1938; CP3100 4-8-4 Montreal 1928; CNR business car "Terra Nova"; CNR 76109 caboose.

**Location/Directions:** Located ten minutes from downtown Ottawa. Queensway (Highway 417) exit St. Laurent south for 2.6 kilometers, left at Lancaster Rd. (at the lighthouse).

**Site Address:** 1867 St. Laurent Blvd., Ottawa, ON
**Mailing Address:** PO Box 9724, Stn. T, Ottawa, ON Canada K1G 5A3
**Telephone:** (613) 991-3044
**Fax:** (613) 993-7923
**E-mail:** scitech@nmstc.ca
**Internet:** www.science-tech.nmstc.ca

# PORT STANLEY TERMINAL RAIL
*Train ride*
*Standard gauge*

AL HOWLETT

**Description:** Three different rides, all from the station in Port Stanley, on the harbor next to the lift bridge. Trains pass over two bridges and northward for up to 3 miles through the Kettle Creek Valley. Port Stanley is a commercial fishing village on the north shore of Lake Erie. Equipment includes cabooses, heavyweight coaches, open coaches, baggage cars, boxcars, flatcars, hopper cars, a snowplow, tank cars, and more. Ticket office and displays are in the former London & Port Stanley station. Open excursion cars; cabooses, former Canadian National, modified into enclosed coaches; standard coaches, former VIA. The "Little Red Caboose" can be chartered for birthday parties and other events with advance reservation.

**Schedule:** Weekends, May through November. Daily, July through August.

**Admission/Fare:** Adults, $9.50; children 2-12, $5.

**Locomotives/Rolling Stock:** GE 25- and 44-ton and converted cabooses.

**Special Events:** Easter, Teddy Bear, Santa, and Entertainment Trains.

**Nearby Attractions/Accommodations:** St. Thomas Elgin Railroad Museum.

**Location/Directions:** Located on the north side of Lake Erie, 25 miles (50 kilometers) south of London, Ontario.

**Radio frequency:** 160.575

**Site Address:** 309 Bridge St., Port Stanley, ON
**Mailing Address:** 309 Bridge St., Port Stanley, ON Canada N5L 1C5
**Telephone:** (519) 782-3730
**Fax:** (519) 782-4385
**Internet:** www.pstr.on.ca/

# ELGIN COUNTY RAILWAY MUSEUM
*Train ride, museum, display*
*Standard gauge*

**Description:** Ongoing restoration and display of engines, rolling stock, and artifacts. Steam train ride in yard, every other Sunday, operated by Southern Ontario Locomotive Restoration Society.

**Schedule:** Daily all summer, 10 a.m. to 4 p.m. Fall through spring, Mondays, Wednesdays, and Saturdays, 10 a.m. to 4 p.m.

**Admission/Fare:** Entrance to museum by donation. Train rides: adults, $5; children, $3; families, $15.

**Locomotives/Rolling Stock:** CN 5700 4-6-4 ? Milwaukee 1930; London & Port Stanley Railway car no. 14, Jewett interurban; Wabash 43T diesel no. 5 General Electric; ? Pacific 8921 Milwaukee RSD 17 (only one ever built); GTW 77137, wooden caboose built 1891; NW 555020 caboose, international steel car; CN 7074 baggage car, national steel car; more.

**Special Events:** Nostalgia Days, early May. Heritage Days, late August.

**Nearby Attractions/Accommodations:** Elgin Pioneer Museum, "Statue of Jumbo"; Elgin Military Museum; Village of Port Stanley and city of London to the north.

**Location/Directions:** From Highways 1101 and 402, south on Highway 4, Wellington Rd. or Highbury Ave. to St. Thomas.

**Site Address:** 255 Wellington St., St. Thomas, ON
**Mailing Address:** PO Box 20062, St. Thomas, ON Canada N5P 4H4
**Telephone:** (519) 637-6284
**Fax:** (519) 631-0662
**E-mail:** ecrmpromo@hotmail.com
**Internet:** http://members.home.net/ecrm5700

# ALGOMA CENTRAL RAILWAY INC.
*Train ride*
*Standard gauge*

STEVE BRADLEY/RAIL INNOVATIONS

**Description:** We operate both tour trains and regular passenger service. Tour trains take you on a one-day wilderness excursion to Agawa Canyon Park. Regular passenger train provides service to Hearst, Ontario, as well as access to a variety of wilderness lodges. Private car and camp car rentals are available.

**Schedule:** Passenger service train–year round. Agawa Canyon train–June through mid-October: daily. Snow train–January through mid-March: weekends. Group rentals available.

**Admission/Fare:** Varies, call for information.

**Locomotives/Rolling Stock:** Refurbished F9s; refurbished 1950s VIA coaches.

**Nearby Attractions/Accommodations:** Depot is located downtown close to hotels, restaurants, shopping.

**Location/Directions:** Located in downtown Sault Ste. Marie, minutes from International Bridge.

**Site Address:** 129 Bay St., Sault Ste. Marie, ON
**Mailing Address:** PO Box 130, Sault Ste. Marie, ON Canada P6A 6Y2
**Telephone:** (705) 946-7300 and (800) 242-9287
**Fax:** (705) 541-2989
**E-mail:** kabooth@wclx.com
**Internet:** www.agawacanyontourtrain.com and www.algomacentralrailway.com

# SMITH FALLS RAILWAY MUSEUM
*Museum*

**Description:** National historic site, walk-through rail cars, inspection car rides, exhibits, gift shop, and children's area.

**Schedule:** July and August, daily 10 a.m. to 4 p.m. September 3 through mid-May, by appointment for groups and researchers. Open weekends May and June.

**Admission/Fare:** Adults, $4; seniors and students, $2.50; children under 6, free.

**Special Events:** Children's Days.

**Nearby Attractions/Accommodations:** Heritage House Museum, Rideau Canal Museum, Hershey's Factory and chocolate shop.

**Location/Directions:** One hour from Ottawa, Kingston, or Ogdensburg.

**Site Address:** 90 William St. W., Smith Falls, ON
**Mailing Address:** PO Box 962, Smith Falls, ON K7A 5A5
**Telephone:** (613) 283-5696
**Fax:** (613-283-7211
**E-mail:** sfrm@superaje.com
**Internet:** www.magna.ca/~sfrm/

**YORK DURHAM
HERITAGE RAILWAY**
*Train ride*
*Standard gauge*

JOHN SKINNER, EAGLE VISION PHOTOGRAPHY

**Description:** Twelve-mile train ride through the beautiful rural area between the towns of Uxbridge and Stouffville.

**Schedule:** Call or write for information.

**Admission/Fare:** Adults, $17; seniors, $13; children 4-12, $9; under age 4 and over age 90 are free.

**Locomotives/Rolling Stock:** No. 3612 Also RS-11; no. 1310 Alco RS-3; nos. 3209 and 3232 cafe cars, former VIA; 1920s heavyweights 4960 and 4977; former rules instruction car; caboose; flatcar.

**Special Events:** Mother's Day, Christmas in July, Father's Day, Teddy Bear Day, Halloween Spook Trains, Christmas Trip (weather permitting). Call or write for dates.

**Nearby Attractions/Accommodations:** Sales Barn. Uxbridge–Uxbridge Scott Museum, Lucy Maude Montgomery Home, restaurants, gift shops.

**Location/Directions:** Thirty minutes northeast of Toronto, Ontario. Take Highway 404 to the Bloomington Sideroad, go east on the Bloomington Sideroad, which becomes Highway 47 into Uxbridge.

**Site Address:** Railway St., Uxbridge, ON
**Mailing Address:** PO Box 462, Stouffville, ON Canada L4A 7Z7
**Telephone:** (905) 852-3696
**E-mail:** lbhill@interhop.net
**Internet:** www.ydhr.on.ca

**SOUTH SIMCOE RAILWAY**
*Train ride*
*Standard gauge*

JOHN SPRING

**Description:** Enjoy a scenic journey through the Beeton Creek Valley aboard South Simcoe Railway's historic steam train. Excursions last just under an hour and are highlighted by the entertaining and informative commentary of the conductor. It's a unique trip into the past the whole family will enjoy!

**Schedule:** May 19 through October 14: Sundays and holidays. Departs 10, 11:30 a.m., 1, 2:30, and 4 p.m. Additional weekday departures during the summer and fall color season. Call or check website for schedule.

**Admission/Fare:** Adults, $10; seniors, $9; children, $6.50.

**Locomotives/Rolling Stock:** Rogers Locomotive Works 4-4-0 no. 136 (built 1883); Canadian Locomotive Co. 4-6-0 no. 1057 (built 1912); vintage open-window day coaches dating from the 1920s.

**Nearby Attractions/Accommodations:** Nearby family attractions include the Falconry Centre, Puck's Farm, and a large Conservation Park with swimming and picnic pavilions. Nearby restaurants, motels, bed and breakfasts and camping.

**Location/Directions:** From Highway 400, take Highway 9 west 20 kilometers to traffic lights at Tottenham Rd. and turn north. Turn left at first traffic lights in Tottenham, follow signs to parking. Driving time from Toronto is approximately 50 minutes.

**Site Address:** Mill St. W., Tottenham, ON
**Mailing Address:** PO Box 186, Tottenham, ON Canada L0G 1W0
**Telephone:** (905) 936-5815
**Fax:** (905) 936-1057
**Internet:** www.steamtrain.com

G. BURBIDGE

**Description:** Scenic 20-mile tour along the shore of the picturesque Gateway river, including a two-hour stop to visit the quaint village of Wakefield, Quebec.

**Schedule:** May to October, five-hour scenic day tour; four-hour sunset dinner train.

**Admission/Fare:** Scenic tour: adults, $29; seniors, $26; children, $14; family, $74 (plus taxes).

**Locomotives/Rolling Stock:** 1907 class Swedish locomotive; 1962 GM diesel electric locomotive; nine 1942 Swedish passenger cars.

**Nearby Attractions/Accommodations:** Located in Canada's capital region Ottawa. Parliament buildings, eight national museums, Casino de Hull Gatineau Park; two hours from Montreal, Quebec.

**Location/Directions:** Via Macdonald Cartier Bridge from Ottawa, exit no. 3, left on Carriere Blvd., left on Deveault St.

*Coupon available, see coupon section.

**Site Address:** 165 Deveault St., Hull, PQ
**Mailing Address:** 165 Deveault St., Hull, PQ Canada J8Z 1S7
**Telephone:** (819) 778-7246 and (800) 871-7246
**Fax:** (819) 778-5007
**E-mail:** info@steamtrain.ca
**Internet:** www.steamtrain.ca

# CANADIAN RAILWAY MUSEUM
*Museum*
*Standard gauge*

KEVIN ROBINSON

**Description:** Canada's finest collection of railway equipment with more than 142 vehicles.

**Schedule:** May 7 through Labor Day, daily, 9 a.m. to 5 p.m.; Labor Day through mid-October, weekends only, 9 a.m. to 5 p.m.

**Admission/Fare:** $6-$12.

**Location/Directions:** South of Montreal via Routes 15 and 132 west.

**Site Address:** 1110 St. Pierre St., St. Constant, PQ
**Mailing Address:** 1110 St. Pierre St., St. Constant, PQ Canada J5A 1G7
**Telephone:** (450) 632-2410
**Fax:** (450) 638-1563
**E-mail:** mfcd@exporail.org
**Internet:** www.exporail.org

461

**Quebec, Vallee-Jonction**

**CHAUDIERE-APPALACIAN**
**TOURIST TRAIN**
*Train ride*
*Standard gauge*

**Description:** 1½-hour, 2-hour, and 2½-hour excursions on passenger train pulled by a diesel engine. Trips are operated between Valley Junction and St. Joseph, St. Marie, and St. Frederic in the Chaudiere River Valley. Museum in the heritage railway station built in 1917.

**Schedule:** May through June 23, weekends 1:30 to 4 p.m. June 23 to Sept. 3, Tuesday through Sunday, 1:30 to 4 p.m. June 23 through August 12, Wednesday through Sunday, 9:45 and 10:15 a.m. September 3 to October 31, weekend afternoons and special excursions on QCR.

**Admission/Fare:** Regular adult fares including taxes. 1½-hour trip, $17.95, 2-hour trip, $19.95, 2½-hour trip $24.95, Canadian funds. Rebates for children 6-11. Children 5 and under, free.

**Locomotives/Rolling Stock:** TTCA Power car no. 616, TTCA Pullman coach nos. 2722, 2709, 2841; more.

**Special Events:** Sugar Bush specials, April. Santa Claus specials, late November.

**Location/Directions:** Highway 20 links Montreal and Quebec City. Exit on Highway 73 south on south shore of Quebec City. Exit 81, Vallee Jonction. Thirty minutes south from Quebec Bridge on Highway 73.

*Coupon available, see coupon section.

**Site Address:** 399 boul. Rousseau, Vallee-Jonction, PQ Canada
**Mailing Address:** 399 boul. Rousseau, Vallee-Jonction, PQ Canada G0S 3J0
**Telephone:** (877) 642-5580
**Fax:** (418) 253-5585
**E-mail:** francoiscliche@videotron.ca
**Internet:** http://beaucerail.iquebec.com

462

**Description:** History of transportation museum with displays of artifacts from rail, land, air, and water transportation.

**Schedule:** April through December: daily 9 a.m. to 6 p.m. January through March: closed Mondays.

**Admission/Fare:** Adults, $6; seniors, $5; students, $4; children 6-12, $2; age 5 and under are free.

**Locomotives/Rolling Stock:** Vulcan 0-4-0 no. 2265; DS-6F no. 6555; G20 no. 2634; combination no. 3321; CPR coach no. 95; CPR caboose no. 6139; 1934 inspector's Buick M-499.

**Special Events:** May long weekend through Labor Day: weekends and holidays, weather permitting, shortline railway 1914 Vulcan runs on museum grounds.

**Nearby Attractions/Accommodations:** Museums, historic sites, camping, motels, spa, variety of cultural and sporting events.

**Location/Directions:** Junction of Highways 1 and 2.

**Site Address:** 50 Diefenbaker Dr., Moose Jaw, SK
**Mailing Address:** 50 Diefenbaker Dr., Moose Jaw, SK Canada S6J 1L9
**Telephone:** (306) 693-5989
**Fax:** (306) 691-0511
**E-mail:** wdm.mj@sk.sympatico.ca
**Internet:** www.wdmuseum.sk.ca

# SASKATCHEWAN RAILWAY MUSEUM
*Museum*
*Standard gauge*

CAL SEXSMITH

**Description:** Museum with ½-mile motor car rides.

**Schedule:** Victoria Day weekend, mid-May through September. Weekends and holidays, May, June, and September 1 to 6 p.m. Daily July and August 1 to 6 p.m. Subject to change.

**Admission/Fare:** Adults, $3; children 6-16, $2; under age 6 are free. Season pass/memberships available.

**Locomotives/Rolling Stock:** CP S-3 no. 6568; caboose no. 434044; no. 434102; sleeping car "Kirkella"; snowplow no. 400657; wash car no. 412718; CN caboose no. 78687; no. 79282; boxcar no. 428980; no. 524418; flatcar no. 57519; no. 59039; GE 23-ton 800-010; UTLX tank car no. 14532; Sask Power generator car; SMR streetcar no. 51; no. 203.

**Special Events:** Railway Days, mid-June. Great Garage Sale, late August.

**Nearby Attractions/Accommodations:** Western Development Museum, Pike Lake Provincial Park.

**Location/Directions:** West on 22nd St. to Highway 7. West on Highway 7 to Highway 60, then 2 kilometers south on Highway 60 at CNR crossing.

**Site Address:** Highway 60, Pike Lake Rd., Saskatoon, SK
**Mailing Address:** Box 19, Site 302, RR 3, Saskatoon, SK Canada S7K 3J6
**Telephone:** (306) 382-9855
**E-mail:** saskrailmuseum@canada.com
**Internet:** www.geocities.com/saskrailmuseum/

## Other Tourist Railroads and Museums
These are additional sites that may be of interest to you. We are unable to provide complete information, so be sure to write or call for details.

**Alaska, Anchorage**
Alaska Railroad Corporation
PO Box 107500, Anchorage, AK 99510
(907) 265-2494 or (800) 544-0552

**Arizona, Clarkdale**
Verde Canyon Railroad
300 N. Broadway, Clarkdale, AZ 86324-2302
(800) 293-7245

**Arkansas, Eureka Springs**
Eureka Springs Model Railroad
127 Spring St., Eureka, AR 72632
(501) 253-2525 or (866) 507-6665

**California, Fremont**
Society for the Preservation of Carter Railroad
34600 Ardenwood Blvd., Fremont, CA 94555
(510) 797-9557

**California, Los Gatos**
Billy Jones Wildcat Railroad
PO Box 234, Los Gatos, CA 95031
(408) 395-7433

**California, McCloud**
McCloud Railway Co.
PO Box 1500, McCloud, CA 96057
(530) 964-2141

**California, McCloud**
Shasta Sunset Dinner Train
PO Box 1199, McCloud, CA 96057
(530) 964-2142 or (800) 733-2141

**California, Santa Clara**
South Bay Historical Railroad Society (SBHRS)
1005 Railroad Ave., Santa Clara, CA 95050-4319
(408) 243-3969

**California, Sunol**
Niles Canyon Railway (Pacific Locomotive Association, Inc.)
Sunol Depot, Sunol, CA 94536-0247
(925) 862-9063

**Florida, Trenton**
Florida West Coast Railroad
PO Box 1267, Trenton, FL 32693
(352) 463-1103

**Georgia, Stone Mountain**
Stone Mountain Scenic Railroad
PO Box 778, Stone Mountain, GA 30086
(770) 498-5600

**Hawaii, Laupahoehoe**
Laupahoehoe Train Museum
PO Box 358, Laupahoehoe, HI 96764
(808) 962-6300

**Idaho, Athol**
Silverwood Central Railway/Theme Park
27843 N. Hwy. 95, Athol, ID 83801
(208) 683-3400

**Illinois, Galesburg**
Galesburg Railroad Museum
PO Box 947, Galesburg, IL 61402
(309) 342-9400

**Indiana, Noblesville**
Indiana Transportation Museum
325 Cicero Rd., Noblesville, IN 46061
(317) 773-6000

**Iowa, Mt. Pleasant**
Midwest Central Railroad
PO Box 102, Mt. Pleasant, IA 52641
(319) 385-2912

**Maryland, Union Bridge**
Western Maryland Railway Historical Society
PO Box 395, Union Bridge, MD 21791
(410) 775-0150

**Michigan, Durand**
Michigan Railroad History Museum
Durand Union Station
PO Box 106, Durand, MI 48429
(989) 288-3561

**Minnesota, Stillwater**
Minnesota Zephyr Limited
PO Box 573, Stillwater, MN 55082
(612) 854-8510

**Minnesota, Two Harbors**
Lake County History & Railroad Museum
PO Box 128, Two Harbors, MN 55616

**Missouri, St. Louis**
Museum of Transportation
3015 Barrett Station Rd., St. Louis, MO 63122
(314) 965-7998

**New Hampshire, North Conway**
Conway Scenic Railroad
PO Box 1947, North Conway, NH 03860
(603) 356-5251 or (800) 232-5251

**New Jersey, Cape May**
Cape May Seashore Lines
PO Box 152, Tuckahoe, NJ 08250-0152
(609) 884-5300

**New York, New York**
Station at Citigroup Center
153 E. 53rd St., New York, NY
(212) 559-MRKT or (212) 559-5350

**North Carolina, Blowing Rock**
Tweetsie Railroad
PO Box 388, Blowing Rock, NC 28605
(828) 264-9061

**North Dakota, Mandan**
North Dakota State Railroad Museum
PO Box 1001, Mandan, ND 58554
(701) 663-9322

**Oklahoma, Cushing**
Cimarron Valley Railroad Museum
PO Box 844, Cushing, OK 74023
(918) 225-1657

**Pennsylvania, Scranton**
Lackawanna County Electric City Trolley
Station & Museum
300 Cliff St., Scranton, PA 18503
(570) 963-6590

**Rhode Island, Newport**
Dinner Trains of New England
PO Box 1081, Newport, RI 02840
(401) 841-8700 or (800) 398-7427

**South Carolina, Charleston**
Best Friend Museum
31 Ann St., Charleston, SC 29403
(843) 724-7174

**Tennessee, Nashville**
Nashville Toy Train Museum
162 8th Avenue N., Nashville, TN 37219
(615) 742-5678

**Texas, Cedar Park**
Austin & Texas Central Railroad
PO Box 1632, Austin, TX 78767
(512) 477-6377

**Texas, Galveston**
Galveston Railroad Museum
123 Rosenberg Ave., Galveston, TX 77550
(409) 765-5700

**Texas, Grapevine**
Tarantula Excursion Train
707 S. Main St., Grapevine, TX 76099
(817) 625-7245

**Utah, Promontory**
Golden Spike National Historic Site
PO Box 897, Brigham City, UT 84032
(435) 471-2209, ext. 18

**Vermont, Bellows Falls**
Green Mountain Railroad
PO Box 498
Bellows Falls, VT 05101
(802) 463-3069

**Washington, Yacolt**
Chelatchie Prairie Railroad
PO Box 1271, Battleground, WA 98604-1271
(360) 686-3559

**Wisconsin, Spooner**
Wisconsin Great Northern Railroad
PO Box 46, Spooner, WI 54801
(715) 635-3200 or (888) 390-0412

**Wyoming, Cheyenne**
Wyoming Transportation Museum
PO Box 704, Cheyenne, WY 82003
(307) 637-3376

**Alberta, Calgary**
Royal Canadian Pacific
133 9th Ave. SW, Calgary, AB
Canada T2T 2M3
(877) 665-3044

**British Columbia, Prince Rupert**
Kwinitsa Railway Station Museum
100 1st Ave. W., Prince Rupert, BC
Canada V8J 1A8
(250) 624-3207

**Manitoba, Winnipeg**
Vintage Locomotive Society, Inc.
PO Box 33021, RPO Polo Park, Winnipeg, MB
Canada R3G 3N4
(204) 832-5258

**Ontario, Brighton**
Memory Junction Museum
PO Box 294, Brighton, ON
Canada K0K 1A0
(613) 475-0379

**Ontario, Port Elgin**
Port Elgin & North Shore Railway
The Station Beach, Port Elgin, ON
Canada N0H 2C0
(519) 389-3919

# Index

# Your satisfaction is guaranteed!

If you're ever dissatisfied—for any reason—you may receive a refund on any unmailed issues.

## To start your railroading adventure, mail this card today!

## We take you there!

NO POSTAGE
NECESSARY
IF MAILED
IN THE
UNITED STATES

## BUSINESS REPLY MAIL
FIRST-CLASS MAIL     PERMIT NO. 16     WAUKESHA, WI

POSTAGE WILL BE PAID BY ADDRESSEE

PO BOX 1612
WAUKESHA WI  53187-9950